THE NEW
BRITISH DRAMA

THE NEW

BRITISH DRAMA

Edited and with an Introduction by

Henry Popkin

GROVE PRESS, INC. | NEW YORK

ACKNOWLEDGMENTS: *Roots* by Arnold Wesker is reprinted from *The Wesker Trilogy* by permission of Random House, Inc.; "Plays for the People" by Joan Littlewood was originally published in *Le Théâtre dans le Mond-World Theatre* and is reprinted by permission of l'Institut International du Théâtre and the author; "The Right to Fail" by George Devine is reprinted by permission of *The Twentieth Century*; "Let Battle Commence!" by Arnold Wesker and "Building the Play," an interview with John Arden are reprinted by permission of *Encore*; an earlier version of "Writing for the Theatre" by Harold Pinter appeared in *The Sunday Times Magazine Section* [London], and is reprinted by permission of the author.

Library of Congress Catalog Card Number: 64-10598

First Printing

MANUFACTURED IN THE UNITED STATES OF AMERICA

CONTENTS

HENRY POPKIN: *Introduction*   7

I. The New British Drama

SHELAGH DELANEY: *A Taste of Honey*   29

BRENDAN BEHAN: *The Hostage*   109

ARNOLD WESKER: *Roots*   203

JOHN ARDEN: *Serjeant Musgrave's Dance*   271

N. F. SIMPSON: *One Way Pendulum*   373

HAROLD PINTER: *The Caretaker*   467

II. Notes on the Theater by Directors and Playwrights

JOAN LITTLEWOOD: *Plays for the People*   557

GEORGE DEVINE: *The Right to Fail*   561

ARNOLD WESKER: *Let Battle Commence!*   566

HAROLD PINTER: *Writing for the Theatre*   574

JOHN ARDEN: *Building the Play*   581

INTRODUCTION

Henry Popkin

THE RECENT REVOLUTION in the British theater is one of the major surprises of modern cultural history, especially for those who like to toy with the idea that the life of nations is like the life of man. The British theater has been in a more or less steady decline ever since its brilliant, vigorous youth came to an end in the first third of the seventeenth century. What would it have been without its Irish recruits—Congreve, Farquhar, Sheridan, Wilde, Synge, O'Casey, Shaw? That list might make us wonder who was the last great *English* dramatist. The man's name was Ben Jonson, and, no doubt, he was known as "rare Ben Jonson" because he was English and not Irish. The current dramatic revival does have its obligatory Irish dramatist in Brendan Behan, but, for once, some English dramatists are also at work.

Who could ever have expected anything from the British theater, dreary and tame as it has been for two centuries now? For most of the nineteenth century, it was no tamer than the rest of European drama. But then, late in that century, Ibsen brought a new intelligence and a more serious realism into the playhouse. The theaters of all the Western nations responded at once. Nearly at once; America's cultural lag has been estimated to be fifty years. Britain gave signs of immediate response with the intellectual dramas of Bernard Shaw and the more insistently reformist plays of John Galsworthy, but it soon settled back into that old lethargy which was the natural atmosphere of its theater. The cultural lag was resumed, and Ibsen might as well have never been born. Comfort was the keynote, and the British stage remained so comfortable for so long that it has only now reached certain outposts that Eugene O'Neill assaulted forty years ago.

London's West End settled down to the drawing-room comedies of Somerset Maugham, Noel Coward, John Van Druten, and Frederick Lonsdale. What else did it have? Detective plays in which an iron-jawed man from the Yard arrived just in time to set things right; the rather obvious character-dramas of the Welsh actor Emlyn Williams; the easy Scottish charm of James Bridie, who was not primarily a product for export, although the *Oxford Companion to the Theatre* gives Bridie a longer entry than Brecht, Pirandello, and Giraudoux put together and gratefully concludes that he "devised plays rich in entertainment and generous in their number of good parts for players." Recognition from so conservative and so respectable a work of reference as the *Oxford Companion* confers a peculiar status upon Bridie, who gets more space than any British contemporary except Shaw. This, the volume implicitly tells us, was the drama of the time—if there was any such thing. To that we may be inclined to reply that there was no such thing. Being bested by such superficial entertainers as these outraged the one serious dramatist who remained once Shaw fell silent; Sean O'Casey spent many angry pages minutely dissecting the work of Emlyn Williams and Noel Coward, from whom it had been suggested that he might learn dramatic craftsmanship. Still, the theater, however unimportant and uninteresting it may have been, was safely solvent. Enough prosperous people bought their seats in the West End each night to pay the theater's way.

These plays of the past decades showed us mainly the upper and upper-middle classes, speaking and behaving charmingly. When some serious emotional crisis arose, their special concern was always to show their good taste and breeding by refusing to express their emotions. Understatement became a sign of grace, and grace was, almost by definition, denied to the lower classes. In these plays, social contrast might be provided by a faithful, whining cockney servant, but woe betide the cockney who forgot class distinctions. Noel Coward, normally a moderate man, had one such presuming creature trampled by runaway horses in *Cavalcade*. Class distinctions prevailed even in the war films, in which the officers were alert, handsome, and David Niven or a facsimile thereof, while the men tended to be dumb, ugly, and Stanley Holloway. Joan Littlewood, the leading director of the new British drama, has effectively expressed the malice that this tradition inspired:

> In the theatre of those dear, departed days when every actress had roses round her vowels, and a butler's suit was an essential part of an actor's equipment, the voice of the Cockney was one long whine of blissful servitude. No play was complete without its moronic maid or faithful batman —rich with that true cockney speech and humor learned in the drama schools.

Obviously, these patronizing portraits were not created for the working classes but for their social superiors, who found the lower classes quaint but fundamentally uninteresting. Most of the plays implied that the serving classes enjoyed their servitude, that they "knew their place" and loved it. Even when James Barrie indicated in *The Admirable Crichton* that class distinctions might undergo some shifting on a desert island, the play conveyed two primary principles: first, class distinctions of some sort are necessary in any circumstances, and, second, the class distinctions that prevail in England are ideally suited to England, if not to other places. The servant who has been a lord on a desert island contentedly goes back to being a servant when he returns to England. Significantly, life in the wilds is not so democratic that the conception of a nobility is lost. Titles are not abolished; all that happens to them is that they change hands. The system itself proves perfect. *The Admirable Crichton* gave this assurance to those beneficiaries of the system who attended the theater, and it assured them also that the lower classes loved the way things were. More recently, William Douglas Home's *The Chiltern Hundreds* gave similar assurances. In this play, a household is torn by political division: a silly young aristocrat stands for Parliament as a Labour candidate, while his profoundly intelligent servant opposes him as a Tory. The point of all this is that the case for the Labour Party is based not upon poverty but upon poverty of intelligence. London audiences loved the play—not surprisingly, in view of the conservative (and Conservative) inclinations of London audiences; but *The Chiltern Hundreds* was incomprehensible in New York.

Did the lower classes love the system? Surely not so much as the playwrights hoped. Even an apparently conservative new writer, Beverley Cross in *One More River,* permits an evil-minded lower-class character to speak of "the films they used to show us in the war where the officers were all heroes and the men stupid clowns with no brains and ugly faces." Speaking in her own person, Shelagh Delaney has told how her friends in Lancashire responded to the way the old-style dramatists would present them on the stage: "We used to object to plays where factory workers come cap in hand and call the boss 'Sir.' Usually North Country people are shown as gormless, whereas in actual fact they are very alive and cynical." But cynicism and intelligence had become, by theatrical fiat, the prerogatives of another class. That class now counts for so little that it has been generally ignored by the new dramatists. Brendan Behan does exhibit an addled aristocrat in *The Hostage,* but only John Osborne consistently pays his respects to those formerly great. His Jimmy Porter casts his cynical darts at the fashionable world in *Look Back in Anger,* and, in *The World of Paul Slickey,* Osborne briefly parodies fashionable drama, offering a scene in which a handsome matron dashes pointlessly around the stage arranging flowers. No doubt some remnants of that charming world still exist, but it is not the function of the new writers to interpret it. They need not bother: the loyal adherents of that old way of life still furnish most of the plays to the West End theaters.

The handsome leads of these old-style plays speak beautifully; they include the actors who display the same beautiful speech when they act in Shakespeare at the Old Vic and at Stratford-on-Avon. Their modern roles hold their eloquence in check but permit them to show their comparable talents at irony, understatement, *savoir-faire,* and *sang-froid.* The peculiar language of these characters is cool, clipped, and shy; the leading British actors have made a fine art of shyness and, in general, of such roles. They are loyal to the plays they know. To this date, Sir Ralph Richardson, Sir Michael Redgrave, Sir Alec Guinness, and Sir John Gielgud have yet to appear in any play by a dramatist of the new school. Their new plays are written chiefly by the old authors—Noel Coward, Terence Rattigan, and Graham Greene—or by the one new author who can satisfy them, Robert Bolt, who differs significantly from what I have called the new school. Paul Scofield is the latest addition to the small number of England's heroic actors. Having appeared in Wolf Mankowitz's *Expresso Bongo* when he was less well established, he went on to act in dramas by Greene and Bolt, and later to play Lear at Stratford. Of all of England's classic actors, only Sir Laurence Olivier has broken with the past—by undertaking the title role in John Osborne's *The Entertainer*.

The long life of this pallid tradition requires some explanation. Why did these conditions prevail? Why has the British drama been so poor for so long? Why were the only original dramatists outsiders like Shaw and O'Casey? I think the answer lies in the class pattern that Joan Littlewood found so infuriating. The theater belonged to the upper and upper-middle classes and the vast army of social climbers, who paid for it and who went to see idealized portraits of themselves—represented as being wittier and yet more serious than in life. They paid the piper, and they called the tune. Economically and socially, the theater was a closed corporation. It belonged to the Establishment, that monster of which British intellectuals speak as if it is a real green-scaled dragon with many arms and many heads. The Establishment is a verbal fiction embodying a truth of sorts. It is that authoritative conservatism that speaks impersonally through such organs as the B.B.C., the *Times* of London, and the West End stages. Questioned about the Establishment at the Drama Desk in New York, Paul Scofield denied its existence, whereupon another British actor protested that it was real enough but that Scofield was silent because he had joined it.

Another reason for the lethargy of the British stage was the severe censorship by which the Lord Chamberlain arbitrarily sets limits to the subjects of drama. The initiation of the present system in 1737 had the immediate effect of driving Henry Fielding out of the theater and into the writing of fiction. We can only conjecture as to how many talented dramatists-to-be the Lord Chamberlain's censorship drove from the stage. If Britain had some embryonic social dramatists in the 1930's, they found little opportunity to speak. Accordingly, a British producer charged in 1934 that, because of the Lord Chamberlain, the British drama was "twenty years behind the times." Just twenty years later, the British theater developed some social dramatists who reminded Americans of their own writers of the 1930's. At last England has, in certain respects, caught up with the American 1930's. Plays must still be submitted for the Lord Chamberlain's approval before they may be performed, but his censorship has become more lenient. This procedure rules out any alteration in the text of a play. The approved text is the one that must be acted, and so, presumably, topical reference and inventive actors are curbed. It is popularly assumed that Joan Littlewood, who encourages spontaneity and inventiveness in her actors, has violated the law in permitting night-to-night alterations in the texts of such plays as *The Hostage* and Frank Norman's *Fings Ain't Wot They Used T'be*. This new boldness with the Lord Chamberlain is another reflection of the new forces that are loose in the British theater.

Why has there been a change? Why have so many talented authors suddenly turned to writing plays? I should think that social mobility is the primary explanation. World War II began the job of jumbling the social classes; war, like death, is a great equalizer. Postwar prosperity furthered the process of breaking social barriers. England has been extraordinarily prosperous since the war, and its prosperity has produced Tory governments and Socialist playwrights. People of humble origin have had better opportunities for education than ever before, and good times have given them leisure in which to write. Prosperity and automation are creating a new and fortunate problem for working people—how to use their leisure time. Accordingly, new dramatists and directors are wresting control of the theater from the Establishment and hopefully offering it

to the newly liberated proletariat. In particular, Joan Littlewood has dedicated herself to establishing a people's theater,
and Arnold Wesker has steadily tried to interest labor unions
in supporting the drama.

The working class has not yet given the theater a new audience, although Joan Littlewood went to some trouble to insist
that the audience at her Stratford Theatre Royal, located far
from the West End in a working-class district, was mainly proletarian. Miss Littlewood's statistics seem convincing, but ob-
servers invariably noted that her audience did not look notably
proletarian. Still, that may be part of the transformation: we
need no longer expect proletarians to look proletarian.

If the theater audience has not yet been transformed and does
not yet spring from new sources, the playwrights have been
transformed. That is, they tend to come from the working class,
and several of them are Jewish. Now, it is true that the playwrights of England's past included a bricklayer named Ben
Jonson and a Jew named Israel Zangwill, but they were rare
intrusions upon the gentile, middle-class domination of the
stage. Among the proletarians turned playwright, Brendan Behan was a house painter, and Arnold Wesker was a plumber's
helper and a kitchen porter before becoming a pastry cook.
Bernard Kops's father made shoes and hoped his son would
follow him in his vocation. Shelagh Delaney was an usherette
in a theater when, at the age of nineteen, she saw *Variations
on a Theme* by Terence Rattigan, announced that she could
write a better play, and promptly went home and did so.
Stephen Lewis, whose *Sparrers Can't Sing* was performed by
Joan Littlewood's Stratford Theatre Royal, was an electrician's
helper until he joined the company as an actor; then, like John
Osborne and Harold Pinter, he turned from acting to playwriting. Another sign of change is the growing number of Jewish
playwrights—Wesker, Pinter, Kops, Lionel Bart (author of
Oliver! and composer of songs for *Fings Ain't Wot They Used
T'be*), Wolf Mankowitz (who dramatized his story *Make Me
an Offer* for Joan Littlewood), and Peter Shaffer (whose *Five
Finger Exercise* is, however, not profoundly linked to the new
movement). Wesker, Kops, and Mankowitz have given promin-

ence to Jewish subjects in their plays; Bart has so freely adapted
Dickens' Fagin that our sense of justice is not outraged when his
Fagin escapes punishment at the end of *Oliver!* The energy of
these new forces in the British theater is reflective, I think, of
their long suppression. The working class, Jewish or otherwise,
had furnished no authors to the British stage, and, but for a
few rare instances, it did not even furnish subjects to the serious
drama. First, a new prosperity and, later, the success of Behan
and Osborne made the stage seem, for the first time, accessible.

The characters of the new drama speak differently because,
for once, their ideal is not based on the B.B.C. and the upper
classes. Their speech reflects native traditions that have survived
all efforts to impose standard vocabularies and pronunciations.
In many of the new plays we hear cockney accents, with a Jewish flavor added in the works of Wesker, Kops, and Mankowitz.
Behan's characters speak with the authentic voice of Dublin.
We hear an assortment of accents in Willis Hall's *The Long and
the Short and the Tall,* Norfolk dialect in Wesker's *Roots,*
North of England speech in John Arden's *Serjeant Musgrave's
Dance,* Lancashire accents in Miss Delaney's *A Taste of Honey,*
and the peculiar tongue of the Liverpool Irish in Alun Owen's
Progress through the Park. No wonder these plays have baffled
traditional actors whose common tongue is standard English.

The new plays may be described as social drama, but of an
odd sort. It is necessarily an odd sort of social drama that arises
not out of bad times but out of prosperity. While most of these
writers are radical critics of society, what we never find is criticism of poverty as a threat to survival. Poverty as we see it here
is never so bad that anyone's existence is threatened. Instead,
the common complaint is that the individual's full development
is prevented. This complaint carries with it the implication
that leisure or the possibility of leisure exists. In *Roots,* the
heroine's father loses his job, but the play's real emphasis falls
upon the family's failure to think, to learn anything, or to
listen to music. The girl in *A Taste of Honey* studies art, but
she is insufficiently resolute to be an artist. The young men of
Osborne's plays, *Look Back in Anger* and *Epitaph for George
Dillon* (written with Anthony Creighton) are, respectively, an

actor and a dramatist; society permits them to survive but not to practice their arts. Behan, in *The Hostage,* attacks those Puritans and killjoys who threaten individual development of another kind. In *Live Like Pigs,* Arden assails the repressive, joyless life of conformist suburban respectability. Bourgeois conformity in its various aspects is surely being lampooned by N. F. Simpson in *One Way Pendulum* and by Harold Pinter in *The Birthday Party.* Continually we see stunted, unfulfilled lives, but we never find the barest level of subsistence. The question is not *whether* these people will survive but *how* they will live.

Individual plays touch upon some of the traditional subjects of the drama of social criticism. Hall's *The Long and the Short and the Tall* and Behan's *The Hostage* attack war, and *Serjeant Musgrave's Dance* makes a particular comment upon colonial war. *The Hostage* criticizes religious and national divisions, while *A Taste of Honey* makes a more tacit criticism of prejudice against Negroes and homosexuals. Behan's *The Quare Fellow* emphatically indicts capital punishment. But the best of these plays are more complex than their causes. They present a distinctive vision of life, and they embody issues that do not fit into any catalog of political grievances.

These plays do not make a case for committed socialism, for in them all of the right questions are asked but none of the easy answers are given, not even by Wesker, who is the most committed socialist of all. Everyone has complaints against the social order; no one has a program, and, in fact, at the heart of many plays we can discern a hard bedrock of anarchism. In general, these dramatists prefer the wild, destructive, foolish rebel to the tame man who conforms. Arden undoubtedly prefers the mad, thieving, antisocial gypsies of *Live Like Pigs* to the good citizens whose premises they invade. In *Serjeant Musgrave's Dance,* he deliberately chooses a religious fanatic to undertake a significant gesture against colonialism. He observes in his preface that "the sympathies of the play . . . turn against" Musgrave, but it is clear that the time's wrongs require a madman. Men like Walsh the labor organizer know the truth, but they do not act; madmen act, in response to a mad order of things. Arden calls the play "a story that is partly one of wish-fulfillment."

In *The Hostage,* we can have no doubt that the eccentric, self-indulgent residents of the brothel are more decent and more lovable than the ostentatiously public-spirited patriots. Behan's radio play *The Big House* celebrates a theft that despoils the effete aristocracy of Ireland. Osborne's heroes sound more antisocial than socialist, and the best man in *The Long and the Short and the Tall* is the worst, most rebellious, most irresponsible soldier. I find a certain kinship to this anarchist pattern in the nostalgia for Stalinism that Wesker reveals in *Chicken Soup with Barley.* Ronnie in that play is too sophisticated to be a Stalinist, but he envies the secure faith of his mother's Stalinism and the warm, if misguided, fellowship of the radical movement in the 1930's. I suggest an analogy with *Serjeant Musgrave's Dance:* might it not be better to be the effective religious fanatic or the effective Stalinist fanatic rather than the uncertain, ineffective intellectual? The dramatists ask the question; they do not answer it.

The new British dramatists make experiments in dramatic form, and in that respect they differ from those American social dramatists of the 1930's with whom they are often compared. To begin with, it is easiest to isolate what might be called the school of Joan Littlewood and to indicate the nature of its revolt against realism. It is well known that Miss Littlewood and her company collaborate on the plays which they produce; not surprisingly, the plays resemble one another in form. They include *The Quare Fellow* (more conventional and more resistant to Miss Littlewood's method than the others), *The Hostage, A Taste of Honey, Make Me an Offer, Fings Ain't Wot They Used T'be,* and *Sparrers Can't Sing.* The plays contain elements of music-hall entertainment, that popular art which Miss Littlewood's working-class audience presumably knows and loves. The characters in these plays stop to sing songs or to dance, to exchange quips irrelevant to the action. They often step out of the action to address us, as any music-hall performer might. Some of the characters are rather broad, obvious, deliberately caricatured types, like certain of the lodgers in *The Hostage,* the Jewish businessmen in *Make Me an Offer,* and the "wide boys" in *Fings*. Inevitably, the combination of this form with radical social criticism reminds us of Bertolt Brecht, but Miss Littlewood, who has played the title role in Brecht's *Mother Courage,* maintains that she has independently worked out her own kind of drama. Her company's skill at improvisation is reflected in the present text of *The Hostage,* which is quite different from the earlier version previously published in this country.

Brecht's influence is clearly present in the songs, the emphasis on episode, the social comment, and the detailed social picture of Arden's plays. *Live Like Pigs,* the most episodic, has seventeen scenes. *Serjeant Musgrave's Dance* concludes, in true Brechtian fashion, with a tribunal that brings all the issues to light; and, at this tribunal, we in the audience constitute the audience at the market place, gathered to hear Musgrave and his men and to be addressed directly by them. Osborne's *Luther* is an historical play in the Brechtian manner, but in his earlier work, Osborne is probably the least experimental of the group. His other plays are conventional in form, unless we consider the music-hall scenes of *The Entertainer* to be departures. Still, how else might the entertainer's act be shown? We are his audience as he performs.

Arnold Wesker observes the conventions of realism, but he gives us some surprises. *Chicken Soup with Barley* is not closely knit together but gives us brief glances at the Kahn family over a period of twenty years. Even though the realistic conventions are maintained, *Roots* manages to break its orderly development with song, dance, and Beatie's self-conscious imitations of Ronnie. The third play of his trilogy, *I'm Talking about Jerusalem,* is the most conservative in form. *The Kitchen* is unusual in its efforts to show an abnormally large scene in intense activity, that is, the kitchen of a large restaurant at mealtimes.

Harold Pinter and N. F. Simpson show much less interest in conventional realism. Individual speeches and acts are real enough in Pinter's plays, but the characters' roots have been torn away, and the men and events are suspended in a mysterious world that we cannot fully comprehend. In Simpson, on the other hand, the bourgeois British environment is plain to us, but the inhabitants of that environment parody the middle-class citizens of the real world. No one has denied Pinter's debt to Samuel Beckett and Simpson's debt to Eugene Ionesco, but each man has applied his foreign inspiration to a product that is distinctively his own.

The new drama has needed not only new forms but new theaters as well. These plays would be inconceivable without the institutions that gave them life. The Royal Court, an independent theater devoted to permitting the dramatist free expression, fostered the first productions of plays by Osborne, Wesker, Arden, and Simpson. Only one of Osborne's plays did not get its first performance at the Royal Court—*The World of Paul Slickey,* a musical which had to succeed on the West End or not at all. The peculiar virtues of productions at the Royal Court was that they were sufficiently modest to keep the cost of failure at a minimum. Then, once the plays had opened in modest circumstances, their reception could be weighed, and they might or might not be taken to the West End.

The theater which Joan Littlewood ran in Stratford East, London, till she resigned in 1961, saw the first productions of *A Taste of Honey* and *The Hostage.* Miss Littlewood's theater was especially committed to social comment and to the presentation of vigorous, roistering, demonstrative life, of whatever sort. Less specifically committed have been the Arts Theatre of London and the Belgrade Theatre of Coventry. *The Caretaker* was first performed at the Arts, which is technically a club and therefore not subject to supervision by the Lord Chamberlain. *Roots* was first done at the Belgrade, before being brought to London by the Royal Court.

Surely England's dramatic renaissance still has its best to give us. Everyone, we are continually reminded, is writing plays. The success of the first new playwrights has inspired others, but even the pioneers are still young and active, still learning their profession, still writing plays. The new dramatists have transformed the British theater, and it gives every evidence that it will remain transformed.

Earliest of the plays in this book is *A Taste of Honey.* In the briefest, plainest terms, any summary of its plot makes the play seem singularly unedifying. The teen-age daughter of "a semi-whore" takes a Negro lover, and, while she waits to bear his child, she is cared for by a homosexual. That sounds like someone's caricature of the grotesque and violent patterns of American drama. But this play is distinguished by many elements that a brief summary must ignore.

First, Miss Delaney offers us the great dramatic and human effectiveness of natural, instinctive action that moves us into surprising situations. The girl, who is in some respects a child of nature, acts naturally if unwisely, without a trace of self-consciousness. It is her lover who quotes from *Othello*, not she. The girl takes a Negro lover because no one taught her anything different; as the old song has it, you have to be taught to hate. But even this girl has been taught that homosexuals are ludicrous; it takes a great deal of the homosexual's instinctive generosity to persuade her otherwise, to teach her that kindness which, in other circumstances, is natural to her. The mother, on her return, reminds us what the world is like. Disastrous as her own life has been, she still feels qualified to express conventional horror at the homosexual and at the prospect of a colored grandchild.

All of this is enacted swiftly to the steady patter of insult jokes that sound rather better in performance than in quotation. The girl is on guard against most people in a world that has treated her badly, and words are her only weapons. "You're just like a big sister to me," the girl tells the homosexual. Describing a dream to her mother, she asks: "Guess what they found planted under a rosebush?" "You?" "No—you." That is how the people of the play protect themselves against human sympathy. The play's paradox is that so much feeling can be generated under these self-protective masks. Beneath it all, the mother has a real concern for her daughter; cynicism and prejudice combined cannot prevent the girl from responding to the homosexual's warm concern for her, and that is a triumph for humanity.

The Hostage was performed at the same theater in the same year, given life on the stage by the same director, Joan Littlewood, with the homosexual of the first play taking the title role of the second. Energy is Behan's first principle, and most of his characters give a full evening's display of energy in action. They interrupt the plot with their songs, dances, and vaudeville lines (like "I'll have you know I had my voice trained by an electrocutionist"), and they address the audience almost as often as they speak to one another. All of this activity may indicate that the plot is secondary, but the plot does, in fact, hold us, and it provides a proper center for the play.

Behan's play has for its subject the continuing warfare between life and death, between lively, extroverted human energy and the inhibitions, prohibitions, and miscellaneous barriers that keep humanity in check. In the brothel, energy is unrestrained, and "inhibition" is a foreign concept. Mr. Mulleady may profess to be a self-righteous soul, but he is, by Behan's standards, better than his word. The world's meanness is brought to the brothel by the civil war and by the I.R.A. officer who has charge of the prisoner. Why should the prisoner be kept in the brothel? For theatrical reasons, primarily, and also so that he may be in the company of the least fettered, the least imprisoned people in the world.

As *The Hostage* develops, the soldier and the servant girl respond to their natural instincts and overcome the barriers that the world has built to separate them. He is a brash Londoner; she is a timid convent girl. He understands nothing of the hostilities that have made a prisoner of him, but the girl harbors some vague nationalistic prejudices against him; he has a few prejudices of his own, against "'bleeding Nigger-boys" and the London Irish. He is a Protestant; she is a Catholic. He speaks cockney, which is nearly a foreign tongue to her. (Behan plays with the barriers of language. A foreign sailor—originally Polish, later Russian—speaks no English, but his pound notes speak a universal language. Monsewer's native tongue is upper-class English, but his Irish nationalism compels him to speak Irish, which the Irish do not understand.) The lovers vault over the obstacles between them. Still, the soldier has seen too much of life to expect any heroism; to his surprise, the girl brings about the ill-fated attempt to rescue him.

While the main plot of *The Hostage* bears down on the evils of war and nationalism, the characters in their incidental remarks pay their respects to the hydrogen bomb, the royal family, the F.B.I., and other bugbears. They urge an intensely personal, practical, nonidealistic philosophy, embodied in the songs that go "There's no place on earth like the world" and "There is no one loves you like yourself." In a certain sense, such notions as these are the hope of the world. It is the idealists who start the wars.

Arnold Wesker's *Roots* is central to the new development in the British theater because Wesker is the dramatist who is most explicit about his socialism, a doctrine of undeniable relevance to the other new plays. But Wesker is self-critical, for he does not give his socialists an easy time of it in any of his works. In the first play of his trilogy, *Chicken Soup with Barley,* only one stubborn Stalinist remains of the ardent socialists of old; the rest have turned respectable. In the second play, *Roots,* the unseen socialist is an opinionated lout and a cad who cruelly and abruptly drops his girl. In the third play, *I'm Talking About Jerusalem,* an effort to establish a William Morris kind of socialism meets with failure. To say the very least, Wesker recognizes the frailties of his socialists. Consequently, the voice of Ronnie Kahn, which, by a kind of ventriloquism, we hear from the mouth of Beatie Bryant, is not to be confused with the voice out of the whirlwind. *Roots* rests upon the interplay between the quixotic Ronnie's equally quixotic disciple and her boorish family. Far from being the vigorous children of nature that Beatie's city-bred lover thinks they are, these farmers are eager consumers of mass culture, of television shows and popular songs. They quarrel over possessions or over nothing at all, with the result that the family is intersected by an elaborate network of feuds. Their lives are marked mainly by the passage of this or that train or oversized truck, by which they note the hours. They indulge their senses principally by overeating. And, less directly, the action reveals to us that Beatie is substantially like the others, in spite of the "culture" that she has picked up in London and repeats in the country. She imitates Ronnie's attitudes rather expertly, but she has never learned anything substantial, perhaps because he has, substantially, so little to teach.

Even though Beatie and her Ronnie are weak vessels and doubtful oracles, at least they aspire, and their aspirations find some authentic expression in Beatie's concluding discourse on mass culture. While Beatie's little speech is neither the first nor the last word on the subject, it is, as she hopefully asserts, a beginning, and it comments directly on the problem of the play, the corruption of the mass mind by mass culture. If it strikes a note of hope, it adds all the necessary qualifications.

Serjeant Musgrave's Dance had a mixed reception and a short run at the Royal Court Theatre. Subsequently, some hostile critics were converted by less professional productions. A few were puzzled by nearly everything and especially by the unlovable spokesman Arden had created for his pacifist doctrine. Others, even if they recognized Arden's need to make Musgrave a specific kind of human being and not merely a paragon of pacifism, thought the attention given to the minor characters to be extraneous. And yet, the indifference and selfishness of the townsfolk are obviously suited to a nation that supports colonial ventures. The soldiers, too, act out a little parable. Only Attercliffe, the dullest of the three, a man half-alive ever since he found himself a cuckold, only he blindly follows Musgrave without serious question. Attercliffe has forsworn passion, and Musgrave has converted his own passion into his pacifist mania. But Sparky and Hurst are more passionate and more normal; in their quarrel over Annie, they recall Billy Hicks, who was Annie's lover. Life distracts them from their cause, as it distracts all of us from causes, except for fanatics like Musgrave. The shrewd labor leader keeps his distance, and that, too, reminds us of the worldliness of sane, sensible people. Musgrave's madness is only half the tragedy here; the indifference of the sane is the other half.

N. F. Simpson, the author of *One Way Pendulum,* is regarded as England's leading disciple of Eugène Ionesco. He has a peculiar added advantage. His insidious and insistent parody of logic recalls Lewis Carroll. When *One Way Pendulum* transferred to the West End from the Royal Court Theatre, that development, surprising for an *avant-garde* play, suggested that Simpson had appealed to the same whimsical natures to which Lewis Carroll had directed *Alice in Wonderland.*

This play is constructed upon such celebrated English traits as idiosyncrasy and logic. The family is obsessed with travel, on camels, rickshaws, wheel chairs or anything else. The son has an artistic bent, reflected in his love of color—just one color, black—and his efforts to coax a concert performance out of speak-your-weight weighing machines. The father's passion for the law combines idiosyncrasy with the traditional British love of justice. It is in the nature of idiosyncrasies to be illogical and never to be pursued to their inevitable conclusions. But the Groomkirbys parody logic by observing it. The woman who comes to eat up surplus food follows the logic of certain stand-ard household arrangements. The son's extraordinary actions are logically inspired by his passionate fondness for the color black, and that leaning has, in its turn, been logically inspired by his parents' natural liking for contrasting colors. The court-room and the trial proceed directly out of the father's hobby; in the London production, the courtroom set looked much more real than the Groomkirbys' home, to indicate that Mr. Groom-kirby's dream life was more real to him than his home life.

Inexorable logic prevails in the trial scene. The mother is the perfect, cautious witness, testifying only to her certain knowl-edge when she refuses to say whether her husband has any Negro blood: "Well—he *has* got one or two bottles up in his room, but he doesn't tell me what's *in* them." The judge, too, shows that he can think straight when he acquits the defendant so that the law will not be deprived of its prerogative of dealing with the malefactor's future crimes. Simpson's target is the logic of the sensible, no-nonsense, businesslike middle-class mind, and the play works beautifully when it is played, as in London, with perfect dignity by actors who might be doing a serious drama of middle-class life. In fact, Alison Leggatt, the mother in the Osborne-Creighton *Epitaph for George Dillon,* played the mother in *One Way Pendulum,* and her mannerisms were not notably different in the more serious role.

The influence of Samuel Beckett upon Harold Pinter is as well publicized as the influence of Ionesco upon Simpson. But, as in any literary comparison, differences are probably more instructive than resemblances. Pinter does, like Beckett, set distinctive, highly theatrical characters down in the precise center of a vague world. They thoroughly expose their relationships with one another, but they reveal next to nothing of their connection with the rest of mankind. In Beckett, we even have reason to wonder if the rest of mankind exists; Pinter leads us to assume, in *The Caretaker* and *The Birthday Party,* the general environment of business life and the city, even though we learn no details about it. What sort of businessman is Mick? What sort of relationship does he have with his brother? We understand the brothers' separate relationships with Davies rather more fully, for no better reason than because that is where Pinter causes the light to fall.

We can understand *The Caretaker* in various ways. Donald Pleasence, who memorably created the part of the tramp, has spoken of it as a play in which "boy meets tramp, boy loses tramp," indicating that it is no more unusual than it would be if the word "girl" were substituted for "tramp." But it is also surely a little moral drama in which good wins a small victory; the victory is small indeed, for it is no more than mere survival. Good is embodied in Aston, the older brother, who is a decent, generous human being; that is to say, he is demented. He has been in a mental institution where society has sought, by shock therapy, to fill him with that violence which abounds in the sane world. Naturally, no one thinks of clapping the tramp or the younger brother into an institution; their selfishness establishes them as model citizens. Just one thing in particular prevents these model citizens from ganging up to destroy the benevolent Aston—an accident of blood relationship. Also, the tramp ruins his own cause by being a caricature of presuming self-importance; even this universally popular trait is capable of being overdone, and he overdoes it. Selfishness is the way of the world, but the world demands a certain finesse in its practice. The tramp is cast out, and that brings us to another departure from Beckett's practice. Pinter goes a step further than Beckett toward resolving his action. Mysteries remain, but

Pinter's plays have a more formal ending and not only a steady drift toward dissolution and oblivion.

New wine requires new vessels, even though Arnold Wesker has been quoted as saying, "We young writers are still writing conventionally constructed plays." Wesker has himself written a play about a kitchen; if he interprets "conventionally constructed" so broadly as to include such works, then no one can quarrel with his observation. The worlds of Simpson and Pinter are clearly not those of conventional realism. While Joan Littlewood enlivens the plays she directs with music-hall songs, John Arden inserts ballads into his works. Even John Osborne, who did indeed write "conventionally constructed plays," has turned Brechtian with *Luther*. In more ways than one, something new has come to the British theater.

THE NEW
BRITISH DRAMA

A TASTE
OF HONEY

Shelagh Delaney

A TASTE OF HONEY was first presented by Theatre Workshop at the Theatre Royal, Stratford, London E.15, on 27 May 1958. On 10 February 1959 it was presented by Donald Albery and Oscar Lewenstein Ltd, at Wyndham's Theatre, London, directed by Joan Littlewood, settings by John Bury, costumes by Una Collins, and with the following cast:

HELEN	Avis Bunnage
JOSEPHINE, *her daughter*	Frances Cuka
PETER, *her friend*	Nigel Davenport
THE BOY	Clifton Jones
GEOFFREY	Murray Melvin
THE APEX JAZZ TRIO	Johnny Wallbank (*cornet*)
	Barry Wright (*guitar*)
	Christopher Capon (*double bass*)

The play is set in Salford, Lancashire, today.

ACT ONE

Scene One

The stage represents a comfortless flat in Manchester and the street outside. Jazz music. Enter HELEN, *a semi-whore, and her daughter,* JO. *They are loaded with baggage.*

HELEN: Well! This is the place.

JO: And I don't like it.

HELEN: When I find somewhere for us to live I have to consider something far more important than your feelings . . . the rent. It's all I can afford.

JO: You can afford something better than this old ruin.

HELEN: When you start earning you can start moaning.

JO: Can't be soon enough for me. I'm cold and my shoes let water . . . what a place . . . and we're supposed to be living off her immoral earnings.

HELEN: I'm careful. Anyway, what's wrong with this place? Everything in it's falling apart, it's true, and we've no heating—but there's a lovely view of the gasworks, we share a bathroom with the community and this wallpaper's contemporary. What more do you want? Anyway it'll do for us. Pass me a glass, Jo.

JO: Where are they?

HELEN: I don't know.

JO: You packed 'em. She'd lose her head if it was loose.

HELEN: Here they are. I put 'em in my bag for safety. Pass me that bottle—it's in the carrier.

JO: Why should I run around after you? (*Takes whisky bottle from bag.*)

HELEN: Children owe their parents these little attentions.

JO: I don't owe you a thing.

HELEN: Except respect, and I don't seem to get any of that.

JO: Drink, drink, drink, that's all you're fit for. You make me sick.

HELEN: Others may pray for their daily bread, I pray for . . .

JO: Is that the bedroom?

HELEN: It is. Your health, Jo.

JO: We're sharing a bed again, I see.

HELEN: Of course, you know I can't bear to be parted from you.

JO: What I wouldn't give for a room of my own! God! It's freezing! Isn't there any sort of fire anywhere, Helen?

HELEN: Yes, there's a gas-propelled thing somewhere.

JO: Where?

HELEN: Where? What were you given eyes for? Do you want me to carry you about? Don't stand there shivering; have some of this if you're so cold.

JO: You know I don't like it.

HELEN: Have you tried it?

JO: No.

HELEN: Then get it down you! (*She wanders around the room searching for fire.*) "Where!" she says. She can never see anything till she falls over it. Now, where's it got to? I know I saw it here somewhere . . . one of those shilling in the slot affairs; the landlady pointed it out to me as part of the furniture and fittings. I don't know. Oh! It'll turn up. What's up with you now?

JO: I don't like the smell of it.

HELEN: You don't smell it, you drink it! It consoles you.

JO: What do you need consoling about?

HELEN: Life! Come on, give it to me if you've done with it. I'll soon put it in a safe place. (*Drinks.*)

JO: You're knocking it back worse than ever.

HELEN: Oh! Well, it's one way of passing time while I'm waiting something to turn up. And it usually does if I drink hard enough. Oh my God! I've caught a shocking cold from somebody. Have you got a clean hanky, Jo? Mine's wringing wet with dabbing at my nose all day.

JO: Have this, it's nearly clean. Isn't that light awful? I do hate to see an unshaded electric light bulb dangling from the ceiling like that.

HELEN: Well, don't look at it then.

JO: Can I have that chair, Helen? I'll put my scarf round it.

JO takes chair from HELEN, *stands on it and wraps her scarf round light bulb—burning herself in the process.*

HELEN: Wouldn't she get on your nerves? Just when I was going to take the weight off my feet for five minutes. Oh! my poor old nose.

JO: Christ! It's hot.

HELEN: Why can't you leave things alone? Oh! she gets me down. I'll buy a proper shade tomorrow. It's running like a tap. This is the third hanky today.

JO: Tomorrow? What makes you think we're going to live that long? The roof's leaking!

HELEN: Is it? No, it's not, it's just condensation.

JO: Was it raining when you took the place?

HELEN: It is a bit of a mess, isn't it.

JO: You always have to rush off into things. You never think.

HELEN: Oh well, we can always find something else.

JO: But what are you looking for? Every place we find is the same.

HELEN: Oh! Every time I turn my head my eyeballs hurt. Can't we have a bit of peace for five minutes?

JO: I'll make some coffee.

HELEN: Do what you like. I feel rotten. I've no business being out of bed.

JO: Where's the kitchen?

HELEN: Where's the—through there. I have to be really bad before I can go to bed, though. It's the only redeeming feature in this entire lodging house. I've got it in my throat now too. I hope you're going to make full use of it.

JO: There's a gas stove in here.

HELEN: It hurts when I swallow. Of course there is!

JO: It looks a bit ancient. How do I light it?

HELEN: How do I—with a match. Wouldn't she drive you mad?

JO: I know that, but which knob do I turn?

HELEN: Turn 'em all, you're bound to find the right one in the end. She can't do a thing for herself, that girl. Mind you don't gas yourself. Every time I comb my hair it goes right through me. I think it's more than a cold, you know—more likely it's 'flu! Did you find it?

Loud bang.

JO: Yes.

HELEN: The way she bangs about! I tell you, my head's coming off.

JO: Won't be long now. Who lives here besides us, Helen? Any young people?

HELEN: Eh? Oh! Yes, I did see a lad hanging around here when I called last week. Handsome, long-legged creature—just the way I like 'em. Perhaps he's one of the fixtures. He'd just do for you, Jo; you've never had a boy friend, have you?

JO: No. I used to like one of your fancy men though.

HELEN: Oh! Which one?

JO: I thought I was in love with him.

HELEN: Which one does she mean?

JO: I thought he was the only man I'd ever love in my life and then he ran off with that landlady's daughter.

HELEN: Oh! Him.

JO: And I cried myself to sleep for weeks.

HELEN: She was a silly cat if ever there was one. You should have seen her. Honest to God! She was a sight for sore eyes. I'll have to tell you about her too sometime.

JO: I saw him again one day, on the street.

HELEN: Did you?

JO: I couldn't believe my eyes. He was thin, weak-chinned, with a funny turned-up nose.

HELEN: It wasn't his nose I was interested in.

Tugboat heard.

JO: Can you smell that river?

HELEN: I can't smell a thing! I've got such a cold.

JO: What's that big place over there?

HELEN: The slaughterhouse. Where all the cows, sheep and pigs go in and all the beef, pork and mutton comes out.

JO: I wonder what it'll be like here in the summer. I bet it'll smell.

HELEN: This whole city smells. Eee, there's a terrible draught in here. Where's it coming from? Look at that! What a damn silly place to put a window. This place is cold enough, isn't it, without giving shelter to the four winds.

JO: Helen, stop sniffing. It sounds awful.

HELEN: I can't help it. You'd sniff if you had a cold like this. She's not got a bit of consideration in her. It's self all the time.

JO: I'm going to unpack my bulbs. I wonder where I can put them.

HELEN: I could tell you.

JO: They're supposed to be left in a cool, dark place.

HELEN: That's where we all end up sooner or later. Still, it's no use worrying, is it?

JO: I hope they bloom. Always before when I've tried to fix up a window box nothin's ever grown in it.

HELEN: Why do you bother?

JO: It's nice to see a few flowers, isn't it?

HELEN: Where did you get those bulbs?

JO: The Park. The gardener had just planted about two hundred. I didn't think he'd miss half a dozen.

HELEN: That's the way to do things. If you see something you want, take it. That's my daughter for you. If you spent half as much time on me as you do on them fiddling bits of greenery I'd be a damn sight better off. Go and see if the kettle's boiling.

JO: See yourself. I've got to find somewhere for my bulbs.

HELEN: See yourself. Do everything yourself. That's what happens. You bring 'em up and they turn round and talk to you like that. I would never have dared talk to my mother like that when I was her age. She'd have knocked me into the middle of next week. Oh! my head. Whenever I walk, you know how it is! What a journey! I never realized this city was so big. Have we got any aspirins left, Jo?

JO: No. I dreamt about you last night, Helen.

HELEN: You're going to have a shocking journey to school each day, aren't you? It must be miles and miles.

JO: Not for much longer.

HELEN: Why, are you still set on leaving school at Christmas?

JO: Yes.

HELEN: What are you going to do?

JO: Get out of your sight as soon as I can get a bit of money in my pocket.

HELEN: Very wise too. But how are you going to get your money in the first place? After all, you're not very fond of work, are you?

JO: No. I take after you.

HELEN (*looking at the aspidistra*): That's nice, isn't it? Puts me in mind of my first job, in a tatty little pub down Whit Lane. I thought it was wonderful . . . You know, playing the piano and all that; a real get-together at weekends. Everybody standing up and giving a song. I used to bring the house down with this one. (*Sings.*)

> I'd give the song birds to the wild wood
> I'd give the sunset to the blind
> And to the old folks I'd give the memory
> of the baby upon their knee.

(*To orchestra:*) Come on, vamp it in with me.

JO: You can't play to that. It's got no rhythm.

HELEN: Oh! They'd tear it up, wouldn't they? (*She sings another verse.*) It's nice though, isn't it?

JO: What would you say if I did something like that?

HELEN: I should have taken up singing—everybody used to tell me. What did you say?

JO: I said what would you say if I got a job in a pub?

HELEN: You can't sing, can you? Anyway, it's your life, ruin it your own way. It's a waste of time interfering with other people, don't you think so? It takes me all my time to look after myself, I know that.

JO: That's what you said, but really you think you could make a better job of it, don't you?

HELEN: What?

JO: Ruining my life. After all, you've had plenty of practice.

HELEN: Yes, give praise where praise is due, I always say. I certainly supervised my own downfall. Oh! This chair's a bit low, isn't it? Could do with a cushion.

JO: Anyway I'm not getting married like you did.

HELEN: Oh!

JO: I'm too young and beautiful for that.

HELEN: Listen to it! Still, we all have funny ideas at that age, don't we—makes no difference though, we all end up same way sooner or later. Anyway, tell me about this dream you had.

JO: What dream?

HELEN: You said you had a dream about me.

JO: Oh that! It was nothing much. I was standing in a garden and there were some policemen digging and guess what they found planted under a rosebush?

HELEN: You.

JO: No—you.

HELEN: Why, had we run short of cemetary space? Well, I've always said we should be used for manure when we're gone. Go and see to that coffee. I'm dying for a hot drink. This bloody cold! It's all over me. I'm sure it's 'flu—I suppose I'd better clear some of this stuff away. She wouldn't think. Well, they don't at that age, do they? Oh! It gets me right here when I try to do anything when I bend, you know. Have you ever had it? I was thinking of washing my hair tonight, but I don't think it's wise to . . . Christ! what the hell's she got in here . . . sooner her than me . . . what's this? *(Seeing drawings.)* Hey, Jo, Jo, what's this?

JO: What's what?

HELEN: Did you do this?

JO: Put it down.

HELEN: I thought you said you weren't good at anything.

JO: It's only a drawing.

HELEN: It's very good. Did you show them this at school?

JO: I'm never at one school long enough to show them anything.

HELEN: That's my fault, I suppose.

JO: You will wander about the country.

HELEN: It's the gipsy in me. I didn't realize I had such a talented daughter. Look at that. It's good, isn't it?

JO: I'm not just talented, I'm geniused.

HELEN: I think I'll hang this on the wall somewhere. Now, where will it be least noticeable? Don't snatch. Have you no manners? What's these?

JO: Self-portraits. Give 'em here.

HELEN: Self-portraits? Oh! Well, I suppose you've got to draw pictures of yourself, nobody else would. Hey! Is that supposed to be me?

JO: Yes.

HELEN: Don't I look a misery? They're very artistic though, I must say. Have you ever thought of going to a proper art school and getting a proper training?

JO: It's too late.

HELEN: I'll pay. You're not stupid. You'll soon learn.

JO: I've had enough of school. Too many different schools and too many different places.

HELEN: You're wasting yourself.

JO: So long as I don't waste anybody else. Why are you so suddenly interested in me, anyway? You've never cared much before about what I was doing or what I was trying to do or the difference between them.

HELEN: I know, I'm a cruel, wicked woman.

JO: Why did we have to come here anyway? We were all right at the other place.

HELEN: I was fed up with the other place.

JO: You mean you're running away from somebody.

HELEN: You're asking for a bloody good hiding, lady. Just be careful. Oh! She'd drive you out of your mind. And my head's splitting. Splitting in two.

JO: What about me? Don't you think I get fed up with all this flitting about? Where's the bathroom? I'm going to have a bath.

HELEN: You're always bathing.

JO: I'm not like you. I don't wait until it becomes necessary before I have a good wash.

HELEN: You'll find the communal latrine and wash-house at the end of the passage. And don't throw your things about, this place is untidy enough as it is.

JO: That's all we do, live out of a travelling-bag.

HELEN: Don't worry, you'll soon be an independent working woman and free to go where you please.

JO: The sooner the better. I'm sick of you. You've made my life a misery. And stop sneezing your 'flu bugs all over me. I don't want to catch your cold.

HELEN: Oh! Get out of my sight. Go and have your bath.

JO: You can get your own coffee too. Why should I do anything for you? You never do anything for me.

Music. Enter PETER, *a brash car salesman, cigar in mouth.*

HELEN: Oh! My God! Look what the wind's blown in. What do you want?

PETER: Just passing by, you know. Thought I'd take a look at your new headquarters.

HELEN: Just passing . . . How did you find my address?

PETER: I found it. Did you think you could escape me, dear?

JO: So that's what she was running away from.

PETER: Who's this?

HELEN: My daughter.

PETER: Oh! Hello there. That puts another ten years on her.

JO: What's this one called?

HELEN: Smith.

JO: You told me not to trust men calling themselves Smith.

HELEN: Oh go and have your bath.

JO: I don't know where the bathroom is.

HELEN: It's in a little hole in the corridor.

JO: Is he staying?

PETER: Yes, I'm staying.

JO: Then I'll go for my bath later.

HELEN: What did you want to follow me here for?

PETER (*fumbling*): You know what I want.

HELEN: Give over! Jo, go and see to that coffee! He would show up just when I've got her hanging round my neck.

PETER: Do what your mother tells you.

JO: Ordering me about like a servant! (*She goes.* PETER *makes another pass at* HELEN.) The kettle's not boiling. I suppose she hasn't told you about me.

PETER: Christ!

HELEN: Go and lay the table.

JO: No.

HELEN: Well, do something. Turn yourself into a bloody termite and crawl into the wall or something, but make yourself scarce.

PETER: Get rid of her.

HELEN: I can't. Anyway, nobody asked you to come here.

PETER: Why did you come here? I had to chase all over town looking for you, only to finish up in this dump.

HELEN: Oh shut up! I've got a cold.

PETER: What on earth made you choose such a ghastly district?

HELEN: I can't afford to be so classy.

PETER: Tenements, cemetery, slaughterhouse.

HELEN: Oh we've got the lot here.

PETER: Nobody could live in a place like this.

JO: Only about fifty thousand people.

PETER: And a snotty-nosed daughter.

HELEN: I said nobody asked you to come. Oh my God! I'll have to have a dose of something. My head's swimming. Why did you?

PETER: Why did I what?

HELEN: Follow me here?

PETER: Now you know you're glad to see me, kid.

HELEN: No I'm not. The only consolation I can find in your immediate presence is your ultimate absence.

PETER: In that case, I'll stay.

HELEN: I warned you. I told you I was throwing my hand in. Now didn't I?

PETER: You did.

HELEN: Oh! Throw that cigar away. It looks bloody ridiculous stuck in your mouth like a horizontal chimney.

PETER: Your nose is damp. Here, have this.

HELEN: Oh go away!

PETER: Give it a good blow.

HELEN: Leave it alone.

PETER: Blow your nose, woman. *(She does.)* And while we're at it blow a few of those cobwebs out of your head. You can't afford to lose a man like me.

HELEN: Can't I?

PETER: This is the old firm. You can't renege on the old firm.

HELEN: I'm a free lance. Besides, I'm thinking of giving it up.

PETER: What?

HELEN: Sex! Men!

PETER: What have we done to deserve this?

HELEN: It's not what you've done. It's what I've done.

PETER: But *(approaching her),* darling, you do it so well.

HELEN: Now give over, Peter. I've got all these things to unpack.

PETER: Send her to the pictures.

HELEN: I don't feel like it.

PETER: What's wrong?

HELEN: I'm tired. It's terrible when you've got a cold, isn't it? You don't fancy anything.

PETER: Well, put your hat on, let's go for a drink. Come on down to the church and I'll make an honest woman out of you.

HELEN *(she goes to put her coat on, then changes her mind):* No, I don't fancy it.

PETER: I'm offering to marry you, dear.

HELEN: You what?

PETER: Come on, let's go for a drink.

HELEN: I told you I don't fancy it.

PETER: You won't find anything better.

HELEN: Listen, love, I'm old enough to be your mother.

PETER (*petting her*): Now you know I like this mother and son relationship.

HELEN: Stop it!

PETER: Aren't you wearing your girdle?

HELEN: Now, Peter.

PETER: Whoops!

HELEN: Well, you certainly liberate something in me. And I don't think it's maternal instincts either.

PETER (*sings*): "Walter, Walter, lead me to the altar!"

HELEN: Some hopes.

PETER: Helen, you don't seem to realize what an opportunity I'm giving you. The world is littered with women I've rejected, women still anxious to indulge my little vices and excuse my less seemly virtues. Marry me, Helen. I'm young, good-looking and well set up. I may never ask you again.

HELEN: You're drunk.

PETER: I'm as sober as a judge.

HELEN: If you ask me again I might accept.

PETER (*sings*): "I see a quiet place, a fireplace, a cosy room."

HELEN: Yes, the tap room at the Red Lion. What are you after?

PETER: You know what I like.

JO (*coughs, enters*): Here's your coffee. Excuse me if I interrupted something. I'm sorry the crockery isn't very elegant, but it's all we've got.

PETER: Don't run away.

JO: I'm not running. (*Sits.*)

PETER: Is she always like this?

HELEN: She's jealous ...

PETER: That's something I didn't bargain for.

HELEN: Can't bear to see me being affectionate with anybody.

JO: You've certainly never been affectionate with me.

PETER: Still, she's old enough to take care of herself. What sort of coffee is this anyway? It can hardly squeeze itself through the spout.

HELEN: She always does that. Makes it as weak as she can because she knows I like it strong. Don't drink that, it isn't worth drinking. Leave it.

JO: She should be in bed.

PETER: I know she should.

JO: You look very pale and sickly, Helen.

HELEN: Thank you.

JO: Is he going?

HELEN: Yes, come on, you'd better go before you catch my cold.

He pulls her to him as she passes.

PETER: Come outside then.

HELEN: No.

PETER: What does the little lady want? An engagement ring?

JO: I should have thought their courtship had passed the stage of symbolism.

HELEN: I always accept the odd diamond ring with pleasure.

PETER: I know it's my money you're after.

HELEN: Are you kidding?

JO: Hey!

He embraces HELEN *at the door and begins to tell her a dirty story.*

PETER: Did I ever tell you about the bookie who married the prostitute?

HELEN: No. Go on.

JO: Hey! What sort of a cigar is that?

PETER: Why don't you go home to your father?

JO: He's dead.

PETER: Too bad. Anyway, this bookie . . .

JO: Is it a Havana?

HELEN: Yes.

PETER: A rich, dark Havana, rolled on the thigh of a coal black mammy.

JO: You want to be careful. You never know where a coal black mammy's thigh's been.

HELEN: Take no notice of her. She think's she's funny.

JO: So does he! I bet he's married.

HELEN *bursts out laughing at his joke.*

You're not really going to marry her, are you? She's a devil with the men.

PETER: Are you Helen?

HELEN: Well, I don't consider myself a slouch. Now come on then, if you've finished what you came for you'd better get going. We've all this to clear away before we go to bed.

PETER: Well, I won't be round tomorrow; the cat's been on the strawberries.

HELEN: Get going.

PETER: Don't forget me.

JO: Shall I withdraw while you kiss her good night?

HELEN: I'll kiss you good night in a minute, lady, and it really will be good night.

PETER: Well, take care of your mother while she's ailing, Jo. You know how fragile these old ladies are.

HELEN: Go on, get! (*Exit* PETER.) Well, I'm going to bed. We'll shift this lot tomorrow. There's always another day.

JO: It's dark out there now. I think I'll have my bath in the morning.

HELEN: Are you afraid of the dark?

JO: You know I am.

HELEN: You should try not to be.

JO: I do.

HELEN: And you're still afraid?

JO: Yes.

HELEN: Then you'll have to try a bit harder, won't you?

JO: Thanks. I'll do that. What's the bed like?

HELEN: Like a coffin only not half as comfortable.

JO: Have you ever tried a coffin?

HELEN: I dare say I will one day. I do wish we had a hot water bottle.

JO: You should have asked him to stay. It wouldn't be the first time I've been thrown out of my bed to make room for one of your . . .

HELEN: For God's sake shut up! Close your mouth for five
 minutes. And you can turn the light off and come to bed.

JO: Aren't we going to clear this lot up?

HELEN: No, it'll look all right in the dark.

JO: Yes, it's seen at its best, this room, in the dark.

HELEN: Everything is seen at its best in the dark—including me.
 I love it. Can't understand why you're so scared of it.

JO: I'm not frightened of the darkness outside. It's the darkness inside houses I don't like.

HELEN: Come on! Hey, Jo, what would you do if I told you I
 was thinking of getting married again?

JO: I'd have you locked up in an institution right away!

HELEN: Come on.

Music. Fade out.

Scene Two

JO *and her* BOY FRIEND, *a coloured naval rating, walking on the
street. They stop by the door.*

JO: I'd better go in now. Thanks for carrying my books.

BOY: Were you surprised to see me waiting outside school?

JO: Not really.

BOY: Glad I came?

JO: You know I am.

BOY: So am I.

JO: Well, I'd better go in.

BOY: Not yet! Stay a bit longer.

JO: All right! Doesn't it go dark early? I like winter. I like it
 better than all the other seasons.

BOY: I like it too. When it goes dark early it gives me more time for— (*He kisses her.*)

JO: Don't do that. You're always doing it.

BOY: You like it.

JO: I know, but I don't want to do it all the time.

BOY: Afraid someone'll see us?

JO: I don't care.

BOY: Say that again.

JO: I don't care.

BOY: You mean it too. You're the first girl I've met who really didn't care. Listen, I'm going to ask you something. I'm a man of few words. Will you marry me?

JO: Well, I'm a girl of few words. I won't marry you but you've talked me into it.

BOY: How old are you?

JO: Nearly eighteen.

BOY: And you really will marry me?

JO: I said so, didn't I? You shouldn't have asked me if you were only kidding me up. (*She starts to go.*)

BOY: Hey! I wasn't kidding. I thought you were. Do you really mean it? You will marry me?

JO: I love you.

BOY: How do you know?

JO: I don't know why I love you but I do.

BOY: I adore you. (*Swinging her through the air.*)

JO: So do I. I can't resist myself.

BOY: I've got something for you.

JO: What is it? A ring!

BOY: This morning in the shop I couldn't remember what sort of hands you had, long hands, small hands or what. I stood there like a damn fool trying to remember what they felt like. (*He puts the ring on and kisses her hand.*) What will your mother say?

JO: She'll probably laugh.

BOY: Doesn't she care who her daughter marries?

JO: She's not marrying you, I am. It's got nothing to do with her.

BOY: She hasn't seen me.

JO: And when she does?

BOY: She'll see a coloured boy.

JO: No, whatever else she might be, she isn't prejudiced against colour. You're not worried about it, are you?

BOY: So long as you like it.

JO: You know I do.

BOY: Well, that's all that matters.

JO: When shall we get married?

BOY: My next leave? It's a long time, six months.

JO: It'll give us a chance to save a bit of money. Here, see... this ring... it's too big; look, it slides about... And I couldn't wear it for school anyway. I might lose it. Let's go all romantic. Have you got a bit of string?

BOY: What for?

JO: I'm going to tie it round my neck. Come on, turn your pockets out. Three handkerchiefs, a safety pin, a screw! Did that drop out of your head? Elastic bands! Don't little boys carry some trash. And what's this?

BOY: Nothing.

JO: A toy car! Does it go?

BOY: Hm hm!

JO: Can I try it? *(She does.)*

BOY: She doesn't even know how it works. Look, not like that.

He makes it go fast.

JO: I like that. Can I keep it?

BOY: Yes, take it, my soul and all, everything.

JO: Thanks. I know, I can use my hair ribbon for my ring. Do it up for me.

BOY: Pretty neck you've got.

JO: Glad you like it. It's my schoolgirl complexion. I'd better tuck this out of sight. I don't want my mother to see it. She'd only laugh. Did I tell you, when I leave school this week I start a part-time job in a bar? Then as soon as I get a full-time job, I'm leaving Helen and starting up in a room somewhere.

BOY: I wish I wasn't in the Navy.

JO: Why?

BOY: We won't have much time together.

JO: Well, we can't be together all the time and all the time there is wouldn't be enough.

BOY: It's a sad story, Jo. Once, I was a happy young man, not a care in the world. Now! I'm trapped into a barbaric cult . . .

JO: What's that? Mau-Mau?

BOY: Matrimony.

JO: Trapped! I like that! You almost begged me to marry you.

BOY: You led me on. I'm a trusting soul. Who took me down to that deserted football pitch?

JO: Who found the football pitch? I didn't even know it existed. And it just shows how often you must have been there, too . . . you certainly know where all the best spots are. I'm not going there again . . . It's too quiet. Anything might happen to a girl.

BOY: It almost did. You shameless woman!

JO: That's you taking advantage of my innocence.

BOY: I didn't take advantage. I had scruples.

JO: You would have done. You'd have gone as far as I would have let you and no scruples would have stood in your way.

BOY: You enjoyed it as much as I did.

JO: Shut up! This is the sort of conversation that can colour a young girl's mind.

BOY: Women never have young minds. They are born three thousand years old.

JO: Sometimes you look three thousand years old. Did your ancestors come from Africa?

BOY: No. Cardiff. Disappointed? Were you hoping to marry a man whose father beat the tom-tom all night?

JO: I don't care where you were born. There's still a bit of jungle in you somewhere. *(A siren is heard.)* I'm going in now, I'm hungry. A young girl's got to eat, you know.

BOY: Honey, you've got to stop eating. No more food, no more make-up, no more fancy clothes; we're saving up to get married.

JO: I just need some new clothes too. I've only got this one coat. I have to use it for school and when I go out with you. I do feel a mess.

BOY: You look all right to me.

JO: Shall I see you tonight?

BOY: No, I got work to do.

JO: What sort of work?

BOY: Hard work, it involves a lot of walking.

JO: And a lot of walking makes you thirsty. I know, you're going drinking.

BOY: That's right. It's one of the lads' birthdays. I'll see you tomorrow.

JO: All right. I'll tell you what, I won't bother going to school and we can spend the whole day together. I'll meet you down by that ladies' hairdressing place.

BOY: The place that smells of cooking hair?

JO: Yes, about ten o'clock.

BOY: Okay, you're the boss.

JO: Good night.

BOY: Aren't you going to kiss me good night?

JO: You know I am. (*Kisses him.*) I like kissing you. Good night.

BOY: Good night.

JO: Dream of me.

BOY: I dreamt about you last night. Fell out of bed twice.

JO: You're in a bad way.

BOY: You bet I am. Be seeing you!

JO (*as she goes*): I love you.

BOY: Why?

JO: Because you're daft.

He waves good-bye, turns and sings to the audience, and goes. HELEN *dances on to the music, lies down and reads an evening paper.* JO *dances on dreamily.*

HELEN: You're a bit late coming home from school, aren't you?

JO: I met a friend.

HELEN: Well, he certainly knows how to put stars in your eyes.

JO: What makes you think it's a he?

HELEN: Well I certainly hope it isn't a she who makes you walk round in this state.

JO: He's a sailor.

HELEN: I hope you exercised proper control over his nautical ardour. I've met a few sailors myself.

JO: He's lovely.

HELEN: Is he?

JO: He's got beautiful brown eyes and gorgeous curly hair.

HELEN: Has he got long legs?

JO: They're all right.

HELEN: How old is he?

JO: Twenty-two. He's doing his national service, but before that he was a male nurse.

HELEN: A male nurse, eh? That's interesting. Where did he do his nursing?

JO: In a hospital, of course! Where else do they have nurses?

HELEN: Does he ever get any free samples? We could do with a few contacts for things like that.

JO: Oh shut up, Helen. Have a look in that paper and see what's on at the pictures tomorrow night.

HELEN: Where is it? Oh yes ... *I was a Teenage* ... what? You can't go there anyway, it's a proper little flea pit. *The Ten Commandments,* here, that'd do you good. *Desire Under the* ... oh! What a funny place to have desire! You might as well have it at home as anywhere else, mightn't you? No, there's nothing here that I fancy.

JO: You never go to the pictures.

HELEN: I used to but the cinema has become more and more like the theatre, it's all mauling and muttering, can't hear what they're saying half the time and when you do it's not worth listening to. Look at that advertisement. It's pornographic. In my opinion such a frank and open display of the female form can only induce little boys of all ages to add vulgar comments in pencil. I ask you, what sort of an inflated woman is that? She's got bosom, bosom and still more bosom. I bet every inch of her chest is worth its weight in gold. Let's have a look at you. I wonder if I could turn you into a mountain of voluptuous temptation?

JO: Why?

HELEN: I'd put you on films.

JO: I'd sooner be put on't streets. It's more honest.

HELEN: You might have to do that yet.

JO: Where did this magazine come from?

HELEN: Woman downstairs give it me.

JO: I didn't think you'd buy it.

HELEN: Why buy when it's cheaper to borrow?

JO: What day was I born on?

HELEN: I don't know.

JO: You should remember such an important event.

HELEN: I've always done my best to forget that.

JO: How old was I when your husband threw you out?

HELEN: Change the subject. When I think of her father and my husband it makes me wonder why I ever bothered, it does really.

JO: He was rich, wasn't he ...

HELEN: He was a rat!

JO: He was your husband. Why did you marry him?

HELEN: At the time I had nothing better to do. Then he divorced me; that was your fault.

JO: I agree with him. If I was a man and my wife had a baby that wasn't mine I'd sling her out.

HELEN: Would you? It's a funny thing but I don't think I would. Still, why worry?

JO (*reading from magazine*): It says here that Sheik Ahmed—an Arabian mystic—will, free of all charge, draw up for you a complete analysis of your character and destiny.

HELEN: Let's have a look.

JO: There's his photograph.

HELEN: Oh! He looks like a dirty little spiv. Listen Jo, don't bother your head about Arabian mystics. There's two w's in your future. Work or want, and no Arabian Knight can tell you different. We're all at the steering wheel of our own destiny. Careering along like drunken drivers. I'm going to get married. *(The news is received in silence.)* I said, I'm going to get married.

JO: Yes, I heard you the first time. What do you want me to do, laugh and throw pennies? Is it that Peter Smith?

HELEN: He's the unlucky man.

JO: You're centuries older than him.

HELEN: Only ten years.

JO: What use can a woman of that age be to anybody?

HELEN: I wish you wouldn't talk about me as if I'm an impotent, shrivelled old woman without a clue left in her head.

JO: You're not exactly a child bride.

HELEN: I have been one once, or near enough.

JO: Just imagine it, you're forty years old. I hope to be dead and buried before I reach that age. You've been living for forty years.

HELEN: Yes, it must be a biological phenomena.

JO: You don't look forty. You look a sort of well-preserved sixty.

Music. Enter PETER *carrying a large bouquet and a box of chocolates and looking uncomfortable.*

HELEN: Oh look, and it's all mine!

JO: Hello, Daddy.

PETER: Oh! So you told her.

HELEN: Of course. Come in and sit down. On second thoughts lie down, you look marvellous.

He gives her the bouquet.

Oh! really, you shouldn't have bothered yourself. I know the thought was there, but . . . here, Jo, have we got a vase, put these in some water.

JO: How did she talk you into it? You must be out of your mind.

PETER: That's possible, I suppose.

JO: Flowers and all the trimmings. Helen can't eat anything sweet and delicious. She's got to watch her figure.

HELEN: Nonsense! My figure hasn't altered since I was eighteen.

JO: Really?

HELEN: Not an inch.

JO: I hope I'm luckier with mine.

HELEN: Do you see anything objectionable about my figure, Peter?

PETER: I find the whole thing most agreeable.

JO: You've got to say that, you're marrying it!

PETER: The chocolates are for you, Jo.

JO: Buying my silence, hey? It's a good idea. I like chocolates.

HELEN: Help yourself to a drink, Peter, and I'll go and put my glad rags on. *(Exit.)*

PETER: Don't let's be long, huh? I've booked a table. Dammit, I thought you'd be ready.

JO: She's got no sense of time.

PETER: Don't sit there guzzling all those chocolates at once.

She throws the lid at him.

What the hell are you playing at . . . sit down and behave yourself, you little snip.

JO: Hey! Don't start bossing me about. You're not my father.

PETER: Christ Almighty! Will you sit down and eat your chocolates. Do what you like but leave me alone.

Suddenly she attacks him, half-laughing, half-crying.

JO: You leave me alone. And leave my mother alone too.

HELEN *enters.*

PETER: Get away! For God's sake go and . . .

HELEN: Leave him alone, Jo. He doesn't want to be bothered with you. Got a cigarette, Peter? Did you get yourself a drink?

PETER: No, I . . .

JO: Do I bother you, Mister Smith, or must I wait till we're alone for an answer?

PETER: Can't you keep her under control?

HELEN: I'll knock her head round if she isn't careful. Be quiet, Jo. And don't tease him.

PETER: Tonight's supposed to be a celebration.

JO: What of?

HELEN: He's found a house. Isn't he marvellous? Show her the photo of it, Peter. I shan't be a tick!

JO: You've certainly fixed everything up behind my back.

HELEN: Don't you think it's nice? One of his pals had to sell, moving into something smaller. (*Goes.*)

PETER *throws snap on to the table.*

JO: It's not bad. White walls, tennis courts. Has it got a swimming pool?

PETER: It has twelve swimming pools.

JO: Can I see the other photos?

PETER: Which photos?

JO: In your wallet. I suppose you thought I didn't notice.

PETER: Oh! These. Yes, well, that's a photograph of my family, my mother, my father, my sister, my brother and . . . (*To himself.*) all the rest of the little bastards.

JO: Is this a wedding group?

PETER: My brother's wedding.

JO: They only just made it, too, from the look of his wife. You can tell she's going to have a baby.

PETER: Oh? Thank you.

JO: You can have it back if I can see the others.

PETER: Which others? What are you talking about?

JO: Do you want me to tell my mother?

PETER: I don't give a damn what you tell your mother.

JO: They're all women, aren't they? I bet you've had thousands of girl friends. What was this one with the long legs called?

PETER: Ah! Yes, number thirty-eight. A charming little thing.

JO: Why do you wear that black patch?

PETER: I lost an eye.

JO: Where?

PETER: During the war.

JO: Were you in the Navy?

PETER: Army.

JO: Officer?

PETER: Private.

JO: I thought you would have been somebody very important.

PETER: A private is far more important than you think. After all, who does all the dirty work?

JO: Yes, a general without any army wouldn't be much use, would he? Can I see your eye? I mean can I see the hole?

PETER: There's nothing to see.

JO: Do you wear that patch when you go to bed?

PETER: That's something about which I don't care to make a public statement.

JO: Tell me.

PETER: Well, there is one highly recommended way for a young girl to find out.

JO (*glancing through photos in wallet*): I don't like this one. She's got too much stuff on her eyes.

PETER: That's the sort of thing your sex goes in for.

JO: I don't. I let my natural beauty shine through.

PETER: Is there no alternative?

JO: Don't you like shiny faces?

PETER: I suppose they're all right on sweet young things but I just don't go for sweet young things—

JO: Do you fancy me?

PETER: Not yet.

JO: You prefer old women.

PETER: She isn't old.

JO: She soon will be.

PETER: Ah well, that's love. (*Sings.*) "That wild, destructive thing called love."

JO: Why are you marrying Helen?

PETER: Why shouldn't I marry Helen?

JO: Your generation has some very peculiar ideas, that's all I can say.

PETER: Could I have my photographs back, please?

JO: There . . .

PETER: You don't like your mother much do you?

JO: She doesn't much care for me either.

PETER: I can understand that.

JO (*looking over his shoulder at photographs*): I like that one with the shaggy hair cut. She's got nice legs too. Nearly as nice as mine.

PETER: Would you care for a smoke?

JO: Thanks.

HELEN *is heard singing off stage:*

HELEN: Jo! Where's my hat?

JO: I don't know. Where you left it. It's no use getting impatient, Peter. The art work takes a long time. Are you sure you lost your eye during the war? What happened?

PETER: Go and tell your mother I'll wait for her in the pub.

JO: Are you married?

PETER: (*going*): No, I'm still available.

HELEN: (*entering*): But only just.

PETER: Helen, you look utterly fantastic.

HELEN: Thanks. Put that cigarette out, Jo, you've got enough bad habits without adding to your repertoire. Do you like my hat, Peter?

PETER: Bang-on, darling!

HELEN: What are all these books doing all over the place? Are you planning a moonlight flit, Jo? Stop it, Peter.

PETER: Got your blue garters on?

HELEN: Now, Peter. Come on, Jo, shift these books.

JO: I'm sorting them.

PETER (*taking* HELEN's *hat*): How do I look?

HELEN: Peter!

JO: Have you forgotten I'm leaving school this week?

HELEN: Peter, give it here. Stop fooling about. It took me ages to get this hat on right. Jo, do as you're told.

JO: All right.

HELEN: Peter! Don't do that. Give it to me. It's my best one. Put it down.

PETER (*to himself*): No bloody sense of humour.

HELEN: What has she got here? Look at 'em. *Selected Nursery Rhymes,* Hans Andersen's *Fairy Tales, Pinocchio.* Well, you certainly go in for the more advanced types of literature. And what's this? The Holy Bible!

JO: You ought to read it. I think it's good.

HELEN: The extent of my credulity always depends on the extent of my alcoholic intake. Eat, drink and be merry—

JO: And live to regret it.

PETER: God! We've got a founder member of the Lord's Day Observance Society here.

JO: What are you marrying him for?

HELEN: He's got a wallet full of reasons.

JO: Yes. I've just seen 'em too.

HELEN: Can you give us a quid, Peter? I'd better leave her some money. We might decide to have a weekend at Blackpool and she can't live on grass and fresh air.

JO: I won't set eyes on her for a week now. I know her when she's in the mood. What are you going to do about me, Peter? The snotty-nosed daughter? Don't you think I'm a bit young to be left like this on my own while you flit off with my old woman?

PETER: She'll be all right, won't she? At her age.

HELEN: We can't take her with us. We will be, if you'll not take exception to the phrase, on our honeymoon. Unless we change our minds.

PETER: I'm not having her with us.

HELEN: She can stay here then. Come on. I'm hungry.

JO: So am I.

HELEN: There's plenty of food in the kitchen.

JO: You should prepare my meals like a proper mother.

HELEN: Have I ever laid claim to being a proper mother? If you're too idle to cook your own meals you'll just have to cut food out of your diet altogether. That should help you lose a bit of weight, if nothing else.

PETER: She already looks like a bad case of malnutrition.

JO: Have you got your key, Helen? I might not be here when you decide to come back. I'm starting work on Saturday.

HELEN: Oh yes, she's been called to the bar.

PETER: What sort of a bar?

JO: The sort you're always propping up. I'm carrying on the family traditions. Will you give me some money for a new dress, Helen?

HELEN: If you really want to make a good investment, you'll buy a needle and some cotton. Every article of clothing on her back is held together by a safety pin or a knot. If she had an accident in the street I'd be ashamed to claim her.

PETER: Are we going?

JO: Can't I come with you?

HELEN: Shut up! You're going to have him upset. You jealous little cat! Come on, Peter.

PETER: All right, all right, don't pull. Don't get excited. And don't get impatient. Those bloody little street kids have probably pulled the car to pieces by now but we needn't worry about that, need we . . .

HELEN: I told you you'd upset him.

PETER: Upset? I'm not upset. I just want to get to hell out of this black hole of Calcutta.

They leave flat. JO *looks after them for a moment then turns to bed—she lies across it, crying. Music.* BLACK BOY *enters.*

BOY *(calling)*: JO!

She doesn't move.

BOY: Joee!

JO: Coming.

They move towards each other as if dancing to the music. The music goes, the lights change.

JO: Oh! It's you! Come in. Just when I'm feeling and looking a mess.

BOY: What's wrong? You been crying?

JO: No.

BOY: You have. Your eyes are red.

JO: I don't cry. I've got a cold.

BOY: I think you have, too. Yes, you've got a bit of a temperature. Have you been eating?

JO: No.

BOY: You're a fine sight. Where's the kitchen?

JO: Through there. What are you going to do?

BOY: Fix you a cold cure. Where do you keep the milk?

JO: Under the sink. I hate milk.

BOY: I hate dirt. And this is just the dirtiest place I've ever seen.
The children round here are filthy.

JO: It's their parents' fault. What are you putting in that milk?

BOY: A pill.

JO: I bet it's an opium pellet. I've heard about men like you.

BOY: There isn't another man like me anywhere. I'm one on
his own.

JO: So am I.

BOY: Who was that fancy bit I saw stepping out of here a few
minutes ago?

JO: If she was dressed up like Hope Gardens it was my mother.

BOY: And who is the Pirate King?

JO: She's marrying him. Poor devil!

BOY: You'll make a pretty bridesmaid.

JO: Bridesmaid! I'd sooner go to my own funeral.

BOY: You'd better drink this first.

JO: I don't like it.

BOY: Get it down you.

JO: But look, it's got skin on the top.

BOY: Don't whine. I'm not spending the evening with a running-
nosed wreck. Finish your milk.

JO: Did you treat your patients in hospital like this?

BOY: Not unless they were difficult. Your mother looks very
young, Jo, to have a daughter as old as you.

JO: She can still have children.

BOY: Well, that's an interesting bit of news. Why should I worry
if she can have children or not?

JO: Do you fancy her?

BOY: That isn't the sort of question you ask your fiancé.

JO: It doesn't really matter if you do fancy her, anyway, because she's gone. You're too late. You've had your chips.

BOY: I'll be gone soon, too. What then?

JO: My heart's broke.

BOY: You can lie in bed at night and hear my ship passing down the old canal. It's cold in here. No fire?

JO: It doesn't work.

BOY: Come and sit down here. You can keep me warm.

JO: Is it warm where you're going?

BOY: I guess so.

JO: We could do with a bit of sunshine. In this country there are only two seasons, winter and winter. Do you think Helen's beautiful?

BOY: Who's Helen?

JO: My mother. Honestly, you are slow sometimes. Well, do you think she's beautiful?

BOY: Yes.

JO: Am I like her?

BOY: No, you're not at all like her.

JO: Good. I'm glad nobody can see a resemblance between us.

BOY: My ring's still round your neck. Wear it. Your mother isn't here to laugh.

JO: Unfasten it, then.

BOY: Pretty neck you've got.

JO: Glad you like it.

BOY: No! Let me put it on.

JO: Did it cost very much?

BOY: You shouldn't ask questions like that. I got it from Woolworth's!

JO: Woolworth's best! I don't care. I'm not proud. It's the thought that counts and I wonder what thought it was in your wicked mind that made you buy it.

BOY: I've got dishonourable intentions.

JO: I'm so glad.

BOY: Are you? *(He embraces her.)*

JO: Stop it.

BOY: Why? Do you object to the "gross clasps of the lascivious Moor"?

JO: Who said that?

BOY: Shakespeare in *Othello.*

JO: Oh! Him. He said everything, didn't he?

BOY: Let me be your Othello and you my Desdemona.

JO: All right.

BOY: "Oh ill-starred wench."

JO: Will you stay here for Christmas?

BOY: If that's what you want.

JO: It's what you want.

BOY: That's right.

JO: Then stay.

BOY: You naughty girl!

JO: I may as well be naughty while I've got the chance. I'll probably never see you again. I know it.

BOY: What makes you say that?

JO: I just know it. That's all. But I don't care. Stay with me now, it's enough, it's all I want, and if you do come back I'll still be here.

BOY: You think I'm only after one thing, don't you?

JO: I know you're only after one thing.

BOY: You're so right. *(He kisses her.)* But I will come back. I love you.

JO: How can you say that?

BOY: Why or how I say these things I don't know, but whatever it means it's true.

JO: Anyway, after this you might not want to come back. After all, I'm not very experienced in these little matters.

BOY: I am.

JO: Anyway, it's a bit daft for us to be talking about you coming back before you've gone. Can I leave that hot milk?

BOY: It would have done you good. Never mind. *(Embraces her.)*

JO: Don't do that.

BOY: Why not?

JO: I like it.

Fade out. Music. Wedding bells. HELEN's *music. She dances on with an assortment of fancy boxes, containing her wedding clothes.*

HELEN: Jo! Jo! Come on. Be sharp now.

JO *comes on in her pajamas. She has a heavy cold.*

For God's sake give me a hand. I'll never be ready. What time is it? Have a look at the church clock.

JO: A quarter past eleven, and the sun's coming out.

HELEN: Oh! Well, happy the bride the sun shines on.

JO: Yeah, and happy the corpse the rain rains on. You're not getting married in a church, are you?

HELEN: Why, are you coming to throw bricks at us? Of course not. Do I look all right? Pass me my fur. Oh! My fur! Do you like it?

JO: I bet somebody's missing their cat.

HELEN: It's a wedding present from that young man of mine. He spends his money like water, you know, penny wise, pound foolish. Oh! I am excited. I feel twenty-one all over again. Oh! You would have to catch a cold on my wedding day. I was going to ask you to be my bridesmaid too.

JO: Don't talk daft.

HELEN: Where did you put my shoes? Did you clean 'em? Oh! They're on my feet. Don't stand there sniffing, Jo. Use a handkerchief.

JO: I haven't got one.

HELEN: Use this, then. What's the matter with you? What are you trying to hide?

JO: Nothing.

HELEN: Don't try to kid me. What is it? Come on, let's see.

JO: It's nothing. Let go of me. You're hurting.

HELEN: What's this?

JO: A ring.

HELEN: I can see it's a ring. Who give it to you?

JO: A friend of mine.

HELEN: Who? Come on. Tell me.

JO: You're hurting me.

HELEN *breaks the cord and gets the ring.*

HELEN: You should have sewn some buttons on your pyjamas
if you didn't want me to see. Who give it you?

JO: My boy friend. He asked me to marry him.

HELEN: Well, you silly little bitch. You mean that lad you've
been knocking about with while we've been away?

JO: Yes.

HELEN: I could choke you.

JO: You've already had a damn good try.

HELEN: You haven't known him five minutes. Has he really asked
you to marry him?

JO: Yes.

HELEN: Well, thank God for the divorce courts! I suppose just
because I'm getting married you think you should.

JO: Have you got the monopoly?

HELEN: You stupid little devil! What sort of a wife do you
think you'd make? You're useless. It takes you all your time
to look after yourself. I suppose you think you're in love.
Anybody can fall in love, do you know that? But what do
you know about the rest of it?

JO: Ask yourself.

HELEN: You know where that ring should be? In the ashcan
with everything else. Oh! I could kill her, I could really.

JO: You don't half knock me about. I hope you suffer for it.

HELEN: I've done my share of suffering if I never do any more.
Oh Jo, you're only a kid. Why don't you learn from my
mistakes? It takes half your life to learn from your own.

JO: You leave me alone. Can I have my ring back, please?

HELEN: What a thing to happen just when I'm going to enjoy
myself for a change.

JO: Nobody's stopping you.

HELEN: Yes, and as soon as my back's turned you'll be off with
this sailor boy and ruin yourself for good.

JO: I'm already ruined.

HELEN: Yes, it's just the sort of thing you'd do. You make me sick.

JO: You've no need to worry, Helen. He's gone away. He may be back in six months, but there again, he may . . .

HELEN: Look, you're only young. Enjoy your life. Don't get trapped. Marriage can be hell for a kid.

JO: Can I have your hanky back?

HELEN: Where did you put it?

JO: This is your fault too.

HELEN: Everything's my fault. Show me your tongue.

JO: Breathing your 'flu bugs all over me.

HELEN: Yes, and your neck's red where I pulled that string.

JO: Will you get me a drink of water, Helen?

HELEN: No, have a dose of this. (*Offering whisky.*) It'll do you more good. I might as well have one myself while I'm at it, mightn't I?

JO: You've emptied more bottles down your throat in the last few weeks than I would have thought possible. If you don't watch it, you'll end up an old down-and-out boozer knocking back the meths.

HELEN: It'll never come to that. The devil looks after his own they say.

JO: He certainly takes good care of you. You look marvellous, considering.

HELEN: Considering what?

JO: The wear and tear on your soul.

HELEN: Oh well, that'll have increased its market value, won't it?

JO: Old Nick'll get you in the end.

HELEN: Thank God for that! Heaven must be the hell of a place. Nothing but repentant sinners up there, isn't it?
All the pimps, prostitutes and politicians in creation trying to cash in on eternity and their little tin god. Where's my hat?

JO: Where's your husband?

HELEN: Probably drunk with his pals somewhere. He was going down to the house this morning to let some air in. Have you seen a picture of the house? Yes, you have. Do you like it? (*She peers and primps into mirror.*)

JO: It's all right if you like that sort of thing, and I don't.

HELEN: I'll like it in a few years, when it isn't so new and clean. At the moment it's like my face, unblemished! Oh look at that, every line tells a dirty story, hey?

JO: Will you tell me something before you go?

HELEN: Oh! You can read all about that in books.

JO: What was my father like?

HELEN *turns away.*

HELEN: Who?

JO: You heard! My father! What was he like?

HELEN: Oh! Him.

JO: Well, was he so horrible that you can't even tell me about him?

HELEN: He wasn't horrible. He was just a bit stupid, you know. Not very bright.

JO: Be serious, Helen.

HELEN: I am serious.

JO: Are you trying to tell me he was an idiot?

HELEN: He wasn't an idiot, he was just a bit—retarded.

JO: You liar!

HELEN: All right, I'm a liar.

JO: Look at me.

HELEN: Well, am I?

JO: No.

HELEN: Well, now you know.

JO: How could you give me a father like that?

HELEN: I didn't do it on purpose. How was I to know you'd materialize out of a little love affair that lasted five minutes?

JO: You never think. That's your trouble.

HELEN: I know.

JO: Was he like a . . . a real idiot?

HELEN: I've told you once. He was nice though, you know, a nice little feller!

JO: Where is he now, locked up?

HELEN: No, he's dead.

JO: Why?

HELEN: Why? Well, I mean, death's something that comes to us all, and when it does come you haven't usually got time to ask why.

JO: It's hereditary, isn't it?

HELEN: What?

JO: Madness.

HELEN: Sometimes.

JO: Am I mad?

HELEN: Decide for yourself. Oh, Jo, don't be silly. Of course you're not daft. Not more so than anybody else.

JO: Why did you have to tell me that story? Couldn't you have made something up?

HELEN: You asked for the truth and you got it for once. Now be satisfied.

JO: How could you go with a half-wit?

HELEN: He had strange eyes. You've got 'em. Everybody used to laugh at him. Go on, I'll tell you some other time.

JO: Tell me now!

HELEN: Mind my scent!

JO: Please tell me. I want to understand.

HELEN: Do you think I understand? For one night, actually it was the afternoon, I loved him. It was the first time I'd ever really been with a man . . .

JO: You were married.

HELEN: I was married to a Puritan—do you know what I mean?

JO: I think so.

HELEN: And when I met your father I was as pure and unsullied as I fondly, and perhaps mistakenly, imagine you to be. It was the first time and though you can enjoy the second, the third, even the fourth time, there's no time like the first, it's always there. I'm off now. I've got to go and find my husband. Now don't sit here sulking all day.

JO: I was thinking.

HELEN: Well, don't think. It doesn't do you any good. I'll see you when the honeymoon's over. Come on, give us a kiss. You may as well. It's a long time since you kissed me.

JO: Keep it for him.

HELEN: I don't suppose you're sorry to see me go.

JO: I'm not sorry and I'm not glad.

HELEN: You don't know what you do want.

JO: Yes, I do. I've always known what I want.

HELEN: And when it comes your way will you recognize it?

JO: Good luck, Helen.

HELEN: I'll be seeing you. Hey! If he doesn't show up I'll be back.

JO: Good luck, Helen.

Exit HELEN. *"Here Comes the Bride" on the cornet.*

Curtain.

ACT TWO

Scene One

As the curtain goes up fairground music can be heard in the distance. JO *and a boy can be heard playing together. When they enter the flat they have been playing about with a bunch of brightly coloured balloons. It is summer now and* JO's *pregnancy is quite obvious.*

JO (*as she falls on a couch in the darkened room*): Let me lie here and don't wake me up for a month.

GEOF: Shall I put the light on?

JO: No. Don't you dare put that light on.

GEOF: Did you enjoy the fair?

JO: Loved it. I haven't been to a fair since Christmas.

GEOF: Those roundabouts are still going. Can you hear 'em?

JO: I should be up at half past seven tomorrow morning. I'll never make it. I'll just have to be late. Anyway, why should I slave away for anybody but me? Haven't you got a home to go to, Geof?

GEOF: Of course.

JO: Well, why are you lurking about? Come in if you want to.

GEOF: Thanks.

JO: There's some biscuits and a flask of coffee in the kitchen only I'm too tired to get 'em. Aren't you hungry?

GEOF: No, but you are.

JO: That's right. Go and get 'em for me, Geof.

GEOF: Where's the kitchen?

JO: Straight on.

GEOF: I'll put the light on.

JO: No, you won't! I like this romantic half-light, it just goes with this Manchester maisonette!

GEOF: Take four paces forward, turn right, turn left, once round the gasworks and straight on up the creek. (*He bangs into a chair or table and cries or swears.*)

JO: Put a match on, you daft thing.

GEOF *strikes a match.*

GEOF: Ee, this place is enormous, isn't it?

JO: I know. I've got to work all day in a shoe shop and all night in a bar to pay for it. But it's mine. All mine.

GEOF: I can tell it's yours from the state it's in. No wonder you won't put the light on. Where do you keep the cups?

JO: In the sink.

GEOF: Isn't this a bit big for one, Jo?

JO: Why? Are you thinking of moving in?

GEOF: Not likely.

JO: You are, you know. Put 'em down here. Don't you want any?

GEOF: No.

JO: Well, hand 'em over to me because I'm starved. Has your landlady thrown you out?

GEOF: Don't be silly.

JO: I've been wondering why you were so anxious to see me home. You didn't fancy sleeping under the arches, did you? Why did your landlady throw you out, Geoffrey? I'll let you stay here if you tell me.

GEOF: I was behind with the rent.

JO: That's a lie for a start.

GEOF: I don't tell lies.

JO: Come on, let's have some truth. Why did she throw you out?

GEOF: I've told you why.

JO (*switches on light*): Come on, the truth. Who did she find you with? Your girl friend? It wasn't a man, was it?

GEOF: Don't be daft.

JO: Look, I've got a nice comfortable couch. I've even got some sheets. You can stay here if you'll tell me what you do. Go on, I've always wanted to know about people like you.

GEOF: Go to hell.

JO: I won't snigger, honest I won't. Tell me some of it, go on. I bet you never told a woman before.

GEOF: I don't go in for sensational confessions.

JO: I want to know what you do. I want to know why you do it. Tell me or get out.

GEOF: Right! (*He goes to the door.*)

JO: Geof, don't go. Don't go, Geof! I'm sorry. Please stay.

GEOF: Don't touch me.

JO: I didn't mean to hurt your feelings.

GEOF: I can't stand women at times. Let go of me.

JO: Come on, Geof. I don't care what you do.

GEOF: Thank you. May I go now, please?

JO: Please stay here Geof. I'll get those sheets and blankets.

GEOF: I can't stand people who laugh at other people. They'd get a bigger laugh if they laughed at themselves.

JO: Please stay, Geof. (*She goes off for the sheets and blankets. He finds her book of drawings on the table and glances through them.*)

GEOF: Are these yours?

JO: No, why? Put them down, Geof.

GEOF: Obviously they are. They're exactly like you.

JO: How do you mean?

GEOF: Well, there's no design, rhythm or purpose.

JO: Hey?

GEOF: Where's the design in that? It's all messy, isn't it? Charcoal. I don't like it.

JO: I do.

GEOF: What made you choose that for a subject?

JO: I like ...

GEOF: They're all sentimental.

JO: Me? Sentimental?

GEOF: No. No. I don't like 'em.

JO: Do you really think they're sentimental?

GEOF: Well, look. I mean . . .

JO: I'm sorry you don't like them.

GEOF: Why don't you go to a decent school?

JO: I've never been to any school.

GEOF: You want taking in hand.

JO: No, thanks.

GEOF: Has anybody ever tried?

JO: What?

GEOF: Taking you in hand.

JO: Yes.

GEOF: What happened to him?

JO: He came in with Christmas and went out with the New Year.

GEOF: Did you like him?

JO: He was all right . . .

GEOF: Did you love him?

JO: I don't know much about love. I've never been too familiar with it. I suppose I must have loved him. They say love creates. And I'm certainly creating at the moment. I'm going to have a baby.

GEOF: I thought so. You're in a bit of a mess, aren't you?

JO: I don't care.

GEOF: You can get rid of babies before they're born, you know.

JO: I know, but I think that's terrible.

GEOF: When's it due?

JO: Reckon it up from Christmas.

GEOF: About September.

JO: Yes.

GEOF: What are you going to do? You can't be on your own.

JO: There's plenty of time.

GEOF: Got any money?

JO: Only my wages and they don't last long. By the time I've bought all I need, stockings and make-up and things, I've got nothing left.

GEOF: You can do without make-up.

JO: I can't. I look like a ghost without it.

GEOF: At your age?

JO: What's age got to do with it? Anyway, I'm not working for much longer. I'm not having everybody staring at me.

GEOF: How are you going to manage then?

JO: There's no need for you to worry about it.

GEOF: Somebody's got to. Anyway, I like you.

JO: I like you too.

GEOF: Your mother should know.

JO: Why?

GEOF: Well, she's your mother. Do you know her address?

JO: No. She was supposed to be marrying some man. They live in a big, white house somewhere.

GEOF: What sort of a woman is she?

JO: She's all sorts of woman. But she's got plenty of money.

GEOF: That's all you need to be interested in. You've got to buy all sorts of things for the baby. Clothes, a cot and a pram. Here, that teddy bear we won tonight'll come in handy, won't it? I can make things too. I'll help . . .

JO: Shut up! I'm not planning big plans for this baby, or dreaming big dreams. You know what happens when you do things like that. The baby'll be born dead or daft!

GEOF: You're feeling a bit depressed, Jo.

JO: I'm feeling nothing.

GEOF: You'll be your usual self soon.

JO: And what is my usual self? My usual self is a very unusual self, Geoffrey Ingram, and don't you forget it. I'm an extraordinary person. There's only one of me like there's only one of you.

GEOF: We're unique!

JO: Young.

GEOF: Unrivalled!

JO: Smashing!

GEOF: We're bloody marvellous!

JO: Hey! Do you like beer?

GEOF: Yes.

JO: Whisky?

GEOF: Yes.

JO: Gin?

GEOF: Yes. Have you got some?

JO: No, but if I had I'd give it all to you. I'd give everything I had to you. Here, have a biscuit. You'll like these. They taste like dog food.

GEOF: Spratts!

JO: You look like a spratt. Jack Spratt, who'd eat no fat, his wife would eat no lean and so between them both, you see, they licked the platter clean. Did you enjoy that dramatic recitation?

GEOF: Very moving.

JO: You say one.

GEOF: There was a young man of Thessaly,
And he was wondrous wise.
He jumped into a quickset hedge
And scratched out both his eyes.
And when he saw his eyes were out,
With all his might and main
He jumped into another hedge
And scratched them in again.

JO: I like that. Do you know any more?

GEOF: As I was going up Pippin Hill,
Pippin Hill was dirty.
And there I met a pretty miss
And she dropped me a curtsy.
Little miss, pretty miss,
Blessings light upon you.
If I had half a crown a day
I'd gladly spend it on you.

JO: Would you?

GEOF: I would.

JO: Silly things nursery rhymes when you weigh them up.

GEOF: I like them. Do you want a cigarette?

JO: How many have you got left?

GEOF: I've got enough for one each.

JO: No, you keep 'em. They don't bother me really. I used to smoke just to annoy my mother. What's that?

GEOF: A free gift coupon.

JO: Everything you buy lately has a free gift coupon in it. It's coming to something when they have to bribe the public to buy their stuff. What's this one for?

GEOF: There's a whole list of things to send for if you have enough coupons. Hee, there's even a car, smoke forty thousand cigarettes a day for the next ten thousand years and you'll get a Lagonda.

JO: What's that?

GEOF: A car.

JO: A nice car?

GEOF: A wonderful car.

JO: I'll buy you one for Christmas. If you ask me nice I'll buy you two.

GEOF: Thanks.

JO: Oh! I'm tired. This couch isn't going to be very comfortable, is it?

GEOF: It'll do.

JO: What are you going to sleep in?

GEOF: My shirt!

JO: I'm that tired! I haven't the energy to get myself to bed. You won't sleep very well on this couch, Geof.

GEOF: It's all right. Beggars can't be choosers.

JO: We're both beggars. A couple of degenerates.

GEOF: The devil's own!

JO (*she goes to bed.* GEOF *starts to undress*): Hey! You'd better turn that light out, or I might be after you. (*He turns the light out and then gets into bed. She begins to sing the song "Black Boy" as she lies on her bed.*)

Black boy, black boy, don't you lie to me.
Where did you stay last night?
In the pines, in the pines where the sun never shines,
I shivered the whole night through.

GEOF: Jo!

JO: Yes.

GEOF: What was that boy like?

JO: Which boy?

GEOF: You know.

JO: Oh! Him. He wasn't a bit like you. He could sing and dance and he was as black as coal.

GEOF: A black boy?

JO: From darkest Africa! A Prince.

GEOF: A what?

JO: A Prince, son of a chieftain.

GEOF: I'll bet he was too.

JO: Prince Ossini!

GEOF: What was he doing here?

JO: He was a male nurse in the Navy.

GEOF: Do you wish he was still here?

JO: Not really. I think I've had enough. I'm sick of love. That's why I'm letting you stay here. You won't start anything.

GEOF: No, I don't suppose I will.

JO: You'd better not. I hate love.

GEOF: Do you, Jo?

JO: Yes, I do.

GEOF: Good night.

JO: Good night.

GEOF: You needn't lock the bedroom door.

JO: I'm in bed. Geoffrey! Geoffrey!

GEOF: What do you want?

JO: What time have you got to be up in the morning?

GEOF: I don't go to school tomorrow. I'll stay here and clear this place up a bit. And make you a proper meal. Now go to sleep, hey?

JO: Geoffrey!

GEOF: What's wrong now?

JO (*laughing*): You're like a big sister to me.

Music to black out. Then quick as lights go up. Waking, GEOF *dances and goes off with bedclothes.* JO *dances off.* GEOF *dances in with props for the next scene, which in reality would be a month or two later.* GEOF *is cutting out a baby's gown.* JO *wanders about the room.*

JO: God! It's hot.

GEOF: I know it's hot.

JO: I'm so restless.

GEOF: Oh, stop prowling about.

JO: This place stinks. (*Goes over to the door. Children are heard singing in the street.*) That river, it's the colour of lead. Look at that washing, it's dirty, and look at those filthy children.

GEOF: It's not their fault.

JO: It's their parents' fault. There's a little boy over there and his hair, honestly, it's walking away. And his ears. Oh! He's a real mess! He never goes to school. He just sits on that front doorstep all day. I think he's a bit deficient.

The children's voices die away. A tugboat hoots.

His mother ought not to be allowed.

GEOF: Who?

JO: His mother. Think of all the harm she does, having children.

GEOF: Sit down and read a book, Jo.

JO: I can't.

GEOF: Be quiet then. You're getting on my nerves. (*Suddenly she yells and whirls across the room.*)

JO: Wheee! Come on rain. Come on storm. It kicked me, Geof. It kicked me!

GEOF: What?

JO: It kicked me. (GEOF *runs to her and puts his head on her belly.*)

GEOF: Will it do it again?

JO: It shows it's alive anyway. Come on, baby, let's see what big sister's making for us.

GEOF: Put it down.

JO: What a pretty little dress.

GEOF: It's got to wear something. You can't just wrap it up in a bundle of newspaper.

JO: And dump it on a doorstep. How did Geoffrey find out the measurements?

GEOF: Babies are born to the same size more or less.

JO: Oh, no, they're not. Some are thin scrappy things and others are huge and covered in rolls of fat.

GEOF: Shut up, Jo, it sounds revolting.

JO: They are revolting. I hate babies.

GEOF: I thought you'd change. Motherhood is supposed to come natural to women.

JO: It comes natural to you, Geoffrey Ingram. You'd make somebody a wonderful wife. What were you talking about to that old mare downstairs?

GEOF: I was giving her the rent. I got my grant yesterday.

JO: You're as thick as thieves, you two.

GEOF: She's going to make the baby a cradle.

JO: What?

GEOF: You know, she makes wicker baskets.

JO: A wicker basket!

GEOF: It's the best we can do, unless you want to go down to the river plaiting reeds.

JO: I don't want her poking her nose into my affairs.

GEOF: You're glad enough to have me dancing attendance on you.

JO: Only because I thought you'd leave me alone. Why don't you leave me alone? *(She cries and flings herself down on the coach.)* I feel like throwing myself in the river.

GEOF: I wouldn't do that. It's full of rubbish.

JO: Well that's all I am, isn't it?

GEOF: Stop pitying yourself.

JO: Don't jump down my throat.

GEOF: How much longer is this going on?

JO: What?

GEOF: Your present performance.

JO: Nobody asked you to stay here. You moved in on me, remember, remember? If you don't like it you can get out, can't you? But you wouldn't do that, would you, Geoffrey? You've no confidence in yourself, have you? You're afraid the girls might laugh ...

GEOF: Read that book and shut up. When the baby comes, if it ever does, you won't know one end of it from the other.

JO: *Looking After Baby*. Isn't that nice? Three months, exercises, constipation. Four months, relaxation. It even tells you how to wash nappies. How lovely. There's a little job for you, Geoffrey.

GEOF: Drink that. (*He hands her a glass of milk.*)

JO (*flirting with him*): Does it tell you how to feed babies, Geoffrey?

GEOF: Even you know that.

JO: I know about that way, breast feeding, but I'm not having a little animal nibbling away at me, it's cannibalistic. Like being eaten alive.

GEOF: Stop trying to be inhuman. It doesn't suit you.

JO: I mean it. I hate motherhood.

GEOF: Well, whether you hate it or not you've got it coming to you so you might as well make a good job of it.

JO: I've got toothache.

GEOF: I've got bloody heartache!

JO: I think you'd like everybody to think this baby's yours, wouldn't you, Geoffrey?

GEOF: Not likely.

JO: After all, you don't show much sign of coming fatherhood, do you? You like babies, don't you, Geof?

GEOF: Yes, I do.

JO (*coquettes with him*): Geoffrey, have you got any of that toothache cure?

He moves away.

Geoffrey, have you got any of that toothache cure?

GEOF: The only cure for the toothache is a visit to the dentist. Drink your milk.

JO: I hate milk. (*She looks out of the window.*) I never thought I'd still be here in the summer. (*She puts her arms round* GEOF *playfully.*) Would you like to be the father of my baby, Geoffrey?

GEOF: Yes, I would.

JO *stands in the doorway. The children can be heard singing again.*

What time is it?

JO: Half-past four by the church clock. Why do you stay here, Geof?

GEOF: Someone's got to look after you. You can't look after yourself.

JO: I think there's going to be a storm. Look at that sky. It's nearly black. And you can hear the kids playing, right over there on the croft.

A silence in the room: we hear the children singing.

GEOF: What would you say if I started something?

JO: Eh!

GEOF: I said what would you say if I started something?

JO: In my condition I'd probably faint.

GEOF: No, I mean after.

JO: I don't want you.

GEOF: Am I repulsive to you?

JO: You're nothing to me. I'm everything to myself.

GEOF: No, you're not. You're going to need me after.

JO: I won't be here after.

GEOF: Do you still think he might come back?

JO: I've forgotten him.

She turns towards him, he to her.

GEOF: You do need me, Jo, don't you?

JO: Let go of me. You're squeezing my arm.

GEOF: I've never kissed a girl.

JO: That's your fault.

GEOF: Let me kiss you.

JO: Let go of me. Leave me alone.

She struggles but he kisses her.

GEOF: How was that for first time?

JO: Practise on somebody else.

GEOF: I didn't mean to hurt you.

JO: Look Geof, I like you, I like you very much, but I don't enjoy all this panting and grunting . . .

GEOF: Marry me, Jo.

JO: Don't breathe all over me like that, you sound like a horse. I'm not marrying anybody.

GEOF: I wouldn't ask you to do anything you didn't want to do.

JO: Yes, you would.

GEOF: Jo, I don't mind that you're having somebody else's baby. What you've done, you've done. What I've done, I've done.

JO: I like you, Geof, but I don't want to marry you.

GEOF: Oh, all right. Anyway, I don't suppose I could live up to that black beast of a prince of yours. I bet you didn't struggle when he made love to you.

JO: It might have been better if I had.

GEOF (*he gives her a bar of chocolate*): Have some chocolate.

JO: Thanks. Do you want some?

GEOF: No.

JO: Go on.

GEOF: I said no.

JO: You like strawberry cream.

GEOF: I don't want any, Jo. I've made my mind up.

JO: Don't be daft, have some chocolate.

GEOF: No . . . (*She gives a piece of chocolate to him just the same.*)

JO: I think it would be best if you left this place, Geof. I don't think it's doing you any good being here with me all the time.

GEOF: I know that, but I couldn't go away now.

JO: You'll have to go some time. We can't stay together like this for ever.

GEOF: I'd sooner be dead than away from you.

JO: You say that as if you mean it.

GEOF: I do mean it.

JO: Why?

GEOF: Before I met you I didn't care one way or the other—I didn't care whether I lived or died. But now . . .

JO: I think I'll go and lie down. (*She goes to bed and lies across it.*)

GEOF: There's no need for me to go, Jo. You said yourself you didn't want anybody else here and I'm only interested in you. We needn't split up need we, Jo?

JO: I don't suppose so.

Music. Enter HELEN.

HELEN: Jo! Your beloved old lady's arrived. Well, where is she, Romeo?

GEOF: Don't tell her I came for you.

HELEN: What? Don't mumble.

GEOF: I said don't tell her I came for you.

HELEN: All right, all right. This place hasn't changed much, has it? Still the same old miserable hole. Well, where's the lady in question?

GEOF: In there.

HELEN: What, lazing in bed, as usual? Come on, get up; plenty of girls in your condition have to go out to work and take care of a family. Come on, get up.

JO: What blew you in?

HELEN: Let's have a look at you.

JO: Who told you about me?

HELEN: Nobody.

JO: How did you get to know then?

HELEN: Come on, aren't you going to introduce me to your boy friend? Who is he?

JO: My boy friend. Oh, it's all right, we're so decent we're almost dead. I said who told you about me?

HELEN: Does it matter?

JO: I told you to keep out of my affairs, Geoffrey. I'm not having anybody running my life for me. What do you think you're running? A "Back to Mother" movement?

GEOF: Your mother has a right to know.

JO: She's got no rights where I'm concerned.

HELEN: Oh, leave him alone. You're living off him, by all accounts.

JO: Who've you been talking to? That old hag downstairs?

HELEN: I didn't need to talk to her. The whole district knows what's been going on here.

JO: And what has been going on?

HELEN: I suppose you think you can hide yourself away in this chicken run, don't you? Well, you can't. Everybody knows.

GEOF: She won't go out anywhere, not even for a walk and a bit of fresh air. That's why I came to you.

HELEN: And what do you think I can do about it? In any case, bearing a child doesn't place one under an obligation to it.

GEOF: I should have thought it did.

HELEN: Well, you've got another think coming. If she won't take care of herself that's her lookout. And don't stand there looking as if it's my fault.

GEOF: It's your grandchild.

HELEN: Oh, shut up, you put years on me. Anyway, I'm having nothing to do with it. She's more than I can cope with, always has been.

GEOF: That's obvious.

HELEN: And what's your part in this little Victorian melodrama? Nursemaid?

JO: Serves you right for bringing her here, Geof.

HELEN: It's a funny-looking set-up to me.

JO: It's our business.

HELEN: Then don't bring me into it. Where's the loving father? Distinguished by his absence, I suppose.

JO: That's right.

HELEN (to GEOF): Did she hear any more of him?

JO: No, she didn't.

HELEN: When I'm talking to the organ grinder I don't expect the monkey to answer.

JO: I could get him back tomorrow if I wanted to.

HELEN: Well, that's nice to know. He certainly left you a nice Christmas box. It did happen at Christmas, I suppose? When the cat's away.

GEOF: You've been away a long time.

HELEN: Oh, you shut up. Sling your hook!

JO: Will you keep out of this, Geoffrey?

HELEN: Well, come on, let's have a look at you. (JO *turns away.*) What's up? We're all made the same, aren't we?

JO: Yes, we are.

HELEN: Well then. Can you cut the bread on it yet? (JO *turns.*) Yes, you're carrying it a bit high, aren't you? Are you going to the clinic regularly? Is she working?

GEOF: No, I told you, she doesn't like people looking at her.

HELEN: Do you think people have got nothing better to do than look at you?

JO: Leave me alone.

HELEN: She'd be better off working than living off you like a little bloodsucker.

GEOF: She doesn't live off me.

JO: No, we share everything, see! We're communists too.

HELEN: That's his influence I suppose.

JO: Get out of here. I won't go out if I don't want to. It's nothing to do with you. Get back to your fancy man or your husband, or whatever you like to call him.

HELEN *begins to chase her.*

Aren't you afraid he'll run off and leave you if you let him out of your sight?

HELEN: I'll give you such a bloody good hiding in a minute, if you're not careful. That's what you've gone short of!

JO: Don't show yourself up for what you are!

HELEN: You couldn't wait, could you? Now look at the mess you've landed yourself in.

JO: I'll get out of it, without your help.

HELEN: You had to throw yourself at the first man you met, didn't you?

JO: Yes, I did, that's right.

HELEN: You're man mad.

JO: I'm like you.

HELEN: You know what they're calling you round here? A silly little whore!

JO: Well, they all know where I get it from too.

HELEN: Let me get hold of her! I'll knock her bloody head round!

JO: You should have been locked up years ago, with my father.

HELEN: Let me get hold of her!

GEOF: Please, Jo, Helen, Jo, please!

HELEN: I should have got rid of you before you were born.

JO: I wish you had done. You did with plenty of others, I know.

HELEN: I'll kill her. I'll knock the living daylights out of her.

GEOF: Helen, stop it, you will kill her!

JO: If you don't get out of here I'll ... jump out of the window.

There is a sudden lull.

GEOF (*yelling*) : Will you stop shouting, you two?

HELEN: We enjoy it.

GEOF: Helen!

HELEN: Now you're going to listen to a few home truths, my girl.

JO: We've had enough home truths!

HELEN: All right, you thought you knew it all before, didn't you? But you came a cropper. Now it's "poor little Josephine, the tragedy queen, hasn't life been hard on her." Well, you fell down, you get up ... nobody else is going to carry you about. Oh, I know you've got this pansified little freak to lean on, but what good will that do you?

JO: Leave Geof out of it!

HELEN: Have you got your breath back? Because there's some more I've got to get off my chest first.

JO: You don't half like the sound of your own voice.

GEOF: If I'd known you were going to bully her like this I'd never have asked you to come here.

HELEN: You can clear off! Take your simpering little face out of it!

JO: Yes, buzz off, Geof! Well, who brought her here? I told you what sort of a woman she was. Go and ... go and make a cup of tea.

He goes.

HELEN: Look at your arms. They're like a couple of stalks! You look like a ghost warmed up. And who gave you that haircut, him? Don't sit there sulking.

JO: I thought it was the tea break.

HELEN: I didn't come here to quarrel.

JO: No?

HELEN: I brought you some money.

JO: You know what you can do with that.

HELEN: All right! You've said your piece. Money doesn't grow on trees. I'll leave it on the table. Have you been collecting your maternity benefit or . . .

JO: Or are you too idle to walk down to the post office? Don't be daft! I'm not entitled to it. I haven't been earning long enough.

HELEN: You've no need to go short of anything.

JO: It's taken you a long time to come round to this, hasn't it?

HELEN: What?

JO: The famous mother-love act.

HELEN: I haven't been able to sleep for thinking about you since he came round to our house.

JO: And your sleep mustn't be disturbed at any cost.

HELEN: There'll be money in the post for you every week from now on.

JO: Until you forget.

HELEN: I don't forget things; it's just that I can't remember anything. I'm going to see you through this whether you like it or not. After all I am . . .

JO: After all you are my mother! You're a bit late remembering that, aren't you? You walked through that door with that man and didn't give me a second thought.

HELEN: Why didn't you tell me?

JO: You should have known. You're nothing to me.

PETER *appears.*

PETER: What the hell's going on? Do you expect me to wait in the filthy street all night?

HELEN: I told you to stay outside.

PETER: Don't point your bloody finger at me.

HELEN: I said I'd only be a few minutes and I've only been a few minutes. Now come on, outside!

PETER: Ah! The erring daughter. There she is. *(Sings.)* "Little Josephine, you're a big girl now." Where d'you keep the whisky?

HELEN: They haven't got any. Now, come on.

PETER *(seeing GEOF)*: What's this, the father? Oh Christ, no!

GEOF: Who's he?

HELEN: President of the local Temperance Society!

PETER *(singing)*: "Who's got a bun in the oven? Who's got a cake in the stove?"

HELEN: Leave her alone.

PETER: Oh, go to hell!

JO: I've got nothing to say . . .

PETER: Go on, have your blasted family reunion, don't mind me! *(Notices GEOF again.)* Who's this? Oh, of course! Where are the drinks, Lana? *(He falls into the kitchen, singing.)* "Getting to know you, getting to know all about you . . ."

HELEN: Jo, come on . . .

There is a loud crash in the kitchen.

And the light of the world shone upon him.

PETER *enters.*

PETER: Cheer up, everybody. I am back. Who's the lily? Look at Helen, well, if she doesn't look like a bloody unrestored oil painting. What's the matter everybody? Look at the sour-faced old bitch! Well, are you coming for a few drinks or aren't you?

HELEN: The pubs aren't open yet.

JO: Do you mind getting out of here?

PETER: Shut your mouth, bubble belly! Before I shut it for you. Hey *(To GEOF)*: Mary, come here. Did I ever tell you about the chappie who married his mother by mistake?

JO: I said get him out of here, Helen. His breath smells.

HELEN: I can't carry him out, can I?

PETER: His name was Oedipus, he was a Greek I think. Well, the old bag turned out to be his mother ...

HELEN: Shut up, Peter, for God's sake!

PETER: So he scratched out both his eyes.

HELEN: Cut the dirty stories!

PETER: But I only scratched out one of mine. Well, are you coming or not?

HELEN: I am not.

PETER: Well, is anybody coming for a few drinks? You staying with the ladies, Jezebel?

GEOF: Listen, mister, this is my friend's flat ...

PETER: And what do you do, Cuddles? Don't worry, I know this district. Look at Helen, isn't she a game old bird? Worn out on the beat but she's still got a few good strokes left.

HELEN: Get out of here, you drunken sot.

PETER: Now I told you to moderate your language. What's this? Giving my money away again?

HELEN: Take your bloody money and get out!

PETER: Thank you.

HELEN: You dirty bastard!

PETER: You should have heard her the other night. You know what happened? Her wandering boy returned. He hadn't been home for two weeks and do you know why? He picked up a couple of grapefruit on a thirty-two bust, rich, young and juicy ... hey! Where's the smallest room?

GEOF: This way.

PETER: And she went off the deep end. (*Sings as he goes. Another crash offstage.*)

HELEN (*to* GEOF): You'd better go with him or Lord knows where he'll end up.

GEOF: I hope the landlady hasn't heard him.

HELEN: Cigarette?

JO: No. Yes, I will. I'll keep it for Geof.

HELEN: You'd better have the whole bloody packet if you're in such a state.

JO: Well, he couldn't hold it any more, could he?

HELEN: No one could hold that much.

JO: How long has he been like this?

HELEN: What does that boy friend of yours do for a living?

JO: He's an art student. I suppose that's what's been keeping you occupied?

HELEN: An art student. I might have known. Does he live here?

JO: Why should I answer your questions? You never answer any of mine.

HELEN: Look at you! Why don't you take a bit of pride in yourself? Grow your hair properly?

JO: Look at you. Look what your pride in yourself has done for you.

HELEN: Come and stay with me, Jo; there's a nice room and plenty of food.

JO: No, thanks.

HELEN: You prefer to stay in this hole with that pansified little freak?

GEOF: Shall I go?

HELEN: I didn't know you'd come.

JO: Would you go and live with her if you were me, Geof?

GEOF: No, I don't think I would.

JO: Neither would anybody in their right mind.

GEOF: She always said you were a pretty rotten sort of woman. I thought she was exaggerating.

HELEN: Look, can't you get it into your stupid head that I'm offering you a decent home?

PETER *enters, more sober, more unpleasant.*

PETER: Bloody cockroaches are playing leapfrog in there.

HELEN: Look, I'll tell you again, in front of him, my home is yours.

PETER: Ah! Shut up!

HELEN: I'll take care of you and see you through it.

JO: The time to have taken care of me was years ago, when I couldn't take care of myself.

HELEN: All right, but we're talking about here and now. When

I really set out to take care of somebody I usually do the job properly.

JO: So I see.

PETER: I'm not having that bloody slut at our place. I'll tell you that for nothing.

HELEN: Take no notice. The house is half mine.

PETER: Like hell it is. I could throw you out tomorrow.

JO: I don't think ...

PETER: And don't bring that little fruitcake parcel either! (*Mumbles.*) I can't stand the sight of him. Can't stand 'em at any price.

HELEN: Oh, keep out of it. Jo, I can't bear to think of you sitting here in this dump!

PETER: Neither can I. Now let's get going.

HELEN: The whole district's rotten, it's not fit to live in.

PETER: Let's go before we grow old sitting here.

HELEN: Shut up, the pubs will be open in ten minutes.

PETER: You're wrong there. (*Looking at his watch.*) They're open now. What time do you make it?

GEOF: There's one thing about this district, the people in it aren't rotten. Anyway, I think she's happier here with me than in that dazzling white house you're supposed to be so ...

PETER: Dazzling bunch of bul ... lot of bloody outsiders, no class at all. What's the time anyway?

HELEN (*to* GEOF): You shut up! I know what she needs if she's not going to finish up in a box.

PETER: What's the time by your watch, sonny?

GEOF: It's never been right since it last went wrong.

PETER: Neither have I. How long are we going to sit around in this room? I don't like the smell of unwashed bodies, woman. I dragged you out of the gutter once. If you want to go back there it's all the same to me. I'm not having this shower at any price. I'm telling you for the last time because I'm getting out of it. Stay if you want, it's all the same to me; it's your own bloody level. Well, are you coming or not?

HELEN: I'm not.

PETER: I said are you coming?

HELEN: And I said I'm not.

PETER: Well, you can just go and take a flying flip out of the window. *(He goes.)*

HELEN: I'll ... I'll ... would you sooner I stayed here with you?

JO: No, thanks.

PETER: Helen ... *(Calling.)* ... come on!

HELEN: I'll send you some money.

JO: Keep it. You might need it.

PETER: Helen!

HELEN: Go to ...

PETER: Are you coming?

HELEN *(yelling)*: Yes. *(To* GEOF.*)* See that she goes to the clinic regularly and be sure she gets enough to eat.

GEOF: She has been doing that.

HELEN: I'll see you around. *(She goes.)*

JO: Well, here endeth the third lesson.

GEOF: At least she left you some money. We can get some ...

JO: He took it back. I got you a cigarette though, love.

GEOF: Oh, smashing! I was out.

Music. They dance together. Fade out.

Scene Two

GEOFFREY *dances in with a mop and bucket and begins to clean the place.* JO *dances back and sits on the table reading. She is wearing a long white housecoat and again, in reality, months have passed between this and the previous scene. Music out.*

JO: "Ninth month, everything should now be in readiness for the little stranger." Where did you find this book, Geoffrey? It reads like *Little Women*.

GEOF: I got it for fourpence off a book barrow.

JO: You've got terrible tendencies, haven't you?

GEOF: How do you mean?

JO: You like everything to be just that little bit out of date, don't you? Clothes, books, women.

GEOF: You've got no choice, have you? I mean you all start by living in the past. Well look, it's all around you, isn't it?

JO: I wonder if we ever catch up with ourselves?

GEOF: I don't know.

JO: Now you're a real Edwardian, aren't you?

GEOF: What's that?

JO: A proper Ted! And me, I'm contemporary.

GEOF: God help us!

JO: I really am, aren't I? I really do live at the same time as myself, don't I?

GEOF: Do you mind? I've just done all that. Oh come on! Get off!

He pushes her with the mop.

JO: Hey, hey!

GEOF: Women!

JO: You haven't noticed my home dressmaking.

GEOF: No. I've been trying to ignore it. What is it?

JO: A housecoat.

GEOF: It looks more like a badly tailored shroud.

JO: What the well-dressed expectant mother is wearing this year. I feel wonderful. Aren't I enormous?

GEOF: You're clever, aren't you?

JO: What's in the oven, Geoffrey?

GEOF: You what?

JO: What's cooking?

GEOF: A cake.

JO: Mm, you're wonderful, aren't you?

GEOF: Pretty good.

JO: I know, you make everything work. The stove goes, now we eat. You've reformed me, some of the time at any rate.

GEOFFREY *shifts the sofa. There is old rubbish and dirt under it.*

GEOF: Oh, Jo!

JO: I wondered where that had got to.

GEOF: Now you know. It's disgusting, it really is.

JO: Oh Geof, the bulbs I brought with me!

GEOF: Haven't you shifted the sofa since then?

JO: They never grew.

GEOF: No, I'm not surprised.

JO: They're dead. It makes you think, doesn't it?

GEOF: What does?

JO: You know, some people like to take out an insurance policy, don't they?

GEOF: I'm a bit young for you to take out one on me.

JO: No. You know, they like to pray to the Almighty just in case he turns out to exist when they snuff it.

GEOF (*brushing under the sofa*): Well, I never think about it. You come, you go. It's simple.

JO: It's not, it's chaotic—a bit of love, a bit of lust and there you are. We don't ask for life, we have it thrust upon us.

GEOF: What's frightened you? Have you been reading the newspapers?

JO: No, I never do. Hold my hand, Geof.

GEOF: Do you mind? Halfway through this?

JO: Hold my hand.

He does.

GEOF: Hey, Jo. Come on, silly thing, it's all right. Come on there.

JO: You've got nice hands, hard. You know I used to try and hold my mother's hands, but she always used to pull them away from me. So silly really. She had so much love for everyone else, but none for me.

GEOF: If you don't watch it, you'll turn out exactly like her.

JO: I'm not like her at all.

GEOF: In some ways you are already, you know.

She pushes his hand away.

Can I go now?

JO: Yes.

GEOF: Thank you very much! *(He is pushing the couch back into position.)*

JO: "And he took up his bed and walked." You can stay here if you tell me what you do. Do you remember, Geoffrey? I used to think you were such an interesting, immoral character before I knew you. I thought you were like that . . . for one thing.

GEOFFREY *chases her with the mop all through this speech.*

You're just like an old woman really. You just unfold your bed, kiss me good night and sing me to sleep. Hey, what's the matter? Don't you like living here with me?

GEOF: It has its lighter moments, but on the whole it's a pretty trying prospect.

JO: Why do you wear black shirts? They make you look like a spiv.

GEOF: They do, Jo, but I can't be too particular. Good clothes cost money.

JO: Well, I weigh in with my share, don't I? That's a nice little job you got me, retouching those bloody photographs. What was it supposed to do, prove I was the artistic type? Of course we can't all be art students, going to our expensive art schools, nursing our little creative genius.

GEOF: Must you shout?

JO: I'm Irish.

GEOF: Never mind, it's not your fault.

JO *(laughing)*: I like you.

GEOF: Do you like me more than you don't like me or don't you like me more than you do?

JO: Now you're being Irish.

GEOF: Fine Irishwoman you are. Where did your ancestors fall, in the Battle of Salford Town Hall?

JO: My mother's father was Irish.

GEOF: You'll find any excuse.

JO: And she had me by an Irishman—the village idiot, from what I can make out.

GEOF: What do you mean?

JO: A frolic in a hayloft one afternoon. You see her husband thought sex was dirty, and only used the bed for sleeping in. So she took to herself an idiot. She said he'd got eyes like me.

GEOF: Are you making it up?

JO: He lived in a twilight land, my daddy. The land of the daft.

GEOF: Did she tell you all this?

JO: Yes.

GEOF: I'm not surprised. It sounds like Ibsen's *Ghosts*. I don't know where Helen gets them from, I don't really.

JO: I had to drag it out of her. She didn't want to tell me.

GEOF: That doesn't mean to say it's the truth. Do people ever tell the truth about themselves?

JO: Why should she want to spin me a yarn like that?

GEOF: She likes to make an effect.

JO: Like me?

GEOF: You said it. You only have to let your hair grow for a week for Helen to think you're a cretin.

JO: What?

GEOF: I said you've only got to let your hair grow for a week for Helen to think you're a cretin. She always looks at me as though I should be put away for treatment, doesn't she?

JO: Yes.

GEOF: I know, you don't have to tell me! Have you been worrying about that all these months?

JO: No.

GEOF: You have.

JO: I haven't.

GEOF: Well, I didn't think you could be so daft. Can you see Helen going out with a real loony!

JO: Well, now you put it like that, no, I can't!

GEOF: No, neither can—I don't know. Anyway, who knows who are the fools and the wise men in this world?

JO: I wouldn't be surprised if all the sane ones weren't in the bin.

GEOF: You're probably right. Anyway everyone knows you're as cracked as an old bedbug.

JO *(laughing)*: Thanks, Geof. You know, you're a cure.

GEOF: I used to be a patrol leader in the Boy Scouts.

JO: So long as you weren't Scoutmaster! You know, I wish she was here all the same.

GEOF: Why? You'd only quarrel. You know you always say you hate the sight of her.

JO: I do.

GEOF: Well then.

JO: She must know my time has almost come. When do your exams finish?

GEOF: On Thursday.

JO: I wonder which day it'll be? Put your arms round me, Geof. I don't want you to be worried while your exams are on.

GEOF: Then you shouldn't have asked me to put my arms round you, should you?

JO: Ah well, it doesn't matter if you fail. In this country the more you know the less you earn.

GEOF: Yes, you're probably right. I've got something for you. Oh Jo, I'm daft at times.

JO: I know that. I was wondering what it was.

GEOF *(from his pack he takes a life-sized doll)*: There—isn't it nice? I thought you could practise a few holds on it over the weekend. You've got to be able to establish your superiority over the little devils. I don't know where that goes. There, look, isn't it good?

JO *(seeing the doll)*: The colour's wrong.

GEOF: Jo.

JO: The colour's wrong. *(Suddenly and violently flinging the doll to the ground.)* I'll bash its brains out. I'll kill it. I

don't want his baby, Geof. I don't want to be a mother. I
don't want to be a woman.

GEOF: Don't say that, Jo.

JO: I'll kill it when it comes, Geof, I'll kill it.

GEOF: Do you want me to go out and find that chap and bring
him back? Is that what you want?

JO: I don't want that. I don't want any man.

GEOF: Well, if you're going to feel like that about it you might
as well have it adopted. I thought you'd feel differently as
time went on.

JO: I won't.

GEOF: Perhaps you will when you see the baby.

JO: No, I won't.

GEOF: Do you still love him?

JO: I don't know. He was only a dream I had. You know, he
could sing and he was so tender. Every Christmas Helen
used to go off with some boy friend or other and leave me
all on my own in some sordid digs, but last Christmas I
had him.

GEOF: Your black prince.

JO: What was his name?

GEOF: Prince Ossini.

JO: No, it was Jimmie!

GEOF: Oh well, the dream's gone, but the baby's real enough.

JO: My mother always used to say you remember the first time
all your life, but until this moment I'd forgotten it.

GEOF: Do you remember when I asked you to marry me?

JO: Yes.

GEOF: Do you?

JO: No. What did I say?

GEOF: You just went and lay on the bed.

JO: And you didn't go and follow me, did you?

GEOF: No.

JO: You see, it's not marrying love between us, thank God.

GEOF: You mean you just like having me around till your next
prince comes along?

JO: No.

GEOF: Oh well, you need somebody to love you while you're looking for someone to love.

JO: Oh Geof, you'd make a funny father. You are a funny little man. I mean that. You're unique.

GEOF: Am I?

JO: I always want to have you with me because I know you'll never ask anything from me. Where are you going?

GEOFFREY *goes to the kitchen.*

GEOF: To see the cake.

JO *follows him.*

JO: I'll set the cups and we'll have a celebration, then you'll have to study for your exams. It's a bit daft talking about getting married, isn't it? We're already married. We've been married for a thousand years.

They march in together from the kitchen, he with the cake, she with the tea things.

GEOF *(putting it down)*: Here, look at that. What are you going to call it?

JO: What, the cake?

GEOF *(laughing)*: No, Jo, the baby.

JO: I think I'll give it to you, Geof. You like babies, don't you? I might call it Number One. It'll always be number one to itself.

HELEN *enters, loaded with baggage as in Act One, Scene one.*

HELEN: Anybody at home? Well, I'm back. You see, I couldn't stay away, could I? There's some flowers for you, Jo. The barrows are smothered in them. Oh! How I carried that lot from the bus stop I'll never know. The old place looks a bit more cheerful, doesn't it? I say, there's a nice homely smell. Have you been doing a bit of baking? I'll tell you one thing, it's a lovely day for flitting.

JO: Would you like a cup of tea, Helen?

HELEN: Have you got anything stronger? Oh no, course you haven't! Go on, I'll have a cup with you. Let's have a look at you, love. I arrived just in time, by the looks of things, didn't I? How are you, love? Everything straightforward? Been having your regular check-up and doing all them exercises and all the things they go in for nowadays? That's a good girl. Have you got everything packed?

JO: Packed?

HELEN: Yes.

JO: But I'm not going into hospital.

HELEN: You're not having it here, are you?

GEOF: Yes, she didn't want to go away.

HELEN: Oh my God, is he still here? I thought he would be.

GEOF: Do you want a piece of cake, Jo?

JO: Yes, please.

HELEN: You can't have a baby in this dump. Why don't you use a bit of sense for once and go into hospital? They've got everything to hand there. I mean, sometimes the first one can be a bit tricky.

GEOF: There's going to be nothing tricky about it; it's going to be perfectly all right, isn't it, Jo?

HELEN: Who do you think you are, the Flying Doctor?

JO: Look, I've made up my mind I want to have it here. I don't like hospitals.

HELEN: Have you ever been in a hospital?

JO: No.

HELEN: Well, how do you know what it's like? Oo! Give me a cup of tea quick.

GEOF: Oh well, we've got a district nurse coming in.

HELEN: Oh my God, my feet are killing me. How I got that lot from the bus stop I'll never know.

JO: Well what are you lugging all the cases about for?

HELEN: I've come to look after you. It's just as well, by the looks of things. (*Whispers to* JO.)

JO: Well, it's going to be a bit crowded, you know. Is your husband coming and all? Is he moving in too?

HELEN: There wouldn't be much room for two of us on that couch, would there?

JO: That's Geoffrey's bed.

GEOF: It's all right, Jo, I don't mind moving out.

JO: For Heaven's sake, you don't have to start wilting away as soon as she barges in.

GEOF: I don't.

HELEN: I could do with a drink.

JO: Start barging around just like a bull in a china shop.

HELEN: I've got some lovely things for the baby, Jo. Where did I put them? Where's that other case, Jo? Oh!

GEOF: Jo, will you sit down. I'll get it.

HELEN: Look, love. I've come here to talk to my daughter. Can you make yourself scarce for a bit?

GEOF: I've got to go, we need some things for the weekend.

JO: You don't have to let her push you around.

GEOF: I don't.

HELEN: Oh I do wish he wouldn't mumble. It does get on my nerves. What's he saying?

GEOF: Where's my pack?

JO: What a couple of old women.

GEOF: Look here, Jo!

JO: Look, just a minute will you. I . . . look I . . . there's nothing . . .

GEOF: How can I stay . . .

HELEN: Come here. How long is he going to stick around here. Bloody little pansy . . .

JO: Look, if you're going to insult Geof . . .

HELEN: I'm not insulting him.

JO: Yes you are.

HELEN: I'm not. I just don't like his style, that's all.

GEOF: It's all right, Mrs. Smith . . .

HELEN: Look, love, I just want five minutes alone with her. Do you mind? Is it too much to ask?

GEOF: Do you want any cotton wool?

HELEN: Good God, does he knit an' all?

JO: You don't have to go.

GEOF: Jo, I've got to go, I'll only be a couple of minutes.

JO: There's plenty of stuff in the kitchen. Now look...

GEOFFREY *goes.*

HELEN: You don't mean to tell me he's really gone?

JO: Now that you've been rude to my friend...

HELEN: What an arty little freak! I wasn't rude to him. I never said a word. I never opened my mouth.

JO: Look, he's the only friend I've got, as a matter of fact.

HELEN: Jo! I thought you could find yourself something more like a man.

JO: Why were you so nasty to him?

HELEN: I wasn't nasty to him. Besides, I couldn't talk to you in front of him, could I? Hey, wait till you see these things for the baby.

JO: You hurt people's feelings and you don't even notice.

HELEN: Jo, I just wanted to get rid of him, that's all. Look at those, Jo. Look, isn't that pretty, eh? The baby's going to be dressed like a prince, isn't he?

JO: We're all princes in our own little kingdom. You're not to insult Geoffrey. Will you leave him alone?

HELEN: Hey, look at this Jo, isn't it pretty? Oh, I love babies—aren't they lovely?

JO: Has your husband thrown you out?

HELEN: Oh come off it, Jo. I had to be with you at a time like this, hadn't I? And what about this sailor lad of yours, have you made any attempt to trace him? He's entitled to keep his child, you know.

JO: I wouldn't do that, it's degrading.

HELEN: What do you call this set-up?

JO: It's all right. There's no need for you to worry about me. I can work for the baby myself.

HELEN: Who's going to look after it when you're out at work? Have you thought about that?

JO: Yes, I have.

HELEN: Well, you can't do two jobs at once, you know. Who's going to nurse it? Him?

JO: That's my business. I can do anything when I set my mind to it.

HELEN: Very clever, aren't you?

JO: There's no need to be so superior. Look where all your swanking's landed you. What does the little lady want— an engagement ring? And now he's thrown you out, hasn't he, and you have to come crawling back here.

HELEN: Well, it was good while it lasted.

JO: Making a fool of yourself over that throw-back.

HELEN: He threw his money about like a man with no arms.

JO: This is my flat now, Helen.

HELEN: It's all right, love, I've got a bit of money put by.

JO: You're a real fool, aren't you?

HELEN: Oh, Jo, look. I'm back aren't I? Forget it. Don't keep on about it.

JO: Do you know what I think?

HELEN: What?

JO: I think you're still in love with him.

HELEN: In love? Me?

JO: Yes.

HELEN: You must be mad.

JO: What happened?

HELEN: He's gone off with his bit of crumpet. Still, it was good while it lasted. Anyway, I'll shift some of this, Jo.

JO: So we're back where we started. And all those months you stayed away from me because of him! Just like when I was small.

HELEN: I never thought about you! It's a funny thing, I never have done when I've been happy. But these last few weeks I've known I should be with you.

JO: So you stayed away—

HELEN: Yes. I can't stand trouble.

JO: Oh, there's no trouble. I've been performing a perfectly normal, healthy function. We're wonderful! Do you know, for the first time in my life I feel really important. I feel as though I could take care of the whole world. I even feel as though I could take care of you, too!

HELEN: Here, I forgot to tell you, I've ordered a lovely cot for you.

JO: We've got one.

HELEN: It's lovely. It's got pink curtains, you know, and frills.

JO gets wicker basket from under bed.

Oh, I don't like that. What is it?

JO: It's wicker work. Geof got it.

HELEN: It's a bit old-fashioned, isn't it?

JO: We like it.

HELEN: Look love, why don't you go and lie down? You look as though you've got a bit of a headache.

JO: Do you wonder?

HELEN: Well, go and have a rest, there's a good girl. I'm going to tidy this place up for you. I'm going to make it just the way you like it. Go on.

JO: Oh no!

HELEN: Go on, Jo. Go on. It looks more like a laundry basket, doesn't it! Oh! The state of this place! We'll never have it right. Living like pigs in a pigsty—

GEOFFREY *enters.*

Oh, you're back are you? Well, come in if you're coming.

GEOF: Where's Jo?

HELEN: She's in bed. Where do you think she is? She's having a little sleep, so don't you dare wake her up.

GEOF: I wouldn't do that. (*He places pack filled with food on the table.*)

HELEN: Don't put that bag on there, I'm cleaning this place up.

GEOF: You know I just did it before you came.

HELEN: It doesn't look like it. Look, son, we're going to have the midwife running in and out of here before long. We want this place all clean and tidy, all hygienic-looking, if that's possible.

GEOF: Well, it's clean.

JO: Is that Geof?

HELEN: Now look what you've done!

GEOF: Yes, Jo.

JO: Have you got any of those headache pills, love?

GEOF: Yes, I'll get you some.

HELEN: If you're going in there take these flowers with you and put them in water. You might as well make yourself useful. They look as though they're withering away. *(She peers into the pack.)* What the devil's he got here? What's that? Spaghetti! I don't know how people can eat it. And that's a funny looking lettuce. What the hell's that? Hey, what's this here?

GEOF: What?

HELEN: All this muck in here?

GEOF: Well, Jo likes that type of food.

HELEN: Since when? She needs proper food down her at a time like this.

GEOF: Oh!

HELEN *points to wicker basket.*

HELEN: Hey, you can throw that bloody thing out for a start.

GEOF: What thing?

HELEN: That thing there. You're not putting my grandchild in a thing like that. Oh, this place! It's filthy! I don't know what you've been doing between the two of you. You might have kept it a bit cleaner than this. Just look at it! Don't stand there looking silly holding that thing, throw it away, or do something with it! I've ordered a proper cot of the latest design, it's got all the etceteras and everything. This place! You're living like pigs in a pigsty. Oh, for God's sake give it here, I'll do something with it.

GEOF: Yes, but Jo likes it.

HELEN: Well, I suppose it will come in handy for something.

(She enters the kitchen.) Oh my God, it's the same in here! Nowhere to put anything ... Are you off now?

GEOF: Yes.

HELEN: Well, take that muck with you as you're going.

GEOF: I don't want it.

HELEN: I'm sure I don't.

GEOF: Mrs. Smith, I ... I ...

HELEN: Are you talking to me?

GEOF: Yes, I wanted to ask you something.

HELEN: Well, get it said. Don't mumble.

GEOF: I don't want you to take offence.

HELEN: Do I look the type that takes offence?

GEOF: Would you not frighten Jo?

HELEN: I thought you said you were going.

GEOF: I said would you not frighten Jo.

HELEN: What are you talking about, frightening her?

GEOF: You know, telling her that it might be tricky or that she might have trouble, because she's going to be all right.

HELEN: Are you trying to tell me what to do with my own daughter?

GEOF: Oh no.

HELEN: Well, are you going?

GEOF: Yes, although she said she didn't want a woman with her when she had it.

HELEN: She said what?

GEOF: She said she wanted me with her when she had it because she said she wouldn't be frightened if I was with her.

HELEN: How disgusting!

GEOF: There's nothing disgusting about it.

HELEN: A man in the room at a time like this!

GEOF: Husbands stay with their wives.

HELEN: Are you her husband?

GEOF: No.

HELEN: Well, get.

GEOF: I'm going. She can't cope with the two of us. Only just don't frighten her, that's all.

HELEN: I've told you we don't want that.

GEOF: Yes I know, but she likes it.

HELEN: You can bloody well take it with you, we don't want it.

> GEOFFREY *empties food from his pack on to the table while* HELEN *thrusts it back.* HELEN *finally throws the whole thing, pack and all, on to the floor.*

GEOF: Yes, the one thing civilisation couldn't do anything about —women. Good-bye Jo, and good luck. *(He goes.)*

> JO *stirs on the bed.*

HELEN: It's all right, love, I'm here and everything's all right. Are you awake now?

JO: Hello. Yes . . . What's it like?

HELEN: What?

JO: Is there much pain?

HELEN: No! It's not so much pain as hard work, love. I was putting my Christmas pudding up on a shelf when you started on me. There I was standing on a chair singing away merry as the day is long . . .

JO: Did you yell?

HELEN: No, I ran.

JO: Do you know, I had such a funny dream just now.

HELEN: Oh, Jo, you're always dreaming, aren't you. Well, don't let's talk about your dreams or we'll get morbid.

JO: Where would you like those flowers put?

HELEN: Over . . . over there . . . Come on, you come and do it, love.

JO: Hasn't Geof come back yet?

HELEN: No, he hasn't.

JO: Well, where are you going to sleep, Helen?

HELEN: It's all right, love. Don't fall over, now.

JO: You know, I've got so used to old Geof lying there on that couch like—like an old watchdog. You aren't . . .

HELEN: It's all right, love, don't you worry about me, I'll find somewhere.

JO: I wonder where he is . . . Oh!

HELEN: Oh Jo, careful . . . Hold on, love, hold on! It'll be all right. The first one doesn't last long. Oh my God, I could do with a drink now. Hold on.

JO *kneels on bed.* HELEN *strokes her hair.*

JO: That's better.

HELEN: Are you all right now? There we are. *(Children sing outside.)* Can you hear those children singing over there on the croft, Jo?

JO: Yes, you can always hear them on still days.

HELEN: You know when I was young we used to play all day long at this time of the year; in the summer we had singing games and in the spring we played with tops and hoops, and then in the autumn there was the Fifth of November, then we used to have bonfires in the street, and gingerbread and all that. Have I ever told you about the time when we went to a place called Shining Clough? Oh, I must have done. I used to climb up there every day and sit on the top of the hill, and you could see the mills in the distance, but the clough itself was covered in moss. Isn't it funny how you remember these things? Do you know, I'd sit there all day long and nobody ever knew where I was. Shall I go and make us a cup of tea?

HELENS *enters kitchen and fiddles with stove.*

Oh Jo, I've forgotten how we used to light this thing.

JO: Turn on all the knobs. Mind you don't gas yourself.

HELEN: I still can't do it.

JO: Geof'll fix it.

HELEN: No, it's all right.

JO: Helen.

HELEN: Yes.

JO: My baby may be black.

HELEN: You what, love?

JO: My baby will be black.

HELEN: Oh, don't be silly, Jo. You'll be giving yourself nightmares.

JO: But it's true. He was black.

HELEN: Who?

JO: Jimmie.

HELEN: You mean to say that ... that sailor was a black man? ... Oh my God! Nothing else can happen to me now. Can you see me wheeling a pram with a ... Oh my God, I'll have to have a drink.

JO: What are you going to do?

HELEN: I don't know. Drown it. Who knows about it?

JO: Geoffrey.

HELEN: And what about the nurse? She's going to get a bit of a shock, isn't she?

JO: Well, she's black too.

HELEN: Good, perhaps she'll adopt it. Dear God in heaven!

JO: If you don't like it you can get out. I didn't ask you to come here.

HELEN: Where's my hat?

JO: On your head.

HELEN: Oh yes ... I don't know what's to be done with you, I don't really. (*To the audience.*) I ask you, what would you do?

JO: Are you going?

HELEN: Yes.

JO: Are you just going for a drink?

HELEN: Yes.

JO: Are you coming back?

HELEN: Yes.

JO: Well, what are you going to do?

HELEN: Put it on the stage and call it Blackbird. (*She rushes out.*)

JO *watches her go, leaning against the doorpost. Then she looks round the room, smiling a little to herself—she remembers* GEOF.

JO: As I was going up Pippin Hill,
Pippin Hill was dirty.
And there I met a pretty miss,
And she dropped me a curtsy.
Little miss, pretty miss,
Blessings light upon you.
If I had half a crown a day,
I'd gladly spend it on you.

Curtain.

THE HOSTAGE

Brendan Behan

THE HOSTAGE was first presented by Theatre Workshop at the Theatre Royal, Stratford, London E.15, on 14 October 1958. A revised version was presented by Theatre Workshop at the Paris Théâtre des Nations Festival on 3 April 1959, and, in conjunction with Donmar Productions Ltd., at Wyndham's Theatre on 11 June 1959. This text is of the later production, produced by Joan Littlewood, setting designed by Sean Kenny, and with the following cast:

PAT, *the caretaker of a lodging-house*	Howard Goorney
MEG DILLON, *his consort*	Eileen Kennally
MONSEWER, *the owner of the house*	Glynn Edwards
RIO RITA, *a homosexual navvy*	Stephen Cato
PRINCESS GRACE, *his coloured boyfriend*	Roy Barnett
MR. MULLEADY, *a decaying Civil Servant*	Brian Murphy
MISS GILCHRIST, *a social worker*	Ann Beach
COLETTE, *a whore*	Yootha Joyce
ROPEEN, *an old whore*	Leila Greenwood
LESLIE WILLIAMS, *a British soldier*	Alfred Lynch
TERESA, *the skivvy, a country girl*	Celia Salkeld
I.R.A. OFFICER, *a fanatical patriot*	James Booth
VOLUNTEER, *Feargus O'Connor, a ticket-collector*	Clive Barker
RUSSIAN SAILOR	Dudley Sutton
KATE, *the pianist*	Kathleen O'Connor

The music for the play was arranged and edited by Kathleen O'Connor and can be obtained from the publishers, Chappell & Co. Ltd., 50 New Bond Street, London, W. 1.

ACT ONE

The action of the play takes place in an old house in Dublin that has seen better days. A middle-aged man wearing carpet slippers, old corduroys and using a walking-stick is holding court. He runs the house. He doesn't own it, although he acts as though he does. This is because the real owner isn't right in his head and thinks he's still fighting in The Troubles or one of the anti-English campaigns before that.

Since the action of the play runs throughout the whole house and it isn't feasible to build it on stage, the setting is designed to represent one room of the house with a window overlooking the street. Leading off from this room are two doors and a staircase leading to the upper part. Between the room and the audience is an area that represents a corridor, a landing, or another room in the house and also serves as an extension of the room when the characters need room to dance and fight in.

The middle-aged man is PATRICK, *an ex-hero and present-time brothel-keeper. During the first act of the play* PATRICK, *with the aid of* MEG DILLON, *his consort, is preparing the room that we can see, for a guest. It contains a table, two chairs and a brass bedstead. During the action of the play the other inhabitants of the house, in search of stout, physical comfort or the odd ballad, drift in and out of the room according to their curiosity and the state of* PAT'S *temper. Like the house, they have seen better times. As the curtain rises, pimps, prostitutes, decayed gentlemen and their visiting "friends" are dancing a wild Irish jig, which is a good enough reason for* MEG *and* PAT *to stop their preparations and sit down for a drink of stout. During the act these rests and drinks occupy more time than the actual work of preparation.*

The jig reaches its climax and the dancers swing off the stage leaving PAT *and* MEG *sitting at the table in the room.*

MEG: Thank God, that's over!

From the end of the passage comes the blast of an off-key bagpiper. The noise recedes into the distance.

MEG: In the name of God, what's that?

PAT: It's Monsewer practising his music. He's taken it into his head to play the Dead March for the boy in Belfast Jail when they hang him in the morning. You know, the one that got copped for his I.R.A. activities.

MEG: I wish he'd kept it in his head. Those bagpipes get on me nerves.

PAT: Get us a drink.

MEG: Get it yourself.

PAT: I can't move my leg.

MEG: There's nothing wrong with your leg. (*She reaches him a bottle of stout.*) Here you are, you old scow.

A homosexual navvy, RIO RITA, attempts to get through the room and up the stairs without PAT seeing him. He is accompanied by a Negro with a kit-bag. PAT spots them.

PAT: Hey! Where's your rent?

RIO RITA: Give me a chance to earn it. (*They scuttle upstairs.*)

MEG: Do you think they will hang him?

PAT: Who, him? (*He indicates RIO RITA's disappearing backside.*) They bloody well ought to!

MEG: No, the boy in Belfast Jail.

PAT: There's no think about it. Tomorrow morning at the hour of eight, he'll hang as high as Killymanjaro.

MEG: What the hell's that?

PAT: It's a noted mountain off the south coast of Switzerland. It would do you no good to be hung as high as that, anyway.

MEG: Do you know what he said? "As a soldier of the Irish Republic, I will die smiling."

PAT: And who asked him to give himself the trouble?

MEG: He only did his duty as a member of the I.R.A.

PAT: Don't have me use a coarse expression, you silly old

bitch. This is nineteen-sixty, and the days of the heroes are over this forty years past. Long over, finished and done with. The I.R.A. and the War of Independence are as dead as the Charleston.

MEG: The old cause is never dead. "Till Ireland shall be free from the centre to the sea. Hurrah for liberty, says the Shan Van Vocht."

PAT *(to the audience)*: She's as bad as that old idiot out there. *(He indicates* MONSEWER.*)* It's bad enough he hasn't got a clock, but I declare to Jesus, I don't think he even has a calendar. And who has the trouble of it all? Me! He wants to have the New I.R.A., so-called in this place now. Prepare a room for them, no less.

COLETTE, *an attractive young whore, enters propelling a* SAILOR *before her. The* SAILOR *obviously speaks no English or Gaelic, and seeing the bed in the room starts to take his trousers off.* COLETTE *drags him away upstairs.*

COLETTE: I've got a right one here, this time. *(They go upstairs.)*

PAT: It's bad enough trying to run this place as a speak-easy and a brockel—

MEG: A what?

PAT: A brockel. That's English for whorehouse.

MEG: I will be thankful to you to keep that kind of talk about whorehouses to yourself. I'm no whore for one.

PAT: Why? Are you losing your union card?

The SAILOR *sings lustily upstairs.*

MEG: Well, if I'm a whore itself, you don't mind taking the best part of my money. So you're nothing but a ponce.

PAT: Well, I'm saving up to be one. And a long time that will take me with the money you earn.

MEG: Well, you know what you can do. And shut that bloody row up there.

COLETTE *(off)*: And you.

PAT *(to* MEG*)*: You ought to know better than to abuse a poor crippled man that lost his leg, three miles outside of Mullingar.

MEG: There's nothing the matter with your leg.

PAT: And how do you think we could keep the house going on what we get from Monsewer? And who would look after him in England or Ireland if I didn't?

MEG: Not me for one.

PAT: Well, I'll stick by him because we were soldiers of Ireland in the old days.

There is a PIANIST *at one end of the passage area with the piano half on stage and half off.* PAT *signals to her and he sings:*

On the eighteenth day of November,
Just outside the town of Macroom,
The Tans in their big Crossley tenders,
Came roaring along to their doom.

But the boys of the column were waiting
With hand grenades primed on the spot,
And the Irish Republican Army
Made shit of the whole mucking lot

The foreign SAILOR *sings on.*

RIO RITA: Oh, shut up, you dirty foreign bastard.

Whilst PAT *is singing all the other inhabitants come on to the stage, join in the song, and stay for a drink.*

MEG: You stand there singing about them ould times and the five glorious years, and yet you sneer and jeer at the boys of today. What's the difference.

PAT: It's the H bomb. It's such a big bomb it's got me scared of the little bombs. The I.R.A. is out of date—

ALL: Shame. No.

PAT:—and so is the R.A.F., the Swiss Guards, the Foreign Legion, the Red Army—

SAILOR: Niet.

PAT:—the United States Marines, the Free State Army, the Coldstream Guards, the Scots Guards, the Welsh Guards, the Grenadier Guards and the bloody fire guards.

MEG: Not the Horse Guards?

A blast on the bagpipes and MONSEWER *enters along the passage looking like Baden Powell in an Irish kilt and flowing cloak. The noise from the bagpipes is terrible. Everyone but* MEG *springs smartly to attention as* MONSEWER *passes and salutes.* MONSEWER *lives in a world of his own, peopled by heroes and enemies. He spends his time making plans for battles fought long ago against enemies long since dead.*

MONSEWER *(greets him in Gaelic):* Cén caoi ina bfuil tu.

PAT: Commandant-General.

MONSEWER: As you were, Patrick.

PAT: Thank you, Monsewer.

PAT *stands at ease. The rest, except for* MEG, *drift away.* MONSEWER *addresses* PAT *with a great show of secrecy.*

MONSEWER: Patrick—preparations.

PAT: Everything's ready for the guest.

MONSEWER: Good, good. The troops will be coming quite soon.

PAT *(aside):* The troops! Good God! *(To* MONSEWER:*)* How many of them are expected, then?

MONSEWER: There will be the two guards and the prisoner.

PAT: The prisoner?

MONSEWER: Yes. Yes, we only have the one at the moment, but it's a good beginning.

PAT: Yes, indeed, as the Scotchman says, "Many a mickle makes a muckle."

MONSEWER: And as we Irish say, "It's one after another they built the castle. Iss in yeeg a Kale-ah shah togeock nuh cashlawn."

PAT *(to the audience)*: Do you hear that? That's Irish. It's a great thing, an Oxford University education! Me, I'm only a poor ignorant Dublin man. I wouldn't understand a word of it. *(To* MONSEWER.*)* About this prisoner, Monsewer.

MONSEWER: Yes. An English laddie to be captured on the Border.

PAT: Armagh?

MONSEWER: Only one at first, but soon we'll have scores of them.

PAT *(aside)*: I hope to God he's not going to bring them all here.

MONSEWER: What's that?

PAT: I say, it's a great thing, the boys being out again, sir.

MONSEWER: Absolutely first-class. Carry on.

MONSEWER *marches off to make more plans.* PAT *retires defeated to have another stout.*

MEG: He's a decent old skin, even if he has got a slate loose.

PAT: Did you hear that? It's bad enough turning this place into an I.R.A. barracks. Monsewer wants to make a glasshouse out of it now.

MEG: A what?

PAT: A kind of private Shepton Mallet of his own.

MEG: We should be proud to help the men that are fighting for Ireland. Especially that poor boy to be hanged in Belfast Jail tomorrow morning.

PAT: Why are you getting so upset over Ireland? Where the hell were you in nineteen-sixteen when the real fighting was going on?

MEG: I wasn't born yet.

PAT: You're full of excuses. Where were you when we had to go out and capture our own stuff off of the British Army?

MEG: Capture it? You told me that you bought it off the Tommies in the pub. You said yourself you got a revolver, two hundreds rounds of ammunition, and a pair of jodhpurs off a colonel's batman for two pints of Bass and fifty Woodbines.

PAT: I shouldn't have given him anything. But I was sorry for him.

MEG: Why?

PAT: He got my sister in the family way.

MEG: Well, she was a dirty no-good . . .

The conversation is interrupted by the rush of feet on the stairs. The SAILOR *enters, minus his trousers, pursued by* COLETTE *in a dressing-gown. The rear is brought up by* MR. MULLEADY, *a decaying Civil Servant. The row brings the other people in and the* SAILOR *is chased into a corner, where a menacing ring of people surrounds him.*

MULLEADY: Mr. Pat, Mr. Pat, that man, he—he's a Russian.

PAT: A what?

MULLEADY: A Russian.

PAT: Well, is he dirty or something?

MULLEADY: He's a Communist.

MEG: A Communist.

COLETTE: Oh now, Pat, it's against my religion to have anything to do with the likes of him.

PAT: You have to pick up trade where you can these days. The only reason I know for throwing a man out is when he has no money to pay.

MEG: Has he got any?

PAT: I'll find out. Have you got any money? Any gelt? Dollars? Pound notes? Money? (PAT *makes a sign for money.*)

SAILOR: Da! Da! (*He produces a big wad of notes.*)

MEG: Do you see the wad he has on him? (*The* SAILOR *throws the money in the air and beams. They all dive for the money.*)

MEG: Sure, pound notes is the best religion in the world.

PAT: And the best politics, too.

As they all scrabble and fight for the money on the floor, a voice thunders from the stairs:

118 / *Brendan Behan*

MONSEWER: Hark a voice like thunder spake,
The west awake, the west awake.
Sing Oh Hurrah, for Ireland's sake,
Let England quake.

SAILOR: Mir y drushva!

MONSEWER: Cén caoi ina bfuil tu. *(He compliments* COLETTE.*)* Carry on, my dear. Ireland needs the work of the women as well, you know. *(Exit.)*

COLETTE: Is it all right now?

PAT: Yes, go on.

COLETTE: Well, I've been to confession three times already and I don't want to make a mistake about it.

> COLETTE *takes the* RUSSIAN SAILOR *upstairs to bed. The excitement over, everyone drifts off, leaving* MR. MULLEADY *with* PAT *and* MEG.

MULLEADY: I'm sorry, Mrs. M.—I mean about the Russian. I felt that as a God-fearing man I could shut my eyes no longer.

MEG: Anybody would think you was doing God a good turn speaking well of him.

MULLEADY: Oh, and another thing—about my laundry, Miss Meg. It was due back three days ago.

PAT: It walked back.

MULLEADY: I have to go to one of my committees this evening and I haven't a shirt to my name.

MEG: Go and ask the Prisoners Aid Society to give you one.

MULLEADY: You know very well that is the committee on which I serve.

MEG: Well, go and wash one.

MULLEADY: You know I can't—

MEG: Get going, or I'll ask you for the money you owe me.

MULLEADY: Please don't bring all that up again. You know that at the end of the month . . .

MEG: Are you going? *(She drives him out.)* Fine thing to be letting rooms to every class of gouger and bowsey in the city.

PAT: Dirty thieves and whores the lot of them. Still, their money is clean enough.

MEG: It's not the whores I mind, it's the likes of that old whited sepulchre that I don't like.

MULLEADY *comes downstairs with a filthy shirt and scoots through the room and out of the kitchen door.*

PAT: You don't mean Monsewer?

MEG: No, I don't. I mean that old Mulleady geezer, though Monsewer is bad enough, giving out about the Republic and living in a brockel.

PAT *(hushing her)*: Monsewer doesn't know anything about these matters.

MEG: Course he does, Pat.

PAT: He doesn't.

MEG: He must know.

PAT: No. He thinks everybody in this house are gaels, patriots or Republicans on the run.

MEG: He doesn't, the old idiot! He's here again.

MONSEWER *enters, on secret service, carrying a sheaf of despatches and plans.*

MONSEWER: Patrick!

PAT: Sir!

MONSEWER: As you were. (PAT *stands at ease.*)

PAT: Thank you, Monsewer.

MONSEWER *(in great confidence)*: Patrick, I trust we may rely on the lads in the billet if anything should go wrong tonight?

PAT: We may put our lives in their hands, Monsewer.

MEG: God help us.

MONSEWER: There was a bit of rumpus in here a minute ago, wasn't there?

PAT: Strain of battle, Commandant.

MONSEWER: Yes, yes. The boys are bound to be a bit restless on a night like this. It's in the air, Patrick—can you smell it? *(Like Wellington on the eve of Waterloo, PAT sniffs.)*

PAT: No, sir, I'm afraid I can't.

MONSEWER: The coming battle. I think you should have a copy of this, Patrick. Battle orders. Plenty of fodder in?

PAT: For the horses, Commandant?

MONSEWER: For the men, damn you! The men.

PAT: Oh yes, Monsewer. This is in Irish, Monsewer.

MONSEWER: At a time like this, we should refuse to use the English language altogether. (MONSEWER *surveys his imaginary battlefield, planning how he will deploy his forces.*)

PAT: Well, you've done your bit on that score, Monsewer. For years Monsewer wouldn't speak anything but Irish.

MEG: Most people wouldn't know what he was saying, surely.

PAT: No, they didn't. When he went on a tram or a bus he had to have an interpreter with him so the conductor would know where he wanted to get off.

MEG: Ah, the poor man.

MONSEWER: Patrick. (*He draws him aside.*) Any letters arrived for me from England lately?

PAT: No, sir.

MONSEWER: Oh dear. I was relying on my allowance for a few necessities.

PAT: Ah, never mind, sir, we'll keep the kip going somehow.

MEG (*to the audience*): Sure, he hasn't had a letter from England since they naturalised the Suez Canal.

MONSEWER: There's another matter: fellow patriot of ours, calls himself Pig-eye—code name, of course. Just served six months in prison for the cause. I told him that, in return, he shall billet here, at our expense, till the end of his days. Carry on. (MONSEWER *marches off.*)

PAT (*to the audience*): Pig-eye! He's just done six months for robbery with violence. "Till the end of his days." If he doesn't pay his rent, he'll reach the end of his days sooner than he expects.

MEG: Don't you talk to me about that Pig-eye. He's as mean as the grave. A hundred gross of nylons he knocked off the other day, from the Hauty Cotture warehouse, and not one did he offer to a girl in the street. No bejasus, not even to the one-legged girl in Number 8. The old hypocrite.

PAT: Who? Pig-eye?

MEG: No, Monsewer. He's not as green as he's cabbage looking. Calling himself "Monsewer," blowing the head off you with his ould pipes, and not a penny to his name.

PAT: Well, he's loyal to the old cause, and he's a decent old skin.

As PAT *begins to tell his story other people from the house edge in:* KATE, *the pianist,* RIO RITA *in a faded silk dressing-gown, and his coloured boy-friend,* MR. MULLEADY, COLETTE *and the* SAILOR *and* OLD ROPEEN, *a retired whore. They egg* PAT *on or mock him, if they dare.*

MEG: Where did he get that monniker for a start? Is it an English name?

PAT: What?

MEG: Monsewer.

PAT: It's French for mister, isn't it?

MEG: I don't know. I'm asking you.

PAT: Well, I'm telling you, it is. At one time all the toffs were going mad, talking Irish and only calling themselves by their Irish names.

MEG: You just said it was a French name.

PAT: Will you let me finish for once? What's the Irish for mister?

ROPEEN: R. Goine Vasal.

MEG *starts laughing.*

PAT: Yes, well it was too Irish for them, too, so they called themselves Monsieur or Madame as the case might be.

MEG: Ah, they're half mad, these high-up ould ones.

PAT: He wasn't half mad the first time I saw him, nor a quarter mad, God bless him. See that? (*He produces a photo.*) Monsewer on the back of his white horse, the Cross of Christ held high in his right hand, like Brian Boru, leading his men to war and glory.

MEG: Will you look at the poor horse.

PAT: That was the day we got captured. We could have got out of it, but Monsewer is terrible strict and honest. You see, he's an Englishman.

MEG: An Englishman, and him going round in a kilt all day playing his big Gaelic pipes.

PAT: He was born an Englishman, remained one for years. His father was a bishop.

MEG: His father was a bishop. *(All good Catholics, they start to leave.)* Well, I'm not sitting here and listening to that class of immoral talk. His father was a bishop, indeed!

PAT: He was a Protestant bishop.

MEG: Ah well, it's different for them. *(They all come back.)*

RIO RITA: They get married, too, sometimes.

PAT: He went to all the biggest colleges in England and slept in the one room with the King of England's son.

MEG: Begad, it wouldn't surprise me if he slept in the one bed with him, his father being a bishop.

PAT: Yes, he had every class of comfort, mixed with dukes, marquises, earls and lords.

MEG: All sleeping in the one room, I suppose?

ROPEEN: In the one bed.

PAT: Will you shut up. As I was saying, he had every class of comfort until one day he discovered he was an Irishman.

MEG: Aren't you after telling me he was an Englishman?

PAT: He was an Anglo-Irishman.

MEG: In the name of God, what's that?

PAT: A Protestant with a horse.

ROPEEN: Leadbetter.

PAT: No, no, an ordinary Protestant like Leadbetter, the plumber in the back parlour next door, won't do, nor a Belfast orangeman, not if he was as black as your boot.

MEG: Why not?

PAT: Because they work. An Anglo-Irishman only works at riding horses, drinking whisky and reading double-meaning books in Irish at Trinity College.

MEG: I'm with you he wasn't born an Irishman. He became one.

PAT: He didn't become one—he was born one—on his mother's

side, and as he didn't like his father much he went with his mother's people—he became an Irishman.

MEG: How did he do that?

PAT: Well, he took it easy at first, wore a kilt, played Gaelic football on Blackheath.

MEG: Where's that?

PAT: In London. He took a correspondence course in the Irish language. And when the Rising took place he acted like a true Irish hero.

MEG: He came over to live in Ireland.

PAT: He fought for Ireland, with me at his side.

MEG: Aye, we've heard that part of the story before.

PAT: Five years' hard fighting.

COLETTE: Ah, God help us.

ROPEEN: Heavy and many is the good man that was killed.

PAT: We had the victory—till they signed that curse-of-God treaty in London. They sold the six counties to England and Irishmen were forced to swear an oath of allegiance to the British Crown.

MEG: I don't know about the six counties, but the swearing wouldn't come so hard on you.

ROPEEN: Whatever made them do it, Mr. Pat?

PAT. Well, I'll tell you, Ropeen. It was Lloyd George and Birkenhead made a fool of Michael Collins and he signed an agreement to have no more fighting with England.

MEG: Then he should have been shot.

PAT: He was.

MEG: Ah, the poor man.

PAT: Still, he was a great fighter and he fought well for the ould cause.

ROPEEN: They called him "The Laughing Boy."

PAT: They did.

RIO RITA: Give us your song, Pat. (*General agreement.*)

PAT: Give us a note, Kate.

PAT *sings the first verse and the others join in, naturally, as they feel moved, into the choruses and the following verses.*

'Twas on an August morning, all in the morning hours,
I went to take the warming air all in the month of flowers,
And there I saw a maiden and heard her mournful cry,
Oh, what will mend my broken heart, I've lost my Laughing Boy.

MEG: So strong, so wide, so brave he was, I'll mourn his loss too sore
When thinking that we'll hear the laugh or springing step no more.
ALL: Ah, curse the time, and sad the loss my heart to crucify,
That an Irish son, with a rebel gun, shot down my Laughing Boy.

Oh, had he died by Pearse's side, or in the G.P.O.,
Killed by an English bullet from the rifle of the foe,
Or forcibly fed while Ashe lay dead in the dungeons of Mountjoy,
I'd have cried with pride at the way he died, my own dear Laughing Boy.

RIO RITA: Now one voice.
MEG: My princely love, can ageless love do more than tell to you
Go raibh mile maith Agath, for all you tried to do,
For all you did and would have done, my enemies to destroy,
ALL: I'll praise your name and guard your fame, my own dear Laughing Boy.
PAT: It's a great story.
MEG: It's better than that show that used to be on the television below in Tom English's Eagle Bar, "This is your life."
PAT: It wasn't the end of the story. Some of us wouldn't accept the treaty. We went on fighting, but we were beat. Monsewer was loyal to the old cause and I was loyal to Monsewer. So when the fighting was done we came back together to this old house.
MEG: This dirty old hole.
PAT: A good hole it was for many a decent man on the run for twenty years after that.

MEG: Who the hell was still running twenty years after that?

PAT: All the Republicans who wouldn't accept the Treaty. We put Cosgrave's government in and he had the police hunting us.

RIO RITA: Then you put de Valera in, and he started hunting us, too.

PAT: I put de Valera in—what the hell are you talking about?

RIO RITA: I ought to know what I'm talking about—I was Michael Collins's runner in the old days.

PAT: He must have had a thousand bloody runners if you were another one.

RIO RITA: Are you calling me a liar?

PAT: Oh, get out.

RIO RITA: You know I was Michael Collins's runner.

MULLEADY: That was over thirty years ago—you weren't even born.

RIO RITA: I did my bit in O'Connell Street, with the rest of them.

ROPEEN: He did his bit up in O'Connell Street.

RIO RITA: You shut your bloody row—you want to take a bucket of water out with you when you go out the back, you do.

ROPEEN: Get out, will you. *(She chases him upstairs.)*

RIO RITA: There you are—look—she's picking on me again. I haven't said a word to her. I won't argue with her—I only upset myself if I argue with that one. I'll go and have a lie down. *(Exits.)*

MEG: Carry on with the coffin, the corpse'll walk.

PAT: Hiding hunted Republicans was all very well, but it didn't pay the rent, so in the end we had to take in all sorts of scruffy lumpers to make the place pay.

RIO RITA *(from the top of the stairs)*: You wouldn't say that to my face.

PAT: This noble old house, which housed so many heroes, was turned into a knocking shop. But I'd you to help me.

MEG: You had me to help you! The curse of God meet and melt you and your rotten lousy leg. You had me to help you, indeed! If I'm a whore itself, sure I'm a true patriot.

PAT: Course you are, course you are. Aren't we husband and wife—nearly?

MEG: Well, nearly.

PAT: Sure, I wasn't referring to you. I was talking about old Ropeen and that musician, and Colette, there's another one.

COLETTE: I don't have to stay here.

MEG: Don't you talk to me about that Colette, not after what she done to the poor old Civil Servant out of the Ministery of Pensions.

PAT: Never mind that now.

MEG: There was the poor old feller kneeling by the bedside saying his prayers. For Colette to go robbing him of all his money and him in the presence of Almighty God, so to speak.

The sound of hymn-singing comes from upstairs. Down the stairs RIO RITA *flies into the room, followed by the* NEGRO, *now in boxing kit with gloves on. The other people in the house flood into the room and listen to the din.*

What the hell's that? What's going on?

RIO RITA *silences the room and tells his story.*

RIO RITA: I've seen everything, dear. I've seen everything. I was upstairs doing a bit of shadow boxing with my friend.

MEG: Where the hell's that row coming from?

RIO RITA: It's that man in the third floor back. He has a strange woman in his room.

MEG: Old Mulleady?

RIO RITA: Three hours he's had her in there, and the noises, it's disgusting. It's all very well you laughing, but it doesn't say much for the rest of us girls in the house.

ROPEEN: No, it doesn't, does it?

MEG: Has he got that one-legged girl from Number 8 in there?

RIO RITA: No, she's not even out of the street, let alone the house. A complete stranger—I don't know the woman.

MEG: Well, what sort of woman is it?

RIO RITA: A female woman.

MEG: Well, the dirty low degenerate old maniac, what does he take this house for?

COLETTE: They're coming.

MR. MULLEADY and MISS GILCHRIST appear on the stairs kneeling and singing their prayers. Their shoes are beside them.

MULLEADY: Let us say a prayer, Miss Gilchrist, and we will be forgiven. (MR. MULLEADY's *hand strays and gooses* MISS GILCHRIST.)

MISS GILCHRIST: In nomine—please, Mr. Mulleady, let us not fall from grace again.

MULLEADY: I'm very sorry, Miss Gilchrist, let not the right hand know what the left hand is doing. Miss Gilchrist, can you—(*The hand strays again and strokes* MISS GIL-CHRIST's *tail.*)

MEG (*calling*): Mr. Mulleady.

MULLEADY:—feel our souls together?

MEG: Mr. Mulleady.

The praying and the stroking stop. MR. MULLEADY *puts on his shoes.* MISS GILCHRIST *smoothes her hair and dress. She looks very prim and proper.*

MULLEADY: Is that you, Mrs. M.?

MEG: Is it me? Who the hell do you think it is? Will you come down here and bring that shameless bitch down with you.

MULLEADY: What do you want? Did you call me, Mrs. M?

MEG: If Mulleady is your name, I called you, and I called that low whore you have up there with you. I didn't call her by her name, for I don't know what it is, if she's got one at all. Come down from there, you whore, whoever you are.

MEG shoos everyone out of the room and hides behind the door. MULLEADY *enters, sees no one and turns to go, only to find* MEG *blocking his path. She thrusts her bosom at him and drives him back on to one of the chairs.*

MULLEADY: Mrs. M., she might have heard you.

MEG: Who's she when she's at home, and what's she got that I haven't got, I should like to know.

MULLEADY: She is a lady.

MEG: The more shame to her, and don't you go calling me your dear Mrs. M. Nor your cheap Mrs. M. either. What do you mean by bringing whores into this house?

PAT: And it's full of them, coals to Newcastle.

COLETTE, ROPEEN, RIO RITA *and* MEG *crowd* MULLEADY *and sit on his knees, ruffle his hair and tickle him. The* NEGRO *shadow boxes, the* SAILOR *falls asleep with a bottle of vodka and* PAT *takes no part in this.*

MEG: Now, Mr. Mulleady, Mr. Mulleady, sir, don't you know you could have got anything like that, that you wanted, here?

RIO RITA: Yes, anything.

MEG: I'm surprised at you, so I am. God knows I've stuck by you. Even when that man there was wanting to cast you out into the streets for the low-down dirty old hypocrite that you are.

MULLEADY: Thank you, Mrs. M. Your blood's worth bottling.

MEG: Are you all right now?

MULLEADY: Oh yes, indeed, thank you.

MEG: Right then. Bring down that brasstitute.

MULLEADY: Oh, is there any need?

MEG: Fetch her down.

MULLEADY *(feebly)*: Miss Gilchrist.

MEG: Louder.

MULLEADY: Miss Gilchrist.

MISS GILCHRIST: Yes, Mr. Mulleady?

MULLEADY: Will you come down here a minute, please.

MISS GILCHRIST: I haven't finished the first novena, Mr. Mulleady.

MEG: I'll give her the first bloody novena!

MULLEADY: Mrs. M., please. I'll get her down.

MR. MULLEADY *climbs the stairs and helps* MISS GILCHRIST *to her feet. Together they prepare to meet their martyrdom and they march resolutely down the stairs singing (to a corrupt version of Handel's Largo).*

MISS GILCHRIST
MULLEADY

> We are soldiers of the Lord, Miss Gilchrist,
> Forward to battle, forward side by side.
> Degenerates and lay-abouts cannot daunt us.
> We are sterilized.

MISS GILCHRIST *takes a firm stand, whilst* MULLEADY *hands out religious tracts.*

MISS GILCHRIST: Save your souls, my brothers, my sisters, save your souls. One more sinner saved today. Jesus lives.

MULLEADY: This is Miss Gilchrist.

MEG: In the name of all that's holy, what kind of a name is Gilchrist?

MISS GILCHRIST: It is an old Irish name. In its original form "Giolla Christ," the servant or gilly of the Lord.

MEG: You're a quare-looking gilly of the lord, you whore.

MISS GILCHRIST: I take insults in the name of our blessed saviour.

MEG: You take anything you can get like a good many more round here. You've been three hours up in his room.

MULLEADY: A quarter of an hour, Mrs. M.

ALL: Three hours.

MISS GILCHRIST: We were speaking of our souls.

MISS GILCHRIST
MULLEADY } *(singing):* Our souls. Our souls. Our souls.

(This is slurred to sound—"Our souls. Are souls. Arseholes.")

MEG: You can leave his soul alone, whatever about your own. And take yourself out of here, before I'm dug out of you.

MISS GILCHRIST: I will give you my prayers.

MEG: You can stuff them up your cathedral.

MISS GILCHRIST: I forgive her. She is a poor sinful person.

MEG: And you're a half-time whore.

PAT: Compliments pass when the quality meet.

MISS GILCHRIST: Mr. Mulleady, come away. This is Sodom and Gomorrah.

MEG (*stops him*): Don't leave us, darlin'.

MULLEADY: I can't, Miss Gilchrist. I haven't paid my rent.

MISS GILCHRIST: I will pray for you, Eustace. My shoes, please.

MULLEADY (*fetching her shoes*): Will you come back, Miss Gilchrist?

MISS GILCHRIST: The Lord will give me the strength. God go with you.

THE RUSSIAN SAILOR *goes to grab her. She runs out.*

MULLEADY: Evangelina!

PAT: Ships that pass in the night.

MEG: Did you ever see anything like that in your life before? Now are you going to ask for an explanation, or am I?

PAT: Leave me out of it. You brought him here in the first place.

MEG: So I did, God help me. And you can take your face out of here, you simpering little get.

MULLEADY *starts to go.*

Not you, him.

RIO RITA: Me—well there's gratitude for you. Who told you about him in the first place? I always knew what he was, the dirty old eye-box.

MULLEADY: Informer! Butterfly! You painted May-pole!

RIO RITA: You filthy old get!

PAT: Hey, what about some rent.

The room clears as if by magic. Only RIO RITA *is trapped on the stairs.*

RIO RITA: I wish you wouldn't show me up when I bring a friend into the house.

PAT: Never mind all that. What about the rent? What's his name, anyway?

RIO RITA: Princess Grace.

PAT: I can't put down Princess Grace, can I?

RIO RITA: That's only his name in religion.

MEG: Don't be giving out that talk about religion.

PAT: Well, what's his real name?

RIO RITA: King Kong. *(Exit.)*

A row erupts in the kitchen between MULLEADY *and* RO-PEEN *and* MULLEADY *enters, holding his dirty shirt.*

MULLEADY: Mr. Pat, Mr. Pat, she has no right to be in there all morning washing her aspidistra. I only wanted to wash my shirt. *(He recovers his dignity.)* All this fuss about Miss Gilchrist. She merely came to talk religion to me.

MEG: That kind is the worst kind. You can take it from me.

PAT: From one who knows.

MULLEADY: You don't seem aware of my antecedents. My second cousin was a Kilkenny from Kilcock.

MEG: I'll cock you. Take this broom and sweep out your room, you scowling little bollix—take it before I ruin you completely.

She throws a broom at him and he disappears, flicking the old whore with the broom as he goes. Things quieten down and PAT *and* MEG *take a rest.*

PAT: If the performance is over I'd like a cigarette.

MEG: I sent the skivvy out for them half an hour ago. God knows where she's got to. Have a gollywog.

PAT: What in the hell's name is that?

MEG: It's a French cigarette. I got them off that young attaché case at the French Embassy—that one that thinks all Irishwomen are his mother.

PAT: I don't fancy those. I'll wait for me twenty Afton. Meanwhile I'll sing that famous old song, "The Hound That Caught the Pubic Hair."

MEG: You're always announcing these songs, but you never get round to singing them.

PAT: Well, there is a song I sing sometimes.

There's no place on earth like the world
Just between you and me.
There's no place on earth like the world,
Acushla, astore and Mother Machree.

TERESA, *the skivvy runs in. She is a strong hefty country girl of nineteen and a bit shy.*

TERESA: Your cigarettes, sir.

PAT: A hundred thousand welcomes. You look lovely. If I wasn't married I'd be exploring you.

TERESA: I'm very sorry I was so late, sir.

MEG: Were you lost in the place?

TERESA: I was, nearly. Shall I get on with the beds, Meg?

MEG: Yes, you might as well.

PAT: Don't be calling me sir, there's only one sir in this house and that's Monsewer. Just call me Pat.

TERESA: Pat, sir, there's a man outside.

MEG: Why doesn't he come in?

TERESA: Well, he's just looking around.

PAT: Is he a policeman?

TERESA: Oh no, sir, he look respectable.

PAT: Where is he now? (TERESA *goes to the window.*)

TERESA: He's over there, sir.

PAT: I can't see without me glasses. Is he wearing a trench coat and a beret.

TERESA: He is, sir. How did you know?

MEG: He's a fortune-teller.

TERESA: And he has a badge to say he only speaks Irish.

PAT: Begod, then him and me will have to use the deaf and dumb language, for the only bit of Irish I know would get us both prosecuted. That badge makes me think he's an officer.

TERESA: He has another to say he doesn't drink.

PAT: That means he's a higher officer.

MEG: Begod, don't be bringing him in here.

PAT: He'll come in, in his own good time. Now, Teresa girl, you haven't been here long but you're a good girl and you can keep your mouth shut.

TERESA: Oh yes, sir.

PAT: Well, someone's coming to stay here and you'll bring him his meals. Now, if you don't tell a living sinner about it, you can stay here for the rest of your life.

MEG: Well, till she's married anyway.

TERESA: Thank you, sir. Indeed, I'm very happy here.

PAT: You're welcome.

TERESA: And I hope you'll be satisfied with my work.

PAT: I'd be more satisfied if you were a bit more cheerful and not so serious all the time.

TERESA: I've always been a very serious girl.

Sings:

Open the door softly,
Shut it—keep out the draught,
For years and years, I've shed millions of tears,
And never but once have I laughed.

'Twas the time the holy picture fell,
And knocked me old Granny cold,
While she knitted and sang an old Irish song,
'Twas by traitors poor old Ulster was sold.

So open the window softly,
For Jaysus' sake, hang the latch,
Come in and lie down, and afterwards
You can ask me what's the catch.

Before these foreign-born bastards, dear,
See you don't let yourself down,
We'll be the Lion and Unicorn,
My Rose unto your Crown.

MEG: Hasn't she got a nice voice, Pat?
PAT: You make a pretty picture. Do you know what you look
like, Meg?
MEG: Yes, a whore with a heart of gold. At least, that's what
you'd say if you were drunk enough.

*Two men enter and begin examining the room, stamping on
the boards, testing the plaster and measuring the walls. The
first is a thin-faced fanatic in a trench coat and black beret.
He is a part-time* OFFICER *in the I.R.A. The second man is*
FEARGUS O'CONNOR, *a* VOLUNTEER. *He wears a rubber mackin-
tosh and a shiny black cap. The* OFFICER *is really a school-
master and the* VOLUNTEER *a railway ticket-collector. They
survey all exits and escape routes.*

RIO RITA: Is it the sanitary inspector, Pat?
OFFICER: Filthy—filthy. The whole place is filthy. (*He sees the*
RUSSIAN SAILOR *asleep.*) Get rid of that, will you?
PAT: Who does this belong to?
COLETTE: That's mine.
RIO RITA: Let me give you a hand with him.
COLETTE: Keep your begrudging hands off him.

COLETTE *exits with* SAILOR.

OFFICER: Who's in charge here?
PAT: I am.
OFFICER: Your cellar's full of rubbish.
PAT: Oh, there's no rubbish there. No, I'll tell you what there is
in there. There's the contents of an entire house which
nearly fell down a couple of weeks ago.
OFFICER: What are these people doing here?

PAT: Well, that's Meg and that's Teresa...

OFFICER: Get 'em out of here.

PAT: You'd better go—get out.

MEG: Come on, Teresa—if they want to play toy soldiers we'll leave them to it.

All leave except PAT, I.R.A. OFFICER *and* VOLUNTEER. *The* VOLUNTEER *makes lists.*

OFFICER: You'll have to get that cellar cleared; it's an escape route.

PAT: Yes, sir.

OFFICER: Here's a list of your instructions; it's in triplicate, one for you, one for me and one for H.Q. When you've read and digested them, append your signature and destroy your copy. Do you have the Gaelic?

PAT: No, I'm afraid I don't.

OFFICER: Then we'll have to speak in English. Have you food sufficient for three people for one day?

PAT: There's always plenty of scoff in this house.

OFFICER: May I see your toilet arrangements, please?

PAT: Oh yes, just through that door—no, not that one—there. There's plenty of paper, and mind your head as you go in. (*The* OFFICER *goes.*)

MONSEWER (*off*): I'm in here. (MONSEWER *comes out.*) No damned privacy in this house at all. Laddie from H.Q.?

PAT: Yes, sir.

MONSEWER: Damned ill-mannered. (*Exit. The* I.R.A. OFFICER *returns.*)

OFFICER: Who the hell was that?

PAT: My old mother.

OFFICER: Can we be serious, please?

PAT: Can I offer you any refreshment?

OFFICER: I neither eat nor drink when I'm on duty.

PAT: A bottle of stout?

OFFICER: Teetotal. I might take a bottle of orange and me after dancing the high caul cap in a Gaelic measurement at an Irish ceilidhe, but not at any other time.

PAT: Well, no one would blame you for that.

OFFICER: Rent book, please.

PAT: Are you thinking of moving in?

OFFICER: I wish to see a list of tenants.

> PAT *takes take out a very old dilapidated rent book.*

PAT: Well, there's Bobo, The Mouse, is Ropeen still here?—Mulleady. *(The people of the house look round the doors and whisper at* PAT.*)* Get out, will you? *(Goes back to book.)* Colette—ey, this one's been dead for weeks, I hope he's not still there. Rio Rita, Kate, Meg . . . Well, that's all I know about—there might be some more about somewhere.

OFFICER: If it was my doings, there'd be no such thing as us coming here at all. And the filthy reputation this house has throughout the city.

PAT: Can't think how you came to hear about it at all, a clean-living man like yourself.

OFFICER: I do charitable work round here for the St. Vincent de Paul Society. Padraig Pearse said, "To serve a cause that is splendid and holy, the man himself must be splendid and holy."

PAT: Are you splendid, or just holy? Rent in advance, four pounds.

OFFICER: Is it money you're looking for?

PAT: We're not all working for St. Vincent de Paul.

OFFICER: Will you leave St. Vincent out of it, please.

PAT: Begod, and I will. *(To the audience.)* St. Vincent de Paul Society! They're all ex-policemen. In the old days we wouldn't go anywhere near them.

OFFICER: In the old days there were nothing but Communists in the I.R.A.

PAT: There were some. What of that?

OFFICER: Today the movement is purged of the old dross. It has found its spiritual strength.

PAT: Where did it find that?

OFFICER: "The man who is most loyal to the faith is the one who is most loyal to the cause."

PAT: Haven't you got your initials mixed up? Are you in the I.R.A. or the F.B.I.?

OFFICER: You're an old man, don't take advantage of it.

PAT: I was out in 1916.

OFFICER: And lost your leg, they tell me.

PAT: More than that. You wouldn't recall, I suppose, the time in County Kerry when the agricultural labourers took over five thousand acres of land from Lord Tralee?

OFFICER: No, I would not.

PAT: 1925 it was. They had it all divided fair and square and were ploughing and planting in great style. I.R.A. H.Q. sent down orders that they were to get off the land. That social question would be settled when we'd won the thirty-two-county republic.

OFFICER: Quite right, too.

PAT: The Kerry men said they weren't greedy, they didn't want the whole thirty-two counties, their own five thousand acres would do 'em for a start.

OFFICER: Those men were wrong on the social question.

PAT: It wasn't the question they were interested in, but the answers. Anyway, I agreed with them. I stayed there and trained a unit. By the time I'd finished we could take on the I.R.A., the Free State Army, or the British bloody Navy, if it came to it.

OFFICER: That was mutiny. You should have been court-martialled.

PAT: I was. Court-martialled in my absence, sentenced to death in my absence. So I said, right, you can shoot me—in my absence.

OFFICER: I was told to come here. They must have known what I was coming to. You can understand their reasons for choosing it, the police would never believe we'd use this place. At least you can't be an informer.

PAT: You're a shocking decent person. Could you give me a testimonial in case I wanted to get a job on the Corporation?

OFFICER: I was sent here to arrange certain business. I intend to conclude that business.

PAT: Very well, let us proceed, shall we? When may we expect the prisoner?

OFFICER: Tonight.

PAT: What time?

OFFICER: Between nine and twelve.

PAT: Where is he now?

OFFICER: We haven't got him yet.

PAT: Are you going to Woolworth's to buy one?

OFFICER: I have no business telling you more than has already been communicated to you. The arrangements are made for his reception.

PAT: All except the five pounds for the rent.

OFFICER: I told you I haven't got it.

PAT: Then you'd better get it before your man arrives, or I'll throw the lot of you, prisoner and escort, out—*shun!*

OFFICER: I wouldn't be too sure about that if I were you.

MEG *and* TERESA *come in.*

MEG: Can we come in now, Pat?

PAT: What do you want?

MEG: We want to put the sheets on the bed.

There is a blurt of mechanical sound and a commotion upstairs. Everyone in the house rushes in to listen to a portable radio that COLETTE *is carrying.*

RIO RITA: Mr. Pat, Mr. Pat!

PAT: What is it?

RIO RITA: It's about the boy in the Belfast Jail. They've refused a reprieve.

MULLEADY: The Lord Lieutenant said tomorrow morning, eight o'clock. No reprieve final.

ROPEEN: The boy—the boy in the Belfast Jail?

MULLEADY: Yes—made on behalf of the Government of Northern Ireland.

COLETTE: I've lost it now.

The radio blurts out music.

PAT: Turn the bloody thing off.

Silence.

MEG: God help us all.

TERESA: The poor boy.

ROPEEN: Eight o'clock in the morning, think of it.

MEG: Ah sure, they might have mercy on him yet. Eighteen years of age—

OFFICER: Irishmen have been hanged by Englishmen at eighteen years of age before now.

PAT: Yes, and Cypriots, Jews and Africans.

MEG: Did you read about them black fellers? Perhaps Mr. de Valera could do something about it.

PAT ⎱ *(together for once, and with great contempt)*:
OFFICER ⎰ Mr. de Valera!

MEG: I'm sure he could stop it if he wanted to. They say he's a very clever man. They say he can speak seven languages.

PAT: It's a terrible pity that English or Irish are not among them, so we'd know what he was saying at odd times.

RIO RITA: Quiet everybody, something's coming through.

COLETTE *repeats the news item from the radio and is echoed by* MULLEADY, ROPEEN, RIO RITA, *and* TERESA:

"Early today a young British soldier was captured as he was coming out of a dance hall in Armagh by the I.R.A. He was put into the back of a car and when last seen was speeding towards the border. All troops have been alerted..."

OFFICER: Turn it off. Patrick, get these people out of here.

PAT: I can't do that without making a show of ourselves.

OFFICER: Then come outside with me.

PAT, I.R.A. OFFICER *and* VOLUNTEER *go out.*

RIO RITA: Who is that man, anyway?

MEG: He's just come about the rent. He's an I.R.A. officer.

MULLEADY: That poor boy waiting all night for the screws coming for him in the morning.

MEG: Shut up, will you?

MULLEADY: I know just how he feels.

MEG: How do you know?

MULLEADY: Well, I was in prison myself once.

MEG: Oh, yes, he was. I forgot.

RIO RITA: Mountjoy?

MULLEADY: As a matter of fact, it was.

RIO RITA: So was I—I'll get you a drink.

They all sit at MULLEADY'S *feet.*

MULLEADY: I was in a cell next to a condemned man.

RIO RITA: What were you in for?

MULLEADY: It was the *Pall Mall Gazette* in 1919.

COLETTE: The what?

MULLEADY: The *Pall Mall Gazette.*

COLETTE: What's that?

MULLEADY: A magazine. There was an advertisement in it for an insurance company and I put all my savings into it. And in return I was to receive an annuity of twenty pounds a year.

MEG: Well, that's not such a vast sum.

ROPEEN: It was in those days.

MULLEADY: Yes, that's the point. When the annuity was due the value of money had declined, so I ran off with the church funds.

MEG: That was a filthy thing to do.

MULLEADY: They put me into prison for that.

RIO RITA: What about the boy in the condemned cell? What had he done?

MULLEADY: Yes, now this is interesting. Flynn, I think his name was. He disposed of his wife and a chicken down a well. Said it was an accident. Said his wife fell down the well trying to retrieve the chicken, but, unfortunately, the police found the wife under the chicken.

COLETTE: How long were you in for?

MULLEADY: Three years.

RIO RITA: You don't look it, dear.

MULLEADY: All this time my younger brother was travelling all over the world.

RIO RITA: They do—don't they?

MULLEADY: Visited every capital in Europe, saw Cardiff, Liverpool, Middlesbrough, went to London—saw Marie Lloyd every night, at the Tivoli.

ROPEEN: Marie Lloyd! She was lovely.

MULLEADY: She may have been, but all that time I was in prison. It broke my poor mother's heart.

MEG: Well, I never caused my poor mother any sorrow, for I never knew her.

MULLEADY: You never had a mother. How very sad.

MEG: I never heard of any living person that didn't have a mother, though I know plenty that don't have fathers. I had one, but I never saw her.

ALL: How sad—I never knew my mother—never to know your mother.

MEG: Are you lot going to sit there all night moaning about your mothers? Did you sweep out your room?

MULLEADY: Well, no.

MEG: Well, go out and get us twelve stout.

MULLEADY *goes and talks with* KATE, *the pianist.*

We've run dry by the look of it. And if you're going to sit there you can give us a hand with the beds.

COLETTE: Do you mind—I've been flat on my back all day.

MULLEADY: Kate says the credit has run out.

MEG: Oh, Kate, I've got a terrible drought on me.

RIO RITA: I'll tell you what I'll do—I'll run down to the docks and see if I can pick up a sailor—and I'll bring back a crate of Guinness. (*Exit.*)

MEG: Bring the beer back here.

ROPEEN: And the sailor.

> ROPEEN, MULLEADY *and* COLETTE *go.* TERESA *and* MEG *start to make the bed.*

TERESA: There's some very strange people in this house.

MEG: There's some very strange people in the world.

TERESA: I like that big feller. There was no one like him in the convent.

MEG: Do you mean Rio Rita?

TERESA: Yes, it's a gas name, isn't it?

MEG: How long have you been out of the convent?

TERESA: I've just had the one job with the family in Drumcondra.

MEG: Why did you leave there? Did you half-inch something?

TERESA: What did you say?

MEG: Did you half-inch something?

TERESA: I never stole anything in my whole life.

MEG: There's no need to get so upset about it. I never stole anything either. The grand chances I had, too! God doesn't give us these chances twice in a lifetime.

TERESA: It wasn't that; you see, there was a clerical student in the house.

MEG: Well, as far as that's concerned, you'll be a lot safer here. Do the nuns know you left that job in Drumcondra?

TERESA: Oh, no, and they wouldn't be a bit pleased.

MEG: Well, don't say anything to Pat about it. It doesn't do to tell men everything. Here he comes now—don't forget.

> PAT *and* MONSEWER *enter from opposite sides along the passage-way.*

Oh, isn't it terrible, Pat? About that poor young man. There's to be no reprieve. Wouldn't it break your heart to be thinking about it?

MONSEWER: It doesn't break my heart.

PAT (*softly*): It's not your neck they're breaking either.

MONSEWER: It doesn't make me unhappy. It makes me proud; proud to know that the old cause is not dead yet, and that there are still young men willing and ready to go out and die for Ireland.

PAT: I'd say that young man will be in the presence of the Irish martyrs of eight hundred years ago just after eight o'clock tomorrow morning.

MONSEWER: He will. He will. With God's help, he'll be in the company of the heroes.

PAT: My life on yer!

MONSEWER: I would give anything to stand in that young man's place tomorrow morning. For Ireland's sake I would hang crucified in the town square.

PAT: Let's hope it would be a fine day for you.

MONSEWER: I think he's very lucky.

PAT: Very lucky—its a great pity he didn't buy a sweepstake ticket. (*Coming to* MONSEWER.) You were always a straight man, General, if I may call you by your Christian name. Well, everything is ready for the guest.

MONSEWER: Good. (*Exit.*)

Exit PAT slowly, singing to himself the third verse of "The Laughing Boy"—"Oh, had he died by Pearse's side, or in the G.P.O."

TERESA: Wasn't that ridiculous talk that old one had out of him?

MEG: Well, Monsewer doesn't look at it like an ordinary person. Monsewer is very given to Ireland and to things of that sort.

TERESA: I think he's an old idiot.

MEG: Monsewer an old idiot? I'll have you know he went to all the biggest colleges in England.

TERESA: It's all the same where he went. He is mad to say that the death of a young man will make him happy.

MEG: Well, the boy himself said when they sentenced him to death that he was proud and happy to die for Ireland.

TERESA: Ah, but sure, Meg, he hasn't lived yet.

MEG: Have you?

TERESA: A girl of eighteen knows more than a boy of eighteen.

MEG: You could easy do that. That poor young man, he gave no love to any, except to Ireland, and instead of breaking his heart for a girl, it was about the Cause he was breaking it.

TERESA: Well, his white young neck will be broken tomorrow morning anyway.

MEG: Well it's no use mourning him before his time. Come on, Kate, give us a bit of music; let's cheer ourselves up.

The pianist plays a reel and MEG *and* TERESA *dance. Gradually everyone else in the house hears the music and comes to join in, until everyone is caught up in a swirling interweaving dance. Through this dance the* SOLDIER *is pushed by the two* I.R.A. *men. He is blindfolded. The dancing falters and the music peters out as the blindfold is whipped from his eyes.*

SOLDIER: Don't stop. I like dancing.

OFFICER: Keep your mouth shut, and get up there.

The SOLDIER *walks slowly up into the room, then turns and sings.*

SOLDIER: There's no place on earth like the world,
                 There's no place wherever you be.

ALL: There's no place on earth like the world,
                 That's straight up and take it from me.

WOMEN: Never throw stones at your mother,
                 You'll be sorry for it when she's dead.

MEN: Never throw stones at your mother,
                 Throw bricks at your father instead.

MONSEWER: The south and the north poles are parted,

MEG: Perhaps it is all for the best.

PAT: Till the H-bomb will bring them together,

ALL: And there we will let matters rest.

Curtain.

ACT TWO

Later in the same day. The SOLDIER *is confined in the room. The passage is dark and the lights in the rest of the house are low. The* I.R.A. OFFICER *and the* VOLUNTEER *march along the passage on alternating beats, peering out into the darkness and waiting for a surprise attack that they fear may come. The* VOLUNTEER *carries an old rifle.*

The house appears to be still, but in the dark corners and doorways, behind the piano and under the stairs, people are hiding, waiting for an opportunity to contact the prisoner, to see what he looks like and to take him comforts like cups of tea, bible tracts, cigarettes and stout. As soon as the OFFICER *and the* VOLUNTEER *turn their backs, a scurry of movement is seen and hisses and low whistles are heard. When the* I.R.A. *men turn to look there is silence and stillness. The* I.R.A. *men are growing more and more nervous.*

SOLDIER (*as the* VOLUNTEER *passes him on his sentry beat*): Psst!

The VOLUNTEER *ignores him, marks time and marches off fast. He re-enters cautiously and marches along his beat.*

Pssst!

The VOLUNTEER *peers into the darkness and turns to go.*

Halt!

The VOLUNTEER *drops his rifle in fright, recovers it and threatens the* SOLDIER *as the* OFFICER *comes dashing in. In the corners there is a faint scuttling as people hide away.*

OFFICER: What's going on here?

SOLDIER: Any chance of a cigarette?

OFFICER: I don't smoke.

SOLDIER: How about you?

VOLUNTEER: I don't indulge meself. *(He waits until the* OFFICER *has left.)* Ey, you'll get a cup of tea in a minute. *(He marches off.)*

SOLDIER: Smashing. "I'll get a nice cuppa tea in the morning. A nice cuppa tea ... "

OFFICER *(rushing back)*: What's the matter now?

SOLDIER: Nothing. *(The* VOLUNTEER *reappears.)*

OFFICER: What's all the noise about?

SOLDIER: I just wondered if she might be bringing my tea.

OFFICER: Who's she?

SOLDIER: You know, the red-headed one—the one we saw first. Bit of all right.

OFFICER: Guard, keep him covered. I'll go and see about his tea.

The OFFICER *goes to see about the prisoner's tea. The* VOLUNTEER *resumes his beat. As he turns to go, all hell breaks loose and everyone tries to get to the* SOLDIER *at once. People hare through the room at breakneck speed, leaving the* SOLDIER *with stout, hymn sheets, aspidistras, and words of comfort.*

COLETTE: Five minutes—upstairs—I won't charge you.

The VOLUNTEER *attempts to stop them all at once and only gets more and more confused until* PAT *enters and drives everyone offstage. The lines of this scene are largely improvised to suit the situation.*

PAT: Come on, out of here, you lot. Get out, will you!

ROPEEN. I'm only going to the piano.

They all go and PAT *calls* TERESA. PAT *and the* VOLUNTEER *leave as* TERESA *comes downstairs with the* SOLDIER's *tea on a tray. She goes to leave straight away, but he stops her.*

SOLDIER: Ey! I liked your dancing . . . you know, the old-knees-up . . . Is that mine?

TERESA: Yes, it's your tea—sure you must be starving. Your belly must be stuck to your back with hunger.

SOLDIER: A bit of all right, isn't it?

TERESA: You're lucky. Meg gave you two rashers.

SOLDIER: Did she now?

TERESA: She said you must have double the meal of a grown person.

SOLDIER: Why's that?

TERESA: Because you have two jobs to do.

SOLDIER: What are they?

TERESA: To grow up big and strong like all lads.

SOLDIER: Here, I'm older than you, I bet.

TERESA: I think you look like a young lad.

SOLDIER: You look like a kid yourself. How old are you?

TERESA: I'm nineteen.

SOLDIER: Are you? I'm nineteen, too. When's your date of birth?

TERESA: January. Twenty-fifth of January. When were you born?

SOLDIER: August. *(He is shamed.)*

TERESA: So you see, I'm older than you.

SOLDIER: Only a few weeks.

TERESA: What name do we call you?

SOLDIER: Leslie. What's yours?

TERESA: Teresa.

SOLDIER: Teresa. That's proper Irish, ain't it?

TERESA: Well, it is Irish.

SOLDIER: Yeah, that's what I said. Teresa, you haven't got a fag have you?

TERESA: A what?

SOLDIER: A fag. *(He makes a gesture with his fingers for a fag which* TERESA *thinks is an invitation to bed.)* Smoke—cigarette.

TERESA: No, thank you. I don't smoke.

SOLDIER: No, not for you—for me.

TERESA: Oh, for you. Wait a minute. Look, it's only a bit crushed. Pat gave it to me. *(She gives him a crumpled cigarette.)*

SOLDIER: Have you got a match—they took mine.

TERESA *gives him matches.*

Hey, don't go. I suppose you couldn't get me a packet?
SOLDIER: I'll get you twenty Afton.
SOLDIER: Oh no. I mean—thanks, anyway. Ten'll do.
TERESA: You don't fancy the Irish cigarettes?
SOLDIER: What? The old Aftons? I love 'em. Smoke 'em by the barrer-load.
TERESA: I'll get you twenty. You've a long night ahead of you.

> TERESA *gets money from* KATE, *the pianist, who is standing offstage. The* SOLDIER, *left completely alone for the first time, has a quick run round the room, looking through doors and windows. He lifts the clothes and looks under the bed.* TERESA *returns.*

TERESA: Are you looking for something?
SOLDIER: No. Yes, an ashtray.
TERESA: Under the bed?
SOLDIER: Well, I might have been looking for the in and the out, mightn't I?
TERESA: What?
SOLDIER: The way out. I'm a prisoner, ain't I?
TERESA: I'd better go.
SOLDIER: You'll be back with the fags?
TERESA: I might. I only work here, you know.

> TERESA *goes and the* SOLDIER *moves to all the doors in turn and calls out:*

SOLDIER: Hey! Charlie! Buffalo Bill!

> *The* VOLUNTEER *rushes on, thinking an attack has started, does not see the* SOLDIER *in the corner of the room and prepares to defend the front. The* SOLDIER *calls him back and whispers to him.* PAT *comes downstairs.*

PAT: What's he saying?

VOLUNTEER: He wants to go round the back, sir.

PAT: Well, he can, can't he?

VOLUNTEER: No, sir. I'm in the same plight myself, but I can't leave me post for two hours yet.

PAT: Why don't you both go?

VOLUNTEER: We'll have to ask the officer.

PAT: Well, I'll call him. Sir, St. Patrick. Sir.

The OFFICER *enters in a panic.*

OFFICER: What the hell's going on here?

PAT: It's your man here . . .

The OFFICER *silences him and leads him out into the passage.* PAT *whispers in his ear. The* OFFICER *comes to attention.*

(To the audience.) A man wants to go round the back and it's a military secret.

OFFICER: Right. Prisoner and escort, fall in. (PAT *and the* VOLUNTEER *fall in on either side of the* SOLDIER.) Prisoner and escort, right turn. By the front, quick march . . . left . . . right. *(They march right round the room to the lavatory door.)* HALT! Prisoner, fall out. You two guard the door. (TERESA *rushes into the room with the twenty Afton, sees the* OFFICER *and starts to rush out again, but he spots her.)* You girl, come back here. What are you doing here?

TERESA: I was just going to give him his cigarettes, sir.

OFFICER: What is this man to you?

TERESA: Nothing, sir.

OFFICER: Give them to me.

TERESA: But they're his.

OFFICER: Give them to me.

She gives him the cigarettes. The parade returns.

PAT: Fall in. Quick march—left right, etc. Halt. One man relieved, sir.

VOLUNTEER: What about me?

OFFICER: Silence.

TERESA: Where has he been?

PAT: Doing a job that no one else could do for him.

TERESA: Leslie, I got you . . .

OFFICER: That's enough. Get along with you, girl. About your business.

Exit TERESA. *The* I.R.A. OFFICER *watches her go.*

Patrick, is that girl all right?

PAT: Oh, come on, sir. You don't want to be thinking about that, and you on duty, too.

OFFICER: I mean will she keep her mouth shut?

PAT: Sure now, you know what women are like. They're always talking about these things—did you have a bit last night? But I don't think she'd fancy you somehow.

OFFICER: I'm asking you if she's to be trusted.

PAT: You mean would she help your man to escape?

OFFICER: Now you have it.

PAT: She'd do nothing to bring the police here. And as for helping him get away, she's all for keeping him here. They're getting along very well, those two.

OFFICER: Yes, a bit too well for my liking.

PAT: Well, she's passing the time for him. Better than having him fighting and all. Sure, they're getting along like a couple of budgeriguards.

OFFICER: This no laughing matter, you idiot.

PAT: You know, there are two kinds of gunmen. The earnest, religious-minded ones like you, and the laughing boys.

OFFICER: Like you.

PAT: Well, you know, in the time of the troubles it was always the laughing boys who were most handy with the skit.

OFFICER: Why?

PAT: Because it's not a natural thing for a man with a sense of humour to be tricking with firearms and fighting. There must be something wrong with him.

OFFICER: There must be something the matter with you, then.

PAT: Of course there is. Ey, what about the money for the rent?

OFFICER: At this moment the hearts of all true Irishmen are beating for us, fighting as we are to save the Belfast martyr, and all you can think about is money.

PAT: Well, you see, I'm not a hero. I'm what you might call an ex-hero. And if we get raided . . .

OFFICER: I refuse to envisage such a possibility.

PAT: All the same, if we are raided, you can say I only did it for the money.

OFFICER: We shall fight to the death.

PAT: You're all in the running for a hero's death.

OFFICER: I hope I would never betray my trust.

PAT: You've never been in prison for the cause.

OFFICER: No. I have not.

PAT: That's easily seen.

OFFICER: You have, of course.

PAT: Nine years, in all.

OFFICER: Nine years in English prisons?

PAT: Irish prisons part of the time.

OFFICER: The loss of liberty is a terrible thing.

PAT: That's not the worst thing, nor the redcaps, nor the screws. Do you know what the worst thing is?

OFFICER: No.

PAT: The other Irish patriots in along with you.

OFFICER: What did you say?

PAT: Your fellow patriots, in along with you. There'd be a split straight away.

OFFICER: If I didn't know you were out in 1916 . . .

Bagpipes have been playing in the distance and the sound comes steadily nearer. Everyone in the house crowds down into the passage area and stares out front as though they are looking through two windows, straining to get a sight of the procession in the street.

MEG: Teresa—Teresa—it's a band!

PAT: What's going on?

MEG: They're marching to the G.P.O. over the boy that's being hung in the Belfast Jail.

PAT: It's like Jim Larkin's funeral.

VOLUNTEER: Plenty of police about.

MONSEWER: By Jove, look at those banners. "Another victim for occupied Ireland."

MEG: "England, the hangman of thousands. In Ireland, in Kenya, in Cyprus."

MULLEADY: "Release the Belfast martyr!"

MEG: The world will see a day when England will be that low you won't be able to walk on her.

RIO RITA: "Eighteen years of age, in jail for Ireland."

ROPEEN
COLETTE } Ah, the poor boy.

MEG: Oh, the murdering bastards.

The SOLDIER *comes down to the front of the stage and tries to explain to the audience what is happening.*

SOLDIER: You know what they're on about, don't you? This bloke in the Belfast Jail who's going to be topped tomorrow morning. You read about it, didn't you? Papers were full of it over here—headliness that big. He's only eighteen, same age as us National Service blokes. Anyway, they got him, and tomorrow they're going to do him in—eight o'clock in the morning.

The pipes fade away and the groups break up.

MEG: That's the end of it.

PAT: Thanks be to God we don't all go that away.

MONSEWER: It was a good turn-out, Patrick. (*He leaves.*)

PAT: It was, sir.

MISS GILCHRIST: I shan't sleep a wink all night.

RIO RITA: Ah, you murdering bastard. Why don't you go back home to your own country?

SOLDIER: You can take me out of it as soon as you like. I never bloody-well asked to be brought here.

The first person to take advantage of the I.R.A. OFFICER's *absence and the* VOLUNTEER's *confusion is* MISS GILCHRIST. *While the* VOLUNTEER *is striving to keep* MULLEADY *and* COLETTE *out of the room,* MISS GILCHRIST *slips behind his back, the* VOLUNTEER *turns, and soon* MULLEADY, COLETTE *and* ROPEEN *are inside the room with* MISS GILCHRIST. *They crowd round the* SOLDIER *and paw and stroke him.*

MISS GILCHRIST: Is this the English boy? May I give him a little gift?

PAT: What is it?

MISS GILCHRIST: It's an article from a newspaper and as it's about his own dear Queen, I thought it might comfort him.

PAT: Come here.

MISS GILCHRIST: No, Mr. Pat, I insist. (*She reads from a paper.*)[1] It's from the *Daily Express* and it's called "Within the Palace Walls." "Within the Palace Walls. So much is known of the Queen's life on the surface, so little about how her life is really run. But now this article has been written with the active help of the Queen's closest advisers."

SOLDIER: No, thank you, ma'am, I don't go in for that sort of mullarkey. Haven't you got something else?

MULLEADY: Evangelina!

MISS GILCHRIST: Who calls?

MULLEADY: Me! Me! Me! Me! Bookie, please! Please!

MISS GILCHRIST: Well, if the boy doesn't want it . . .

SOLDIER: Quite sure, thank you, ma'am.

MULLEADY: May I read on, please?

MISS GILCHRIST: Go on, Eustace.

MULLEADY (*savouring and drooling over each phrase*): "Because it is completely fresh, probing hitherto unreported aspects of her problems, this intriguing new serial lays before you

---

[1] This extract was varied to keep it as topical as possible within the context of the scene.

the true pattern of the Queen's life with understanding, intimacy and detail." Oh may I keep it, Miss Gilchrist?

PAT: Give it here. *(He snatches the paper from MULLEADY.)* We don't go in for that sort of nonsense. *(He looks at the article).* Would you believe it. It's by an Irishman. Dermot Morah!

RIO RITA: I don't believe it.

MEG: Never! And she calls herself an Irishwoman, the silly bitch.

The Irish patriots leave the stage. Those remaining in the room are pro-English, sentimental, or both. MISS GILCHRIST *comes down to address the audience.*[2]

MISS GILCHRIST: I have nothing against the Royal Family, I think they're all lovely, especially that Sister Rowe and Uffa Fox. I get all the Sunday papers to follow them up. One paper contradicts another, but you put two and two together—and you might almost be in the yacht there with them. And there's that Mrs. Dale, she's a desperate nice woman. I always send her a bunch of flowers on her birthday. They even have an Irishman in it, a Mr. O'Malley. He keeps a hotel, like you, Mr. Pat. *(PAT has gone long ago.)*

MULLEADY *(picking up the paper from where PAT threw it)*: I'll get this paper every day. It will be my Bible.

SOLDIER: Well, personally mate, I'd sooner have the Bible. I read it once on jankers.

MISS GILCHRIST: Is this true?

SOLDIER: It's blue, ma'am.

MISS GILCHRIST *(enraptured)*: My favourite colour.

SOLDIER: You'd like it then, ma'am. All you've got to do is sort out the blue bits from the dreary bits and you're laughing.

MISS GILCHRIST: May we sing to you?

SOLDIER: If you like?

---

[2] Uffa Fox and Sister Rowe were two examples of people whose names were so closely linked with royalty that the distinctions became blurred. Other names used were Armstrong-Jones before his marriage, several Maharajahs and Billy Wallace.

MISS GILCHRIST *and* MULLEADY *assemble themselves on either side of the table and pose.* ROPEEN *places an aspidistra in the centre of the table. They sing to the tune of "Danny Boy".*

MISS GILCHRIST:
You read the Bible, in its golden pages,
You read those words and talking much of love.
You read the works of Plato and the sages,
They tell of hope, and joy, and peace and love.
MULLEADY:
But I'm afraid it's all a lot of nonsense,
About as true as leprechaun or elf.
BOTH:
You realize, when you want somebody,
That there is no one, no one, loves you like yourself.
MULLEADY:
I did my best to be a decent person,
I drove a tram for Murphy in 'thirteen.
I failed to pass my medical for the Army,
But loyally tried to serve my King and Queen.
Through all the troubled times I was no traitor,
Even when the British smashed poor mother's Delft.
And when they left, I became a loyal Free-Stater.
But, I know there is no one, no one loves you like yourself.
MULLEADY WITH MISS GILCHRIST *(crooning in harmony)*:
I really think us lower-middle classes,
Get thrown around just like snuff at a wake.
Employers take us for a set of asses,
The rough, they sneer at all attempts we make
To have nice manners and to speak correctly,
And in the end we're flung upon the shelf.
We have no unions, cost of living bonus,
BOTH:
It's plain to see that no one, no one loves you like yourself.

PAT *catches them singing and drives everyone off the stage except the* SOLDIER.

PAT: Come on, get out, will you? *(To the* SOLDIER.*)* Never mind
    that old idiot, if you want to go round the back again, just
    give me a shout.
SOLDIER: What if you're asleep?
PAT: I haven't slept a wink since 8th May 1921.
SOLDIER: Did you have an accident?
PAT: I had three. I was bashed, booted and bayoneted in Ar-
    bourhill Barracks.
SOLDIER: Redcaps. Bastards, aren't they?
PAT: They are, each and every one.

> PAT *goes off.*

TERESA *(entering)*: Leslie, Leslie, hey, Leslie.
SOLDIER: Hello, Ginger—come into me castle.
TERESA: Did you get your cigarettes?
SOLDIER: No.
TERESA: Did the officer not give them to you?
SOLDIER: No.

> TERESA *swears in Irish.*

'Ere, 'ere, 'ere, you mustn't swear. Anyway, you should never
    trust officers.
TERESA: Well, I got you a few anyway.

> *There is a mournful blast off from* MONSEWER'S *pipes.*

SOLDIER: What's that?
TERESA: It's Monsewer practising his pipes.
SOLDIER: He's what?
TERESA: He's practising his pipes. He's going to play a lament.
SOLDIER: A lament?
TERESA: For the boy in Belfast Jail.
SOLDIER: You mean a dirge. He's going to need a lot of practice.
TERESA: Don't make a jeer about it. *(The bagpipes stop.)*
SOLDIER: I'm not jeering. I feel sorry for the poor bloke, but
    that noise won't help him, will it?

TERESA: Well, he's one of your noble lot, anyway.

SOLDIER: What do you mean, he's one of our noble lot?

TERESA: Monsewer is—he went to college with your king.

SOLDIER: We ain't got one.

TERESA: Maybe he's dead now, but you had one one time, didn't you?

SOLDIER: We got a duke now. He plays tiddlywinks.

TERESA: Anyway, he left your lot and came over here and fought for Ireland.

SOLDIER: Why, was somebody doing something to Ireland?

TERESA: Wasn't England, for hundreds of years?

SOLDIER: That was donkey's years ago. Everybody was doing something to someone in those days.

TERESA: And what about today? What about the boy in Belfast Jail? Do you know that in the six counties the police walk the beats in tanks and armoured cars.

SOLDIER: If he was an Englishman they'd hang him just the same.

TERESA: It's because of the English being in Ireland that he fought.

SOLDIER: And what about the Irish in London? Thousands of them. Nobody's doing anything to them. We just let them drink their way through it. That's London for you. That's where we should be, down the 'dilly on a Saturday night.

TERESA: You're as bad as the Dublin people here.

SOLDIER: You're one of them, aren't you?

TERESA: I'm no Dubliner.

SOLDIER: What are you—a country yokel?

TERESA: I was reared in the convent at Ballymahon.

SOLDIER: I was reared down the Old Kent Road.

TERESA: Is that where your father and mother live?

SOLDIER: I ain't got none.

TERESA: You're not an orphan, are you?

SOLDIER: Yes, I'm one of the little orphans of the storm.

TERESA: You're a terrible chancer.

SOLDIER: Well, actually, my old lady ran off with a Pole, not that you'd blame her if you knew my old man.

The bagpipes are heard again, louder and nearer.

TERESA: He's coming in.

> MONSEWER *and* PAT *enter from opposite sides of the stage and slow march towards each other.*

SOLDIER: Cor, look at that, skirt and all.

> MONSEWER *stops to adjust the pipes and continues.*

You know the only good thing about them pipes? They don't smell.

> PAT *and* MONSEWER *meet and halt. The bagpipes fade with a sad belch.*

MONSEWER: Not so good, eh, Patrick?
PAT: No, sir.
MONSEWER: Never mind, we'll get there.
PAT: Yes, sir.
MONSEWER (*gives* PAT *the pipes*): Weekly troop inspection, Patrick.
PATRICK: Oh, yes, sir. (*Shouts.*) Come on, fall in. Come on, all you Gaels and Republicans on the run, get fell in.

> *Everyone in the house, except* MEG *and the* I.R.A. OFFICER, *rushes on and lines up.*

SOLDIER: Me an' all?
PAT: Yes, get on the end. Right dress. (*The "troops" stamp their feet and someone shouts "Ole."*) Attention. All present and correct, sir.
MONSEWER: Fine body of men. (*He walks down the line, inspecting. To* PRINCESS GRACE.) Colonials, eh? (*To* RIO RITA.) Keep the powder dry, laddie.
RIO RITA: I'll try, sir.
MONSEWER (*to* COLETTE): You're doing a great job, my dear.
COLETTE: Thank you, sir.
MONSEWER (*to the* VOLUNTEER): Name?

VOLUNTEER: O'Connor, sir.

MONSEWER: Station?

VOLUNTEER: Irish State Railways, Central Station, No. 3 platform.

MONSEWER *(to the* SOLDIER*)*: Name?

SOLDIER: Williams, sir, Leslie A.

MONSEWER: Station?

SOLDIER: Armagh, sir.

MONSEWER: Like it?

SOLDIER: No, sir, it's a dump, sir. *(To* PAT:*)* It is, you know, mate, shocking. Everything closes down at ten. You can't get a drink on a Sunday.

The parade dissolves into a shambles.

PAT: Can't get a drink?

SOLDIER: No.

MONSEWER: Patrick, is this the English laddie?

PAT: Yes, sir.

MONSEWER: Good God! We've made a bloomer. Dismiss the troops.

PAT: Troops, dismiss. Come on, there's been a mistake. Get off.

They go, except TERESA.

SOLDIER: *(to* PAT*)*: She don't have to go, does she?

PAT: No, she's all right.

MONSEWER: What's that girl doing, fraternizing?

PAT: Not at the moment, sir. She's just remaking the bed.

MONSEWER: I'm going to question the prisoner, Patrick.

PAT: Yes, sir.

MONSEWER: Strictly according to the rules laid down by the Geneva Convention.

PAT: Oh yes, sir.

MONSEWER *(to the* SOLDIER*)*: Name?

SOLDIER: Williams, sir. Leslie A.

MONSEWER: Rank?

SOLDIER: Private.

MONSEWER: Number?

SOLDIER: 23774486.

MONSEWER: That's the lot, carry on.

SOLDIER: Can I ask you a question, guv?

MONSEWER: Can he, Patrick?

PAT: Permission to ask question, sir. One step forward, march.

SOLDIER: What are those pipes actually for?

MONSEWER: Those pipes, my boy, are the instrument of the ancient Irish race.

SOLDIER: Permission to ask another question, sir.

PAT: One step forward, march.

SOLDIER: What actually is a race, guv?

MONSEWER: A race occurs when a lot of people live in one place for a long period of time.

SOLDIER: I reckon our old sergeant-major must be a race; he's been stuck in that same depot for about forty years.

MONSEWER (*in Irish*): Focail, Focaileile uait.

SOLDIER: Smashing-looking old geezer, ain't he? Just like our old Colonel back at the depot. Same face, same voice. Gorblimey, I reckon it is him.

MONSEWER: Sleachta—sleachta.

SOLDIER: Is he a free Hungarian, or something?

MONSEWER: Sleachta—sleachta.

SOLDIER: Oh. That's Garlic, ain't it?

MONSEWER: That, my dear young man, is Gaelic. A language old before the days of the Greeks.

SOLDIER: Did he say Greeks?

PAT: Yes, Greeks.

SOLDIER: Excuse me, guv. I can't have you running down the Greeks. Mate of mine's a Greek, runs a caffee down the Edgware Road. Best Rosy Lee and Holy Ghost in London.

MONSEWER: Rosy Lee and Holy Ghost . . .? What abomination is this?

SOLDIER: C. of E., guv.

PAT: Cockney humour, sir.

MONSEWER: The language of Shakespeare and Milton.

SOLDIER: He can't make up his mind, can he?

MONSEWER: That's the trouble with the fighting forces today. No background, no tradition, no morale.

SOLDIER: We got background—we got tradition. They gave us all that at the Boys' Home. They gave us team spirit, fair play, cricket.

MONSEWER: Are you a cricketer, my boy?

SOLDIER: Yes, sir. Do you like a game?

MONSEWER: By jove, yes.

SOLDIER: Mind you, I couldn't get on with it at the Boys' Home. They gave us two sets of stumps, you see, and I'd always been used to one, chalked up on the old wall at home.

MONSEWER: That's not cricket, my boy.

SOLDIER: Now there you are, then. You're what I call a cricket person and I'm what I call a soccer person. That's where your race lark comes in.

MONSEWER: Ah, cricket. By Jove, that takes me back. Strange how this uncouth youth has brought back memories of summers long past. Fetch the pianist, Patrick. A little light refreshment. (ROPEEN *brings him tea.*) Thank you, my dear, two lumps.

*As he sings of summers long forgotten, the genteel people of the house sip tea and listen—*MULLEADY, MISS GILCHRIST *and* ROPEEN.

He sings:

I remember in September,
When the final stumps were drawn,
And the shouts of crowds now silent
And the boys to tea were gone.
Let us, oh Lord above us,
Still remember simple things,
When all are dead who love us,
Oh the Captains and the Kings,
When all are dead who love us,
Oh the Captains and the Kings.

We have many goods for export,
Christian ethics and old port,
But our greatest boast is that
The Anglo-Saxon is a sport.
On the playing-fields of Eton
We still do thrilling things,
Do not think we'll ever weaken
Up the Captains and the Kings!
Do not think we'll ever weaken
Up the Captains and the Kings!

Far away in dear old Cyprus,
Or in Kenya's dusty land,
Where all bear the white man's burden
In many a strange land.
As we look across our shoulder
In West Belfast the school bell rings,
And we sigh for dear old England,
And the Captains and the Kings.
And we sigh for dear old England,
And the Captains and the Kings.

In our dreams we see old Harrow,
And we hear the crow's loud caw,
At the flower show our big marrow
Takes the prize from Evelyn Waugh.
Cups of tea or some dry sherry,
Vintage cars, these simple things,
So let's drink up and be merry
Oh, the Captains and the Kings.
So let's drink up and be merry
Oh, the Captains and the Kings.

I wandered in a nightmare
All around Great Windsor Park,
And what do you think I found there
As I stumbled in the dark?

'Twas an apple half-bitten,
And sweetest of all things,
Five baby teeth had written
Of the Captains and the Kings.
Five baby teeth had written
Of the Captains and the Kings.

By the moon that shines above us
In the misty morn and night,
Let us cease to run ourselves down
But praise God that we are white.
And better still we're English—
Tea and toast and muffin rings,
Old ladies with stern faces,
And the Captains and the Kings.
Old ladies with stern faces,
And the Captains and the Kings.[3]

A quavering bugle blows a staggering salute offstage.

PAT: Well, that's brought the show to a standstill.
OFFICER: Patrick, get that old idiot out of here.

The two I.R.A. *men have been listening horror-stricken to the last verse of the song.*

Guard!
VOLUNTEER: Sir.
OFFICER: No one is to be allowed in here, do you understand?
No one.
VOLUNTEER: I understand, sir. Might I be relieved from my post?
OFFICER: Certainly not. (*The* VOLUNTEER *is bursting.*)
VOLUNTEER: Two minutes, sir.

[3] Actually, he never sings all of this song, as there isn't time. The usual order is to sing verses 1, 4, and 6, with one of the other verses optional.

OFFICER: No, certainly not. Get back to your post. This place is like a rabbit warren with everyone skipping about.

The VOLUNTEER *hobbles off.*

MONSEWER: Ah, the laddie from headquarters. There you are.

OFFICER: Yes, here I am. You being an old soldier will understand the need for discipline.

MONSEWER: Quite right, too.

OFFICER: I must ask you what you were doing in here.

MONSEWER: Inspecting the prisoner.

OFFICER: I'm afraid I must ask you to keep out of here in future.

MONSEWER: Patrick, I know this young man has been working under a strain, but—there's no need to treat me like an Empire Loyalist. You know where to find me when you need me, Patrick. (*He sweeps off.*)

PAT: Yes, sir.

MONSEWER (*as he goes*): Chin up, sonny.

SOLDIER: Cheerio, sir.

OFFICER: I've had enough of this nonsense. I'll inspect the prisoner myself. (TERESA *is seen to be under the bed.*)

PAT: Yes, sir. Stand by your bed.

OFFICER: One pace forward, march.

SOLDIER: Can I ask you what you intend to do with me, sir?

OFFICER: You keep your mouth shut and no harm will come to you. Have you got everything you want?

SOLDIER: Oh yes, sir.

OFFICER: Right. Take over, Patrick. I'm going to inspect the outposts.

PAT: Have you got the place well covered, sir?

OFFICER: I have indeed. Why?

PAT: I think it's going to rain.

OFFICER: No more tomfoolery, please.

I.R.A. OFFICER *and* PATRICK *depart, leaving* TERESA *alone with* LESLIE.

SOLDIER: You can come out now.

TERESA: No, he might see me.

SOLDIER: He's gone, he won't be back for a long time. Come on, sit down and tell me a story—the Irish are great at that, aren't they?

TERESA: Well, not all of them. I'm not. I don't know any stories.

SOLDIER: Anything'll do. It doesn't have to be funny. It's just something to pass the time.

TERESA: Yes, you've a long night ahead of you, and so has he.

SOLDIER: Who?

TERESA: You know, the boy in Belfast.

SOLDIER: What do you have to mention him for?

TERESA: I'm sorry, Leslie.

SOLDIER: It's all right, it's just that everybody's been talking about the boy in the Belfast Jail.

TERESA: Will I tell you about when I was a girl in the convent?

SOLDIER: Yeah, that should be a bit of all right. Go on.

TERESA: Oh, it was the same as any other school, except you didn't go home. You played in a big yard which had a stone floor; you'd break your bones if you fell on it. But there was a big meadow outside the wall, we used to be let out there on our holidays. It was lovely. We were brought swimming a few times, too, that was really terrific, but the nuns were terrible strict, and if they saw a man come within a mile of us, well we ...

SOLDIER: What? ... Aw, go on, Teresa, we're grownups now, aren't we?

TERESA: We were not allowed to take off our clothes at all. You see, Leslie, even when we had our baths on Saturday nights they put shifts on all the girls.

SOLDIER: Put what on yer?

TERESA: A sort of sheet, you know.

SOLDIER: Oh yeah.

TERESA: Even the little ones four or five years of age.

SOLDIER: Oh, we never had anything like that.

TERESA: What did you have?

SOLDIER: Oh no, we never had anything like that. I mean, in our place we had all showers and we were sloshing water over each other—and blokes shouting and screeching and making a row—it was smashing! Best night of the week, it was.

TERESA: Our best time was the procession for the Blessed Virgin.

SOLDIER: Blessed who?

TERESA: Shame on you, the Blessed Virgin. Anyone would think you were a Protestant.

SOLDIER: I am, girl.

TERESA: Oh, I'm sorry.

SOLDIER: That's all right. Never think about it myself.

TERESA: Anyway, we had this big feast.

SOLDIER: Was the scoff good?

TERESA: The—what?

SOLDIER: The grub. The food. You don't understand me half the time, do you?

TERESA: Well, we didn't have food. It was a feast day. We just used to walk around.

SOLDIER: You mean they didn't give you nothing at all? Well, blow that for a lark.

TERESA: Well are you going to listen to me story? Well, are you? Anyway, we had this procession, and I was looking after the mixed infants.

SOLDIER: What's a mixed infant.

TERESA: A little boy or girl under five years of age. Because up until that time they were mixed together.

SOLDIER: I wish I'd been a mixed infant.

TERESA: Do you want to hear my story? When the boys were six they were sent to the big boys' orphanage.

SOLDIER: You're one, too—an orphan? You didn't tell me that.

TERESA: Yes, I did.

SOLDIER: We're quits now.

TERESA: I didn't believe your story.

SOLDIER: Well, it's true. Anyway, never mind. Tell us about this mixed infant job.

TERESA: There was this little feller, his father was dead, and his mother had run away or something. All the other boys were laughing and shouting, but this one little boy was all on his own and he was crying like the rain. Nothing would stop him. So, do you know what I did, Leslie? I made a crown of daisies and a daisy chain to put round his neck and told him he was King of the May. Do you know he forgot everything except that he was King of the May.

SOLDIER: Would you do that for me if I was a mixed infant?

They have forgotten all about Belfast Jail and the I.R.A. LESLIE takes TERESA's hand and she moves away. She goes to the window to cover her shyness.

TERESA: There's a clock striking somewhere in the city.

SOLDIER: I wonder what time it is?

TERESA: I don't know.

SOLDIER: Will you give me a picture of yourself, Teresa?

TERESA: What for?

SOLDIER: Just to have. I mean, they might take me away in the middle of the night and I might never see you again.

TERESA: I'm not Marilyn Monroe or Jayne Mansfield.

SOLDIER: Who wants a picture of them? They're all old.

TERESA: I haven't got one anyway.

She pulls out a medal which she has round her neck.

SOLDIER: What's that?

TERESA: It's a medal. It's for you, Leslie.

SOLDIER: I'm doing all right, ain't I? In the army nine months and I get a medal already.

TERESA: It's not that kind of medal.

SOLDIER: Let's have a look . . . looks a bit like you.

TERESA *(shocked)*: No, Leslie.

SOLDIER: Oh, it's that lady of yours.

TERESA: It's God's mother.

SOLDIER: Yes, that one.

TERESA: She's the mother of everyone else in the world, too. Will you wear it round your neck?

SOLDIER: I will if you put it on.

She puts it over his head and he tries to kiss her.

TERESA: Leslie. Don't. Why do you have to go and spoil everything—I'm going.

SOLDIER: Don't go! Let's pretend we're on the films, where all I
have to say is "Let me," and all you have to say is "Yes."

TERESA: Oh, all right.

SOLDIER: Come on, Kate.

They sing and dance.

I will give you a golden ball,
To hop with the children in the hall,

TERESA: If you'll marry, marry, marry, marry,
If you'll marry me.

SOLDIER: I will give you the keys of my chest,
And all the money that I possess,

TERESA: If you'll marry, marry, marry, marry,
If you'll marry me.

SOLDIER: I will give you a watch and chain,
To show the kids in Angel Lane,

TERESA: If you'll marry, marry, marry, marry,
If you'll marry me.
I will bake you a big pork pie,
And hide you till the cops go by,

BOTH: If you'll marry, marry, marry, marry,
If you'll marry me.

SOLDIER: But first I think that we should see,
If we fit each other,

TERESA *(to the audience)*: Shall we?

SOLDIER: Yes, let's see.

They run to the bed. The lights black out. MISS GILCHRIST
rushes on and a spotlight comes up on her.

MISS GILCHRIST *(horrified)*: They're away. *(To* KATE.*)* My music,
please!

She sings: Only a box of matches
I send, dear mother, to thee.

Only a box of matches,
Across the Irish sea.
I met with a Gaelic pawnbroker,
From Killarney's waterfalls,
With sobs he cried, "I wish I had died,
The Saxons have stolen my—"

PAT *rushes on to stop her saying "balls" and drags her off,
curtsying and singing again—*

Only a box of matches— —

MEG *enters the darkened passage.*

MEG: Teresa! Teresa!

The VOLUNTEER *enters in hot pursuit.*

VOLUNTEER: Ey, you can't go in there. Sir! Sir!

The OFFICER *enters and blocks* MEG'S *passage.*

Sir, there's another woman trying to get in to him.

OFFICER: You can't go in there. Security forbids it.

VOLUNTEER: Common decency forbids it. He might not have his
trousers on.

MEG: Auah, do you think I've never seen a man with his trousers
off before?

OFFICER: I'd be very much surprised if you'd ever seen one with
them on.

MEG: Thanks.

VOLUNTEER: He's a decent boy, for all he's a British soldier.

MEG: Ah, there's many a good heart beats under a khaki tunic.

VOLUNTEER: There's something in that. My own father was in
the Royal Irish Rifles.

OFFICER: Mine was in the Inniskillings.

MEG: And mine was the parish priest.

OFFICER (*horrified*): God forgive you, woman. After saying that, I won't let you in at all.

MEG: I'm not that particular. I was going about my business till he stopped me.

PAT: You might as well let her go in—cheer him up a bit.

OFFICER: I don't think we should. He's in our care and we're morally responsible for his spiritual welfare.

VOLUNTEER: Well, only in a temporal way, sir.

MEG: I only wanted to see him in a temporal way.

OFFICER: Jesus, Mary and Joseph, it would be a terrible thing for him to die with a sin of impurity on his—

The lights go up.

SOLDIER (*running downstage from the bed*): Die. What's all this talk about dying? Who's going to die?

MEG: We're all going to die, but not before Christmas, we hope.

PAT: Now look what you've done. You'll have to let her in now. You should have been more discreet, surely.

OFFICER: Two minutes then.

The I.R.A. OFFICER and the VOLUNTEER move away. TERESA stands by the bed. MEG goes into the room.

MEG: She's there, she's been there all the time.

TERESA: I was just dusting, Meg.

MEG: What's wrong with a bit of comfort on a dark night? Are you all right, lad?

SOLDIER: Mum, what are they going to do with me?

MEG: I don't know—I only wish I did.

SOLDIER: Will you go and ask them, because I don't think they know themselves.

MEG: Maybe they don't know, maybe a lot of people don't know, or maybe they've forgotten.

SOLDIER: I don't know what you mean.

MEG: There are some things you can't forget.

SOLDIER: Forget?

MEG: Like here in Russell Street, right next to the place where I was born, the British turned a tank and fired shells into people's homes.

SOLDIER: I suppose it was war, missus.

MEG: Yes, it was war. Do you know who it was against?

SOLDIER: No.

MEG: Old men and women, the bedridden and the cripples, and mothers with their infants.

SOLDIER: Why them?

MEG: Everybody that was able to move had run away. In one room they found an old woman, her son's helmet and gas mask were still hanging on the wall. He had died fighting on the Somme.

SOLDIER: I don't know nothing about it, lady.

MEG: Would you like to hear some more? Then listen.

A military drum beats, the piano plays softly, and MEG *chants rather than sings:*

Who fears to speak of Easter Week
That week of famed renown,
When the boys in green went out to fight
The forces of the Crown.

With Mausers bold, and hearts of gold,
The Red Countess dressed in green,
And high above the G.P.O.
The rebel flag was seen.

Then came ten thousand khaki coats,
Our rebel boys to kill,
Before they reached O'Connell Street,
Of fight they got their fill.

As she sings everyone else in the house comes slowly on to listen to her.

They had machine-guns and artillery,
And cannon in galore,
But it wasn't our fault that e'er one
Got back to England's shore.

For six long days we held them off,
At odds of ten to one,
And through our lines they could not pass,
For all their heavy guns.

And deadly poison gas they used,
To try to crush Sinn Fein,
And burnt our Irish capital,
Like the Germans did Louvain.

They shot our leaders in a jail,
Without a trial, they say,
They murdered women and children,
Who in their cellars lay,

And dug their grave with gun and spade,
To hide them from our view.
Because they could neither kill nor catch,
The rebel so bold and true.

The author should have sung that one.

PAT: That's if the thing has an author.

SOLDIER: Brendan Behan, he's too anti-British.

OFFICER: Too anti-Irish, you mean. Bejasus, wait till we get him
back home. We'll give what-for for making fun of the
Movement.

SOLDIER *(to audience)*: He doesn't mind coming over here and
taking your money.

PAT: He'd sell his country for a pint.

*What happens next is not very clear. There are a number of
arguments all going on at once. Free-Staters against Re-*

publican, Irish against English, homosexual against hetero-
sexuals, and in the confusion all the quarrels get mixed up
and it looks as though everyone is fighting everyone else. In
the centre of the melee, MISS GILCHRIST *is standing on the*
table singing "Land of Hope and Glory." The I.R.A. OFFICER
has one chair and is waving a Free State flag and singing
"The Soldier's Song," while the RUSSIAN SAILOR *has the other*
and sings the Soviet National Anthem. The NEGRO *parades*
through the room carrying a large banner inscribed "KEEP
IRELAND BLACK." The piano plays throughout. Suddenly
the VOLUNTEER *attacks the* SOLDIER *and the* RUSSIAN *joins in*
the fight. The VOLUNTEER *knocks* MULLEADY'S *bowler hat*
over his eyes and ROPEEN *flattens the* VOLUNTEER. MULLEADY
is now wandering around blind with his hat over his eyes,
and holding ROPEEN'S *aspidistra. The* VOLUNTEER, *somewhat*
dazed, sees the RUSSIAN'S *red flag and thinks he has been pro-*
moted to guard. He blows his railway whistle and the fight
breaks up into a wild dance in which they all join on the
train behind the VOLUNTEER *and rush round the room in*
a circle. All this takes about a minute and a half and at the
height, as they are all chugging round and round LESLIE,
PAT *interrupts.*

PAT: Stop it a minute. Hey, Leslie, have you seen this?

The train stops and the dancers are left in the position of
forming a ring round LESLIE *which resembles a prison cage.*
PAT *hands* LESLIE *a newspaper and everyone is quiet. The*
Irish, British, and Russian flags lie on the ground.

SOLDIER: Let's have a look. "The Government of Northern Ireland have issued a statement that they cannot find a reason
for granting a reprieve in the case of the condemned youth.
The I.R.A. have announced that Private Leslie Alan Williams"—hey, that's me, I've got me name in the papers.
PAT: You want to read a bit further.
MISS GILCHRIST: I'm afraid it's impossible—you're going to be shot.

SOLDIER: Who are you?

MISS GILCHRIST: I am a sociable worker. I work for the St. Vincent de Paul Society and I have one question to ask you: have you your testament?

The SOLDIER *checks his trousers.*

SOLDIER: I hope so.

MISS GILCHRIST: I feel for him like a mother. *(She sings.)* Only a box of matches—

SOLDIER: Shut up, this is serious. "In a statement today delivered to all newspaper offices and press agencies—he has been taken as a hostage—If . . . executed—the I.R.A. declare that Private Leslie Alan Williams will be shot as a reprisal." Does it really mean they're going to shoot me?

MULLEADY: I'm afraid so.

SOLDIER: Why?

MONSEWER: You are the hostage.

SOLDIER: But I ain't done nothing.

OFFICER: This is war.

SOLDIER: Surely one of you would let me go?

They all move backwards away from him, leaving him alone in the room. They disappear.

Well, you crowd of bleeding—Hey, Kate, give us some music.

He sings:
I am a happy English lad, I love my royal-ty,
And if they were short a penny of a packet of fags,
Now they'd only have to ask me.

I love old England in the east, I love her in the west,
From Jordan's streams to Derry's Walls,
I love old England best.

I love my dear old Notting Hill, wherever I may roam,
But I wish the Irish and the niggers and the wogs,
Were kicked out and sent back home.

A bugle sounds and he salutes.

Curtain.

ACT THREE

Late the same night. The SOLDIER *sits alone in his room.* PAT *and* MEG *sit at the table down by the piano.* TERESA, COLETTE, RIO RITA *and* PRINCESS GRACE *are sitting or sprawling on the stairs or in the passage.* ROPEEN *sits, knitting, on a beer barrel near* PAT, *and the* RUSSIAN *is fast asleep on the far side of the stage. Before the curtain rises there is the sound of keening as the women sit mourning for* LESLIE *and the boy in Belfast Jail. The atmosphere is one of death and dying. The curtain rises and* PAT *seizes a bottle of stout from the crate beside him and bursts into wild song.*

PAT: On the eighteenth day of November,
      Just outside the town of Macroom,
      Here, have a drink. *(He gives* LESLIE *the stout.)*
SOLDIER: What's the time?
PAT: I don't know. Ask him.
VOLUNTEER: My watch has stopped.
PAT *(sings)*: The Tans in their big Crossley tenders,
      Came roaring along to their doom.
MEG: Shut up, will you, Pat!

The keening stops.

PAT: What's the matter with you?
MEG: You'll have that Holy Joe down on us.
PAT: Who are you talking about?
MEG: That I.R.A. general, or whatever he is.
PAT: Him a general? He's a messenger boy. He's not fit to be a batman.

MEG: I've heard they're all generals nowadays.

PAT: Like their mothers before them.

> MISS GILCHRIST *in her nightclothes attempts to sneak into* LESLIE'S *room, but the* VOLUNTEER, *who is mounting guard, sees her and challenges.*

MISS GILCHRIST: Leslie—Leslie—

VOLUNTEER: Hey, where are you going?

PAT: Come on, come and sit down. (PAT *drags a protesting* MISS GILCHRIST *to sit at the table with them.*)

MISS GILCHRIST: Well, you must excuse the way I'm dressed.

PAT: You look lovely. Have a drink, Miss Gilchrist.

MISS GILCHRIST: Oh no, thank you, Mr. Pat.

PAT: Get it down you.

MISS GILCHRIST: No, really, Mr. Pat. I never drink.

MEG: She doesn't want it.

PAT: Shut up, you. Are you going to drink?

MISS GILCHRIST: No, Mr. Pat.

PAT (*shouts*): Drink. (*She drinks*). Are you aware, Miss Gilchrist, that you are speaking to a man who was a commandant at the times of the troubles.

MEG: Fine bloody commandant he was.

PAT: Commandant of "E" battalion, second division, Dublin brigade. Monsewer was the Captain.

MEG: What the hell's "E" battalion?

PAT: You've heard of A B C D E, I suppose?

MEG: Certainly I have.

PAT: Well, it's as simple as that.

MISS GILCHRIST: Wasn't that nice? It must be a lovely thing to be a captain.

PAT: Can I get on with my story or not?

MEG: I defy anyone to stop you.

PAT: Now where was I?

VOLUNTEER. Tell us about Mullingar, sir.

PAT: Shut up. Leslie, you want to listen to this. It was in Russell Street in Dublin—

MEG: That's my story and I've already told him.

PAT: Oh, then give us a drink.

MEG: Get it yourself.

PAT: Give us a drink!

MISS GILCHRIST *gives* PAT *a drink.*

MISS GILCHRIST: Please go on, Mr. Pat.

PAT: I intend to. It was at Mullingar, at the time of the troubles, that I lost my leg . . .

MEG: You told me it was at Cork.

PAT: It doesn't matter what I told you, it was at Mullingar, in the Civil War.

MISS GILCHRIST: Well if that's the kind of war you call a civil war, I wouldn't like to see an uncivil one.

PAT: The fightin', Miss Gilchrist, went on for three days without ceasing, three whole days . . .

MISS GILCHRIST: And how did you lose your poor left foot, Mr. Pat?

PAT: It wasn't me left foot, but me right foot. Don't you know your left from your right? Don't you know how to make the sign of the cross?

MISS GILCHRIST: I do, thank you, but I don't make it with me feet.

PAT *retreats to join* LESLIE *and the* VOLUNTEER *inside the room.*

PAT: What the hell difference does it make, left or right? There were good men lost on both sides.

VOLUNTEER: There's good and bad on all sides, sir.

The I.R.A. OFFICER *crosses through the room and out again.*

PAT: It was a savage and barbarous battle. All we had was rifles and revolvers. They had Lewis guns, Thompsons, and landmines—bloody great landmines—the town was nothing but red fire and black smoke and the dead were piled high on the roads . . .

MEG: You told me there was only one man killed.

PAT: What?

MEG: And he was the County Surveyor out measuring the road and not interfering with politics one way or another.

PAT: You're a liar!

MEG: You told me that when the fighting was over both sides claimed him for their own.

PAT: Liar!

MEG: Haven't I seen the Celtic crosses on either side of the road where they both put up memorials to him?

PAT: It's all the same what I told you.

MEG: That's your story when you're drunk, anyway, and like any other man, that's the only time you tell the truth.

PAT: Have you finished?

MEG: No, begod, if whisky and beer were the prewar prices, the father of lies would be out of a job.

PAT: I lost my leg—did I or did I not?

MEG: You lost the use of it, I know that.

MISS GILCHRIST: These little lovers' quarrels.

PAT: Shut up! I lost my leg. Did I or did I not? And these white-faced loons with their berets and trench coats and teetotal badges have no right to call themselves members of the I.R.A.

MISS GILCHRIST: They're only lads, Mr. Pat.

MEG: He begrudges them their bit of sport now that he's old and beat himself.

PAT: What sport is there in that dreary loon out there?

MEG: They've as much right to their drilling and marching, their rifles and revolvers and crucifixes and last dying words and glory as ever you had.

PAT: I'm not saying they haven't, did I? *(There is general disagreement.)*

VOLUNTEER: Oh yes, you did, Pat.

MISS GILCHRIST: I heard you distinctly.

MEG: Weren't you young yourself once?

PAT: That's the way they talk to you, nowadays.

He sulks. The keening starts again.

MISS GILCHRIST: I always say that a general and a bit of shooting makes one forget one's troubles.

MEG: Sure, it takes your mind off the cost of living.

MISS GILCHRIST: A poor heart it is that never rejoices.

PAT: I'll tell you one thing, they've no right to be going up to the border and kidnapping young men like this and bringing them down here.

MEG: They've as much right to leave their legs and feet up on the border as ever you had at Mullingar or Cork or wherever it was.

MISS GILCHRIST *gets up to take a drink to* LESLIE. *The* VOLUNTEER *throws her out of the room.*

VOLUNTEER: I've warned you before you can't come in here.

MEG: Leave her alone.

PAT: She's coming on, you know, to be making smart remarks to a poor crippled man that never harmed anyone in his life.

MEG: Away with you.

PAT: Let alone the years I spent incarcerated in Mountjoy with the other Irish patriots, God help me.

MEG: Ah, Mountjoy and the Curragh Camp were universities for the likes of you. But I'll tell you one thing, and that's not two, the day you gave up work to run this house for Monsewer and take in the likes of this lot, you became a butler, a Republican butler, a half-red footman—a Sinn Fein skivvy—

MISS GILCHRIST: What a rough-tongued person.

PAT: Go on, abuse me, your own husband that took you off the streets on a Sunday morning, when there wasn't a pub open in the city.

MEG: Go and get a mass said for yourself. The only love you ever

had you kept for Mother Ireland and for leaving honest
employment.

PAT: Why did you stop with me so long?

MEG: God knows. I don't. God knows.

On the stairs and in the passage people are dozing off. PAT
and MEG *are not speaking. The* SOLDIER *is thinking about
tomorrow morning and to cheer himself up, sings. The* I.R.A.
OFFICER *passes on his rounds.*

SOLDIER: Abide with me, fast falls the eventide,
The darkness deepens, Lord with me abide.

MISS GILCHRIST *places a black lace scarf on her head, lights a
candle and starts walking slowly towards the* SOLDIER, *keening. The* VOLUNTEER *is struck helpless.*

MEG: She's starting a wake for the poor lad and he's not dead
yet.

As she passes PAT, *he blows out the candle and* MISS GIL-
CHRIST *suffers a great shock.*

PAT (*to* LESLIE): If you must sing, sing something cheerful.

SOLDIER: I don't know anything cheerful.

VOLUNTEER: Then shut up!

Having got into the room, MISS GILCHRIST *stays there.*

MISS GILCHRIST: I know what it is to be in exile. Dublin is not
my home.

MEG: That's one thing in its favour.

MISS GILCHRIST: I came here to work in a house, Mr. Pat.

MEG: I told you what she was.

MISS GILCHRIST: It was in a very respectable district. We only took
in clerical students. They were lovely boys, so much more
satisfactory than the medical students.

PAT: Oh yes, the medicals is more for the beer.

MISS GILCHRIST: Of course, my boys had renounced the demon drink. Being students of divinity they had more satisfactory things to do.

MEG: Such as?

PAT: You know what they go in for, reading all this stuff about "Mat begat Pat" and "This one lay with that one" and the old fellow that lay with his daughters—

MEG: And getting the best of eating and drinking, too. It's a wonder they're in any way controllable at all.

MISS GILCHRIST: Sometimes they were not. Life has its bitter memories. Since then I've had recourse to doing good works, recalling the sinner, salvaging his soul.

MEG: Well, you can leave his soul alone, whatever about your own, or I'll set fire to you.

MISS GILCHRIST (*standing on her dignity*): Our Blessed Lord said, "Every cripple has his own way of walking, so long as they don't cause strikes, rob, steal, or run down General Franco." Those are my principles.

MEG: Your principal is nothing but a pimp.

MISS GILCHRIST: To whom are you referring?

MEG: That creeping Jesus on the third floor back.

MISS GILCHRIST: Oh, you mean Mr. Mulleady.

MEG: I do.

MISS GILCHRIST: But he is a fonctionnaire.

MEG: Is that what they call it nowadays?

MISS GILCHRIST: I strove to save him, together we wrestled against the devil, but here I feel is a soul worth the saving. (*She sings.*) "I love my fellow creatures."

MISS GILCHRIST *chases* LESLIE *round the table and the* VOLUNTEER *chases* MISS GILCHRIST.

PAT: Leave him alone, he's too young for you.

MISS GILCHRIST: Mr. Pat, I'm as pure as the driven snow .

The VOLUNTEER *taps her on the backside with his rifle. She jumps.*

MEG: You weren't driven far enough.

MISS GILCHRIST *returns to the table near the piano.*

PAT: Hey, Feargus. Have a drink and take one up for Leslie. Hey Leslie, don't be paying any attention to her. She's no use to you.

The VOLUNTEER *takes* LESLIE *a bottle of stout.*

SOLDIER: Here, it's all very well you coming the old acid, and giving me all this stuff about nothing going to happen to me. I'm not a complete bloody fool, you know.

PAT: Drink your beer and shut up.

SOLDIER: What have I ever done to you that you should shoot me?

PAT: I'll tell you what you've done. Some time ago there was a famine in this country and people were dying all over the place. Well, your Queen Victoria, or whatever her bloody name was, sent five pounds to the famine fund and at the same time she sent five pounds to the Battersea Dogs' Home so no one could accuse her of having rebel sympathies.

MEG: Good God, Pat, that was when Moses was in the Fire Brigade.

PAT: Let him think about it.

MISS GILCHRIST: They might have given us this little island that we live on for ourselves.

SOLDIER: Will you answer me one thing man to man? Why didn't they tell me why they took me?

PAT: Didn't they? Didn't they tell you?

SOLDIER: No.

MEG: There's a war on.

PAT: Exactly. There's a war going on in the north of Ireland. You're a soldier. You were captured.

SOLDIER: All right, so I'm a soldier. I'm captured. I'm a prisoner of war.

PAT: Yes.

SOLDIER: Well, you can't shoot a prisoner of war.

PAT: Who said anything about shooting?

SOLDIER: What about that announcement in the newspapers?

PAT: Bluff. Haven't you everything you could wish for? A bottle of stout, a new girl-friend bringing you every class of comfort?

SOLDIER: Yeah, till that bloke in Belfast is topped in the morning; then it's curtains for poor old Williams. I'm due for a week-end's leave an' all.

PAT: It's bluff, propaganda! All they'll do is hold you for a few days.

MEG: Sure, they might give him a last-minute reprieve.

SOLDIER: Who, me?

MEG: No. The boy in Belfast Jail.

SOLDIER: Some hopes of that.

PAT: The British Government might think twice about it now that they know we've got you.

VOLUNTEER: They know that if they hang the Belfast martyr, their own man here will be plugged.

SOLDIER: Plug you.

PAT: Be quiet, you idiot.

They all turn on the VOLUNTEER.

SOLDIER: You're as barmy as him if you think that what's happening to me is upsetting the British Government. I suppose you think they're all sitting round in their West End clubs with handkerchiefs over their eyes, dropping tears into their double whiskies. Yeah, I can just see the Secretary of State for War now waking up his missus in the night: "Oh Isabel-Cynthia love, I can hardly get a wink of sleep wondering what's happening to that poor bleeder Williams."

MISS GILCHRIST: Poor boy! Do you know, I think they ought to put his story in the *News of the World*. Ah, we'll be seeing you on the telly yet. He'll be famous like that Diana Dors, or the one who cut up his victim and threw the bits out of an aeroplane. I think he has a serial running somewhere.

SOLDIER: I always heard the Irish were barmy, but that's going it, that is.

PAT: Eh, let's have a drink.

MEG: I want me bed, Pat. Never mind a drink.

SOLDIER: Here mum, listen—*(Coming out of the room.)*

PAT *(to the* SOLDIER*)*: Where are you going?

SOLDIER: I'm just going to talk to . . .

PAT: I'm going to fix you . . . Leslie.

MEG *starts to sing softly*:

"I have no mother to break her heart,
I have no father to take my part.
I have one friend and a girl is she,
And she'd lay down her life for McCaffery."

Now, I'm going to draw a circle round you, with this piece of chalk. Now, you move outside that circle and you're a dead man. Watch him, Feargus.

He draws a circle round LESLIE *and the* VOLUNTEER *points his gun at him.*

SOLDIER: I bet that fellow in Belfast wouldn't want me plugged.

PAT: Certainly he wouldn't.

SOLDIER: What good's it going to do him?

MEG: When the boy's dead, what good would it be to croak this one? It wouldn't bring the other back to life now, would it?

The VOLUNTEER *comes away from* LESLIE *to sit near the piano.*

SOLDIER: What a caper! I'm just walking out of a dance hall—

He tries to walk out of the circle and the VOLUNTEER *grabs his gun.*

PAT: Walk in.

SOLDIER *(back inside)*: I was just walking out of a dance hall, when this geezer nabs me. "What do you want?" I says. "Information," he says. "I ain't got no information," I says, "apart from me name and the addresses of the girls in the N.A.A.F.I." "Right," he says, "we're taking you to Dublin. Our Intelligence wants to speak to you."

PAT: Intelligence! Holy Jesus, wait till you meet 'em. This fellow here's an Einstein compared to them.

SOLDIER: Well, when will I be meeting them?

PAT: Maybe they'll come tomorrow morning to ask you a few questions.

SOLDIER: Yeah, me last bloody wishes, I suppose.

MISS GILCHRIST (*sings*):
I have no mother to break her heart,
I have no father to take my part.

MEG: Pat, will you do something about that one?

PAT: Can you see that circle?

MISS GILCHRIST: Yes.

PAT: Well, get in.

He rushes MISS GILCHRIST *into the room.*

MISS GILCHRIST *carries on singing.*

MISS GILCHRIST:
I have one friend, and a girl is she,
And she'd lay down her life for McCaffery.

PAT: Leslie, come down here. The old idiot would put years on you. I can't stand your bloody moaning.

MISS GILCHRIST: I'll have you know, Mr. Pat, I had my voice trained by an electrocutionist.

MEG: It sounds shocking.

VOLUNTEER (*jumping to attention*): Sir, it's neither this nor that, sir, but if you're taking charge of the prisoner, I'll carry out me other duties and check the premises.

PAT: Yes, you do that, Feargus.

VOLUNTEER: It's only a thick would let the job slip between his fingers.

PAT: You may be blamed, Einstein, but you never will be shamed.

VOLUNTEER: I hope not, sir. Of course, sir, God gives us the brains, it's no credit to ourselves.

PAT: Look—I don't wish to come the sergeant-major on you, but will you get about what you came for?

VOLUNTEER: I will, sir, directly.

He salutes smartly and marches off into the growing dark, getting more and more frightened as he goes.

MISS GILCHRIST: I have such a thirst on me, Mr. Pat. *(She looks at the crate of empties.)* Oh, Mr. Pat, you gave that twelve of stout a very quick death.

PAT: You could sing that if you had an air to it. Leslie, pop out and get us twelve of stout. Go on—just out there and round the corner—go on—you can't miss it. Tell 'em it's for me.

LESLIE takes some persuading, but finally, seeing his chance to escape, leaves quietly. Everyone else is falling asleep. There is a long silence, then a terrific clatter.

VOLUNTEER: Hey, where do you think you're going?

LESLIE: He told me I could . . .

LESLIE runs back, hotly pursued by the VOLUNTEER. Everyone wakes up in alarm. PAT is furious.

PAT: You're a bloody genius, Einstein. *(The VOLUNTEER beams.)* If you're so fond of that circle, you get in it. *(He takes a swipe at the VOLUNTEER with his walking stick and drives him into the circle. The VOLUNTEER is puzzled.)* Leslie, come and sit over here.

LESLIE: Oh yeah, you're just leading me up the garden path, sending me out for beer. All of a sudden, I turn round and cop a bullet in my head. Anyway, I can tell you this, an Englishman can die as well as an Irishman any day.

PAT: Don't give me all that old stuff about dying. You won't

die for another fifty years, barring you get a belt of an
atom bomb, God bless you.

LESLIE *comes down to sit with* PAT *and* MEG, *as* MONSEWER
enters at the back of the room with the I.R.A. OFFICER. *The*
VOLUNTEER *reports to them about the disturbance.*

MONSEWER: Have you checked his next-of-kin?
VOLUNTEER: He hasn't got none, sir.

The I.R.A. OFFICER *and* VOLUNTEER *synchronize watches and
the* OFFICER *and* MONSEWER *depart. The* VOLUNTEER *sits at
the table with his gun trained on* LESLIE'S *back.*

PAT: Come and sit down here and don't pay any attention to
them.
MEG: Ignore them. Come on, lad.
SOLDIER: You know, up till tonight I've enjoyed myself here.
It's better than square bashing. You know what they say?
(Sings.)

When Irish eyes are smiling,
Sure, it's like a morn in Spring,
In the lilt of Irish laughter
You can hear the angels sing.
When Irish eyes are happy—

*None of the Irish know the words, but they all hum and
whistle.* MISS GILCHRIST *starts keening and the singing stops.*

PAT: It's all right, it's one of ours.
MISS GILCHRIST: Jesus, Mary and Joseph, I feel for this boy as
if I were his mother.
MEG: That's remarkable, that is.
MISS GILCHRIST: It would be more remarkable if I were his father.
MEG: Were his father? How many of you are there? I never
heard you were married.

MISS GILCHRIST: You never heard the Virgin Mary was married.

MEG: That was done under the Special Powers Act by the Holy Ghost.

MISS GILCHRIST: Oh, Miss Meg, I repulse your prognostications. It would answer you better to go and clean your carpet.

MEG: How dare you? When I was ill I lay prostituted on that carpet. Men of good taste have complicated me on it. Away, you scruff hound, and thump your craw with the other hippo-crites.

MISS GILCHRIST: Pray do not insult my religiosity.

MEG: Away, you brass.

MISS GILCHRIST: I stand fast by my lord, and will sing my hymn now:

I love my dear Redeemer,
My Creator, too, as well,
And, oh, that filthy Devil,
Should stay below in Hell.
I cry to Mr. Khrushchev
Please grant me this great boon,
Don't muck about, don't muck about,
Don't muck about with the moon.

I am a little Christ-ian,
My feet are white as snow,
And every day, my prayers I say,
For Empire Lamb I go.
I cry unto Macmillan,
That multi-racial coon,
I love him and those above him,
But don't muck about with the moon,

ALL: Don't muck about, don't muck about,
Don't muck about with the moon.

MEG: Get off the stage, you castle Catholic bitch.

MISS GILCHRIST: She is a no-class person. Things haven't been the same since the British went.

SOLDIER: They've not all gone yet—I'm still here. Perhaps you
can tell me what these people are going to do me in for?

MEG: Maybe you voted wrong.

SOLDIER: I'm too young to have a vote for another three years.

MEG: Well, what are you doing poking your nose into our
affairs?

SOLDIER: In what affairs? What do I know about Ireland or
Cyprus, or Kenya or Jordan or any of those places?

OFFICER (*as he crosses the stage*): You may learn very shortly
with a bullet in the back of your head.

RIO RITA: You'll put a bullet in the back of nobody's head, mate.

WHORES: Oh no, it's not his fault.

MULLEADY: He should never have been brought here in the first
place. It means trouble. I've been saying so all day. It's
illegal.

*The action takes a very sinister turn. At the mention of
bullets there is a rush by everyone to blanket* LESLIE *from
the* OFFICER. MULLEADY *appears as if by magic and summons*
RIO RITA *and* PRINCESS GRACE *to him. They go into a huddle.
The other inhabitants of the house are mystified. All that
can be seen are three pairs of twitching hips, as they mutter
and whisper to each other.*

MEG: What are they up to?

PAT: I wouldn't trust them as far as I could fling them.

COLETTE: What are you up to?

RIO RITA: We've made a pact.

There is much homosexual by-play between MULLEADY *and
the two queers.*

COLETTE: What sort of a pact? Political or—?

MULLEADY: One might as well be out of the world as out of
the fashion.

MISS GILCHRIST *is horrified.*

MISS GILCHRIST: Eustace, what are you doing with those persons?

MULLEADY: Oh, we're speaking now, are we, Miss Gilchrist? That's a change. Ever since you've been interested in that young man's soul, a poor Civil Servant's soul means nothing to you.

MISS GILCHRIST: Eustace, what has happened to you?

MULLEADY: You can't do what you like with us, you know.

RIO RITA: Don't you know? *(He comes down to the audience.)* Do you? Well, for the benefit of those who don't understand we'll sing our ancient song, won't we, Uncle? *(MULLEADY and GRACE join him.)* Blanche? *(This to the NEGRO.)* Isn't he lovely? I met him at a whist drive. He trumped my ace. Give us a note, Kate. Will you try another one, please? We'll have the first one, I think.

RIO RITA, MULLEADY, PRINCESS GRACE *(sing)*:
When Socrates in Ancient Greece,
Sat in his Turkish bath,
He rubbed himself, and scrubbed himself,
And steamed both fore and aft.

He sang the songs the sirens sang,
With Oscar and Shakespeare,
We're here because we're queer,
Because we're queer because we're here.

MULLEADY:
The highest people in the land
Are for or they're against,
It's all the same thing in the end,
A piece of sentiment.

PRINCESS GRACE:
From Swedes so tall to Arabs small,
They answer with a leer,

ALL THREE:
We're here because we're queer
Because we're queer because we're here.

PRINCESS GRACE: The trouble we had getting that past the nice Lord Chamberlain. This next bit's even worse.

The song ends and the three queers gyrate across the stage, twisting their bodies sinuously and making suggestive approaches to LESLIE. LESLIE *is about to join in when* MISS GILCHRIST *throws herself at him.*

MISS GILCHRIST: Leslie, come away, this is no fit company for an innocent boy.

SOLDIER: No, mum.

MISS GILCHRIST: Leave off this boy. He's not used to prostitutes, male, female or *Whiston Mail.*

MEG: Get out, you dirty low things. A decent whore can't get a shilling with you around.

RIO RITA: Shut up, Meg Dillon, you're just bigoted.

MEG: Don't you use language like that to me.

MISS GILCHRIST: Leave off this boy. He is not a ponce.

SOLDIER: No, I'm a builder's labourer. At least, I was.

MISS GILCHRIST: Honest toil.

SOLDIER: It's a mug's game.

MISS GILCHRIST: Oh, my boy!

They sing a duet, LESLIE *speaking his lines. As the song goes on, the whores and queers sort themselves out into a dance for all the outcasts of this world. It is a slow sad dance in which* ROPEEN *dances with* COLETTE *and* PRINCESS GRACE *dances first with* MULLEADY *and then with* RIO RITA. *There is jealousy and comfort in the dance.*

MISS GILCHRIST:
Would you live on a woman's earnings,
Would you give up work for good?
For a life of prostitution?

SOLDIER:
Yes, too bloody true, I would.

MISS GILCHRIST:
Would you have a kip in Soho?
Would you be a West End ponce?

SOLDIER:
I'm fed up with pick and shovel,
And I'd like to try it once.

MISS GILCHRIST:

Did you read the Wolfenden Report
On whores and queers?

SOLDIER:

Yeah, gorblimey, it was moving,
I collapsed meself in tears.

Well, at this poncing business,
I think I'll have a try,
And I'll drop the English coppers,
They're the best money can buy.

MISS GILCHRIST:

Good-bye, my son. God bless you,
Say your prayers each morn and night,
And send home your poor old mother,
A few quid—her widow's mite.

At the end of the dance the RUSSIAN *silently and smoothly removes* MISS GILCHRIST. *The whores and queers melt away, quietly cooing "Leslie!" There is a moment of stillness and quiet, when* TERESA *comes down into the darkened room and calls.*

TERESA: Leslie, Leslie!

The VOLUNTEER *is asleep at* LESLIE's *table. He wakes up and sees* TERESA.

VOLUNTEER: You can call me Feargus! *(He leers lecherously.)*
PAT *(to* VOLUNTEER*)*: Hey, you'll have us all in trouble. Attention! Quick march—left, right, left, right . . . Come on, leave 'em in peace.

PAT *throws out the* VOLUNTEER *and takes* MEG *away, to leave* LESLIE *alone with* TERESA.

TERESA: That strict officer is coming back and I won't get a chance of a word with you.

SOLDIER: Well, what do you want?

TERESA: Don't be so narky. I just wanted to see you.

SOLDIER: Well, you'd better take a good look, hadn't you?

TERESA: What's eating you? I only wanted to talk to you.

SOLDIER: You'd better hurry up, I mightn't be able to talk so well with a hole right through me head.

TERESA: Don't be talking like that.

SOLDIER: Why not? Eh, why not?

TERESA: Maybe I could get you a cup of tea?

SOLDIER: No, thanks, I've just had a barrel of beer.

TERESA: Well, I'll go then.

SOLDIER: Eh, just before you go, don't think you've taken me for a complete bloody fool, will you? All this tea and beer lark: you even obliged with that. *(Indicating the bed.)*

TERESA: Leslie, for God's sake! Do you want the whole house to hear?

LESLIE *takes her to the window.*

SOLDIER: Come here—I'll show you something. Can you see him over there, and that other one opposite? There are more than these two idiots guarding me. Look at those two, by the archway, pretending they're lovers. That should be right up your street, that, pretending they're lovers. That's a laugh.

TERESA: I wasn't pretending.

SOLDIER: How can I believe you, you and your blarney?

TERESA: The boys won't harm you. Pat told me himself; they only wanted to question you . . .

SOLDIER: Do you think he's going to tell you the truth, or me? After all—if you were really sorry for me, you might call the police. Well, would you, Teresa?

TERESA: I'm not an informer.

SOLDIER: How long have I got? What time is it?

TERESA: It's not eleven yet.

SOLDIER: Eleven o'clock. They'll just be waking up at home, fellows will be coming out of the dance halls.

TERESA *(still at the window)*: Look, there's an old fellow, half jarred, trying to sober up before he gets back home.

SOLDIER: Back home, couple of hundred miles away, might just as well be on another bloody planet.

TERESA: Leslie, the chip shop is still open, maybe I could go out—

SOLDIER: I couldn't eat chips. Could you eat chips if you knew you were going to be done in? You're thinking of that poor bloke in Belfast. What about me—here now, Muggins?

TERESA: If I really thought they'd do anything to you—

SOLDIER: If you thought—I'm a hostage. You know what that means? What's the point of taking a hostage if you don't intend to do him in?

TERESA: Leslie, if they do come for you, shout to me.

SOLDIER: Shout! I wouldn't get a chance.

TERESA: I can't be sure.

SOLDIER: Oh, go away and leave me in peace. At least that bloke in Belfast has peace, and tomorrow he'll have nuns and priest and the whole works to see him on his way.

TERESA: What do you want?

SOLDIER: Nothing—this bloke'll do the best he can on his own. Perhaps I'll meet that Belfast geezer on the other side. We can have a good laugh about it.

TERESA: Here's that officer coming. I'd better go.

She starts to leave him.

LESLIE *(frightened)*: Teresa! Don't go yet. I know I wasn't much good to you, but say goodbye properly, eh?

TERESA *goes to him and they clasp in each other's arms.*

If I get away, will you come and see me in Armagh?

TERESA: I will, Leslie.

SOLDIER: I want all the blokes in the billet to see you. They all got pictures on the walls. Well, I never had any pictures, but now I've got you. Then we could have a bloody good time in Belfast together.

TERESA: It would be lovely, astore.

SOLDIER: I'm due for a week-end's leave an' all . . .

TERESA: I could pay my own way, too.

SOLDIER: No, you needn't do that. I've got enough for both of us . . .

TERESA: They're coming.

PAT *and the* I.R.A. OFFICER *come down the stairs.*

OFFICER: What's she doing here? Sleeping with him?

PAT: Mind your own business. She's not interfering with you. You should be in bed now, girl. Where are you going?

TERESA: I'm just going to the chip shop, to get some chips for him.

She starts to go but the OFFICER *stops her.*

OFFICER: You can't go out there now.

PAT: It's too late, girl.

TERESA: It's only eleven.

PAT: It's nearer one.

TERESA: It's not the truth you're telling me.

PAT: Didn't you hear the clock strike?

TERESA: I did.

OFFICER: Patrick, get her to her room or I will.

TERESA: You're lying to me. The chip shop is open till twelve.

OFFICER: Go to your room, girl.

TERESA: Do I have to go?

PAT: Yes, go to your room.

LESLIE *is left alone in his room until* MISS GILCHRIST *creeps from under the stairs to join him.*

MISS GILCHRIST: Oh, Leslie, what's going to become of you?

SOLDIER: I don't know, mum, do I?

MISS GILCHRIST: I've brought you a little gift. (*She gives him a photograph.*)

SOLDIER: Oh, she's nice!

MISS GILCHRIST: Oh, don't you recognize me, Leslie? It's me with me hair done nice.

SOLDIER: Oh, it's you. 'Ere, mum—I think you'd better go. Things might start warming up here.

MISS GILCHRIST: God go with you, Leslie. God go with you.

She goes.

SOLDIER *(to the audience)*: Well, that's got rid of her. Now the thing is will Teresa go to the cops? Even if old Einstein is half sozzled there's still the other two to get through. Will they shoot me? Yeah, I s'pose so. Will Teresa go to the cops? No.

There is an explosion which shakes the house and smoke wreathes the stage. Sirens blow, whistles scream and all the lights go out. PAT and MEG rush into the room and they and the SOLDIER hide behind the table. Pandemonium breaks out. What is actually happening is that MULLEADY has informed on PAT and MONSEWER and has brought the police to rescue LESLIE. He has involved RIO RITA and PRINCESS GRACE in his schemes and they have corrupted his morals. The RUSSIAN has been a police spy all along. The police are now attacking the house and MULLEADY and RIO RITA are guiding them in.

PAT: Take cover, there's a raid on.

MEG: I want to see what's going on.

PAT: Get your head down. They'll open fire any minute.

MULLEADY *(from the roof)*: Stand by. Two of you stay on the roof. The rest come down through the attic with me.

RIO RITA *(from the cellar)*: Six round the front, six round the back, and you two fellers follow me.

PAT: And take your partners for the eightsome reel. *(The piano plays.)*

MULLEADY: O'Shaunessy!

O'SHAUNESSY *(from the rear of the house)*: Sir!

MULLEADY: O'Shaunessy, shine a light for Jesus' sake.

O'SHAUNESSY *(off)*: I will, sir.

MULLEADY: Shine a light. I can't see a bloody thing.

O'SHAUNESSY *(off)*: I can't sir, the battery's gone.

MULLEADY: To hell with the battery.

RIO RITA: Charge!

> *His party go charging across the stage, but don't know where they're going or what they're doing. After confusion, they all charge back again.*

MULLEADY *(off)*: Right, down you go, O'Shaunessy.

O'SHAUNESSY: After you, sir.

MULLEADY: After you, man.

O'SHAUNESSY: After you, sir; I'm terrified of heights.

MULLEADY: Then close your eyes, man. This is war.

> *Pandemonium as the battle intensifies. Whistles and sirens blow, drums beat, bombs explode, bugles sound the attack, bullets ricochet and a confusion of orders are shouted all over the place. Bodies hurtle from one side of the stage to the other and, in the midst of all the chaos, the kilted figure of* MONSEWER *slow marches, serene and stately, across the stage, playing on his bagpipes a lament for the boy in Belfast Jail.* PAT *screams at him in vain.*

PAT: Sir! Sir! Get your head down. Get down, sir—there's a raid on. *(He touches* MONSEWER.*)*

MONSEWER: What? *(He stops playing and the din subsides.)*

PAT: There's a raid on.

MONSEWER: Then why the devil didn't you tell me? Man the barricades. Get the Mills bombs. Don't fire, laddie, till you see the whites of their eyes.

SOLDIER: I've only got a bottle.

MONSEWER: Up the Republic!

PAT: Get your head down, sir; they'll blow it off.

RIO RITA *(from under the stairs)*: Pat, do you want to buy a rifle?

PAT: Get out will you? (RIO RITA *goes.*)

The din subsides and the battle dies down. Inside the room are MONSEWER, *in command,* PAT *by the window, and* MEG, COLETTE, ROPEEN *and* LESLIE *crawling round on the floor. Around the room the shadowy shapes of the forces of law and order flit in and out, darting across the stage and under the stairs.*

MONSEWER: What's happening, Patrick?

PAT: I'll just find out, sir. (*He looks out of the window and improvises a running commentary on the events outside.*) They're just taking the field. The secret police is ready for the kick off, but the regulars is hanging back. Mr. Mulleady has placed himself at the head of the forces of law and order and Miss Gilchrist is bringing up his rear. Princess Grace has joined the police ... (*A whistle blows.*) The whistle's gone and they're off. (MULLEADY *crawls past the window on the window-sill.*) There's a man crawling along the gutter. He's going, he's going, he's gone! (*Crash of falling body, and a quarrel below.*)

SOLDIER: Teresa! Teresa! (*He thinks he's found her.*)

MEG: Shut up or I'll plug you, and your informer bitch when she comes in.

SOLDIER: Sorry, mum, I didn't know it was you.

There is an ominous silence. The piano is playing sinisterly.

MONSEWER: Where's that officer chap?

PAT: I can't see him anywhere, sir.

MONSEWER: Do you mean to say he's deserted in the face of fire?

Suddenly a bugle sounds the attack. Figures run to take up positions surrounding the room.

PAT: They're coming in.

MEG: Let's run for it.

MONSEWER: Hold fast!

PAT: I'm running. *(He runs.)*

MULLEADY: Halt, or I fire.

PAT: I'm halting. *(He stops with his hands up.)*

MONSEWER: Up the Republic!

SOLDIER: Up the Arsenal!

MULLEADY: Hands up, we're coming in.

MONSEWER: If you come in, we'll shoot the prisoner.

TERESA *(offstage)*: Run, Leslie, run.

> *The* SOLDIER *makes a break for it, zig-zagging across the stage, but every door is blocked. The drum echoes his runs with short rolls. As he makes his last run there is a deafening blast of gunfire and he drops.*

MULLEADY: Right, boys, over the top. *(*MULLEADY'S *men storm into the room and round up the defenders.* MULLEADY *is masked.)*

MONSEWER: Patrick, we're surrounded.

MEG *(to* PRINCESS GRACE*)*: Drop that gun or I'll kick you up the backside.

MONSEWER: Who are you?

MULLEADY: I'm a secret policeman and I don't care who knows it. *(He reveals himself. Two nuns scurry across the room and up the stairs, praying softly.)* Arrest those women. *(They are the two* I.R.A. *men in disguise.* TERESA *rushes into the room.)*

TERESA: Leslie! Leslie! Where's Leslie?

> *They all look around. No one has seen him.*

PAT: He was here a minute ago. *(He sees the body and goes down to it.)*

TERESA: Where is he? Leslie. *(She sees him.)*

MEG: There he is.

PAT: He's dead. Take his identification disc.

RIO RITA *(kneeling to do it)*: I'll do it, sir. *(Finding the medal.)* I didn't know he was a Catholic boy.

TERESA: I gave it to him. Leave it with him.

MULLEADY: Cover him up.

> RIO RITA *covers the body with one of the nun's cloaks.* TERESA *kneels by the body. The others bare their heads.*

TERESA: Leslie, my love. A thousand blessings go with you.

PAT: Don't cry, Teresa. It's no one's fault. Nobody meant to kill him.

TERESA: But he's dead.

PAT: So is the boy in Belfast Jail.

TERESA: It wasn't the Belfast Jail or the Six Counties that was troubling you, but your lost youth and your crippled leg. He died in a strange land, and at home he had no one. I'll never forget you, Leslie, till the end of time.

> *She rises and everyone turns away from the body. A ghostly green light glows on the body as* LESLIE WILLIAMS *slowly gets up and sings*:

The bells of hell,
Go ting-a-ling-a-ling,
For you but not for me,
Oh death, where is thy sting-a-ling-a-ling?
Or grave thy victory?
If you meet the undertaker,
Or the young man from the Pru,
Get a pint with what's left over,
Now I'll say goodbye to you.

> *The stage brightens, and everyone turns and comes down towards the audience, singing*:

The bells of hell,
Go ting-a-ling-a-ling,
For you but not for him,
Oh death, where is thy sting-a-ling-a-ling!
Or grave thy victory.

Curtain.

ROOTS

Arnold Wesker

ROOTS was first presented at the Belgrade Theatre, Coventry, on 25 May 1959. In the initial presentation of the complete Wesker trilogy, it was presented at the Royal Court Theatre, London, 28 July 1960, directed by John Dexter, designed by Jocelyn Herbert, and with the following cast:

BEATIE BRYANT, *a young woman aged twenty-two, a friend of Ronnie Kahn*	Joan Plowright
JENNY BEALES, *her sister*	Patsy Byrne
JIMMY BEALES, *her brother-in-law*	Charles Kay
MRS. BRYANT, *her mother*	Gwen Nelson
MR. BRYANT, *her father*	John Colin
FRANKIE BRYANT, *her brother*	Alan Howard
PEARL BRYANT, *her sister-in-law*	Cherry Morris
STAN MANN, a neighbour of the Bealses	Frank Finlay
MR. HEALEY, *a manager at the farm*	Anthony Hall

Act I: *An isolated cottage in Norfolk, the house of the Bealeses.*

Act II, Scene 1: *Two days later at the cottage of Mr. and Mrs. Bryant, in the kitchen.*

Act II, Scene 2: *The same a couple of hours later.*

Act III: *Two weeks later in the front room of the Bryants.*

Time: *The present.*

NOTE ON PRONUNCIATION

This is a play about Norfolk people; it could be a play about any country people and the moral could certainly extend to the metropolis. But as it is about Norfolk people it is important that some attempt is made to find out how they talk. A very definite accent and intonation exists and personal experience suggests that this is not difficult to know. The following may be of great help:

When the word "won't" is used, the "w" is left out. It sounds the same but the "w" is lost.

Double "ee" is pronounced "i" as in "it"—so that "been" becomes "bin," "seen" becomes "sin," etc.

"Have" and "had" become "hev" and "hed" as in "head."

"Ing" loses the "g" so that it becomes "in."

"Boy" is a common handle and is pronounced "bor" to sound like "bore."

Instead of the word "of" they say "on," e.g. "I've hed enough on it" or "What do you think on it?"

Their "yes" is used all the time and sounds like "year" with a "p"—"yearp."

"Blast" is also common usage and is pronounced "blust," a short sharp sound as in "gust."

The cockney "ain't" becomes "ent"—also short and sharp.

The "t" in "what" and "that" is left out to give "thaas" and "whaas," e.g. "Whaas matter then?"

Other idiosyncrasies are indicated in the play itself.

ACT ONE

A rather ramshackle house in Norfolk where there is no water laid on, nor electricity, nor gas. Everything rambles and the furniture is cheap and old. If it is untidy it is because there is a child in the house and there are few amenities, so that the mother is too over-worked to take much care.

An assortment of clobber lies around: papers and washing, coats and basins, a tin wash-tub with shirts and underwear to be cleaned, tilly lamps and primus stoves. Washing hangs on a line in the room. It is September.

JENNY BEALES is by the sink washing up. She is singing a recent pop song. She is short, fat and friendly, and wears glasses. A child's voice is heard from the bedroom crying "Sweet, Mamma, sweet."

JENNY (*good-naturedly*): Shut you up Daphne and get you to sleep now. (*Moves to get a dishcloth.*)

CHILD'S VOICE: Daphy wan' sweet, sweet, sweet.

JENNY (*going to cupboard to get sweet*): My word child, Father come home and find you awake he'll be after you. (*Disappears to bedroom with sweet.*) There—now sleep, gal, don't wan' you grumpy wi' me in mornin'.

Enter JIMMY BEALES. Also short, chubby, blond though hardly any hair left, ruddy complexion. He is a garage mechanic. Wears blue dungarees and an army pack slung over his shoulder. He wheels his bike in and lays it by the wall. Seems to be in some sort of pain—around his back. JENNY returns.

Waas matter wi' you then?

JIMMY: I don' know gal. There's a pain in my guts and one a'tween my shoulder blades I can hardly stand up.

JENNY: Sit you down then an' I'll git you your supper on the table.

JIMMY: Blust gal! I can't eat yit.

JIMMY *picks up a pillow from somewhere and lies down on sofa holding pillow to stomach.* JENNY *watches him a while.*

JENNY: Don't you know what 'tis yit?

JIMMY: Well, how should *I* know what 'tis.

JENNY: I told Mother about the pain and she says it's indigestion.

JIMMY: What the hell's indigestion doin' a'tween my shoulder blades then?

JENNY: She say some people get indigestion so bad it go right through their stomach to the back.

JIMMY: Don't be daft.

JENNY: That's what I say. Blust Mother, I say, you don't git indigestion in the back. Don't you tell me, she say, I hed it!

JIMMY: What hevn't she hed.

JENNY *returns to washing up while* JIMMY *struggles a while on the sofa.* JENNY *hums. No word. Then—*

JENNY: Who d'you see today?

JIMMY: Only Doctor Gallagher.

JENNY (*wheeling round*) : You see who?

JIMMY: Gallagher. His wife driv him up in the ole Armstrong.

JENNY: Well I go t'hell if that ent a rum thing.

JIMMY (*rising and going to table; pain has eased*) : What's that then?

JENNY (*moving to get him supper from oven*) : We was down at the whist drive in the village and that Judy Maitland say he were dead. 'Cos you know he've hed a cancer this last year and they don't give him no longer'n three weeks don't you?

JIMMY: Ole crows. They don't wan' nothin' less than a death to wake them up.

JENNY: No. No longer'n three weeks.

GIRL'S VOICE (*off*) : Yoo-hoo! Yoo-hoo!

JIMMY: There's your sister.

JENNY: That's her.

GIRL'S VOICE (*off*) : Yoo-hoo! Anyone home?

JENNY (*calling*) : Come you on in gal, don't you worry about yoo-hoo.

Enter BEATIE BRYANT, *an ample, blonde, healthy-faced young woman of twenty-two years. She is carrying a case.*

JIMMY: Here she is.

JENNY (*with reserve, but pleased*) : Hello, Beatrice—how are you?

BEATIE (*with reserve, but pleased*) : Hello, Jenny—how are you? What's that lovely smell I smell?

JENNY: Onions for supper and bread for the harvest festival.

BEATIE: Watcha Jimmy Beales, how you doin' bor?

JIMMY: Not so bad gal, how's yourself?

BEATIE: All right you know. When you comin' to London again for a football match?

JIMMY: O blust gal, I don' wanna go to any more o' those things. Ole father Bryant was there in the middle of that crowd and he turn around an' he say (*imitating*), Stop you a-pushin' there, he say, stop you a-pushin'.

JENNY: Where's Ronnie?

BEATIE: He's comin' down at the end of two weeks.

JIMMY: Ent you married yit?

BEATIE: No.

JIMMY: You wanna hurry then gal, a long engagement don't do the ole legs any good.

JENNY: Now shut you up Jimmy Beales and get that food down you. Every time you talk, look, you miss a mouthful? That's why you complain of pain in your shoulder blades.

BEATIE: You bin hevin' pains then Jimmy?

JIMMY: Blust yes! Right a'tween my shoulder blades.

JENNY: Mother says it's indigestion.

BEATIE: What the hell's indigestion doin' a'tween his shoulder blades?

JENNY: Mother reckon some people get indigestion so bad it go right through their stomach to the back.

BEATIE: Don't talk daft!

JENNY: That's what I say. Blust Mother, I say, you don' git indigestion in the back. Don't you tell me, she say, I hed it!

BEATIE: What hevn't she hed. How is she?

JENNY: Still the same you know. How long you staying this time?

BEATIE: Two days here—two weeks at home.

JENNY: Hungry gal?

BEATIE: Watcha got?

JENNY: Watcha see.

BEATIE: Liver? I'll hev it!

BEATIE *makes herself at home. Near by is a pile of comics. She picks one up and reads.*

JENNY: We got some ice-cream after.

BEATIE *(absorbed)* : Yearp.

JENNY: Look at her. No sooner she's in than she's at them ole comics. You still read them ole things?

JIMMY: She don't change much do she?

BEATIE: Funny that! Soon ever I'm home again I'm like I always was—it don' even seem I bin away. I do the same lazy things an' I talk the same. Funny that!

JENNY: What do Ronnie say to it?

BEATIE: He don't mind. He don't even know though. He ent never bin here. Not in the three years I known him. But I'll tell you *(she jumps up and moves around as she talks)* I used to read the comics he bought for his nephews and he used to get riled—

Now BEATIE *begins to quote Ronnie, and when she does she imitates him so well in both manner and intonation that in fact as the play progresses we see a picture of him through her.)*

"Christ, woman, what can they give you that you can *be* so absorbed?" So you know what I used to do? I used to get a

copy of the *Manchester Guardian* and sit with that wide open
—and a comic behind!

JIMMY: *Manchester Guardian*? Blimey Joe—he don' believe in
hevin' much fun then?

BEATIE: That's what I used to tell him. "Fun?" he say, "fun?
Playing an instrument is fun, painting is fun, reading a book
is fun, talking with friends is fun—but a comic? A comic?
for a young woman of twenty-two?"

JENNY (*handing out meal and sitting down herself*) : He sound a
queer bor to me. Sit you down and eat gal.

BEATIE (*enthusiastically*) : He's alive though.

JIMMY: Alive? Alive you say? What's alive about someone who
can't read a comic? What's alive about a person that reads
books and looks at paintings and listens to classical music?

*There is a silence at this, as though the question answers
itself—reluctantly.*

JIMMY: Well, it's all right for some I suppose.

BEATIE: And then he'd sneak the comic away from me and read
it his-self!

JENNY: Oh, he didn't really mind then?

BEATIE: No—'cos sometimes I read books as well. "There's nothing
wrong with comics," he'd cry—he stand up on a chair when
he want to preach but don't wanna sound too dramatic.

JIMMY: Eh?

BEATIE: Like this, look. (*Stands on a chair.*) "There's nothing
wrong with comics only there's something wrong with comics
all the time. There's nothing wrong with football, only there's
something wrong with *only* football. There's nothing wrong
with rock 'n' rolling, only God preserve me from the girl that
can do nothing else!" (*She sits down and then stands up
again, remembering something else.*) Oh yes, "and there's
nothing wrong with talking about the weather, only don't
talk to me about it!" (*Sits down.*)

JIMMY *and* JENNY *look at each other as though she, and no
doubt Ronnie, is a little barmy.* JIMMY *rises and begins to*

*strap on boots and gaiters ready for going out to an allot-
ment.*

JENNY: He never really row with you then?

BEATIE: We used to. There was a time when he handled all official
things for me you know. Once I was in between jobs and I
didn't think to ask for my unemployment benefit. *He* told me
to. But when I asked they told me I was short on stamps and
so I wasn't entitled to benefit. *I* didn't know what to say but
he did. He went up and argued for me—he's just like his
mother, she argues with everyone—and I got it. I didn't know
how to talk see, it was all foreign to me. Think of it! An
English girl born and bred and I couldn't talk the language
—except for to buy food and clothes. And so sometimes when
he were in a black mood he'd start on me. "What can you
talk of?" he'd ask. "Go on, pick a subject. Talk. Use the
language. Do you know what language is?" Well, I'd never
thought before—hev you?—it's automatic to you isn't it, like
walking? "Well, language is words," he'd say, as though he
were telling me a secret. "It's bridges, so that you can get
safely from one place to another. And the more bridges you
know about the more places you can see!" (*To* JIMMY) And
do *you* know what happens when you can see a place but you
don't know where the bridge is?

JIMMY (*angrily*) : Blust gal, what the hell are you on about.

BEATIE: Exactly! You see, you hev a row! Still, rows is all right. I
like to row. So then he'd say: "Bridges! bridges! bridges! Use
your bridges woman. It took thousands of years to build them,
use them!" And that riled me. "Blust your bridges," I'd say.
"Blust you and your bridges—I want a row." Then he'd grin
at me. "You want a row?" he'd ask. "No bridges this time?"
"No bridges," I'd say—and we'd row. Sometimes he hurt me
but then, slowly, he'd build the bridge up *for* me—and then
we'd make love! (*Innocently continues her meal.*)

JENNY: You'd what, did you say?

BEATIE: Make love. Love in the afternoon gal. Ever had it? It's
the only time *for* it. Go out or entertain in the evenings;
sleep at night, study, work and chores in the mornings; but

love—alert and fresh, when you got most energy—love in the afternoon.

JIMMY: I suppose you take time off from work every afternoon to do it?

BEATIE: I'm talking about week-ends and holidays—daft.

JENNY: Oh, Beatie, go on wi' you!

BEATIE: Well, go t'hell Jenny Beales, you're blushin'. Ent you never had love in the afternoon? Ask Jimmy then.

JENNY (*rising to get sweet*) : Shut you up gal and get on wi' your ice-cream. It's strawberry flavour. Want some more James?

JIMMY (*taking it in the middle of lacing up boots*) : Yes please, vanilla please. (*Eating*) Good cream ent it? Made from the white milk of a Jersey cow.

BEATIE: This is good too—made from pink milk ent it?

Pause.

JIMMY: Yearp! (*Pause.*) Come from a pink cow!

Pause. They are all enjoying the cream.

JENNY (*eating*) : You remember Dickie Smart, Beatie?

BEATIE (*eating*) : Who?

JENNY (*eating*) : We had a drink wi' him in the Storks when you was down last.

BEATIE (*eating*) : Yearp.

JENNY (*eating*) : Well, he got gored by a bull last Thursday. His left ear was nearly off, his knee were gored, his ribs bruised, and the ligaments of his legs torn.

Pause as they finish eating.

BEATIE (*euphemistically*) : He had a rough time then!

JENNY: Yearp. (*To* JIMMY) You off now?

JIMMY: Mm.

JENNY *collects dishes.*

BEATIE: Still got your allotment Jimmy?

JIMMY: Yearp.

BEATIE: Bit heavy going this weather.

JIMMY: That ent too bad just yit—few more weeks an' the old mowld'll cling.

BEATIE: Watcha got this year?

JIMMY: Had spuds, carrots, cabbages you know. Beetroot, lettuces, onions, and peas. But me runners let me down this year though.

JENNY: I don't go much on them old things.

BEATIE: You got a fair owle turn then?

JIMMY: Yearp.

JIMMY *starts to sharpen a reap hook.*

BEATIE (*jumping up*): I'll help you wash.

JENNY: That's all right gal.

BEATIE: Where's the cloth?

JENNY: Here 'tis.

BEATIE *helps collect dishes from table and proceeds to help wash up. This is a silence that needs organizing. Throughout the play there is no sign of intense living from any of the characters—*BEATIE's *bursts are the exception. They continue in a routine rural manner. The day comes, one sleeps at night, there is always the winter, the spring, the autumn, and the summer—little amazes them. They talk in fits and starts mainly as a sort of gossip, and they talk quickly too, enacting as though for an audience what they say. Their sense of humour is keen and dry. They show no affection for each other—though this does not mean they would not be upset were one of them to die. The silences are important—as important as the way they speak, if we are to know them.*

JENNY: What about that strike in London? Waas London like wi'out the buses?

BEATIE: Lovely! No noise—and the streets, you should see the streets, flowing with people—the city looks human.

JIMMY: They wanna call us Territorials out—we'd soon break the strike.

BEATIE: That's a soft thing for a worker to say for his mates.

JIMMY: Soft be buggered, soft you say? What they earnin' those busmen, what they earnin'? And what's the farm worker's wage? Do you know it gal?

BEATIE: Well, let the farm workers go on strike too then! It don't help a farm labourer if a busman don't go on strike do it now?

JENNY: You know they've got a rise though. Father Bryant's go up by six and six a week as a pigman, and Frank goes up seven 'n' six a week for driving a tractor.

JIMMY: But you watch the Hall sack some on 'em.

JENNY: Thaas true Beatie. They're such sods, honest to God they are. Every time there's bin a rise someone get sacked. Without fail. You watch it—you ask father Bryant when you get home, ask him who's bin sacked since the rise.

BEATIE. One person they 'ont sack is him though. They 'ont find many men 'd tend to pigs seven days a week and stay up the hours he do.

JENNY: Bloody fool! (*Pause.*) Did Jimmy tell you he've bin chosen for the Territorials' Jubilee in London this year?

BEATIE: What's this then? What'll you do there?

JIMMY: Demonstrate and parade wi' arms and such like.

BEATIE: Won't do you any good.

JIMMY: Don't you reckon? Gotta show we can defend the country you know. Demonstrate arms and you prevent war.

BEATIE (*she has finished wiping up*): Won't demonstrate anything bor. (*Goes to undo her case.*) Present for the house! Have a hydrogen bomb fall on you and you'll find them things silly in your hands. (*Searches for other parcels.*)

JIMMY: So you say gal? So you say? That'll frighten them other buggers though.

BEATIE: Frighten yourself y'mean. (*Finds parcels.*) Presents for the kid.

JIMMY: And what do you know about this all of a sudden?

JENNY (*revealing a tablecloth*): Thank you very much Beatie. Just what I need.

BEATIE: You're not interested in defending your country Jimmy, you just enjoy playing soldiers.

JIMMY: What did I do in the last war then—*sing* in the trenches?

BEATIE (*explaining—not trying to get one over on him*): Ever heard of Chaucer, Jimmy?

JIMMY: No.

BEATIE: Do you know the M.P. for this constituency?

JIMMY: What you drivin' at gal—don't give me no riddles.

BEATIE: Do you know how the British Trade Union Movement started? And do you believe in strike action?

JIMMY: No to both those.

BEATIE: What you goin' to war to defend then?

JIMMY (*he is annoyed now*): Beatie—you bin away from us a long time now—you got a boy who's educated an' that and he's taught you a lot maybe. But don't you come pushin' ideas across at us—we're all right as we are. You can come when you like an' welcome but don't bring no discussion of politics in the house wi' you 'cos that'll only cause trouble. I'm telling you. (*He goes off.*)

JENNY: Blust gal, if you hevn't touched him on a sore spot. He live for them Territorials he do—that's half his life.

BEATIE (*she is upset now*): What's he afraid of talking for?

JENNY: He ent afraid of talking Beatie—blust he can do that, gal.

BEATIE: But not talk, not really talk, not use bridges. I sit with Ronnie and his friends sometimes and I listen to them talk about things and you know I've never heard half of the words before.

JENNY: Don't he tell you what they mean?

BEATIE: I get annoyed when he keep tellin' me—and he want me to ask. (*Imitates him half-heartedly now.*) "Always ask, people love to tell you what they know, always ask and people will respect you."

JENNY: And do you?

BEATIE: No! I don't! An' you know why? Because I'm stubborn, I'm like Mother, I'm stubborn. Somehow I just can't bring myself to ask, and you know what? I go mad when I listen to them. As soon as they start to talk about things I don't know about or I can't understand I get mad. They sit there, casually talking, and suddenly they turn on you, abrupt. "Don't you think?" they say. Like at school, pick on you and

ask a question you ent ready for. Sometimes I don't say anything, sometimes I go to bed or leave the room. Like Jimmy—
just like Jimmy.

JENNY: And what do Ronnie say to that then?

BEATIE: He get mad too. "Why don't you ask me woman, for
God's sake why don't you ask me? Aren't I dying to tell you
about things? Only ask!"

JENNY: And he's goin' to marry you?

BEATIE: Why not?

JENNY: Well I'm sorry gal, you mustn't mind me saying this,
but it don't seem to me like you two got much in common.

BEATIE (*loudly*) : It's not true! We're in love!

JENNY: Well, you know.

BEATIE (*softly*) : No, I don't know. I won't know till he come here.
From the first day I went to work as waitress in the Dell
Hotel and saw him working in the kitchen I fell in love—
and I thought it was easy. I thought everything was easy. I
chased him for three months with compliments and presents
until I finally give myself to him. He never said he love me
nor I didn't care but once he had taken me he seemed to
think he was responsible for me and I told him no different.
I'd *make* him love me I thought. I didn't know much about
him except he was different and used to write most of the
time. And then he went back to London and I followed him
there. I've never moved far from home but I did for him
and he felt all the time he couldn't leave me and I didn't tell
him no different. And then I got to know more about him.
He was interested in all the things I never even thought
about. About politics and art and all that, and he tried to
teach me. He's a socialist and he used to say you couldn't
bring socialism to a country by making speeches, but perhaps
you could pass it on to someone who was near you. So I pre-
tended I was interested—but I didn't understand much. All
the time he's trying to teach me but I can't take it Jenny.
And yet, at the same time, I want to show I'm willing. I'm
not used to learning. Learning was at school and that's finished with.

JENNY: Blust gal, you don't seem like you're going to be happy then. Like I said.

BEATIE: But I love him.

JENNY: Then you're not right in the head then.

BEATIE: I couldn't have any other life now.

JENNY: Well, I don't know and that's a fact.

BEATIE (*playfully mocking her*): Well I don't know and that's a fact! (*Suddenly*) Come on gal, I'll teach you how to bake some pastries.

JENNY: Pastries?

BEATIE: Ronnie taught me.

JENNY: Oh, you learnt that much then?

BEATIE: But he don't know. I always got annoyed when he tried to teach me to cook as well—Christ! I had to know something—but it sank in all the same.

By this time it has become quite dark and JENNY *proceeds to light a tilly lamp.*

JENNY: You didn't make it easy then?

BEATIE: Oh don't you worry gal, it'll be all right once we're married. Once we're married and I got babies I won't need to be interested in half the things I got to be interested in now.

JENNY: No you won't will you! Don't need no education for babies.

BEATIE: Nope. Babies is babies—you just have 'em.

JENNY: Little sods!

BEATIE: You gonna hev another Jenny?

JENNY: Well, course I am. What you on about? Think Jimmy don't want none of his own?

BEATIE: He's a good man Jenny.

JENNY: Yearp.

BEATIE: Not many men 'd marry you after you had a baby.

JENNY: No.

BEATIE: He didn't ask you any questions? Who was the father? Nor nothing?

JENNY: No.

BEATIE: You hevn't told no one hev you Jenny?

JENNY: No, that I hevn't.

BEATIE: Well, that's it gal, don't you tell me then!

By this time the methylated spirit torch has burned out and JENNY *has finished pumping the tilly lamp and we are in brightness.*

JENNY (*severely*) : Now Beatie, stop it. Every time you come home you ask me that question and I hed enough. It's finished with and over. No one don't say nothing and no one know. You hear me?

BEATIE: Are you in love with Jimmy?

JENNY: Love? I don't believe in any of that squit—we just got married, an' that's that.

BEATIE (*suddenly looking around the room at the general chaos*) : Jenny Beales, just look at this house. Look at it!

JENNY: I'm looking. What's wrong?

BEATIE: Let's clean it up.

JENNY: Clean what up?

BEATIE: Are you going to live in this house all your life?

JENNY: You gonna buy us another?

BEATIE: Stuck out here in the wilds with only ole Stan Mann and his missus as a neighbour and sand pits all around. Every time it rain look you're stranded.

JENNY: Jimmy don't earn enough for much more 'n we got.

BEATIE: But it's so untidy.

JENNY: You don' wan' me bein' like sister Susan do you? 'Cos you know how clean she is don' you—she's so bloody fussy she's gotten to polishing the brass overflow pipe what leads out from the lavatory.

BEATIE: Come on gal, let's make some order anyway—I love tidying up.

JENNY: What about the pastries? Pastries? Oh my sainted aunt, the bread! (*Dashes to the oven and brings out a most beautiful-looking plaited loaf of bread. Admiring it*) Well, no one wanna complain after that. Isn't that beautiful Beatie?

BEATIE: I could eat it now.

JENNY: You hungry again?

BEATIE (*making an attack upon the clothes that are lying around*) : "I'm always hungry again. Ronnie say I eat more'n I need. "If you get fat woman I'll leave you—without even a discussion!"

JENNY (*placing bread on large oval plate to put away*) : Well, there ent nothin' wrong in bein' fat.

BEATIE: You ent got no choice gal. (*Seeing bike*) A bike! What's a bike doin' in a livin' room—I'm putting it outside.

JENNY: Jimmy 'ont know where it is.

BEATIE: Don't be daft, you can't miss a bike. (*Wheels it outside and calls from there.*) Jenny! Start puttin' the clothes away.

JENNY: Blust gal, I ent got nowhere to put them.

BEATIE (*from outside*) : You got drawers—you got cupboards.

JENNY: They're full already.

BEATIE (*entering—energy sparks from her*) : Come here—let's look. (*Looks.*) Oh, go away—you got enough room for ten families. You just bung it all in with no order, that's why. Here—help me.

They drag out all manner of clothes from the cupboard and begin to fold them up.

BEATIE: How's my Frankie and Pearl?

JENNY: They're all right. You know she and Mother don't talk to each other?

BEATIE: What, again? Whose fault is it this time?

JENNY: Well, Mother she say it's Pearl's fault and Pearl she say it's Mother.

BEATIE: Well, they wanna get together quick and find whose fault it is 'cos I'm going to call the whole family together for tea to meet Ronnie.

JENNY: Well, Susan and Mother don't talk neither so you got a lot of peace-making to do.

BEATIE: Well go t'hell, what's broken them two up?

JENNY: Susan hev never bin struck on her mother, you know that don't you—well, it seems that Susan bought something off the club from Pearl and Pearl give it to Mother and Mother sent it to Susan through the fishmonger what live next door her in the council houses. And of course Susan were riled 'cos she didn't want her neighbours to know that she bought anything off the club. So they don't speak.

BEATIE: Kids! It make me mad.

JENNY: And you know what 'tis with Pearl don't you—it's 'cos Mother hev never thought she was good enough for her son Frankie.

BEATIE: No more she wasn't neither!

JENNY: What's wrong wi' her then? I get on all right.

BEATIE: Nothing's wrong wi' her, she just wasn't good enough for our Frankie, that's all.

JENNY: Who's being small-minded now?

BEATIE: Always wantin' more'n he can give her.

JENNY: An' I know someone else who always wanted more'n she got.

BEATIE (*sulkily*) : It's not the same thing.

JENNY: Oh yes 'tis.

BEATIE: 'Tent.

JENNY: 'Tis my gal. (*Mimicking the child* BEATIE) I wan' a 'nana, a 'nana, a 'nana. Frankie's got my 'nana, 'nana, 'nana.

BEATIE: Well, I liked bananas.

JENNY: You liked anything you could get your hands on and Mother used to give in to you 'cos you were the youngest. Me and Susan and Frankie never got nothing 'cos o' you— 'cept a clout round the ear.

BEATIE: 'Tent so likely. You got everything and I got nothing.

JENNY: All we got was what we pinched out the larder and then you used to go and tell tales to Mother.

BEATIE: I never did.

JENNY: Oh, didn't you my gal? Many's the time I'd've willingly strangled you—with no prayers—there you are, no prayers whatsoever. Strangled you till you was dead.

BEATIE: Oh go on wi' you Jenny Beales.

By now they have finished folding the clothes and have put away most of the laundry and garments that have till this moment cluttered up the room. BEATIE *says* "There," *stands up and looks around, finds some coats sprawled helter-skelter, and hangs them up behind the door.*

BEATIE: I'll buy you some coat hangers.

JENNY: You get me a couple o' coats to hang on 'em first please.

BEATIE (*looking around*): What next. Bottles, jars, nicknacks, saucepans, cups, papers—everything anywhere. Look at it! Come on!

BEATIE *attempts to get these things either into their proper place or out of sight.*

JENNY: You hit this place like a bloody whirlwind you do, like a bloody whirlwind. Jimmy'll think he've come into the wrong house and I shan't be able to find a thing.

BEATIE: Here, grab a broom. (*She is now gurgling with sort of animal noises signifying excitement. Her joy is childlike.*) How's Poppy?

JENNY: Tight as ever.

BEATIE: What won't he give you now?

JENNY: 'Tent nothing wi' me gal. Nothing he do don't affect me. It's Mother I'm referring to.

BEATIE: Don't he still give her much money?

JENNY: Money? She hev to struggle and skint all the time—*all* the time. Well it ent never bin no different from when we was kids hev it?

BEATIE: No.

JENNY: I tell you what. It wouldn't surprise me if Mother were in debt all the time, that it wouldn't. No. It wouldn't surprise me at all.

BEATIE: Oh, never.

JENNY: Well, what do you say that for Beatie—do you know how much he allow her a week look?

BEATIE: Six pounds?

JENNY: Six pounds be buggered. Four pounds ten! An' she hev to keep house *an'* buy her own clothes out of that.

BEATIE: Still, there's only two on 'em.

JENNY: You try keepin' two people in food for four pound ten. She pay seven an' six a week into Pearl's club for clothes, two and six she hev on the pools, and a shilling a week on the Labour Tote. (*Suddenly*) Blust! I forgot to say. Pearl won the Tote last week.

BEATIE: A hundred pounds?

JENNY: A hundred pounds! An' ole Mrs. Dyson what used to live Startson way, she come up second wi' five pounds and seventy.

BEATIE: Well no one wrote me about it.

JENNY: 'Cos you never wrote no one else.

BEATIE: What she gonna do wi' it—buy a TV?

JENNY: TV? Blust no. You know she hevn't got electricity in that house. No, she say she's gonna get some clothes for the kids.

There is a sound now of a drunk old man approaching, and alongside of it the voice of JIMMY. *The drunk is singing:* "I come from Bungay Town. I calls I Bungay Johnnie."

Well I go t'hell if that ent Stan Mann drunk again. And is that Jimmy wi' him? (*Listens.*)

BEATIE: But I thought Stan Mann was paralysed.

JENNY: That don't stop him getting paralytic drunk. (*Listens again.*) That's Jimmy taking him into the house I bet. A fortune that man hev drunk away—a whole bleedin' fortune. Remember the fleet of cars he used to run and all that land he owned, and all them cattle he had and them fowl? Well, he've only got a few acres left and a few ole chickens. He drink it all away. Two strokes he've had from drinking and now he's paralysed down one side. But that don't stop him getting drunk—no it don't.

JIMMY *enters and throws his jacket on the couch, takes off his boots and gaiters, and smiles meanwhile.*

JIMMY: Silly ole bugger.

JENNY: I was just telling Beatie how he've drunk a fortune away hevn't he?

JIMMY: He wanna drink a little more often and he'll be finished for good.

JENNY: Didn't he hev all them cows and cars and land Jimmy? And didn't he drink it all away bit by bit?

JIMMY: Silly ole sod don't know when to stop.

JENNY: I wished I had half the money he drink.

JIMMY: He messed his pants.

JENNY: He what? Well where was this then?

JIMMY: By the allotment.

JENNY: Well, what did *you* do then?

JIMMY: He come up to me—'course I knowed he were drunk the way he walk—he come up to me an' he say, "Evenin' Jimmy Beales, thaas a fine turnover you got there." An' I say, "Yearp 'tis." An' then he bend down to pick a carrot from the ground an' then he cry, "Oops, I done it again!" An' 'course, soon ever he say "done it again" I knowed what'd happened. So I took his trousers down and ran the ole hose over him.

BEATIE: Oh, Jimmy, you never did.

JIMMY: I did gal. I put the ole hose over him and brought him home along the fields with an ole sack around his waist.

BEATIE: He'll catch his death.

JIMMY: Never—he's strong as an ox.

JENNY: What'd you do with his trousers and things!

JIMMY: Put it on the compost heap—good for the land!

Now STAN MANN *enters. He's not all that drunk. The cold water has sobered him a little. He is old—about seventy-five —and despite his slight stoop one can see he was a very strong upright man. He probably looks like everyman's idea of a farmer—except that he wears no socks or boots at this moment and he hobbles on a stick.*

STAN: Sorry about that ole son.

JIMMY: Don't you go worrying about that my manny—get you along to bed.

JENNY: Get some shoes on you too Stan, or you'll die of cold *and* booze.

STAN (*screwing up his eyes across the room*): Is that you Jenny? Hello ole gal. How are you?

JENNY: It's you you wanna worry about now ole matey. I'm well enough.

STAN (*screwing his eyes still more*) : Who's that next to you?

JENNY: Don't you recognize her? It's our Beatie, Stan.

STAN: Is that you Beatie? Well blust gal, you gotten fatter since I seen you last. You gonna be fat as Jenny here? Come on over an' let's look at you.

BEATIE (*approaching*) : Hello Stan Mann, how are you?

STAN (*looking her up and down*) : Well enough gal, well enough. You married yit?

BEATIE: No.

STAN: You bin courtin' three years. Why ent you married yit?

BEATIE (*slightly embarrassed*) : We ent sure yit.

STAN: You ent sure you say? What ent you sure of? You know how to do it don't you?

JENNY: Go on wi' you to bed Stan Mann.

STAN: Tell your boy he don't wanna waste too much time or I'll be hevin' yer myself for breakfast—on a plate.

JENNY: Stan Mann, I'm sendin' you to your bed—go on now, off wi' you, you can see Beatie in the mornin'.

STAN (*as he is ushered out—to* BEATIE) : She's fat ent she? I'm not sayin' she won't do mind, but she's fat. (*As he goes out*) All right ole sweetheart, I'm goin'. I'm just right for bed. Did you see the new bridge they're building? It's a rum ole thing isn't it . . . (*out of sound.*)

JIMMY: Well, I'm ready for bed.

BEATIE: I can't bear sick men. They smell.

JIMMY: Ole Stan's all right—do anythin' for you.

BEATIE: I couldn't look after one you know.

JIMMY: Case of hevin' to sometimes.

BEATIE: Ronnie's father's paralysed like that. I can't touch him.

JIMMY: Who see to him then?

BEATIE: His mother. She wash him, change him, feed him. Ronnie help sometimes. I couldn't though. Ronnie say, "Christ, woman, I hope you aren't around when I'm ill." (*Shudders.*) Ole age terrify me.

JIMMY: Where you sleepin' tonight gal?

BEATIE: On the couch in the front room I suppose.

JIMMY: You comfortable sleepin' on that ole thing? You wanna sleep with Jenny while you're here?

BEATIE: No thanks, Jimmy. (*She is quite subdued now.*) I'm all right on there.

JIMMY: Right, then I'm off. (*Looking around*) Where's the *Evening News* I brought in?

JENNY (*entering*) : You off to bed?

JIMMY: Yearp. Reckon I've had 'nough of this ole day. Where's my *News*?

JENNY: Where'd you put it Beatie?

JIMMY (*suddenly seeing the room*) : Blust, you movin' out?

BEATIE: Here you are Jimmy Beales. (*Hands him paper.*) It's all tidy now.

JIMMY: So I see. Won't last long though will it? 'Night. (*Goes to bed.*)

JENNY: Well I'm ready for my bed too—how about you Beatie?

BEATIE: Yearp.

JENNY (*taking a candle in a stick and lighting it*) : Here, take this with you. Your bed's made. Want a drink before you turn in?

BEATIE: No thanks gal.

JENNY (*picking up tilly lamp and making towards one door*) : Right then. Sleep well gal.

BEATIE (*going to other door with candle*) : Good night Jenny. (*She pauses at her door. Loud whispers from now on.*) Hey Jenny.

JENNY: What is it?

BEATIE: I'll bake you some pastries when I get to Mother's.

JENNY: Father won't let you use his electricity for me, don't talk daft.

BEATIE: I'll get Mother on to him. It'll be all right. Your ole ovens weren't big 'nough anyways. Good night.

JENNY: Good night.

BEATIE (*an afterthought*) : Hey Jenny.

JENNY: What now?

BEATIE: Did I tell you I took up painting?

JENNY: Painting?

BEATIE: Yes—on cardboard and canvases with brushes.

JENNY: What kind of painting?

BEATIE: Abstract painting—designs and patterns and such like. I can't do nothing else. I sent two on 'em home. Show you when you come round—if Mother hevn't thrown them out.

JENNY: You're an artist then?

BEATIE: Yes. Good night.

JENNY: Good night.

They enter their bedrooms, leaving the room in darkness.[1]
Perhaps we see only the faint glow of moonlight from outside,
and then

The curtain falls.

---

[1] It might be better for Jenny to have previously made up Beatie's bed in the couch on the set. Then Beatie would not have to leave the stage at all.

ACT TWO

Scene One

Two days have passed. BEATIE *will arrive at her own home, the home of her parents. This is a tied cottage on a main road between two large villages. It is neat and ordinary inside. We can see a large kitchen—where most of the living is done—and attached to it is a large larder; also part of the front room and a piece of the garden where some washing is hanging.*

MRS. BRYANT *is a short, stout woman of fifty. She spends most of the day on her own, and consequently when she has a chance to speak to anybody she says as much as she can as fast as she can. The only people she sees are the tradesmen, her husband, the family when they pop in occasionally. She speaks very loudly all the time so that her friendliest tone sounds aggressive, and she manages to dramatize the smallest piece of gossip into something significant. Each piece of gossip is a little act done with little looking at the person to whom it is addressed. At the moment she is at the door leading to the garden, looking for the cat.*

MRS. BRYANT: Cossie, Cossie, Cossie, Cossie, Cossie, Cossie! Here Cossie! Food Cossie! Cossie, Cossie, Cossie! Blust you cat, where the hell are you. Oh hell on you then, I ent wastin' my time wi' you now.

She returns to the kitchen and thence the larder, from which she emerges with some potatoes. These she starts peeling. STAN MANN *appears round the back door. He has a handker-*

chief to his nose and is blowing vigorously, as vigorously as his paralysis will allow. MRS. BRYANT *looks up, but continues her peeling.*

STAN: Rum thing to git a cold in summer, what you say Daphne?

MRS. BRYANT: What'd you have me say my manny. Sit you down bor and rest a bit. Shouldn't wear such daf' clothes.

STAN: Daf' clothes? Blust woman! I got on half a cow's hide, what you sayin'! Where's the gal?

MRS. BRYANT: Beatie? She 'ent come yit. Didn't *you* see her?

STAN: Hell, I was up too early for her. She always stay the week-end wi' Jenny 'fore comin' home?

MRS. BRYANT: Most times.

STAN *sneezes.*

What you doin' up this way wi' a cold like that then? Get you home to bed.

STAN: Just come this way to look at the vicarage. Stuff's comin' up for sale soon.

MRS. BRYANT: You still visit them things then?

STAN: Yearp. Pass the ole time away. Pass the ole time.

MRS. BRYANT: Time drag heavy then?

STAN: Yearp. Time drag heavy. She do that. Time drag so slow, I get to thinkin' it's Monday when it's still Sunday. Still, I had my day gal I say. Yearp, I had that all right.

MRS. BRYANT: Yearp. You had that an' a bit more ole son. I shan't grumble if I last as long as you.

STAN: Yearp. I hed my day. An' I'd do it all the same again, you know that? Do it all the same I would.

MRS. BRYANT: Blust! All your drinkin' an' that?

STAN: Hell! Thaas what kep' me goin' look. Almost anyways. None o' them young 'uns'll do it, hell if they will. There ent much life in the young 'uns. Bunch o' weak-kneed ruffians. None on 'em like livin' look, none on 'em! You read in them ole papers what go on look, an' you wonder if they can see. You do! Wonder if they got eyes to look around them. Think they know where they live? 'Course they don't, they don't you know, not one. Blust! the winter go an' the spring come on after an' they don't see buds an' they don't smell no breeze an' they don't see gals, an' when they see gals they don't know whatta do wi' 'em. They don't!

MRS. BRYANT: Oh hell, they know *that* all right.

STAN: Gimme my young days an' I'd show 'em. Public demonstrations I'd give!

MRS. BRYANT: Oh shut you up Stan Mann.

STAN: Just gimme young days again Daphne Bryant an' I'd mount you. But they 'ont come again will they gal?

MRS. BRYANT: That they 'ont. My ole days working in the fields with them other gals, thems 'ont come again, either.

STAN: No, they 'ont that! Rum ole things the years ent they? (*Pause.*) Them young 'uns is all right though. Long as they don't let no one fool them, long as they think it out theirselves. (*Sneezes and coughs.*)

MRS. BRYANT (*moving to help him up*): Now get you back home Stan Mann. (*Good-naturedly*) Blust, I aren't hevin' no dead 'uns on me look. Take a rum bor, take a rum an' a drop o' hot milk and get to bed. What's Mrs. Mann thinking of lettin' you out like this.

She pulls the coat round the old man and pushes him off. He goes off mumbling and she returns, also mumbling, to her peeling.

STAN: She's a good gal, she's right 'nough, she don't think I got it this bad. I'll pull this ole scarf round me. Hed this scarf a long time, hed it since I started wi' me cars. *She* bought it me. Lasted a long time. Shouldn't need it this weather though. ... (*Exits.*)

MRS. BRYANT (*mumbling same time as* STAN): Go on, off you go. Silly ole bugger, runnin' round with a cold like that. Don't know what 'e's doin' half the time. Poor ole man. Cossie? Cossie? That you Cossie? (*Looks through door into front room and out of window at* STAN.) Poor ole man.

After peeling some seconds she turns the radio on, turning the dial knob through all manner of stations and back again until she finds some very loud dance music which she leaves blaring on. Audible to us, but not to MRS. BRYANT, *is the call of "Yoo-hoo Mother, yoo-hoo."* BEATIE *appears round the garden and peers into the kitchen.* MRS. BRYANT *jumps.)*

MRS. BRYANT: Blust, you made me jump.

BEATIE (*toning radio down*) : Can't you hear it? Hello, Mother. (*Kisses her.*)

MRS. BRYANT: Well, you've arrived then.

BEATIE: Didn't you get my card?

MRS. BRYANT: Came this morning.

BEATIE: Then you knew I'd arrive.

MRS. BRYANT: 'Course I did.

BEATIE: My things come?

MRS. BRYANT: One suitcase, one parcel in brown paper—

BEATIE: My paintings.

MRS. BRYANT: And one other case.

BEATIE: My pick-up. D'you see it?

MRS. BRYANT: I hevn't touched a thing.

BEATIE: Bought myself a pick-up on the H.P.

MRS. BRYANT: Don't you go telling that to Pearl.

BEATIE: Why not?

MRS. BRYANT: She'll wanna know why you didn't buy off her on the club.

BEATIE: Well, hell, Mother, I weren't gonna hev an ole pick-up sent me from up north somewhere when we lived next door to a gramophone shop.

MRS. BRYANT: No. Well, what bus you come on—the half-past-ten one?

BEATIE: Yearp. Picked it up on the ole bridge near Jenny's.

MRS. BRYANT: Well I looked for you on the half-past-nine bus and you weren't on that so I thought to myself I bet she come on the half-past-ten and you did. You see ole Stan Mann?

BEATIE: Was that him just going up the road?

MRS. BRYANT: Wearin' an ole brown scarf, that was him.

BEATIE: I see him! Just as I were comin' off the bus. Blust! Jimmy

Beales give him a real dowsin' down on his allotment 'cos he had an accident.

MRS. BRYANT: What, another?

BEATIE: Yearp.

MRS. BRYANT: Poor ole man. Thaas what give him that cold then. He come in here sneezin' fit to knock hisself down.

BEATIE: Poor ole bugger. Got any tea Ma? I'm gonna unpack.

BEATIE *goes into front room with case. We see her take out frocks, which she puts on hangers, and underwear and blouses, which she puts on couch.*

MRS. BRYANT: Did you see my flowers as you come in? Got some of my hollyhocks still flowering. Creeping up the wall they are—did you catch a glimpse on 'em? And my asters and geraniums? Poor ole Joe Simonds gimme those afore he died. Lovely geraniums they are.

BEATIE: Yearp.

MRS. BRYANT: When's Ronnie coming?

BEATIE: Saturday week—an' Mother, I'm heving all the family along to meet him when he arrive so you patch your rows wi' them.

MRS. BRYANT: What you on about gal? What rows wi' them?

BEATIE: You know full well what rows I mean—them ones you hev wi' Pearl and Susan.

MRS. BRYANT: 'Tent so likely. They hev a row wi' me gal but I give 'em no heed, that I don't. (*Hears van pass on road.*) There go Sam Martin's fish van. He'll be calling along here in an hour.

BEATIE (*entering with very smart dress*): Like it Mother?

MRS. BRYANT: Blust gal, that's a good 'un ent it! Where d'you buy that then?

BEATIE: Swan and Edgar's.

MRS. BRYANT: Did Ronnie choose it?

BEATIE: Yearp.

MRS. BRYANT: He've got good taste then.

BEATIE: Yearp. Now listen Mother, I don't want any on you to let me down. When Ronnie come I want him to see we're proper. I'll buy you another bowl so's you don't wash up in the same one as you wash your hands in and I'll get some more tea cloths so's you 'ont use the towels. And no swearin'.

MRS. BRYANT: Don't he swear then?

BEATIE: He swear all right, only I don't want him to hear *you* swear.

MRS. BRYANT: Hev you given it up then?

BEATIE: Mother, I've never swore.

MRS. BRYANT: Go to hell, listen to her!

BEATIE: I never did, now! Mother, I'm *telling* you, listen to me. Ronnie's the best thing I've ever had and I've tried hard for three years to keep hold of him. I don't care what you do when he's gone but don't show me up when he's here.

MRS. BRYANT: Speak to your father gal.

BEATIE: Father too. I don't want Ronnie to think I come from a small-minded family. "I can't bear mean people," he say. "I don't care about their education, I don't care about their past as long as their minds are large and inquisitive, as long as they're generous."

MRS. BRYANT: Who say that?

BEATIE: Ronnie.

MRS. BRYANT: He *talk* like that?

BEATIE: Yearp.

MRS. BRYANT: Sounds like a preacher.

BEATIE (*standing on a chair*): "I don't care if you call me a preacher, I've got something to say and I'm going to say it. I don't care if you don't like being told things—we've come to a time when you've got to say this is right and this is wrong. God in heaven, have we got to be wet all the time? Well, have we?" Christ, Mother, you've got them ole wasps still flying around. (*She waves her arms in the air flaying the wasps.*) September and you've still got wasps. Owee! shoo-shoo! (*In the voice of her childhood*) Mammy, Mammy, take them ole things away. I doesn't like the—ooh! Nasty things.

BEATIE *jumps off chair and picks up a coat hanger. Now both she and her mother move stealthily around the room "hunting" wasps. Occasionally* MRS. BRYANT *strikes one dead or* BEATIE *spears one against the wall.* MRS. BRYANT *conducts herself matter-of-fact-like but* BEATIE *makes a fiendish game of it.*

MRS. BRYANT: They're after them apples on that tree outside. Go on! Off wi' you! Outside now! There—that's got 'em out, but I bet the buggers'll be back in a jiffy look.

BEATIE: Oh yes, an' I want to have a bath.

MRS. BRYANT: When d'you want that then?

BEATIE: This morning.

MRS. BRYANT: You can't hev no bath this morning, that copper won't heat up till after lunch.

BEATIE: Then I'll bake the pastries for Jenny this morning and you can put me water on now. (*She returns to sort her clothes.*)

MRS. BRYANT: I'll do that now then. I'll get you the soft water from the tank.

MRS. BRYANT *now proceeds to collect bucket and move back and forth between the garden out of view and the copper in the kitchen. She fills the copper with about three buckets of water and then lights the fire underneath it. In between buckets she chats.*

(*Off—as she hears lorry go by*) There go Danny Oakley to market. (*She returns with first bucket.*)

BEATIE: Mother! I dreamt I died last night and heaven were at the bottom of a pond. You had to jump in and sink and you know how afeared I am of water. It was full of film stars and soldiers and there were two rooms. In one room they was playing skiffle and—and—I can't remember what were goin' on in the other. Now who was God? I can't remember. It was someone we knew, a she. (*Returns to unpacking.*)

MRS. BRYANT (*entering with second bucket; automatically*): Yearp. (*Pause.*) You hear what happened to the headache doctor's patient? You know what they say about him—if you've got a headache you're all right but if you've got something more you've had it! Well he told a woman not to worry about a lump she complained of under her breast and you know what that were? That turned out to be thrombosis! There! Thrombosis! She had that breast off. Yes, she did. Had to hev it cut off. (*Goes for next bucket.*)

BEATIE (*automatically*): Yearp. (*She appears from front room with two framed paintings. She sets them up and admires them. They are primitive designs in bold masses, rather well-balanced shapes and bright poster colours—red, black, and yellow—see Dusty Bicker's work.*) Mother! Did I write and tell you I've took up painting? I started five months ago. Working in gouache. Ronnie says I'm good. Says I should carry on and maybe I can sell them for curtain designs. "Paint girl," he say. "Paint! The world is full of people who don't do the things they want so you paint and give us all hope!"

MRS. BRYANT *enters.*

BEATIE: Like 'em?

MRS. BRYANT (*looks at them a second*): Good colours ent they. (*She is unmoved and continues to empty a third bucket while* BEATIE *returns paintings to other room.*) Yes gal, I ent got no row wi' Pearl but I ask her to change my Labour Tote man 'cos I wanted to give the commission to Charlie Gorleston and she didn't do it. Well, if she can be like that I can be like that too. You gonna do some baking you say?

BEATIE (*enters from front room putting on a pinafore and carrying a parcel*): Right now. Here y'are Daphne Bryant, present for you. I want eggs, flour, sugar, and marg. I'm gonna bake a sponge and give it frilling. (*Goes to larder to collect things.*)

MRS. BRYANT (*unpacking parcel; it is a pinafore*): We both got one now.

MRS. BRYANT *continues to peel potatoes as* BEATIE *proceeds to separate four eggs, the yolks of which she starts whipping with sugar. She sings meanwhile a ringing folk song.*

BEATIE:

Oh a dialogue I'll sing you as true as me life.
Between a coal owner and poor pitman's wife
As she was a-walking along the highway
She met a coal owner and to him did say
Derry down, down, down Derry down.
Whip the eggs till they're light yellow he says.

MRS. BRYANT: Who says?

BEATIE: Ronnie.

Good morning Lord Firedamp the good woman said
I'll do you no harm sir so don't be afraid
If you'd been where I'd been for most of my life
You wouldn't turn pale at a poor pitman's wife,
Singing down, down, down Derry down.

MRS. BRYANT: What song's that?

BEATIE: A coalmining song.

MRS. BRYANT: I tell you what I reckon's a good song, that "I'll wait
for you in the heavens blue." I reckon that's a lovely song I
do. Jimmy Samson he sing that.

BEATIE: It's like twenty other songs, it don't mean anything and
it's sloshy and sickly.

MRS. BRYANT: Yes, I reckon that's a good song that.

BEATIE (*suddenly*): Listen Mother, let me see if I can explain
something to you. Ronnie always say that's the point of
knowing people. "It's no good having friends who scratch
each other's back," he say. "The excitement in knowing people is to hand on what you know and to learn what you don't
know. Learn from me," he say, "I don't know much but learn
what I know." So let me try and explain to you what he
explain to me.

MRS. BRYANT (*on hearing a bus*): There go the half-past-eleven
bus to Diss—blust that's early. (*Puts spuds in saucepan on
oven and goes to collect runner beans, which she prepares.*)

BEATIE: Mother, I'm *talking* to you. Blust woman it's not often
we get together and really talk, it's nearly always me listening
to you telling who's dead. Just listen a second.

MRS. BRYANT: Well go on gal, but you always take so long to say it.

BEATIE: What are the words of that song?

MRS. BRYANT: I don't know all the words.

BEATIE: I'll tell you.

Recites them.

> I'll wait for you in the heavens blue
> As my arms are waiting now.
> Please come to me and I'll be true
> My love shall not turn sour.
> I hunger, I hunger, I cannot wait longer,
> My love shall not turn sour.

There! Now what do that mean?

MRS. BRYANT (*surprised*) : Well, don't you know what that mean?

BEATIE: I mean what do they do to you? How do the words affect you? Are you moved? Do you find them beautiful?

MRS. BRYANT: Them's as good words as any.

BEATIE: But do they make you feel better?

MRS. BRYANT: Blust gal! That ent meant to be a laxative!

BEATIE: I must be mad to talk with you.

MRS. BRYANT: Besides it's the tune I like. Words never mean anything.

BEATIE: All right, the tune then! What does *that* do to you? Make your belly go gooey, your heart throb, make your head spin with passion? Yes, passion, Mother, know what it is? Because you won't find passion in that third-rate song, no you won't!

MRS. BRYANT: Well all right gal, so it's third-rate you say. Can you say why? What make that third-rate and them frilly bits of opera and concert first-rate? 'Sides, did I write that song? Beatie Bryant, you do go up and down in your spirits, and I don't know what's gotten into you gal, no I don't.

BEATIE: I don't know either, Mother. I'm worried about Ronnie I suppose. I have that same row with him. I ask him exactly the same questions—what make a pop song third-rate. And he answer and I don't know what he talk about. Something about registers, something about commercial world blunting our responses. "Give yourself time woman," he say. "Time! You can't learn how to live overnight. *I* don't even know," he say, "and half the world don't know but we got to try.

Try," he say, " 'cos we're still suffering from the shock of two world wars and we don't know it. Talk," he say, "and look and listen and think and ask questions." But Jesus! I don't know what questions to ask or *how* to talk. And he gets so riled—and yet sometimes so nice. "It's all going up in flames," he say, "but I'm going to make bloody sure I save someone from the fire."

MRS. BRYANT: Well I'm sure *I* don't know what he's on about. Turn to your baking gal look and get you done, Father'll be home for his lunch in an hour.

A faint sound of an ambulance is heard. MRS. BRYANT *looks up but says nothing.* BEATIE *turns to whipping the eggs again and* MRS. BRYANT *to cleaning up the runner beans. Out of this pause* MRS. BRYANT *begins to sing "I'll wait for you in the heavens blue," but on the second line she hums the tune incorrectly.*)

BEATIE (*laughs*): No, no, hell Mother, it don't go like that. It's—

BEATIE *corrects her and in helping her mother she ends by singing the song, with some enthusiasm, to the end.*

MRS. BRYANT: Thank God you come home sometimes gal—you do bring a little life with you anyway.

BEATIE: Mother, I ent never heard you express a feeling like that.

MRS. BRYANT (*she is embarrassed*): The world don't want no feelings gal. (*Footsteps are heard.*) Is that your father home already?

MR. BRYANT *appears at the back door and lays a bicycle against the wall. He is a small shrivelled man wearing denims, a peaked cap, boots, and gaiters. He appears to be in some pain.*

BEATIE: Hello poppy Bryant.
MR. BRYANT: Hello Beatie. You're here then.

MRS. BRYANT: What are you home so early for?

MR. BRYANT: The ole guts ache again. (*Sits in armchair and grimaces.*)

MRS. BRYANT: Well, what is it?

MR. BRYANT: Blust woman, I don't know what 'tis n'more'n you, do I?

MRS. BRYANT: Go to the doctor man I keep telling you.

BEATIE: What is it father Bryant?

MRS. BRYANT: He got guts ache.

BEATIE: But what's it from?

MR. BRYANT: I've just said I don't know.

MRS. BRYANT: Get you to a doctor man, don't be so soft. You don't want to be kept from work do you?

MR. BRYANT: That I don't, no I don't. Hell, I just see ole Stan Mann picked up an' thaas upset me enough.

MRS. BRYANT: Picked up you say?

MR. BRYANT: Well, didn't you hear the ambulance?

MRS. BRYANT: There! I hear it but I didn't say narthin'. Was that for Stan Mann then?

MR. BRYANT: I was cycling along wi' Jack Stones and we see this here figure on the side o' the road there an' I say, thaas a rum shape in the road Jack, and he say, blust, that's ole Stan Mann from Heybrid, an' 'twere. 'Course soon ever he see what 'twere, he rushed off for 'n ambulance and I waited alongside Stan.

BEATIE: But he just left here.

MRS. BRYANT: I see it comin'. He come in here an' I shoved him off home. Get you to bed and take some rum an' a drop o' hot milk, I tell him.

BEATIE: Is he gonna die?

MR. BRYANT: Wouldn't surprise me, that it wouldn't. Blust, he look done in.

MRS. BRYANT: Poor ole fellah. Shame though ent it?

MR. BRYANT: When d'you arrive Beatie?

MRS. BRYANT: She come in the half-past-ten bus. I looked for her on the nine-thirty bus and she weren't on that, so I thought to myself I bet she come on the half-past-ten. She did.

MR. BRYANT: Yearp.

MRS. BRYANT: You gonna stay away all day?

MR. BRYANT: No I aren't. I gotta go back 'cos one of the ole sows is piggin'. 'Spect she'll be hevin' them in a couple of hours. (*To* BEATIE) Got a sow had a litter o' twenty-two. (*Picks up paper to read.*)

BEATIE: Twenty-two? Oh Pop, can I come see this afternoon?

MR. BRYANT: Yearp.

MRS. BRYANT: Thought you was hevin' a bath.

BEATIE: Oh yes, I forgot. I'll come tomorrow then.

MR. BRYANT: They'll be there. What you doin' gal?

MRS. BRYANT: She's baking a sponge, now leave her be.

MR. BRYANT: Oh, you learnt something in London then.

BEATIE: Ronnie taught me.

MR. BRYANT: Well where *is* Ronnie then?

MRS. BRYANT: He's comin' on Saturday a week an' the family's goin' to be here to greet him.

MR. BRYANT: All on 'em?

MRS. BRYANT *and* BEATIE: All on' em!

MR. BRYANT: Well that'll be a rum gatherin' then.

MRS. BRYANT: And we've to be on our best behaviour.

MR. BRYANT: No cussin' and swearin'?

MRS. BRYANT *and* BEATIE: No.

MR. BRYANT: Blust, I shan't talk then.

A young man, MR. HEALEY, *appears round the garden—he is the farmer's son, and manager of the estate* BRYANT *works for.*

MRS. BRYANT (*seeing him first*) : Oh, Mr. Healey, yes. Jack! It's Mr. Healey.

MR. BRYANT *rises and goes to the door.* HEALEY *speaks in a firm, not unkind, but business-is-business voice. There is that apologetic threat even in his politeness.*

MR. HEALEY: You were taken ill.

MR. BRYANT: It's all right, sir, only guts ache, won't be long goin'. The pigs is all seen to, just waiting for the ole sow to start.

MR. HEALEY: What time you expecting it?

MR. BRYANT: Oh, she 'ont come afore two this afternoon, no she 'ont be much afore that.

MR. HEALEY: You're sure you're well, Jack? I've been thinking that it's too much for you carting those pails round the yard.

MR. BRYANT: No, that ent too heavy, sir, 'course 'tent. You don't wanna worry, I'll be along after lunch. Just an ole guts ache that's all—seein' the doctor tonight—eat too fast probably.

MR. HEALEY: If you're sure you're all right, then I'll put young Daniels off. You can manage without him now we've fixed the new pump in.

MR. BRYANT: I can manage, sir—'course I can.

MR. HEALEY (*moving off outside*): All right then, Jack. I'll be with you around two o'clock. I want to take the old one out of number three and stick her with the others in seventeen. The little ones won't need her, will they? Then we'll have them sorted out tomorrow.

MR. BRYANT: That's right, sir, they *can* go on their own now, they can. I'll see to it tomorrow.

MR. HEALEY: Right then, Jack. Oh—you hear Stan Mann died?

MR. BRYANT: He died already? But I saw him off in the ambulance no more'n half-hour ago.

MR. HEALEY: Died on the way to hospital. Jack Stones told me. Lived in Heybrid, didn't he?

MR. BRYANT: Alongside my daughter.

MR. HEALEY (*calling*): Well, good morning, Mrs. Bryant.

MRS. BRYANT (*calling*): Good morning, Mr. Healey.

The two men nod to each other, MR. HEALEY *goes off.* MR. BRYANT *lingers a second.*

MRS. BRYANT (*to* BEATIE): That was Mr. Healey, the new young manager.

BEATIE: I know it Mother.

MR. BRYANT (*returning slowly*): He's dead then.

MRS. BRYANT: Who? Not Stan Mann?

MR. BRYANT: Young Healey just tell me.

MRS. BRYANT: Well I go t'hell. An' he were just here look, just here alongside o' me not more'n hour past.

MR. BRYANT: Rum ent it?

BEATIE (*weakly*) : Oh hell, I hate dying.

MRS. BRYANT: He were a good ole bor though. Yes he was. A good ole stick. There!

BEATIE: Used to ride me round on his horse, always full o' life an' jokes. "Tell your boy he wanna hurry up and marry you," he say to me, "or I'll hev you meself on a plate."

MRS. BRYANT: He were a one for smut though.

BEATIE: I was talkin' with him last night. Only last night he was tellin' me how he caught me pinchin' some gooseberries off his patch an' how he gimme a whole apron full and I went into one o' his fields near by an' ate the lot. "Blust," he say, "you had the ole guts ache," and he laugh, sat there laughin' away to hisself.

MRS. BRYANT: I can remember that. Hell, Jenny'll miss him—used always to pop in an' out o' theirs.

BEATIE: Seem like the whole world gone suddenly dead don' it?

MR. BRYANT: Rum ent it?

Silence.

MRS. BRYANT: You say young Healey tell you that? *He's* a nice man Mr. Healey is, yes he is, a good sort, I like him.

BEATIE: Sound like he were threatening to sack Father; don't know about being nice.

MR. BRYANT: That's what I say see, get a rise and they start cutting down the men or the overtime.

MRS. BRYANT: The Union magazine's come.

MR. BRYANT: I don't want that ole thing.

BEATIE: Why can't you do something to stop the sackings?

MR. BRYANT: You can't, you can't—that's what I say, you can't. Sharp as a pig's scream they are—you just *can't* do nothin'.

BEATIE: Mother, where's the bakin' tin?

MR. BRYANT: When we gonna eat that?

BEATIE: You ent! It's for Jenny Beales.

MR. BRYANT: You aren't making that for Jenny are you?

BEATIE: I promised her.

MR. BRYANT: Not with my electricity you aren't.

BEATIE: But I promised, Poppy.

MR. BRYANT: That's no matters. I aren't spendin' money on electricity bills so's you can make every Tom, Dick 'n' Harry a sponge cake, that I aren't.

MRS. BRYANT: Well, don't be so soft man, it won't take more'n half-hour's bakin'.

MR. BRYANT: I don't care what it'll take I say. I aren't lettin' her. Jenny wants cakes, she can make 'em herself. So put that away Beatie and use it for something else.

MRS. BRYANT: You wanna watch what you're sayin' of 'cos I live here too.

MR. BRYANT: I know all about that but I pay the electricity bill and I says she isn't bakin'.

BEATIE: But Poppy, one cake.

MR. BRYANT: No I say.

BEATIE: Well, Mummy, do something—how can he be so mean.

MRS. BRYANT: Blust me if you ent the meanest ole sod that walks this earth. Your own daughter and you won't let her use your oven. You bloody ole hypercrite.

MR. BRYANT: You pay the bills and then you call names.

MRS. BRYANT: What I ever seen in you God only knows. Yes! an' he never warn me. Bloody ole hypercrite!

MR. BRYANT: You pay the bills and then you call names I say.

MRS. BRYANT: On four pounds ten a week? You want me to keep you *and* pay bills? Four pound ten he give me. God knows what he do wi' the rest. I don't know how much he've got. I don't, no I don't. Bloody ole hypercrite.

MR. BRYANT: Let's hev grub and not so much o' the lip woman.

BEATIE *begins to put the things away. She is on the verge of the tears she will soon let fall.*

MRS. BRYANT: That's how he talk to me—when he do talk. 'Cos you know he don't ever talk more'n he hev to, and when he do say something it's either "how much this cost" or "lend us couple o' bob." He've got the money but sooner than break into that he borrow off me. Bloody old miser. (*To* BEATIE) What you wanna cry for gal? 'Tent worth it. Blust, you don't wanna let an ole hypercrite like him upset you, no you don't. I'll get my back on you my manny, see if I don't. You won't get away with no tricks on me.

BEATIE *has gone into the other room and returned with a small packet.*

BEATIE (*throwing parcel in father's lap*) : Present for you.
MRS. BRYANT: I'd give him presents that I would! I'd walk out and disown him! Beatie, now stop you a-cryin' gal—blust, he ent worth cryin' for, that he ent. Stop it I say and we'll have lunch. Or you lost your appetite gal?

BEATIE *sniffs a few tears back, pauses, and—*

BEATIE: No—no, that I ent. Hell, I can eat all right!

Curtain.

Scene Two

Lunch has been eaten. MR. BRYANT *is sitting at the table rolling himself a cigarette.* MRS. BRYANT *is collecting the dishes and taking them to a sink to wash up.* BEATIE *is taking things off the table and putting them into the larder—jars of sauce, plates of sliced bread and cakes, butter, sugar, condiments, and bowl of tinned fruit.*

MRS. BRYANT (*to* BEATIE): Ask him what he want for his tea.

MR. BRYANT: She don't ever ask me before, what she wanna ask me now for?

MRS. BRYANT: Tell him it's his stomach I'm thinking about—I don't want him complaining to me about the food I cook.

MR. BRYANT: Tell her it's no matters to me—I ent go no pain now besides.

BEATIE: Mother, is that water ready for my bath?

MRS. BRYANT: Where you hevin' it?

BEATIE: In the kitchen of course.

MRS. BRYANT: Blust gal, you can't bath in this kitchen during the day, what if someone call at the door?

BEATIE: Put up the curtain then, I shan't be no more'n ten minutes.

MR. BRYANT: 'Sides, who want to see her in her dickey suit.

BEATIE: I know men as 'ould pay to see me in my dickey suit. (*Posing her plump outline*) Don't you think I got a nice dickey suit?

MR. BRYANT *makes a dive and pinches her bottom.*

Ow! Stoppit Bryants, stoppit!

He persists.

Daddy, stop it now!

MRS. BRYANT: Tell him he can go as soon as he like, I want your bath over and done with.

BEATIE: Oh Mother, stop this nonsense do. If you want to tell him something tell him—not me.

MRS. BRYANT: *I* don't want to speak to him, hell if I do.

BEATIE: Father, get the bath in for me please. Mother, where's them curtains.

MR. BRYANT *goes off to fetch a long tin bath—wide at one end, narrow at the other—while* MRS. BRYANT *leaves washing up to fish out some curtains which she hangs from one wall to*

*another concealing thus a corner of the kitchen. Anything
that is in the way is removed.* BEATIE *meanwhile brings out a
change of underwear, her dressing-gown, the new frock, some
soap, powder, and towel. These she lays within easy reach of
the curtain.*

BEATIE: I'm gonna wear my new dress and go across the fields to
see Frankie and Pearl.

MRS. BRYANT: Frankie won't be there, what you on about? He'll
be gettin' the harvest in.

BEATIE: You makin' anything for the harvest festival?

MR. BRYANT (*entering with bath, places it behind curtain*) : Your
mother don't ever do anything for the harvest festival—don't
you know that by now.

BEATIE: Get you to work father Bryant, I'm gonna plunge in
water and I'll make a splash.

MRS. BRYANT: Tell him we've got kippers for tea and if he don'
want none let him say now.

BEATIE: She says it's kippers for tea.

MR. BRYANT: Tell her I'll eat kippers. (*Goes off collecting bike on
the way.*)

BEATIE: He says he'll eat kippers. Right now, Mother, you get cold
water an' I'll pour the hot.

Each now picks up a bucket. MRS. BRYANT *goes off out to
collect the cold water and* BEATIE *plunges bucket into boiler
to retrieve hot water. The bath is prepared with much childlike glee.* BEATIE *loves her creature comforts and does with
unabashed, almost animal, enthusiasm that which she enjoys.
When the bath is prepared,* BEATIE *slips behind the curtain
to undress and enter.*

MRS. BRYANT: You hear about Jimmy Skelton? They say he've bin
arrested for accosting some man in the village.

BEATIE: Jimmy Skelton what own the pub?

MRS. BRYANT: That's him. I know all about Jimmy Skelton though.
He were a young boy when I were a young girl. I always

partner him at whist drives. He's been to law before you know. Yes! An' he won the day too! Won the day he did. I don't take notice though, him and me gets on all right. What do Ronnie's mother do with her time?

BEATIE: She've got a sick husband to look after.

MRS. BRYANT: She an educated woman?

BEATIE: Educated? No. She's a foreigner. Nor ent Ronnie educated neither. He's an intellectual, failed all his exams. They read and things.

MRS. BRYANT: Oh, they don't do nothing then?

BEATIE: Do nothing? I'll tell you what Ronnie do, he work till all hours in a hot ole kitchen. An' he teach kids in a club to act and jive and such. And he don't stop at weekends either 'cos then there's political meetings and such and I get breathless trying to keep up wi' him. OOOhh, Mother it's hot . . .

MRS. BRYANT: I'll get you some cold then.

BEATIE: No—ooh—it's lovely. The water's so soft Mother.

MRS. BRYANT: Yearp.

BEATIE: It's so soft and smooth. I'm in.

MRS. BRYANT: Don't you stay in too long gal. There go the twenty-minutes-past-one bus.

BEATIE: Oh Mother, me bath cubes. I forgot me bath cubes. In the little case by me pick-up.

MRS. BRYANT *finds bath cubes and hands them to* BEATIE.

MRS. BRYANT (*continuing her work*) : I shall never forget when I furse heard on it. I was in the village and I was talking to Reggie Fowler. I say to him, there've bin a lot o' talk about Jimmy ent there? Disgustin', I say. Still, there's somebody wanna make some easy money, you'd expect that in a village wouldn't you? Yes, I say to him, a lot of talk. An' he stood there, an' he were a-lookin' at me an' a-lookin' as I were a-talkin' and then he say, missus, he say, I were one o' the victims! Well, you could've hit me over the head wi' a hammer. I was one o' the victims, he say.

BEATIE: Mother, these bath cubes smell beautiful. I could stay here all day.

MRS. BRYANT: Still, Jimmy's a good fellow with it all—do anything for you. I partner him at whist drives; he bin had up scores o' times though.

BEATIE: Mother, what we gonna make Ronnie when he come?

MRS. BRYANT: Well, what do he like?

BEATIE: He like trifle and he like steak and kidney pie.

MRS. BRYANT: We'll make that then. So long as he don't complain o' the guts ache. Frankie hev it too you know.

BEATIE: Know why? You all eat too much. The Londoners think we live a healthy life but they don't know we stuff ourselves silly till our guts ache.

MRS. BRYANT: But you know what's wrong wi' Jimmy Beales? It's indigestion. He eat too fast.

BEATIE: What the hell's indigestion doin' a'tween his shoulder blades?

MRS. BRYANT: 'Cos some people get it so bad it go right through their stomach to the back.

BEATIE: You don't get indigestion in the back Mother, what you on about?

MRS. BRYANT: Don't you tell me gal, I hed it!

BEATIE: Owee! The soap's in me eyes—Mother, towel, the towel, quickly the towel!

> MRS. BRYANT *hands in towel to* BEATIE. *The washing up is probably done by now, so* MRS. BRYANT *sits in a chair, legs apart and arms folded, thinking what else to say.*

MRS. BRYANT: You heard that Ma Buckley hev been taken to Mental Hospital in Norwich? Poor ole dear. If there's one thing I can't abide that's mental cases. They frighten me—they do. Can't face 'em. I'd sooner follow a man to a churchyard than the mental hospital. That's a terrible thing to see a person lose their reason—that 'tis. Well, I tell you what, down where I used to live, down the other side of the Hall, years ago we moved in next to an old woman. I only had Jenny and Frank then—an' this woman she were the sweetest of people. We used to talk and do errands for each other—Oh she was a sweet ole dear. And then one afternoon I was going out to get my washin' in and I saw her. She was standin' in a tub of water up to her neck. She was! Up to her neck. An' her eyes had that glazed, wonderin' look and she stared straight at me she did. Straight at me. Well, do you know what? I was struck *dumb*. I was *struck* dumb wi' shock. What wi' her bein' so nice all this while, the sudden comin' on her like that in the tub fair upset me. It did! And people tell me afterwards that she's bin goin' in an' out o' hospital for years. Blust, that scare me. That scare me so much she nearly took me round the bend wi' her.

BEATIE *appears from behind the curtain in her dressing-gown, a towel round her head.*

BEATIE: There! I'm gonna hev a bath every day when I'm married.

BEATIE *starts rubbing her hair with towel and fiddles with radio. She finds a programme playing Mendelssohn's Fourth Symphony, the slow movement, and stands before the mirror, listening and rubbing.*

BEATIE (*looking at her reflection*) : Isn't your nose a funny thing, and your ears. And your arms and your legs, aren't they funny things—sticking out of a lump.

MRS. BRYANT (*switching off radio*) : Turn that squit off!

BEATIE (*turning on her mother violently*) : Mother! I could kill you when you do that. No wonder I don't know anything about anything. I never heard nothing but dance music because you always turned off the classics. I never knowed anything about the news because you always switched off after the headlines. I never read any good books 'cos there was never any in the house.

MRS. BRYANT: What's gotten into you now gal?

BEATIE: God in heaven Mother, you live in the country but you got no—no—no majesty. You spend your time among green fields, you grow flowers and you breathe fresh air and you got no majesty. Your mind's cluttered up with nothing and you shut out the world. What kind of a life did you give me?

MRS. BRYANT: Blust gal, I weren't no teacher.

BEATIE: But you hindered. You didn't open one door for me. Even
his mother cared more for me than what you did. Beatie, she
say, Beatie, why don't you take up evening classes and learn
something other than waitressing. Yes, she say, you won't ever
regret learnin' things. But did you care what job I took up
or whether I learned things? You didn't even think it was
necessary.

MRS. BRYANT: I fed you. I clothed you. I took you out to the sea.
What more d'you want. We're only country folk you know.
We ent got no big things here you know.

BEATIE: Squit! Squit! It makes no difference country or town. *All*
the town girls I ever worked with were just like me. It makes
no difference country or town—that's squit. Do you know
when I used to work at the holiday camp and I sat down with
the other girls to write a letter we used to sit and discuss
what we wrote about. An' we all agreed, all on us, that we
started: "Just a few lines to let you know," and then we get
on to the weather and then we get stuck so we write about
each other and after a page an' half of big scrawl end up:
"Hoping this finds you as well as it leaves me." There! We
couldn't say any more. Thousands of things happening at this
holiday camp and we couldn't find words for them. All of us
the same. Hundreds of girls and one day we're gonna be
mothers, and you *still* talk to me of Jimmy Skelton and the
ole woman in the tub. Do you know I've heard that story a
dozen times. A dozen times. Can't you hear yourself Mother?
Jesus, how can I bring Ronnie to this house.

MRS. BRYANT: Blust gal, if Ronnie don't like us then he—

BEATIE: Oh, he'll like you all right. He like people. He'd've loved
ole Stan Mann. Ole Stan Mann would've understood everything Ronnie talk about. Blust! That man liked livin'. Besides, Ronnie say it's too late for the old 'uns to learn. But
he says it's up to us young 'uns. And them of us that know
hev got to teach them of us as don't know.

MRS. BRYANT: I bet he hev a hard time trying to change you gal!

BEATIE: He's *not* trying to change me Mother. You can't change
people, he say, you can only give them some love and hope

they'll take it. And he's tryin' to teach me and I'm tryin' to understand—do you see that Mother?

MRS. BRYANT: I don't see what that's got to do with music though.

BEATIE: Oh my God! (*Suddenly*) I'll show you. (*Goes off to front room to collect pick-up and a record.*) Now sit you down gal and I'll show you. Don't start ironing or reading or nothing, just sit there and be prepared to learn something. (*Appears with pick-up and switches on.*) You aren't too old, just you sit and listen. That's the trouble you see, we ent ever prepared to learn anything, we close our minds the minute anything unfamiliar appear. *I* could never listen to music. I used to like some on it but then I'd lose patience, I'd go to bed in the middle of a symphony, or my mind would wander 'cos the music didn't mean anything to me so I'd go to bed or start talking. "Sit back woman," he'd say, "listen to it. Let it happen to you and you'll grow as big as the music itself."

MRS. BRYANT: Blust he talk like a book.

BEATIE: An' sometimes he talk as though you didn't know where the moon or the stars was. (BEATIE *puts on record of Bizet's L'Arlésienne Suite.*) Now listen. This is a simple piece of music, it's not highbrow but it's full of living. And that's what he say socialism is. "Christ," he say. "Socialism isn't talking all the time, it's living, it's singing, it's dancing, it's being interested in what go on around you, it's being concerned about people and the world." Listen Mother. (*She becomes breathless and excited.*) Listen to it. It's simple isn't it? Can you call that squit?

MRS. BRYANT: I don't say it's all squit.

BEATIE: You don't have to frown because it's alive.

MRS. BRYANT: No, not all on it's squit.

BEATIE: See the way the other tune comes in? Hear it? Two simple tunes, one after the other.

MRS. BRYANT: I aren't saying it's all squit.

BEATIE: And now listen, listen, it goes together, the two tunes together, they knit, they're perfect. Don't it make you want to dance? (*She begins to dance a mixture of a cossack dance and a sailor's hornpipe.*)

The music becomes fast and her spirits are young and high.

Listen to that Mother. Is it difficult? Is it squit? It's light. It make me feel light and confident and happy. God, Mother, we could all be so much more happy and alive. Wheeeee . . .

BEATIE *claps her hands and dances on and her mother smiles and claps her hands and—*

The curtain falls.

ACT THREE

Two weeks have passed. It is Saturday, the day Ronnie is to arrive. One of the walls of the kitchen is now pushed aside and the front room is revealed. It is low-ceilinged, and has dark brown wooden beams. The furniture is not typical country farmhouse type. There may be one or two Windsor-type straight-back chairs, but for the rest it is cheap utility stuff. Two armchairs, a table, a small bamboo table, wooden chairs, a small sofa, and a swivel bookcase. There are a lot of flowers around—in pots on the window ledge and in vases on the bamboo table and swivel case.

It is three in the afternoon, the weather is cloudy—it has been raining and is likely to start again. On the table is a spread of food (none of this will be eaten). There are cakes and biscuits on plates and glass stands. Bread and butter, butter in a dish, tomatoes, cheese, jars of pickled onions, sausage rolls, dishes of tinned fruit— it is a spread! Round the table are eight chairs. BEATIE'S *paintings are hanging on the wall. The room is empty because* BEATIE *is upstairs changing and* MRS. BRYANT *is in the kitchen.* BEATIE— *until she descends—conducts all her conversation shouting from upstairs.*

BEATIE: Mother! What you on at now?

MRS. BRYANT *(from kitchen)* : I'm just puttin' these glass cherries on the trifle.

BEATIE: Well come on look, he'll be here at four thirty.

MRS. BRYANT *(from kitchen)* : Don't you fret gal, it's another hour 'n' half yet, the postman hevn't gone by. *(Enters with an enormous bowl of trifle.)* There! He like trifle you say?

BEATIE: He love it.

MRS. BRYANT: Well he need to 'cos there's plenty on it. *(To herself, surveying the table)* Yes, there is, there's plenty on it. *(It starts to rain.)* Blust, listen to that weather.

BEATIE: Rainin' again!

MRS. BRYANT (*looking out of window*) : Raining? It's rainin' fit to drowned you. (*Sound of bus.*) There go the three-o'clock.

BEATIE: Mother get you changed, come on, I want us ready in time.

MRS. BRYANT: Blust you'd think it were the bloody Prince of Egypt comin'. (*Goes upstairs.*)

The stage is empty again for a few seconds. People are heard taking off their macs and exclaiming at the weather from the kitchen. Enter FRANK *and* PEARL BRYANT. *He is pleasant and dressed in a blue pin-striped suit, is ruddy-faced and blond-haired. An odd sort of shyness makes him treat everything as a joke. His wife is a pretty brunette, young, and ordinarily dressed in plain, flowered frock.*

FRANK (*calling*) : Well, where are you all? Come on—I'm hungry.

PEARL: Shut you up bor, you only just had lunch.

FRANK: Well I'm hungry again. (*Calling*) Well, where is this article we come to see?

BEATIE: He ent arrived.

FRANK: Well, he want to hurry, 'cos I'm hungry.

BEATIE: You're always hungry.

FRANK: What do you say he is—a strong socialist?

BEATIE: Yes.

FRANK: And a Jew boy?

BEATIE: Yes.

FRANK (*to himself*) : Well, that's a queer mixture then.

PEARL (*calling*) : I hope he don't talk politics all the time.

FRANK: Have you had a letter from him yet?

PEARL: Stop it Frank, you know she hevn't heard.

FRANK: Well that's a rum boy friend what don't write. (*Looks at paintings, pauses before one of them and growls.*)

PEARL: Watch out or it'll bite you back.

BEATIE *comes down from upstairs. She is dressed in her new frock and looks happy, healthy, and radiant.*

FRANK: Hail there, sister! I was then contemplating your masterpiece.

BEATIE: Well don't contemplate too long 'cos you aren't hevin' it.

FRANK: Blust! I'd set my ole heart on it.

PEARL: That's a nice frock Beatie.

FRANK: Where's the rest of our mighty clan?

BEATIE: Jenny and Jimmy should be here soon and Susie and Stan mightn't come.

FRANK: What's wrong wi' them?

BEATIE: Don't talk to me about it 'cos I hed enough! Susie won't talk to Mother.

PEARL: That make nearly eighteen months she hevn't spoke.

BEATIE: Why ever did *you* and Mother fall out Pearl?

FRANK: 'Cos Mother's so bloody stubborn that's why.

PEARL: Because one day she said she wanted to change her Labour Tote man, that's why, and she asked me to do it for her. So I said all right, but it'll take a couple of weeks; and then she got riled because she said I didn't want to change it for her. And then I ask her why didn't she change him herself and she say because she was too ill to go all the way to see John Clayton to tell him, and then she say to me, why, don't you think I'm ill? And I say—I know this were tactless o' me—but I say, no Mother, you don't look ill to me. And she didn't speak to me since. I only hope she don't snub me this afternoon.

BEATIE: Well, she tell me a different story.

FRANK: Mother's always quarrelling.

PEARL: Well I reckon there ent much else she *can* do stuck in this ole house on her own all day. And father Bryant he don't say too much when he's home you know.

FRANK: Well blust, she hevn't spoke to her own mother for three years, not since Granny Dykes took Jenny in when she had that illegitimate gal Daphne.

BEATIE: Hell! What a bloody family!

FRANK: A mighty clan I say.

JIMMY *and* JENNY BEALES *now enter.*

JENNY: Hello Frankie, hello Pearl, hello Beatie.

FRANK: And more of the mighty clan.

JENNY: Mighty clan you say? Mighty bloody daft you mean. Well, where is he?

FRANK: The mysterious stranger has not yet come—we await.

JENNY: Well, I aren't waitin' long 'cos I'm hungry.

PEARL: That's all this family of Bryants ever do is think o' their guts.

FRANK (*to* JIMMY): Have you formed your association yit?

JENNY: What association is this?

FRANK: What! Hevn't he told you?

JIMMY: Shut you up Frank Bryant or you'll get me hung.

FRANK: Oh, a might association—a mighty one! I'll tell ye. One day you see we was all sittin' round in the pub—Jimmy, me, Starkie, Johnny Oats, and Bonky Dawson—we'd hed a few drinks and Jimmy was feelin'—well, he was feelin'—you know what, the itch! He hed the itch! He started complaining about ham, ham, ham all the time. So then Bonky Dawson say, blust, he say, there must be women about who feel the same. And Starkie he say, well 'course they are, only how do you tell? And then we was all quiet a while thinkin' on it when suddenly Jimmy says, we ought to start an association of them as need a bit now and then and we all ought to wear a badge he say, and when you see a woman wearin' a badge you know she need a bit too.

JIMMY: Now that's enough Frank or I'll hit you over the skull.

FRANK: Now, not content wi' just that, ole Jimmy then say, and we ought to have a password to indicate how bad off you are. So listen what he suggest. He suggest you go up to any one o' these women what's wearin' a badge and you say, how many lumps of sugar do you take in your tea? And if she say "two" then you know she ent too badly off, but she's willin'. But if she say "four" then you knows she's in as bad a state as what you are, see?

Long pause.

JENNY: He'd hev a fit if she said she took sixteen lumps though wouldn't he?

Pause.

PEARL: Where's mother Bryant?
BEATIE: Upstairs changin'.
PEARL: Where's father Bryant?
BEATIE: Tendin' the pigs.
FRANK: You're lucky to hev my presence you know.
BEATIE: Oh?
FRANK: A little more sun and I'd've bin gettin' in the harvest.
PEARL: Well, what did you think of that storm last night? All that thunder 'n' lightnin' and it didn't stop once.
BEATIE: Ronnie love it you know. He sit and watch it for bloody hours.
FRANK: He's a queer article then.
JENNY: He do sound a rum 'un don't he?
BEATIE: Well you'll soon see.
JIMMY: Hev he got any sisters?
BEATIE: One married and she live not far from here.
PEARL: She live in the country? A town girl? Whatever for?
BEATIE: Her husband make furniture by hand.
PEARL: Can't he do that in London?
BEATIE: Ronnie say they think London's an inhuman place.
JIMMY: So 'tis, so 'tis.
BEATIE: Here come father Bryant.

> MR. BRYANT *enters. He is in denims and raincoat, tired, and stooped slightly.*

FRANK: And this be the male head of the mighty Bryant clan!
MR. BRYANT: Blust, you're all here soon then.
BEATIE: Get you changed quick Father—he'll be along any minute look.
MR. BRYANT: Shut you up gal, I'll go when I'm ready, I don't want you pushin' me.

> MRS. BRYANT *comes from upstairs. She looks neat and also wears a flowered frock.*

FRANK: And this be the female head o' the mighty Bryant clan!

MRS. BRYANT: Come on Bryant, get you changed—we're all ready look.

MR. BRYANT: Blust, there go the other one. Who is he this boy, that's what I wanna know.

MRS. BRYANT: He's upset! I can see it! I can tell it in his voice. Come on Bryants, what's the matters.

MR. BRYANT: There ent much up wi' me, what you on about woman. (*Makes to go.*) Now leave me be, you want me changed look.

MRS. BRYANT: If there ent much up wi' you, I'll marry some other.

FRANK: Healey bin at you Pop?

BEATIE: The pigs dyin'?

MRS. BRYANT: It's something serious or he wouldn't be so happy lookin'.

MR. BRYANT: I bin put on casual labour.

JENNY: Well isn't that a sod now.

MRS. BRYANT: Your guts I suppose.

MR. BRYANT: I tell him it's no odds, that there's no pain. That don't matters Jack, he says, I aren't hevin' you break up completely on me. You go on casual, he say, and if you gets better you can come on to the pigs again.

MRS. BRYANT: That's half pay then?

BEATIE: Can't you get another job?

FRANK: He've bin wi' them for eighteen years.

BEATIE: But you must be able to do something else—what about cowman again!

MR. BRYANT: Bill Waddington do that see. He've bin at it this last six 'n' half years.

JENNY: It's no good upsettin' yourself Beatie. It happen all the time gal.

JIMMY: Well, we told her when she was at ours didn't we.

MRS. BRYANT (*to* MR. BRYANT): All right, get you on up, there ent nothin' we can do. We'll worry on it later. We always manage. It's gettin' late look.

MR. BRYANT: Can he swim? 'Cos he bloody need to. It's rainin' fit to drowned you. (*Goes off upstairs.*)

MRS. BRYANT: Well, shall we have a little cup o' tea while we're waitin'? I'll go put the kettle on. (*Goes to kitchen.*)

Everyone sits around now. JENNY *takes out some knitting and* JIMMY *picks up a paper to read. There is a silence. It is not an awkward silence, just a conversationless room.*

PEARL (*to* JENNY) : Who's lookin' after your children?

JENNY: Old mother Mann next door.

PEARL: Poor ole dear. How's she feelin' now?

JENNY: She took it bad. (*Nodding at* JIMMY) Him too. He think he were to blame.

PEARL: Blust that weren't his fault. Don't be so daft Jimmy Beales. Don't you go fretting yourself or you'll make us all feel queer look. You done nothin' wrong bor—he weren't far off dying 'sides.

FRANK: They weren't even married were they?

JENNY: No, they never were—she started lookin' after him when he had that first stroke and she just stayed.

JIMMY: Lost her job 'cos of it too.

FRANK: Well, yes, she would, wouldn't she—she was a State Registered Nurse or something weren't she? (*To* BEATIE) Soon ever the authorities got to hear o' that they told her to pack up livin' wi' him or quit her job, see?

JENNY: Bloody daft I reckon. What difference it make whether she married him or not.

PEARL: I reckon you miss him Jenny?

JENNY: Hell yes—that I do. He were a good ole bor—always joking and buying the kid sweets. Well, do you know I cry when I heard it? I did. Blust, that fair shook me—that it did, there!

JIMMY: Who's lookin' after *your* kid then, Pearl?

PEARL: Father.

Pause.

JIMMY (*to* FRANK): Who do you think'll win today?

FRANK: Well Norwich won't.

JIMMY: No.

Pause. MRS. BRYANT *enters and sits down.*

MRS. BRYANT: Well the kettle's on.

PEARL (*to* BEATIE): Hev his sister got any children?

BEATIE: Two boys.

JIMMY: She wanna get on top one night then they'll hev girls.

JENNY: Oh shut you up Jimmy Beales.

MRS. BRYANT: Hed another little win last night.

JENNY: When was this?

MRS. BRYANT: The fireman's whist drive. Won seven 'n' six in the knockout.

JENNY: Yearp.

FRANK (*reading the paper*): I see that boy what assaulted the ole woman in London got six years.

MRS. BRYANT: Blust! He need to! I'd've given him six years and a bit more. Bloody ole hooligans. Do you give me a chance to pass sentence and I'd soon clear the streets of crime, that I would. Yes, that I would.

BEATIE (*springing into activity*): All right Mother—we'll give you a chance. (*Grabs* JIMMY's *hat and umbrella. Places hat on mother's head and umbrella in her arms.*) There you are, you're a judge. Now sum up and pass judgment.

MRS. BRYANT: I'd put him in prison for life.

FRANK: You gotta sum up though. Blust, you just can't stick a man in prison and say nothing.

MRS. BRYANT: Goodbye, I'd say.

BEATIE: Come on Mother, speak up. Anybody can say "go to prison," but *you* want to be a judge. Well, you show a judge's understanding. Talk! Come on Mother, talk!

Everyone leans forward eagerly to hear Mother talk. She looks startled and speechless.

MRS. BRYANT: Well I—I—yes I—well I—Oh, don't be so soft.

FRANK: The mighty head is silent.

BEATIE: Well yes, she would be wouldn't she.

MRS. BRYANT: What do you mean, I would be? You don't expect me to know what they say in courts do you? I aren't no judge.

BEATIE: Then why do you sit and pass judgment on people? If someone do something wrong you don't stop and think why. No discussin', no questions, just (*snap of fingers*) —off with his head. I mean look at Father getting less money. I don't see the family sittin' together and discussin' it. It's a problem! But which of you said it concerns you?

MRS. BRYANT: Nor don't it concern them. I aren't hevin' people mix in my matters.

BEATIE: But they aren't just people—they're your family for hell's sake!

MRS. BRYANT: No matters, I aren't hevin' it!

BEATIE: But Mother I—

MRS. BRYANT: Now shut you up Beatie Bryant and leave it alone. I shall talk when I hev to and I never shall do, so there!

BEATIE: You're so stubborn.

MRS. BRYANT: So you keep saying.

MR. BRYANT *enters, he is clean and dressed in blue pin-striped suit.*

MR. BRYANT: You brewed up yit?

MRS. BRYANT (*jumping up and going to kitchen*) : Oh hell, yes—I forgot the tea look.

MR. BRYANT: Well, now we're all waitin' on him.

JENNY: Don't look as if Susie's comin'.

BEATIE: Stubborn cow!

Silence.

JENNY: Hev you seen Susie's television set yit?

BEATIE: I seen it.

FRANK: Did you know also that when they first hed it they took it up to bed wi' them and lay in bed wi' a dish of chocolate biscuits?

PEARL: But now they don't bother—they say they've had it a year now and all the old programmes they saw in the beginning they're seein' again.

MRS. BRYANT (*entering with tea*) : Brew's up!

BEATIE: Oh, for Christ's sake let's stop gossiping.

PEARL: I aren't gossiping. I'm making an intelligent observation about the state of television, now then.

MR. BRYANT: What's up wi' you now?

BEATIE: You weren't doin' nothin' o' the sort—you was gossiping.

PEARL: Well that's a heap sight better'n quotin' all the time.

BEATIE: I don't quote all the time, I just tell you what Ronnie say.

FRANK: Take it easy gal—he's comin' soon—don't need to go all jumpin' an' frantic.

BEATIE: Listen! Let me set you a problem.

JIMMY: Here we go.

BEATIE: While we're waitin' for him I'll set you a moral problem. You know what a moral problem is? It's a problem about right and wrong. I'll get you buggers thinking if it's the last thing I do. Now listen. There are four huts—

FRANK: What?

BEATIE: Huts. You know—them little things you live in. Now there are two huts on one side of a stream and two huts on the other side. On one side live a girl in one hut and a wise man in the other. On the other side live Tom in one hut and Archie in the other. Also there's a ferryman what run a boat across the river. Now—listen, concentrate—the girls loves Archie but Archie don't love the girl. And Tom love the girl but the girl don't go much on Tom.

JIMMY: Poor bugger.

BEATIE: One day the girl hears that Archie—who don't love her, remember—is going to America, so she decides to try once more to persuade him to take her with him. So listen what she do. She go to the ferryman and ask him to take her across. The ferryman say, I will, but you must take off all your clothes.

MRS. BRYANT: Well, whatever do he wanna ask that for?

BEATIE: It don't matters why—he do! Now the girl doesn't know what to do so she ask the wise man for advice, and he say, you must do what you think best.

FRANK: Well that weren't much advice was it!

BEATIE: No matters—he give it. So the girl thinks about it and being so in love she decides to strip.

PEARL: Oh I say!

MR. BRYANT: Well, this is a rum ole story ent it?

BEATIE: Shut up Father and listen. Now, er—where was I?

MR. BRYANT: She was strippin'.

BEATIE: Oh yes! So, the girl strips and the ferryman takes her over —he don't touch her or nothing—just takes her over and she rushes to Archie's hut to implore him to take her with him and to declare her love again. Now Archie promises to take her with him and so she sleeps with him the night. But when she wake up in the morning he've gone. She's left alone. So she go across to Tom and explain her plight and ask for help. But soon ever he knowed what she've done, he chuck her out see? So there she is. Poor little gal. Left alone with no clothes and no friends and no hope of staying alive. Now —this is the question, think about it, don't answer quick— who is the person most responsible for her plight?

JIMMY: Well, can't she get back?

BEATIE: No, she can't do anything. She's finished. She've hed it! Now, who's to blame?

There is a general air of thought for the moment and BEATIE *looks triumphant and pleased with herself.*

MRS. BRYANT: Be you a-drinkin' on your tea look. Don't you worry about no naked girls. The gal won't get cold but the tea will.

PEARL: Well I say the girl's most responsible.

BEATIE: Why?

PEARL: Well, she made the choice didn't she?

FRANK: Yes, but the old ferryman made her take off her clothes.

PEARL: But she didn't hev to.

FRANK: Blust woman, she were in love!

BEATIE: Good ole Frank.

JENNY: Hell if I know.

BEATIE: Jimmy?

JIMMY: Don't ask me gal—I follow decisions, I aren't makin' none.

BEATIE: Father?

MR. BRYANT: I don't know what you're on about.

BEATIE: Mother?

MRS. BRYANT: Drink you your tea gal—never you mind what I think.

This is what they're waiting for.

PEARL: Well—what do Ronnie say?

BEATIE: He say the gal is responsible only for makin' the decision to strip off and go across and that she do that because she's in love. After that she's the victim of two phoney men—one who don't love her but take advantage of her and one who say he love her but don't love her enough to help her, and that the man who say he love her but don't do nothin' to help her is most responsible because he were the last one she could turn to.

JENNY: He've got it all worked out then!

BEATIE (*jumping on a chair thrusting her fist into the air like Ronnie, and glorying in what is the beginning of a hysteric outburst of his quotes*). "No one do that bad that you can't forgive them."

PEARL: He's sure of himself then?

BEATIE: "We can't be sure of everything but certain basic things we must be sure about or we'll die."

FRANK: He think everyone is gonna listen then?

BEATIE: "People *must* listen. It's no good talking to the converted. *Everyone* must argue and think or they will stagnate and rot and the rot will spread."

JENNY: Hark at that then.

BEATIE (*her strange excitement growing; she has a quote for everything*): "If wanting the best things in life means being a snob then glory hallelujah I'm a snob. But I'm not a snob Beatie, I just believe in human dignity and tolerance and co-operation and equality and—"

JIMMY (*jumping up in terror*): He's a communist!

BEATIE: "I'm a socialist!"

There is a knock on the front door.

BEATIE (*jumping down joyously as though her excited quotes have been leading to this one moment*) : He's here, he's here! (*But at the door it is the postman, from whom she takes a letter and a parcel.*) Oh, the silly fool, the fool. Trust him to write a letter on the day he's coming. Parcel for you Mother.

PEARL: Oh, that'll be your dress from the club.

MRS. BRYANT: What dress is this then? I didn't ask for no dress from the club.

PEARL: Yes you did, you did ask me, didn't she ask me Frank? Why, we were looking through the book together Mother.

MRS. BRYANT: No matters what we was doin' together I aren't hevin' it.

PEARL: But Mother you distinctly—

MRS. BRYANT: I aren't hevin' it so there now!

BEATIE *has read the letter—the contents stun her. She cannot move. She stares around speechlessly at everyone.*

MRS. BRYANT: Well, what's the matter wi' you gal? Let's have a read. (*Takes letter and reads contents in a dead flat but loud voice—as though it were a proclamation.*) "My dear Beatie. It wouldn't really work would it? My ideas about handing on a new kind of life are quite useless and romantic if I'm really honest. If I were a healthy human being it might have been all right but most of us intellectuals are pretty sick and neu-rotic—as you have often observed—and we couldn't build a world even if we were given the reins of government—not yet any-rate. I don't blame you for being stubborn, I don't blame you for ignoring every suggestion I ever made—I only blame myself for encouraging you to believe we could make a go of it and now two weeks of your not being here has given me the cowardly chance to think about and decide and I—"

BEATIE (*snatching letter*) : Shut up!

MRS. BRYANT: Oh—so we know now do we?

MR. BRYANT: What's this then—ent he comin'?

MRS. BRYANT: Yes, we know now.

MR. BRYANT: Ent he comin' I ask?

BEATIE: *No he ent comin'.*

An awful silence ensues. Everyone looks uncomfortable.

JENNY (*softly*) : Well blust gal, didn't you know this was going to happen?

BEATIE *shakes her head.*

MRS. BRYANT: So *we're* stubborn are we?

JENNY: Shut you up Mother, the girl's upset.

MRS. BRYANT: Well I can see that, I can see that, he ent coming, I can see that, and we're here like bloody fools, I can see that.

PEARL: Well did you quarrel all that much Beatie?

BEATIE (*as if discovering this for the first time*) : He always wanted me to help him but I never could. Once he tried to teach me to type but soon ever I made a mistake I'd give up. I'd give up every time! I couldn't bear making mistakes. I don't know why, but I couldn't bear making mistakes.

MRS. BRYANT: Oh—so we're hearin' the other side o' the story now are we?

BEATIE: He used to suggest I start to copy real objects on to my paintings instead of only abstracts and I never took heed.

MRS. BRYANT: Oh, so you never took heed.

JENNY: Shut you up I say.

BEATIE: He gimme a book sometimes and I never bothered to read it.

FRANK (*not maliciously*) : What about all this discussion we heard of?

BEATIE: I *never* discussed things. He used to beg me to discuss things but I never saw the point on it.

PEARL: And he got riled because o' that?

BEATIE (*trying to understand*) : I didn't have any patience.

MRS. BRYANT: Now it's coming out.

BEATIE: I couldn't help him—I never knew patience. Once he looked at me with terrified eyes and said, "We've been together for three years but you don't know who I am or what I'm trying to say—and you don't care do you?"

MRS. BRYANT: And there she was tellin' me.

BEATIE: I never knew what he wanted—I didn't think it mattered.

MR. BRYANT: And there she were gettin' us to solve the moral problem and now we know she didn't even do it herself. That's a rum 'un, ent it?

MRS. BRYANT: The apple don't fall far from the tree—that it don't.

BEATIE (*wearily*) : So you're proud on it? You sit there smug and you're proud that a daughter of yours wasn't able to help her boy friend? Look at you. All of you. You can't say anything. You can't even help your own flesh and blood. Your daughter's bin ditched. It's your problem as well isn't it? I'm part of your family aren't I? Well, help me then! Give me words of comfort! Talk to me—for God's sake, someone talk to me. (*She cries at last.*)

MR. BRYANT: Well, what do we do now?

MRS. BRYANT: We sit down and we eat that's what we do now.

JENNY: Don't be soft Mother, we can't leave the girl crying like that.

MRS. BRYANT: Well, blust, 'tent my fault she's cryin'. I did what I could—I prepared all this food, I'd've treated him as my own son if he'd come but he hevn't! We got a whole family gathering specially to greet him, all on us look, but he hevn't come. So what am I supposed to do?

BEATIE: My God, Mother, I hate you—the only thing I ever wanted and I weren't able to keep him, I didn't know how. I hate you, I hate . . .

MRS. BRYANT *slaps* BEATIE'S *face. Everyone is a little shocked at this harsh treatment.*

MRS. BRYANT: There! I hed enough!

MR. BRYANT: Well what d'you wanna do that for?

MRS. BRYANT: I hed enough. All this time she've bin home she've
bin tellin' me I didn't do this and I didn't do that and I
hevn't understood half what she've said and I've hed enough.
She talk about bein' part o' the family but she've never lived
at home since she've left school look. Then she go away from
here and fill her head wi' high-class squit and then it turn
out she don't understand any on it herself. It turn out she do
just the same things she say I do. (*Into* BEATIE's *face*) Well,
am I right gal? I'm right ent I? When you tell me I was stubborn, what you mean was that *he* told you *you* was stubborn
—eh? When you tell me I don't understand you mean *you*
don't understand isn't it? When you tell me I don't make
no effort you mean *you* don't make no effort. Well, what you
blaming me for? Blaming me all the time! I haven't bin responsible for you since you left home—you bin on your own.
She think I like it, she do! Thinks I like it being cooped up
in this house all day. Well I'm telling you my gal—I don't!
There! And if I had a chance to be away working somewhere
the whole lot on you's could go to hell—the lot on you's. All
right so I am a bloody fool—all right! So I know it! A whole
two weeks I've bin told it. Well, so then I can't help you my
gal, no that I can't, and you get used to that once and for all.
BEATIE: No you can't Mother, I know you can't.
MRS. BRYANT: I suppose doin' all those things for him weren't
enough. I suppose he weren't satisfied wi' goodness only.
BEATIE: Oh, what's the use.
MRS. BRYANT: Well, don't you sit there an' sigh gal like you was
Lady Nevershit. I ask you something. Answer me. You do
the talking then. Go on—you say you know something we
don't so *you* do the talking. Talk—go on, talk gal.
BEATIE (*despairingly*): I can't Mother, you're right—the apple
don't fall far from the tree do it? You're right, I'm like you.
Stubborn, empty, wi' no tools for livin'. I got no roots in
nothing. I come from a family o' farm labourers yet I ent got
no roots—just like town people—just a mass o' nothin'.
FRANK: Roots, gal? What do you mean, roots?
BEATIE (*impatiently*): Roots, roots, roots! Christ, Frankie, you're

in the fields all day, you should know about growing things. Roots! The things you come from, the things that feed you. The things that make you proud of yourself—roots!

MR. BRYANT: You got a family ent you?

BEATIE: I am not talking about family roots—I mean—the—I mean —Look! Ever since it begun the world's bin growin' hasn't it? Things hev happened, things have bin discovered, people have bin thinking and improving and inventing but what do we know about it all?

JIMMY: What is she on about?

BEATIE (*various interjection*): What do you mean, what am I on about? I'm talking! Listen to me! I'm tellin' you that the world's bin growing for two thousand years and we hevn't noticed it. I'm telling you that we don't know what we are or where we come from. I'm telling you something's cut us off from the beginning. I'm telling you we've got no roots. Blimey Joe! We've all got large allotments, we all grow things around us so we should know about roots. You know how to keep your flowers alive don't you Mother? Jimmy—you know how to keep the roots of your veges strong and healthy. It's not only the corn that need strong roots, you know, it's us too. But what've we got? Go on, tell me, what've we got? We don't know where we push up from and we don't bother neither.

PEARL: Well, I aren't grumbling.

BEATIE: You say you aren't—oh yes, you say so, but look at you. What've you done since you come in? Hev you said anythin'? I mean really said or done anything to show you're alive? Alive! Blust, what do it mean? Do you know what it mean? Any of you? Shall I tell you what Susie said when I went and saw her? She say she don't care if that ole atom bomb drop and she die—that's what she say. And you know why she say it? I'll tell you why, because if she had to care she'd have to do something about it and she find *that* too much effort. Yes she do. She can't be bothered—she's too bored with it all. That's what we all are—we're all too bored.

MRS. BRYANT: Blust woman—bored you say, bored? You say Susie's bored, with a radio and television an' that? I go t'hell if she's bored!

BEATIE: Oh yes, we turn on a radio or a TV set maybe, or we go to the pictures—if them's love stories or gangsters—but isn't that the easiest way out? Anything so long as we don't have to make an effort. Well, am I right? You know I'm right. Education ent only books and music—it's asking questions, all the time. There are millions of us, all over the country, and no one, not one of us, is asking questions, we're all taking the easiest way out. Everyone I ever worked with took the easiest way out. We don't fight for anything, we're so mentally lazy we might as well be dead. Blust, we are dead! And you know what Ronnie say sometimes? He say it serves us right! That's what he say—it's our own bloody fault!

JIMMY: So that's us summed up then—so we know where *we* are then!

MRS. BRYANT: Well if he don't reckon we count nor nothin', then it's as well he didn't come. There! It's as well he didn't come.

BEATIE: Oh, *he* thinks we count all right—living in mystic communion with nature. Living in mystic bloody communion with nature (indeed). But us count? Count Mother? I wonder. Do we? Do you think we really count? You don' wanna take any notice of what them ole papers say about the workers bein' all-important these days—that's all squit! 'Cos we aren't. Do you think when the really talented people in the country get to work they get to work for us? Hell if they do! Do you think they don't know we 'ont make the effort? The writers don't write thinkin' we can understand, nor the painters don't paint expecting us to be interested—that they don't, nor don't the composers give out music thinking we can appreciate it. "Blust," they say, "the masses is too stupid for us to come down to them. Blust," they say, "if they don't make no effort why should we bother?" So you know who come along? The slop singers and the pop writers and the film makers and women's magazines and the Sunday papers and the picture strip love stories—that's who come along, and you don't have to make no effort for them, it come easy. "We know where the money lie," they say, "hell we do! The workers've got it so let's give them what they want. If they want slop songs and film idols we'll give 'em that then. If they want words of one syllable, we'll give 'em that then. If they want the third-rate, *blust!* We'll give 'em *that* then. Anything's good enough for them 'cos they don't ask for no more!" The whole stinkin' commercial world insults us and we don't care a damn. Well, Ronnie's right—it's our own bloody fault. We want the third-rate—we got it! We got it! We got it! We . . .

Suddenly BEATIE *stops as if listening to herself. She pauses, turns with an ecstatic smile on her face—*

D'you hear that? D'you hear it? Did you listen to me? I'm talking. Jenny, Frankie, Mother—I'm not quoting no more.

MRS. BRYANT (*getting up to sit at table*) : Oh hell, I hed enough of her—let her talk a while she'll soon get fed up.

The others join her at the table and proceed to eat and murmur.

BEATIE: Listen to me someone. (*As though a vision were revealed to her*) God in heaven, *Ronnie!* It does work, it's happening to me, I can feel it's happened, I'm beginning, on my own two feet—I'm beginning . . .

The murmur of the family sitting down to eat grows as BEATIE'*s last cry is heard. Whatever she will do they will continue to live as before. As* BEATIE *stands alone, articulate at last—*

The curtain falls.

SERJEANT
MUSGRAVE'S
DANCE

An Unhistorical Parable

John Arden

SERJEANT MUSGRAVE'S DANCE was first performed at the Royal Court Theatre on 22 October 1959, produced by Lindsay Anderson, music by Dudley Moore, decor by Jocelyn Herbert, and with the following cast:

PRIVATE SPARKY	Donal Donnelly
PRIVATE HURST	Alan Dobie
PRIVATE ATTERCLIFFE	Frank Finlay
BLUDGEON, *a bargee*	James Bree
SERJEANT MUSGRAVE	Ian Bannen
THE PARSON	Richard Caldicot
MRS. HITCHCOCK	Freda Jackson
ANNIE	Patsy Byrne
THE CONSTABLE	Michael Hunt
THE MAYOR	Stratford Johns
A SLOW COLLIER	Jack Smethurst
A PUGNACIOUS COLLIER	Colin Blakely
WALSH, *an earnest collier*	Harry Gwynn Davies
A TROOPER OF DRAGOONS	Barry Wilsher
AN OFFICER OF DRAGOONS	Clinton Greyn

The play is set in a mining town in the north of England eighty years ago. It is winter.

INTRODUCTION

This is a realistic, but not a naturalistic, play. Therefore the design of the scenes and costumes must be in some sense stylised. The paintings of L. S. Lowry might suggest a suitable mood. Scenery must be sparing—only those pieces of architecture, furniture, and properties actually *used* in the action need be present: and they should be thoroughly realistic, so that the audience sees a selection from the details of everyday life rather than a generalised impression of the whole of it. A similar rule should also govern the direction and the acting. If this is done, the obvious difficulties, caused by the mixture of verse, prose, and song in the play, will be considerably lessened.

The exact date of the play is deliberately not given. In the London production, the details of costume covered approximately the years between 1860 and 1880. For instance, the soldiers wore the scarlet tunics and spiked helmets characteristic of the later (or "Kipling") epoch, while the Constable was dressed in tall hat and tail coat as an early Peeler—his role in the play suggesting a rather primitive type of police organisation.

The songs should be sung to folk-song airs. There are many available tunes which equally well suit the various songs—perhaps these are as good as any:

Sparky's song (Act One, Scene 1): "Six Jolly Wee Miners"—Scottish.

Sparky's song and chorus (Act Two, Scene 2): "Blow away the Morning Dew"—English.

Sparky's song (Act Two, Scene 3): "The Black Horse"—Irish.

Attercliffe's song (Act Three, Scene 2): First three stanzas—"John Barleycorn"—English Air. Final stanza—"John Barleycorn"—Irish Air.

Musgrave's song (Act Three, Scene 1) proved in production

to be more satisfactory if the words were spoken against a background of drum rolls and recorded music.

The characters perhaps need a few notes of description:

The Soldiers: these are regulars and seasoned men. They should all have moustaches and an ingrained sense of discipline. Musgrave is aged between thirty and forty, tall, swart, commanding, sardonic but never humorous; he could well have served under Cromwell. Attercliffe is aged about fifty, grey-haired, melancholy, a little embittered. He is the senior O.R. of the party and conscious of his responsibility. Hurst, in his twenties, is bloody-minded, quick-tempered, handsome, cynical, tough, but not quite as intelligent as he thinks he is. Sparky, also in his twenties, is easily led, easily driven, inclined to hide from himself behind a screen of silly stories and irritating clownishness. The Dragoon Officer is little more than the deus-ex-machina at the end of the play. All he needs to be is tall, calm, cold and commanding. His Trooper is a tough, reliable soldier.

The Townsmen: The Mayor is a bustling, shrewd, superficially jovial man with a coarse accent and an underlying inclination to bully. The Parson is very much a gentleman: he is conscious of the ungentlemanly nature of the community in which he lives. He must have the accent and manners of a balked aristocrat rather than a stage-clergyman. He too has some inclination to bully. The Constable has a continual inclination to bully, except when in the presence of his superiors. He is as inefficient as he is noisy. The Colliers are all embittered but not so as to make them unpleasant. Walsh is a strong man, physically and morally. He knows what he wants and is entirely impatient with those who are not so single-minded. The Slow Collier is not particularly intelligent but has a vacuous good humour. The Pugnacious Collier is pugnacious, and very quick to show it. The Bargee is something of a grotesque, a hunchback (though this should not be over-emphasized), very rapid in his movements, with a natural urge towards intrigue and mischief.

The Women: The Landlady is a large, immobile widow of about fifty. She sits behind her bar and watches everything that happens. She is clearly a woman of deep sympathies and intelligence, which she disguises with the normal north-country sombre pessimism. Annie is a big-boned girl, not particularly attractive, but in an aggressive sort of way she provokes the men. Her emotional confusion expresses itself in a deliberately enigmatic style of speech and behaviour. Her voice is harsh.

As for the "Meaning of the Play": I do not think that an introductory note is a suitable place for a lengthy analysis of the work, but in view of the obvious puzzlement with which it was greeted by the critics, perhaps a few points may be made. This is not a nihilistic play. This is not (except perhaps unconsciously) a symbolist play. Nor does it advocate bloody revolution. I have endeavoured to write about the violence that is so evident in the world, and to do so through a story that is partly one of wish-fulfilment. I think that many of us must at some time have felt an overpowering urge to match some particularly outrageous piece of violence with an even greater and more outrageous retaliation. Musgrave tries to do this: and the fact that the sympathies of the play are clearly with him in his original horror, and then turn against him and his intended remedy, seems to have bewildered many people. I would suggest, however, that a study of the roles of the women, and of Private Attercliffe, should be sufficient to remove any doubts as to where the "moral" of the play lies. Accusations of nihilism seem to derive from the scene where the Colliers turn away from Musgrave and join in the general dance around the beer barrel. Again, I would suggest, that an unwillingness to dwell upon unpleasant situations that do not immediately concern us is a general human trait, and recognition of it need imply neither cynicism nor despair. Complete pacifism is a very hard doctrine: and if this play appears to advocate it with perhaps some timidity, it is probably because I am naturally a timid man—and also because I know that if I am hit I very easily hit back: and I do not care to preach too confidently what I am not sure I can practise.

J.A.

ACT ONE

Scene One

A canal wharf. Evening.

HURST *and* ATTERCLIFFE *are playing cards on the top of a side-drum. A few yards away* SPARKY *stands, as though on guard, clapping himself to keep warm. There is a pile of three or four heavy wooden boxes with the WD broad arrow stencilled on them, and a lantern set on top.*

SPARKY: Brrr, oh a cold winter, snow, dark. We wait too long, that's the trouble. Once you've started, keep on travelling. No good sitting to wait in the middle of it. Only makes the cold night colder. *(He sings):*

> One day I was drunk, boys, on the Queen's Highway
> When a recruiting party come beating that way.
> I was enlisted and attested before I did know
> And to the Royal Barracks they forced me to go.

Brrr! And they talk of the Crimea! Did I ever tell you that one about the field kitchens at Sebastopol? Well, there was this red-haired provost-sarnt, y'see ... and then the corporal-cook—now *he'd* got no hair at all ... now the Commissary in that Regiment was—oh ... *(He finds no one paying attention.)* Who's winning?

HURST: I'm winning.

ATTERCLIFFE: Oho, no you're not. The black spades carry the day. Jack, King and Ace. *We* throw the red Queen over. That's another shilling, you know. Let's have it.

HURST: All right. Deal agen, boy. Or no, no, *my* deal, this game. Now let's see if I can't turn some good cards on to *my* side for a difference. Here: one, two, three, four . . . *(He deals the cards.)*

SPARKY: How much longer we got to wait, I'd like to know. I want to be off aboard that damned barge and away. What's happened to our Black Jack Musgrave, eh? Why don't he come and give us the word to get going?

ATTERCLIFFE: He'll come on the stroke, as he said. He works his life to bugle and drum, this serjeant. You ever seen him late?

SPARKY: No. *(He sings)*:

> When first I deserted I thought myself free
> Till my cruel sweetheart informed upon me—

ATTERCLIFFE *(sharply)*: I don't think you ought to sing *that* one.

SPARKY: Why not? It's true, isn't it? *(He sings)*:

> Court martial, court martial, they held upon me
> And the sentence they passed was the high gallows tree.

HURST *(dropping cards and springing up in a rage)*: Now shut it, will you! God-damned devil of a song to sing on this sort of a journey! He said you didn't ought to, so don't! *(He glances nervously around.)*

SPARKY: Ha, there's nobody to hear us. You're safe as a bloody blockhouse out here—I'm on the sentry, boy, *I'm* your protection.

ATTERCLIFFE *(irritably)*: You make sure you are then. Go on: keep watching.

SPARKY *(returns to his guard)*: Ah. Ha-ha . . . Or did you think *he* could hear you? *(He gestures towards the boxes.)* Maybe, maybe . . . *I* thought I heard him laugh.

ATTERCLIFFE: Steady, boy.

SPARKY *(a little wildly)*: Steady yourself, you crumbling old cuckold. He might laugh, who knows? Well, make a rattling any road. Mightn't he, soldier boy?

HURST: Are you coming funny wi' me—

SPARKY: Funny? About *him*? You don't tell me he don't know

what we're at. Why shouldn't he have a laugh at it, if that's how he feels?

HURST: Arrh, you're talking daft.

SPARKY: Now don't you be nervous, boy: not for *you* to be nervous. You're a man and a soldier! Or an old red rag stretched over four pair o' bones—well, what's the odds? Eh?

HURST (*after glaring angrily, sits down again*): All right . . . All right, play.

> *They play in silence.* SPARKY *hums and blows his knuckles. Then he starts.*

SPARKY: Who goes there!

> *The* BARGEE *enters with a lantern, whistling "Michael Finnegan."*

BARGEE: Hooroar, my jolly buckos! It's only old Joe Bludgeon, the Captain of the Lugger. Crooked old Joe. Heh heh. And what's the news with you? Are we ready yet, are we?

SPARKY: Ready for what?

BARGEE: Ready for off, of course, what do you think? Are we?

ATTERCLIFFE: No.

BARGEE: Why not, then?

ATTERCLIFFE: 'Cos it's not time, that's why not. Half-past seven, you was told.

BARGEE: Oh, it's as near as—

ATTERCLIFFE: No begod it's not, and he won't be here till it is.

BARGEE: Ah, the serjeant, eh?

ATTERCLIFFE: Aye, the serjeant. Is your barge up yet?

BARGEE: It's up. And the old horse waiting.

ATTERCLIFFE: Then we'll start to load.

HURST: Hey, we've not finished the game.

ATTERCLIFFE: Save it, mucker. You heard what Black Jack said.

HURST: All right. All right.

BARGEE: You can load these smaller cases 'side of the cabin. What you got in 'em, for Godsake? Ten ton and a half here.

SPARKY *(kicking one of them)*: There's a Gatling gun in that one. You know what a Gatling gun is, friend?

BARGEE: I don't, and I don't care neither, tell you truth of it. By Lordy, what a life, the bloody Army. Do they still tie you fellers up and stripe you across with the cat-o'-nine-tails, eh?

HURST: No they don't.

ATTERCLIFFE *and* HURST *start carrying the cases out.*

BARGEE *(gloating)*: Heheh, when I wor a young lad they told me, they did. Whack, whack, whack. Ooh, cruel it was. You know what they used to call 'em in them days—soldiers, I mean? Eh?

SPARKY: I know a lot o' names for calling soldiers.

BARGEE: I'll bet you don't know this one, though. Heh. Bloodred roses, that was it. What d'you think o' that, eh? Whack, whack, whack. Bloodred roses, eh? *(He calls offstage.)* Not there, don't put it there, give me some room to swing me tiller, can't you! Soldiers. Get 'em aboard a barge, you'd be as well off wi' a row of deaf niggers from Peru. That's right, now leave it where you've dropped it, and come ashore before you capsize her—you bloodred bloody roses, you!

HURST *re-enters.*

HURST: That's enough of that, matey. Watch it.

MUSGRAVE *enters.*

MUSGRAVE *(to the* BARGEE*)*: Aye, you watch it. Now I'll tell you just once, old man, and that's all. We travel on your barge, passengers: we pay our fare. So don't you talk to my men like they're deck-hands. Clear?

BARGEE: Oh it's clear, serjeant. I only wanted a little joke.

MUSGRAVE: Aye. And now you've had one. So be thankful.

ATTERCLIFFE *re-enters.*

ATTERCLIFFE (*as he and* HURST *pick up the remaining smaller boxes*): We got the Gatling loaded on serjeant, and we're fetching the rest of it. Then there's just the drum and the other box left. Any news?

MUSGRAVE (*quietly to him*): We're all all right. Don't worry.

ATTERCLIFFE *and* HURST *go out with their load.* MUSGRAVE *taps the drum meditatively and turns to the* BARGEE.

I say, you, bargee. Is it going to snow again before to-morrow?

BARGEE: Likely. There's ice coming on the water too. Give her another day and this canal'll be closed. They say the road over the moors is fast already with the drifts. You've chose a merry time o' year beating up for recruities, haven't you? What you got in here? Another Gatling gun? (*He smacks the last box.*)

MUSGRAVE: Why not? Show 'em all the best equipment, gla-mourise 'em, man, fetch 'em in like conies ... Now get this last box loaded, and be careful. And then we're all ready. You can start.

ATTERCLIFFE *and* HURST, *having returned, pick up the box and carry it out,* SPARKY *going with them, the drum slung on his shoulder.* MUSGRAVE *takes the soldiers' lantern and makes a rapid circuit of the stage to see if anything is left. He stands for a moment looking out in the direction from which he has come in.*

BARGEE (*waiting for him*): This your first trip to the coal-mining towns, serjeant?

MUSGRAVE: It is.

BARGEE: Ooh, brr, bitter and bleak: hungry men for the Queen. If you're used to a full belly, you'll want it when you get there.

MUSGRAVE *(curtly)*: It's not material. We have our duty. A soldier's duty is a soldier's life.

BARGEE: Ah, duty.

> The Empire wars are far away
> For duty's sake we sail away
> Me arms and legs is shot away
> And all for the wink of a shilling and a drink . . .

Come on, me cheery serjeant, you've not left nowt behind.

They go out after the soldiers.

Scene Two

The bar of a public house.

MRS. HITCHCOCK *is sitting in the body of the room, talking to the* PARSON, *who is very much at his ease, with a glass of brandy in his hand.* ANNIE *is polishing glasses etc. behind the bar.*

PARSON: No. No, madam, no. I cannot be seen to countenance idleness, pauperism, beggary. If no one comes to buy your drink, I am sorry for you. But the fact is, madam, a little less drunkenness and disorder will do this town no harm. The Church is not a speculative bank, you know, to subsidise pot-houses.

MRS. HITCHCOCK *(sulkily)*: Always a respectable house.

PARSON: What?

MRS. HITCHCOCK: Always a respectable house, reverend. Aye. If not, why renew the licence? You're a magistrate, you know. You could have spoke agen me on me application. But you didn't.

PARSON: That is not to the purpose, Mrs. Hitchcock. The Bench allows that there have to be public houses to permit an outlet for the poorer sort of people, but in times of regrettable industrial conflict it is better that as many of them as possible remain empty. If the colliers cannot afford drink because of the strike—because of their own stupidity—then there is the less likelihood of their being inflamed to acts of violence. I am not at all certain that the Bench ought not to withdraw all licences altogether until the pits are working.

MRS. HITCHCOCK: That'd be grand. See half a dozen publicans going on the parish—beer-dregs from the workhouse served to the Trade—ooh, talk of arsy-versy! *(She laughs throatily.)*

PARSON: I'm quite sure that would not be necessary.

MRS. HITCHCOCK *(reasonably)*: Now, look, reverend, you've been taking me crossroads since the minute I began. All I asked you in to say is this: this strike is bad for the town. Well, I mean, of course, that means me. But it means you too. *And* it means His Worship the Mayor: oh aye, aye:

> I am a proud coal owner
> And in scarlet here I stand.
> Who shall come or who shall go
> Through all my coal-black land?

(She laughs again.) Eh, if we can't have a laugh, we'll starve!

PARSON: You are impertinent. I have nothing more to say.

MRS. HITCHCOCK: Ah, but I come to you because you're Church, you're charity. Go on, reverend, you tell the Mayor to agree with his men and give them a good price, then they'll buy and sell in the town and they'll drink in this taproom, and —ho-hoo—who knows, they might even come to church! That'll be the day.

The PARSON *turns irritably from her and goes to the door. The* BARGEE *enters and confronts him.*

BARGEE *(touching his cap mockingly)*: Parson.

PARSON *(coldly)*: Good afternoon.

BARGEE: Cold enough for you, eh?

PARSON *(trying to pass)*: It is cold, yes.

BARGEE: How's the strike?

PARSON: It is not yet settled.

BARGEE: No, I bet it's not, and all. Hey missus!

MRS. HITCHCOCK: Hello.

BARGEE: A quart o' taddy. Best!

MRS. HITCHCOCK *(impassive)*: Can you pay for it?

BARGEE: 'Course I can pay—wait a minute, Parson, just a minute, all under control—I'm not one of your colliery agitators, you know. *I'm* still in work. I've news for you.

MRS. HITCHCOCK *(to ANNIE)*: He says he can pay. Draw him his quart.

BARGEE *(to the PARSON)*: I didn't think, like, to find you here, but, eh, well, seeing as how here you are—canal's froze up, you know.

PARSON: Well?

BARGEE: Well. Last barge come in this morning. *My* barge. There was passengers.

PARSON: I am not really interested.

BARGEE *(significantly)*: Four on 'em, Parson. Soldiers.

ANNIE *hands the* BARGEE *his tankard.*

PARSON *(in some alarm)*: Soldiers! Already? Who sent for them? Why was I not told? This could be very dangerous—

BARGEE: They're not here for what you think, you know. Not yet, any road. You see, they've come recruiting.

PARSON *(relieved, but vexed)*: Oh ... Well, what if they have? Why bother me with it? You're just wasting time, man. Come on, get out of my way ...

BARGEE *(still detaining him)*: Eh, but, Parson, you're a magistrate.

PATSON: Of course I'm a magistrate.

BARGEE: You're a power, you are: in a town of trouble, in a place of danger. Yes. You're the word and the book, aren't you? Well then: soldiers. Recruiting. Useful?

PARSON *(beginning to follow his drift)*: H'm. I do not think the

Bench is in any real need of *your* suggestions. But I am
obliged to you for the news. Thank you.

He gives the BARGEE *a coin and leaves.*

BARGEE *(flipping the coin)*: Heh, heh, I said I could pay.

He gives it to ANNIE *and starts whistling "Michael Finnegan."*
ANNIE *goes back to the bar.* MRS. HITCHCOCK *takes the coin
from her and tests it between her teeth.*

MRS. HITCHCOCK: Soldiers. Annie, love, you could tell us what
soldiers is good for.
ANNIE *(sullen)*: Why should I tell you?
BARGEE *(gleefully)*: Go on, go on, lassie, tell us about the soldiers.
She knows the good redcoat button-to-back, I'll bet. Go on,
it's a cold day, warm it up for us. Heh, heh, our strong
Annie's the champion, eh?

He smacks her on the bottom. She swerves angrily.

ANNIE: *When* I've given you leave: and not afore. You bloody
dog, sit down.
BARGEE *(subsiding in mock terror)*: Ooh, sharp, sharp.
MRS. HITCHCOCK: Aye, so sit down . . . Go on, Annie, tell us.
ANNIE: I'll tell you for what a soldier's good:

> To march behind his roaring drum,
> Shout to us all: "Here I come
> I've killed as many as I could—
> I'm stamping into your fat town
> From the war and to the war
> And every girl can be my whore
> Just watch me lay them squealing down."
> And that's what he does and so do we.
> Because we know he'll soon be dead
> We strap our arms round the scarlet red

Then send him weeping over the sea.
Oh he will go and a long long way.
Before he goes we'll make him pay
Between the night and the next cold day—
By God there's a whole lot more I could say—

What good's a bloody soldier 'cept to be dropped into a slit in the ground like a letter in a box. How many did you bring with you—is it four?

BARGEE: Aye. Four.

ANNIE: That's four beds in this house?

MRS. HITCHCOCK: I should hope it's in this house. It's the best house in town.

ANNIE (*in a sudden outburst*): Then you'd do well to see they stay four nights because I'll not go with more nor one in one night, no, not for you nor for all of Egypt!

She lets out a howl and rushes out of the door behind the bar, clattering a tin tray full of tankards on to the floor.

BARGEE: Ooh, Lordy! Champion, strong, and sharp. Annie! Tell us some more!

MRS. HITCHCOCK (*crossly*): Let her alone. She's said enough for you, hasn't she? It's not right to set her off . . . I suppose they *are* coming to this house?

BARGEE: Oh surely, aye, surely. *I* told 'em: *I* took care.

A rat-tat-tat on the drum heard, off.

There, you see, they're coming.

SPARKY *enters magnificently, beating the drum.*

SPARKY: Ho-ho, atten-tion! Stand by your beds! Name of the Queen, missus—has he told you—there's four on us: we three, we'll settle for palliasses in the loft, but the serjeant he wants a big brass bed with knobs on, that's his fancy! Can you do it?

MRS. HITCHCOCK: So here they are, the gay recruiters. Aye, I can do it, young man. I've only one room in the house. The serjeant can have that. The three of you'll have to doss down in me old stable, out back, but there's a good stove, you'll be warm. Now, who's going to pay? You or the Queen?

SPARKY: Oh, Queen at end of it all, I suppose.

MRS. HITCHCOCK: But you at beginning, eh?

SPARKY: Oh-oh, chalk it up, you know ... we've brought some gear with us too.

BARGEE: Ten and a half ton. Nigh foundered the old barge, it did, I can tell you.

SPARKY: But we got here, friend, didn't we? Like we get our-selves to everywhere we go, we do. No question o' that, y'see.

BARGEE: Heh, heh, none.

SPARKY (*calls to offstage*): Serjeant! We're fixed!

MUSGRAVE (*off*): And the equipment?

SPARKY: And the equipment, missus?

MRS. HITCHCOCK: There's a coach-house across the yard.

SPARKY (*calls to offstage*): Coach-house across the yard, serjeant! ... While they're taking it round there, missus, let's have a pint apiece drawn ready. Like what *he* drinks, eh? Re-commend it, friend?

BARGEE: You could stand your bayonet up in this, you could.

SPARKY: Right, then. And we'll give you another while we're at it. That's five on 'em, pints, unless *you're* drinking with us too, are you?

MRS. HITCHCOCK: Why not, soldier? Queen as pays ... Annie! Hey Annie!

As there is no reply, she goes herself behind the bar and starts filling the tankards. MUSGRAVE *enters.*

MUSGRAVE: Is the padlock on your coach-house door a strong one, ma'am?

MRS. HITCHCOCK: Likely so.

MUSGRAVE: Valuable equipment, y'see. Your window in there's barred, I notice.

MRS. HITCHCOCK: That's right.

MUSGRAVE *(picking up a tankard)*: Good ... This for me?

MRS. HITCHCOCK: If you want it.

The other two soldiers enter.

ATTERCLIFFE: The cases are all locked up and safe, serjeant.

MUSGRAVE *(indicates drinks)*: Very good. Here you are.

HURST and ATTERCLIFFE: Thank you serjeant.

BARGEE *(raising his drink)*: Good health to Her Majesty; to Her Majesty's wars; to the girls we leave behind us. Drink!

They all drink.

MRS. HITCHCOCK *(raising her drink)*:

> Into the river, out of the river
> Once I was dry, now I am wet
> But hunger and cold they hold me yet.

They drink again, with a certain puzzlement at the toast.

MRS. HITCHCOCK: They hold this town today, any road, serjeant; or had you been told?

MUSGRAVE: What's the matter?

MRS. HITCHCOCK: No work in the colliery. The owner calls it a strike, the men call it a lockout, we call it starvation.

The CONSTABLE *enters violently.*

CONSTABLE: His Worship the Mayor.

MRS. HITCHCOCK: Eh?

CONSTABLE: I said, His Worship the Mayor!

BARGEE: Oho, *now,* me jolly buckos, give attention, stand-to, to the present!

CONSTABLE *(to the* BARGEE*)*: Ssssh—ssh—

BARGEE: Heh, heh, heh—

The MAYOR *enters at speed, wearing his gold chain. After him comes the* PARSON. MUSGRAVE *calls his men to attention.*

MAYOR: Mrs. Hitchcock, I'm seeking the soldiers. Ah, here they are! Well, I'm the Mayor of this town, I own the colliery, I'm a worried man. So I come seeking you when I could send for you, what do you think to that? Let's have a look at you . . . Ah. Haha . . . Clear the snug a minute, missus. I want a private word with the Parson. Serjeant, be ready outside when I send for you.

MUSGRAVE: At your service, sir . . . Come on.

Beckoned by MRS. HITCHCOCK, *he leads his party out behind the bar.*

CONSTABLE *(propelling the* BARGEE *to the street door)*: Go on, you, out this road.

BARGEE *(dodging him)*: Oo-er—

    Constable Constable alive or dead
    His head is of leather and his belly's of lead.

Go—whoops . . . How are you, Parson?

He ducks out, whistling "Michael Finnegan."

MRS. HITCHCOCK *(sourly, to the* MAYOR*)*: Do you want a drink?

MAYOR: No.

MRS. HITCHCOCK: *At* your service, when you do.

She curtsies and goes out behind the bar.

MAYOR: What do you think to 'em, Parson?

PARSON: Fine strong men. They make me proud of my country. Mr. Mayor, Britain depends upon these spirits. It is a great pity that their courage is betrayed at home by sulkers and shirkers. What do *you* think?

MAYOR *(looking at him sideways)*: I think we'll use 'em, Parson. Temporary expedient, but it'll do. The price of coal has fell, I've had to cut me wages, I've had to turn men off. They say they'll strike, so I close me gates. We can't live like that for ever. There's two ways to solve this colliery— one is build the railway here and cut me costs of haulage, *that* takes two years and an Act of Parliament, though God knows I want to do it. The other is clear out half the population, stir up a diversion, turn their minds to summat else. The Queen's got wars, she's got rebellions. Over the sea. All right. Beat these fellers' drums high around the town, I'll put one pound down for every Royal Shilling the serjeant pays. Red coats and flags. Ged rid o' the troublemakers. Drums and fifes and glory.

PARSON *(severely)*: The soldier's calling is one of honour.

MAYOR: It's more than that. It's bloody convenient. Town Constable, fetch that serjeant in!

CONSTABLE *(nervously)*: Er, excuse me, Your Worship. A point. Soldiers, you see. Now, I've got a very small force in this town. Only one other regular officer, you know: the rest is them deputy-specials—I can't trust *that* lot to stand fast and fear nowt when the time comes.

PARSON: What time?

CONSTABLE: There's been stone-throwing this morning. Two of my office windows is broke. And I'm nervous—that's frank, you know—I *am*.

MAYOR: Well?

CONSTABLE: Your Worship. I want these soldiers added to my force. It's all right recruiting. But what we need's patrols.

MAYOR: Not yet.

CONSTABLE: Your Worship. I'm asking you formal. You've got agitators here, and they won't stop at throwing stones: that's frank.

MAYOR *(angrily)*: I said not yet. We'll try it my road first. Godsake, man, what's four soldiers agen the lot of 'em?

This town's wintered up, you'll get no more help till there's a thaw. So work on that. Call in the serjeant.

CONSTABLE: Right, Your Worship. Serjeant! Come in here!

MUSGRAVE *re-enters.*

MUSGRAVE. Sir?

MAYOR: Serjeant, we're very glad to have you. I speak for the Council, I speak for the magistrates. Now listen: there's loyal hearts and true here, and we're every man-jack of us keen to see our best lads flock to the colours. Isn't that so, Parson?

PARSON *(taken a little by surprise)*: Ha-h'm— with great pride, yes.

MAYOR: Right. For every Queen's Shilling you give out, I give out a golden sovereign—no, two. One for the recruit, and one to be divided among you and your three good lads. What do you say to that?

MUSGRAVE: That's most handsome, sir.

MAYOR: I should damn well think it is. How do you propose to work?

MUSGRAVE: Sir?

MAYOR: Aye, I mean, d'you tramp around the streets drumming, or set on your fannies in a pub—or what?

MUSGRAVE: Depends what's most appropriate, sir, according to the type of town. I've not had time for a look at yours yet. But the pubs seem pretty empty, if this one's owt to go by.

PARSON: They *are* empty.

MUSGRAVE: Aye. Well, in that case, I'll have to make a reconnaissance, won't I? When I'm decided, I'll let you know.

CONSTABLE: And let *me* know, serjeant. I'll see you get facilities.

MUSGRAVE: Thank you, mister.

MAYOR: And while you're on about them facilities, Constable, perhaps you might let in the serjeant on a few likely names for his list, eh? Could you pick him some passable strong-set men, could you?

CONSTABLE *(significantly)*: I could have a try, Your Worship.

MAYOR: Right. Then if that's settled, I'll be off back to town hall. I've not got time to waste wi' nattering, snug and all though it is in here. Come along, Constable. I want a little word wi' you about them stones.

MAYOR *and* CONSTABLE *go out.*

PARSON (*severely*): I think I ought to make one thing clear, serjeant. I know that it is customary for recruiting-parties to impress themselves upon the young men of the district as dashingly as possible, and no doubt upon the young women also. Now I am not having any of that. There's enough trouble in the place as it is. So remember.

MUSGRAVE: Yes, sir. I'll remember.

PARSON: I want no drunkenness, and no fornication, from your soldiers. Need I speak plainer?

MUSGRAVE: No, sir. There will be none. I am a religious man.

PARSON: Very well. Good day to you.

MUSGRAVE: Good day, sir.

The PARSON *goes.* MUSGRAVE *sits down, takes out a small pocket bible and reads.* MRS. HITCHCOCK *enters.*

MRS. HITCHCOCK: What, they've not all gone, already?

MUSGRAVE: They have, ma'am.

MRS. HITCHCOCK: Just like, in't it? Use my bar for a council-parlour, leave nowt behind 'em but bad breath and a shiny bench—*they* take care. I'm giving your three their dinners in back. You eating with 'em?

MUSGRAVE (*off-handed*): No. I'll have a hand of bread and cheese and eat it here.

MRS. HITCHCOCK: Drink with it?

MUSGRAVE (*still at his book*): No ... Thanks, no. Just the cheese.

MRS. HITCHCOCK (*sourly*): H'm, another on 'em ... Hey, Annie! Slice o' bread and a piece o' cheese in here for this one! Pickles?

MUSGRAVE: Eh?

MRS. HITCHCOCK (*annoyed*): Pickles!

MUSGRAVE: No ... (*He looks up suddenly.*) Tell me, ma'am, is there many from this town lately have gone for a soldier?

MRS. HITCHCOCK: Some. It's not a common pleasure here—not as long as the coal wor right to sell, any road. But there was some. You'll know the sort o' reasons, I daresay?

> The yellow-haired boy lay in my bed
> A-kissing me up from me toes to me head.
> But when my apron it did grow too short
> He thought it good time to leave his sport.

> *Enter* ANNIE *with the bread and cheese. She gives it to* MUSGRAVE.

MUSGRAVE: Thank you.

ANNIE (*confronting him*): Serjeant you are.

MUSGRAVE: That's right.

ANNIE: You seem a piece stronger than the rest of 'em.

> *He nods.*

And they call you Black Jack Musgrave?

> *He looks at her.*

Well, I'm looking at your face, mister serjeant. Now do you know what I'd say?

MUSGRAVE: What?

ANNIE: The North Wind in a pair of millstones
> Was your father and your mother.
> They got you in a cold grinding.
> God help us all if they get you a brother.

> *She looks at him another minute, then nods her head and goes out.*

MUSGRAVE (*wryly*): She talks a kind of truth, that lassie. Is she daft?

MRS. HITCHCOCK: No, no, no, I wouldn't say daft. But there's not many would let her bide in their house.

MUSGRAVE: Tell me, ma'am. It sticks on my mind that I once had a sort of a comrade came from this town ... Long, yellow-haired lad, like in your little verse. Name of, oh, Hickson, was it, Hickman?

MRS. HITCHCOCK *(astonished and disturbed)*: Ey, ey—

MUSGRAVE: What was it now, his name—Billy—Billy—

MRS. HITCHCOCK *(very upset)*: Billy Hicks. Hicks. Aye, oh, strange, serjeant, strange roads bringing you along, I'd not wonder.

MUSGRAVE: What do you mean? ... It *was* Hicks—I remember.

MRS. HITCHCOCK *(reminiscently)*: Not what you'd call a bad young feller, you know—but he weren't no good neither. He'd come in here pissed of a Satdy night—I'd tell him straight out, "You needn't reckon on to get any more here." But he'd lean on this bar and he'd look at me, and he'd sing, You know—*hymns*—"Uplift your heads, you gates of brass"—church hymns, he'd sing. Like he'd say to me, "I'll sing for me drinking, missus" ... hymns ...

She hums the tune of "Uplift your heads" and breaks off sharply.

He gave her a baby, and he went straight off to the war. Or the rebellions, they called it. They told us he was killed.

MUSGRAVE *(without emotion)*: Aye, he was killed. He was shot dead last year ... Gave a baby to who?

MRS. HITCHCOCK *(jerks her thumb to door behind bar)*: Her.

MUSGRAVE *(truly surprised)*: Go on?

MRS. HITCHCOCK: True. But when it wor born, it came a kind of bad shape, pale, sick: it wor dead and in the ground in no more nor two month. About the time they called *him* dead, y'see. What d'you reckon to that?

MUSGRAVE *(carelessly)*: It's not material. He was no great friends to me. But maybe, as you said, strange. He did use to sing. And yellow hair he had, didn't he? *(He goes to the door behind the bar and calls.)* Have ye finished your dinners? Because we'll take a look at the town before it gets dark. *(Confidentially to* MRS. HITCHCOCK.*)* What you've just been telling me, don't tell it to these. Dead men and dead children should bide where they're put and not be rose up to the thoughts of the living. It's bad for discipline ...*(He calls again.)* Come on, let's be having you!

The SOLDIERS *come in.* MUSGRAVE *points to each one as they enter.*

East; south; west; I'll go north; I'm told it suits my nature. Then meet at the churchyard rail and tell me what you've seen. Let's make it sharp.

They go out.

Scene Three

The churchyard.

Sunset. HURST *enters and walks about, whistling nervously. The* SLOW COLLIER *enters and looks at him. They pass each other, giving each other good hard stares. The* SLOW COLLIER *is about to leave the stage when he turns round and calls.*

SLOW COLLIER: Hey! Soldier!

HURST: Aye?

SLOW COLLIER: How many on you is there?

HURST: Four.

SLOW COLLIER: Four ... Four dead red rooks and be damned.

HURST: What? What's that?

SLOW COLLIER (*contemptuously*): Arrh . . .

> *He slouches out.*
> HURST *makes to follow, but decides not to, and continues walking about.*
> MUSGRAVE *enters.*

MUSGRAVE: Coldest town I ever was in. What did you see?

HURST: Hardly a thing. Street empty, windows shut, two old wives on a doorstep go indoors the minute I come. Three men on one corner, two men on another, dirty looks and no words from any on 'em. There's one man swears a curse at me just now. That's all.

MUSGRAVE: H'm . . .

> *He calls to offstage.*

Hello! We're over here!

> ATTERCLIFFE *enters.*

What did you see?

ATTERCLIFFE: Hardly a thing. Street empty, doors locked, windows blind, shops cold and empty. A young lass calls her kids in from playing in the dirt—she sees *me* coming, so she calls 'em. There's someone throws a stone—

MUSGRAVE: A stone?

ATTERCLIFFE: Aye. I don't know who did it and it didn't hit me, but it was thrown.

HURST: It's a cold poor town, I'm telling you, serjeant.

MUSGRAVE: Coldest town I ever was in. And here's the fourth of us.

> *Enter* SPARKY.

What did you see?

SPARKY: Hardly a thing. Street empty, no chimneys smoking,

no horses, yesterday's horsedung frozen on the road. Three men at a corner-post, four men leaning on a wall. No words but some chalked up on a closed door—they said: "Soldiers go home."

HURST: Go home?

SPARKY: That's it, boy: home. It's a place they think we have somewhere. And what did *you* see, serjeant?

MUSGRAVE: Nothing different from you . . . So, here is our town and here are we. All fit and appropriate.

HURST *(breaking out suddenly)*: Appropriate? Serjeant, now we've come with you so far. And every day we're in great danger. We're on the run, in red uniforms, in a black-and-white coalfield; and it's cold; and the money's running out that you stole from the Company office; and we don't know who's heard of us or how much they've heard. Isn't it time you brought out clear just what you've got in mind?

MUSGRAVE *(ominously)*: Aye? Is it? And any man else care to tell me what the time is?

ATTERCLIFFE *(reasonably)*: Now serjeant, please, easy—we're all your men, and we agreed—

HURST: All right: if we *are* your men, we've rights.

MUSGRAVE *(savagely)*: The only right *you* have is a rope around your throat and six foot six to drop from. On the run? Stolen money? I'm talking of a murdered officer, shot down in a street fight, shot down in one night's work. They put that to the rebels, but *I* know *you* were the man. We deserted, but you killed.

HURST: I'd a good reason . . .

MUSGRAVE: I know you had reason, else I'd not have left you alive to come with us. All I'm concerned about this minute is to tell you how you stand. And you stand in my power. But there's more to it than a bodily blackmail—isn't there? —because my power's the power of God, and that's what's brought me here and all three of you with me. You know my words and purposes—it's not just authority of the orderly room, it's not just three stripes, it's not just given to me by the reckoning of my mortal brain—well, *where* does it come from?

He flings this question fiercely at HURST.

HURST (*trying to avoid it*): All right, I'm not arguing—
MUSGRAVE: *Where!*
HURST (*frantically defensive*): I don't believe in God!
MUSGRAVE: You don't? Then what's this!

He jabs his thumb into HURST'S *cheek and appears to scrape something off it.*

HURST: Sweat.
MUSGRAVE: The coldest winter for I should think it's ten years, and the man sweats like a bird-bath!
HURST (*driven in a moral corner*): Well, why not, because—
MUSGRAVE (*relentless*): Go on—because?
HURST (*browbeaten into incoherence*): All right, because I'm afraid. 'Cos I thought when I met you, I thought we'd got the same motives. To get out, get shut o' the Army—with its "treat-you-like-dirt-but-you-do-the-dirty-work"—"kill *him,* kill *them,* they're all bloody rebels, State of Emergency, high standard of turnout, military bearin"—so *I* thought up some killing, I said I'll get me own in. I thought o' the Rights of Man. Rights o' the Rebels: that's *me!* Then I *went.* And here's a serjeant on the road, he's took two men, he's deserted same as me, he's got money, he can bribe a civvy skipper to carry us to England . . . It's nowt to do wi' God. I don't understand all that about God, why d'you bring God into it! You've come here to tell the people and then there'd be no more war—
MUSGRAVE (*taking him up with passionate affirmation*): Which *is* the word of God! Our message without God is a bad belch and a hiccup. You three of you, without me, are a bad belch and a hiccup. How d'you think you'd do it, if I wasn't here? Tell me, go on, tell me!
HURST (*still in his corner*): Why then I'd—I'd—I'd tell 'em, Sarnt Musgrave, I'd bloody stand, and tell 'em, and—
MUSGRAVE: Tell 'em *what!*
HURST (*made to appear more stupid than he really is*): All right:

like, the war, the Army, colonial wars, we're treated like
dirt, out there, and for to do the dirty work, and—
MUSGRAVE *(with withering scorn)*: And they'd run you in and
run you up afore the clock struck five! You don't understand about God! But you think, yourself, you, alone, stupid,
without a gill of discipline, illiterate, ignorant of the Scrip-
tures—you think you can make a whole town, a whole nation, understand the cruelty and greed of armies, what it
means, and how to punish it! You hadn't even took the
precaution to find the cash for your travel. I paid your fare!
HURST *(knuckling under)*: All right. You paid . . . You're the Serjeant . . . All right. Tell us what to do.
MUSGRAVE *(the tension eased)*: Then we'll sit down, and we'll be
easy. It's cold atween these tombs, but it's private. Sit down.
Now: you can consider, and you can open your lugs and
you can listen—ssh! Wait a minute . . .

The SLOW COLLIER *enters at one side, the* PUGNACIOUS *and*
EARNEST COLLIERS *at the other. All three carry pick-hefts as*
clubs.

SLOW COLLIER *(calls to the other two)*: Four on 'em, you see.
They're all here together.
PUGNACIOUS COLLIER: Setting in the graveyard, eh, like a coffin-
load o' sick spooks.
EARNEST COLLIER *(coming towards the soldiers)*: Which one's the
Serjeant?
MUSGRAVE *(standing up)*: Talk to me.
EARNEST COLLIER: Aye and I will too. There's a Union made
at this colliery, and we're strong. When we say strike, we
strike, all ends of us: that's fists, and it's pick-hefts and it's
stones and it's feet. If you work in the coal-seam you carry
iron on your clogs—see!

He thrusts up his foot menacingly.

PUGNACIOUS COLLIER: And you fight for your life when it's
needed.

MUSGRAVE: So do some others of us.

EARNEST COLLIER: Ah, no, lobster, *you* fight for pay. You go sailing on what they call punitive expeditions, against what you call rebels, and you shoot men down in streets. But not here. These streets is *our* streets.

MUSGRAVE: Anything else?

EARNEST COLLIER: No. Not this evening. Just so as you know, that's all.

PUGNACIOUS COLLIER: Setting in the graveyard. Look at 'em for Godsake. Waiting for a riot and then they'll have a murder. Why don't *we* have one *now*: it's dark enough, ent it?

EARNEST COLLIER: Shut up. It'll do when it's time. Just so as they know, that's all.

The COLLIERS *turn to go.*

MUSGRAVE: Wait a minute.

They pause.

Who told you we'd come to break the strike?

EARNEST COLLIER: Eh?

MUSGRAVE: Who told you?

EARNEST COLLIER: Nobody told us. We don't need to be told. You see a strike: you see soldiers: there's only one reason.

MUSGRAVE: Not this time there isn't. We haven't been sent for—

PUGNACIOUS COLLIER: And all soldiers aren't alike, you know. Some of us is human.

SLOW COLLIER: ⎫ Arrh—

PUGNACIOUS COLLIER: ⎭ *(laughs)*

MUSGRAVE: Now I'm in Mrs. Hitchcock's bar tonight until such time as she closes it. There'll be my money on the counter, and if you want to find what I'm doing here you can come along and see. I speak fair; you take it fair. Right?

EARNEST COLLIER: No, it's not right, Johnny Clever. These streets is our streets, so you learn a warning . . . Come on, leave 'em be, *we* know what they're after. Come on . . .

The COLLIERS *go, growling threateningly.*

ATTERCLIFFE: They hate us, Serjeant, don't they? Wouldn't you
    say that's good?
MUSGRAVE: Because of the bad coal-trade they hate us; the rest
    just follows. True, there's one man talks of shooting rebels
    down in streets, but the others only think of bayonets turned
    on pitmen, and that's no good. At the present, they believe
    we've come to kill them. Soon they'll find we haven't, so
    they'll stop hating. Maybe even some o' them'll come and
    sign on. You'll see: His Worship's sovereigns—they'll fall
    too damned heavy into these boys' pockets. But we'll watch
    and take count, till we know the depth of the corruption.
    'Cos all that we know now is that we've had to leave behind
    us a colonial war that is a war of sin and unjust blood.
ATTERCLIFFE (*sharply*): All wars is sin, serjeant ...
MUSGRAVE (*impatient*): I'm not discussing that. Single purpose
    at a single time: your generalities aren't material: this is
    particular—one night's work in the streets of one city, and
    it damned all four of us and the war it was part of. We're
    each one guilty of particular blood. We've come to this town
    to work that guilt back to where it began.

He turns to SPARKY.

    Why to this town? Say it, say it!
SPARKY (*as with a conditioned reflex*): Billy. Billy's dead. He
    wor my mucker, back end of the rear rank. He wor killed
    dead. He came from this town.
MUSGRAVE (*relentless*): Go on.
SPARKY (*appealing*): Serjeant—
MUSGRAVE: Use your clear brain, man, and tell me what you're
    doing here! Go on.
SPARKY (*incoherent with recollecting what he wants to forget*):
    I'm doing here? I'm doing ... Serjeant, you know it. 'Cos
    he died. That wor Billy. I got drunk. Four days and four
    nights. After work of one night. Absent. Not sober. Im-
    properly dressed.

He tries to turn it into one of his jokes.

> Stick me in a cell, boys,
> Pull the prison bell
> Black Jack Musgrave
> To call the prison roll—

Sarnt, no offence—"First ye'll serve your punishment," he says. "Then I'll show you how," he says, the Serjeant. I says, "You'll show me what?" He says, "I'll show you how your Billy can be paid for." . . . I didn't want to pay for him— what had I to care for a colonial war? . . .

He meets MUSGRAVE'S *eye and takes a grip on his motives.*

But I *did* want to pay for him, didn't I? 'Cos that's why I'm here. "You go down, I'll follow" . . . You, Serjeant, ent it?

> Black Jack Musgrave
> He always calls the roll.

He says:

> Go down to Billy's town
> Tell 'em how he died.

And that's what I'm doing here. The Serjeant pays the fare. Here I am, I'm paid for. Next turn's for Billy. Or all that's left of Billy. Who'll give me an offer for his bones? Sixpence for a bone, for a bone of my dead mucker . . .

He again avoids emotion by turning on HURST, *jeeringly.*

You didn't even know him when he lived, you weren't in his squad, what do *you* care that he's dead? To you he's like God, ent that the truth, you don't care and you're not bothered!

HURST (*angrily*): Hold your noise, you dirty turd! Who are you telling!

SPARKY: You. Oh you, me boy, you. A man and a soldier—

He meets MUSGRAVE'S *eye again, and his voice trails away.*

—a man and a soldier . . .

MUSGRAVE *(emphatically)*: Aye. And *you're* a soldier. Don't forget that. You're my man and you'll hear me. You're not on any drunk now. Now you've got discipline. You've got grief, but good order, and it's turned to the works of God!

SPARKY *(submissively)*: Yes, Sarnt.

MUSGRAVE *(to* HURST*)*: Turned to the works of God!

HURST *(submissively)*: Yes, Sarnt.

MUSGRAVE *(in a more encouraging voice)*: There was talk about danger. Well, I never heard of no danger yet that wasn't comparative. Compare it against your purposes. And compare it against my strategy. Remember: the roads are closed, the water's frozen, the telegraph wires are weighted down with snow, they haven't *built* the railway. We came here safe, and here we are, safe here. The winter's giving us one day, two days, three days even—that's clear safe for us to hold our time, take count of the corruption, then stand before this people with our white shining word, and let it dance! It's a hot coal, this town, despite that it's freezing—choose your minute and blow: and whoosh, she's flamed your roof off! They're trembling already into the strikers' riots. Well, their riots and our war are the same one corruption. This town is ours, it's ready for us: and its people, when they've heard us, and the Word of God, crying the murders that we've done—I'll tell you they'll turn to us, and they'll turn against that war!

ATTERCLIFFE *(gravely)*: All wars, Serjeant Musgrave. They've got to turn against all wars. Colonial wars, do we say, no war of honour? I'm a private soldier, I never had no honour, I went killing for the Queen, I did it for me wages, that wor my life. But I've got a new life. There was one night's work, and I said: no more killing.

HURST *(with excitement)*: It's time we did our *own* killing.

ATTERCLIFFE: No, boy, it isn't.

HURST: Aye, and I mean it. We're all on the run, and we're all of us deserters. We're wild-wood mad and raging. We caught it overseas and now we've got to run around the English streets biting every leg to give it *them*—that can't be done without—

MUSGRAVE *(interrupting)*: Listen to me!

HURST *(subsiding)*: Serjeant.

MUSGRAVE *(with angry articulation)*: We are here with a word. That's all. That's particular. Let the word dance. That's all that's material, this day and for the next. What happens afterwards, the Lord God will provide. I am with you, He said. Abide with Me in Power. A Pillar of Flame before the people. What we show here'll lead forward forever, against dishonour, and greed, and murder-for-greed! There is our duty, the new, deserter's duty: God's dance on this earth: and all that we are is His four strong legs to dance it ... Very well. That'll do. It's dark. We'll go in. Now we'll be likely buying drinks around and so on, in the public tonight. I don't want to see any o' you with more nor you can hold. When there's danger, there's temptation. So keep it gay, but that's all. Off you go now! Take 'em in.

ATTERCLIFFE *(as the senior)*: All right then, smartly now, walking up the street. Remember, we're recruiting. I'll give you the time—left right left right.

They walk out briskly, leaving MUSGRAVE *alone. As they go, the* BARGEE *enters, and gives them a parody salute in passing.* MUSGRAVE *doesn't see him, walks downstage, crosses his hands on his chest and stands to pray. The* BARGEE *parodies his attitude behind his back.*

MUSGRAVE: God, my Lord God. Have You or have You not delivered this town into my hands? All my life a soldier I've made You prayers and made them straight, I've reared my one true axe against the timber and I've launched it true. My regiment was my duty, and I called Death honest, killing by the book—but it all got scrawled and mucked about and I could not think clear ... Now I have my duties different. I'm in this town to change all soldiers' duties. My prayer is: keep my mind clear so I can weigh Judgement against the Mercy and Judgement against the Blood, and make this Dance as terrible as You have put it into my brain. The Word alone is terrible: the Deed must be worse. But I know it is Your Logic, and You will provide.

He pauses for a moment, then turns sharply on his heel and strides away after the soldiers. He still fails to see the BAR-GEE. *The latter has whipped off his hat at the conclusion of* MUSGRAVE'S *prayer, and now he stands looking solemnly up to Heaven. He gives a sanctimonious smirk and breathes "Amen."*

ACT TWO

Scene One

The bar of the public house.
  A scene of noise and conviviality, crowded confusion. MRS.
HITCHCOCK *is seated behind the bar, drinking tea with brandy
in it.* ANNIE *is going backwards and forwards in the room carrying drinks and empties.* MUSGRAVE *is sitting with a tankard,
calmly watching.* SPARKY *is wearing his drum and alternately
beating it and drinking and singing. The* SLOW *and* PUGNACIOUS
COLLIERS, *well-oiled, are drinking and dancing. The* BARGEE *is
drinking and dancing and playing a mouth-organ and beating
time to the singing.* ATTERCLIFFE *is drinking and dancing and
pinning cockades to the hats of the* COLLIERS. *At intervals one of
the dancers grabs hold of* ANNIE *and swirls her around, but she
retains a contemptuous aloofness and carries on with her work.
As the scene opens the men (save* MUSGRAVE) *are all joining in
the chorus:*

CHORUS   Blow your morning bugles
         Blow your calls ey-ho
         For platoon and dress the ranks
         And blow boys blow!

   *This chorus is sung (with progressively less correctness) by
most of the men at the end of each verse of the song.*

SPARKY *(singing)*:

         When first I came to the barracks
         My heart it grieved full sore

For leaving of my old true love
That I would see no more.

chorus

SLOW COLLIER (*to* MUSGRAVE, *who is studying a notebook*): I'm
not signing nowt. Provisional, I said, provisional.
MUSGRAVE: Aye, aye, provisional. No one makes it different.
SPARKY (*sings*):

They made us drill and muster
And stand our sentries round
And I never thought I'd lay again
A girl upon the ground.

chorus

PUGNACIOUS COLLIER (*to* ATTERCLIFFE): That's *my* point, *my* point,
too . . . all right enlisting, aye . . . but I'm a married man—
SPARKY (*sings*):

But soon we were paraded
And marching to the war
And in every town the girls lay down
And cried out loud for more.

chorus

PUGNACIOUS COLLIER (*to* ATTERCLIFFE): I'm not so sure I like
your looks, aye, *you!*
SPARKY: Me?
PUGNACIOUS COLLIER (*pointing to* ATTERCLIFFE): You!
SPARKY (*sings*):

And when we'd lodge in billets
We'd beer in every can
And the landlord's wife and daughters learnt
Just how to love a man.

chorus

PUGNACIOUS COLLIER (*going at* SPARKY): I'm a married man,
bedamn, I've got a wife, I've got a wife, a wife . . .

SPARKY: No one's taking her from you.

PUGNACIOUS COLLIER: Not you?

SPARKY: No.

MUSGRAVE *(interrupting)*: All right, steady, friend, *no one.*

SLOW COLLIER: *I'll* take her from you when you go to the war, I'll take her—

PUGNACIOUS COLLIER: You?

SLOW COLLIER: Me! Or no, no, no: I'll make do with our Annie!

He makes a drunken lurch at her which she more or less evades.

Come on then, mucker!

Foiled by ANNIE, *he seizes the* PUGNACIOUS COLLIER *and they do a clog dance together while the* BARGEE *plays. Chorus while they dance, and general cheer.*

BARGEE: Bring 'em in some more, Annie, it's all on the Queen tonight—how many have you listed, serjeant!

MUSGRAVE: I'm not listing no one tonight. *(He bangs with his tankard for silence.)* Now then, boys, everybody—

BARGEE *(officiously)*: Everybody listen!

A roll on the drum.

BARGEE: Listen!

MUSGRAVE *(expansively)*: This is Her Majesty's hospitality— that's *all* that it is, boys, on a soldier's honour, so! Any man that drinks tonight—

BARGEE: Any man that drinks tonight—

MUSGRAVE: He drinks at the Queen's pleasure, and none of you need fear to find a shilling in your mug at end of it—that like o' lark's finished and gone with the old days—the Army only wants good men, that's free men, of your own true will for the Empire—so drink and welcome: and all men in this town—

BARGEE: All men in this town—

MUSGRAVE: When we hold our meeting and the drum beats and we bring out our colours, then you can make your return in the signing of your names—but only those men willing! That's all: drink and away!

A roll on the drum.

BARGEE: Drink and away, me boys, hurray!
PUGNACIOUS COLLIER: Serjeant, you're a bleeding lobster, but you're a man! Shake me by the hand!

The BARGEE *gives a whoop and starts to dance, playing a mouth-organ. He stumbles, and everybody laughs.*

ANNIE *(scornfully)*: And what regiment's *that* one, serjeant? The Backwards-Mounted-Foot?
BARGEE: I'll tell you, me lovely, why not? The Queen's Own Randy Chancers: or the Royal Facing-Both-Ways—hey, me clever monkeys:

> Old Joe looks out for Joe
> Plots and plans and who lies low?
> But the Lord provides, says Crooked Old Joe.

MUSGRAVE *(looking sharply at him)*: Eh?

The BARGEE *shrugs and grins.* MUSGRAVE *dismisses the question.*

BARGEE: Just a little joke ... little joke: little dog, I'll be with you ...

He whistles "Michael Finnegan" and ducks out of the pub. Meanwhile SPARKY *has taken off his drum and come downstage to intercept* ANNIE. ATTERCLIFFE *is drinking with the* COLLIERS *and one or other of these plays the drum at intervals. The going of the* BARGEE *has made the room somewhat quieter for a while.*

SPARKY (*to* ANNIE): Little dog—bow-wow, *I'm* a little dog, any trick for a bit of biscuit, Annie, bit o' meat—look:

He takes a pack of cards out of his pocket and presents it.

Take one, go on, take one.

She obeys.

Well?

ANNIE: Queen o' Spades.

SPARKY (*laughing*): That's a hell of a card to take: I think there's treacle on it, sticks to all fingers out o' this pack, I call her Grandma, makes her gentle, y'see—hope she'll kiss me whiskers and leave it at that.

He has replaced the cards and shuffles.

Now then, take first four cards on top. Tell me what they are.

ANNIE (*obeying*): Eight Nine Ten Jack, all spades.

SPARKY (*triumphantly*): Right, right, calls the roll straight up to the one you took, the Queen, and where's the one you took? On the bottom—take it!

ANNIE (*obeying*): It is the Queen and all!

SPARKY: 'Course it is: I *told* you. That's what I call life—it all turns up in the expected order, but not when you expect it. And that's what sets your two teeth laughing, click-clack, doesn't it, ha ha ha! Oh I'm a clever lad, you see, they call me Sparky, lots o' games, lots o' jokes . . .

ANNIE (*not impressed*): Lots of liquor too. Now get out of me road while I fetch some more—*I've* got *work,* you know.

SPARKY (*going after her and again intercepting her*): Hey, but lovey, listen: there was an Englishman, a Welshman and a drunk. Now the Orderly Sarnt, he says, "One, Two, Three, all we want's a Scotchman." And a voice in the guardroom-yard says: "Hoots awa', man, I'm taking back the empties fairst."

She avoids him and goes away to the bar, thus ruining the climax of his tale. He tries to follow her up, but this time he is intercepted by MUSGRAVE. HURST *appears in the doorway.* ANNIE *looks up at him and follows him with her eyes for the rest of this dialogue.*

MUSGRAVE *(to* SPARKY*)*: You've had enough.

SPARKY: I'm not drunk.

MUSGRAVE: No and you won't be neither. This is no time.

SPARKY *(pointing to* HURST*)*: No—and *here* he comes, look at him.

MUSGRAVE *(striding angrily over to* HURST*)*: Where have you been?

HURST *(surlily)*: Down by the canal.

MUSGRAVE: Why?

HURST: All right, I'd got things on my mind. And I'll tell you this, Serjeant, it isn't enough.

MUSGRAVE: What isn't enough?

HURST: What you and that old cuckold are reckoning to do. It's all soft, it's all flat, it's all—God and the Word! Tchah! What good's a word, what good's a bloody word, they can *all* talk bloody words—it isn't enough: we've got to be strong!

MUSGRAVE: Leave it alone, boy. *I* hold the logic. *You* hold some beer and get on with your work.

MUSGRAVE *walks away from* HURST.

HURST *(shouts after him)*: It isn't enough!

He turns to find ANNIE *standing at his elbow, looking into his face and handing him a tankard of beer. He takes it and drinks it rapidly, without looking at her.*

MRS. HITCHCOCK *(calling from the bar)*: The Queen's in debt, Serjeant!

MUSGRAVE: Hello, ma'am?

MRS. HITCHCOCK: I said the Queen's in debt!

MUSGRAVE: Chalk it up, ma'am, and another round for us all.

MRS. HITCHCOCK: No more chalk.
MUSGRAVE: Easily found though.

*He plunges his hand in his pocket and pulls out a quantity
of money. He does a rapid count, whistles in consternation,
and selects a few coins.*

ATTERCLIFFE (*watching him*): Not so much of it left, is there?
MUSGRAVE: Easy, easy.

He goes over to the bar and pays. SPARKY *is now showing
his card tricks to the* COLLIERS. ANNIE *plucks at the sleeve of
the pensive* HURST.

ANNIE (*simply*): You're the best to look at of all the four, aren't
you?
HURST: Eh? What's that?
ANNIE: Tell you again? Why? You know it, don't you?
HURST (*preoccupied*): I'd forgot it. I'd other matter beyond won-
dering what you'd think to our looks.

*He studies her closer, and snaps out of his gloomy mood into
an attitude of lady-killing arrogance.*

Why, I don't need to think o' women. I let them think of
me. I've knocked greasier ones than you between me por-
ridge and me bacon. Don't flatter yourself.
ANNIE: I'm not, soldier: I'm flattering you. I'll come to you
tonight.
HURST (*pleased, though trying not to show it*): Will you? That's
a good choice, you've got sense.
ANNIE (*meaningly*): But you forget them other matters, eh?
HURST (*decidedly warming to her*): I'll try . . . I'd rather. I hope
I can . . . Stand straight: let's see . . . Gay and greasy, like I
like 'em! You're big, and you're bonny. A good shape, I'd
call it. And you've got good hair, but wants a comb in it.
You ought to wash your face. And your neck smells of soot,
don't it?

ANNIE (*accepting this in the spirit in which it's meant*): I've been blowing up the fire.

HURST (*boastfully*): Ah, the last I had was a major's daughter. I've got standards, Lovely.

ATTERCLIFFE *comes across to them.*

ATTERCLIFFE: You said he was the best looker. I heard you. But it's not true.

ANNIE: Then who is? You?

ATTERCLIFFE: I'll tell you a tale about that. That pitman over there—he said to me he thought I'd steal his wife. By God, I'd sooner steal his nightsoil . . . I've got a wife. Ask me to tell you one o' these days—Sparky'd make a joke of it—wouldn't you, Sparky!

The last phrases are shouted across the room.

SPARKY (*shouts back*): Not any more—we're all going too fast.

He turns back to the COLLIERS.

Down, down—any card, any card, mate—tell me its name—down.

PUGNACIOUS COLLIER: Six o' Hearts!

SPARKY: Right, right—*and* we shuffle and cut—

Enter the BARGEE.

BARGEE (*shouts*): Time, gennelmen please, everybody time, last orders everybody!

MRS. HITCHCOCK (*angrily*): Who's given *you* leave to do the calling here!

BARGEE (*singing*):

Blow your morning bugles
Blow your calls ey-ho—

If it's not me and it's not you, there'll be somebody else—
look!

Enter CONSTABLE.

CONSTABLE: All right, Mrs. Hitchcock, it's time you closed your bar.

MRS. HITCHCOCK: What are you talking about!

CONSTABLE: Magistrates' orders, missus. All public houses to close at nine o'clock sharp, pending settlement of colliery dispute.

MRS. HITCHCOCK: It's the first I've heard of it.

SLOW COLLIER (*to the* CONSTABLE): Get out of it.

PUGNACIOUS COLLIER (*ditto*): Go home, you closhy bluebottle, and sweep your bloody chimney.

CONSTABLE: That'll do there.

MUSGRAVE: That'll do, lads, keep it easy.

PUGNACIOUS COLLIER (*to* MUSGRAVE): We're not in the Army yet, y'know!

ATTERCLIFFE: Steady, matey, steady. All friends, y'know: married men together.

PUGNACIOUS COLLIER: But, Serjeant, you're a man, and I'll *shake* you by the hand.

CONSTABLE (*now things seem quiet again*): Magistrates issued the order only this evening, missus. I've let you stay open a lot longer than the others—it's nigh on a quarter to ten already—and I'm in my rights to allow an exception for this house, on account of the Army. Question of facilities. I trust you've made good use of the extra time, Sarnt Musgrave?

MUSGRAVE: H'm.

PUGNACIOUS COLLIER (*with great friendliness*): Have the last drink on me, bluebottle!

CONSTABLE (*curtly*): The last drink's been had already. Close your bar, please, missus.

PUGNACIOUS COLLIER (*an angry idea occurring to him*): Wait a minute . . . Suppose I join your Army. Suppose I bloody 'list. What does my wife do?

BARGEE: Cock-a-doodle-doo!

PUGNACIOUS COLLIER (*finding his own answer*): She goes to bed with the Peeler! I'll break his wooden head off.

He goes for the CONSTABLE *with a tankard, the* CONSTABLE *staggers backwards and falls, the* COLLIER *raises his tankard to smash it into his face.* ATTERCLIFFE *and* MUSGRAVE, *being nearest, jump to prevent him.*

ATTERCLIFFE (*pulling the* COLLIER *fiercely back*): Hey, ey, ey, ey-ey, hold it there, boy, hold it there! My God, you might ha' killed him. No . . .

ATTERCLIFFE is trembling all over.

SLOW COLLIER: Why shouldn't he if he wants to?

ATTERCLIFFE (*with great passion*): We've had enough o' that already—no more, no more, no more of it.

MUSGRAVE (*holding* ATTERCLIFFE *to quiet him*): Stop it there!

CONSTABLE (*getting up slowly*): Stand back, stand back. By God, it's *time* this place was closed. Turn out into the street, go on with you, get home. D'ye want me to whistle up me specials? Go on.

He hurls the COLLIERS *and* BARGEE *out of the pub.*

ATTERCLIFFE: He was going to, Serjeant. He would have, he'd have killed him. It's always here. Kill him. Kill.

MUSGRAVE (*roughly*): That'll do . . . We've all had enough, Mr. Constable. I'll get this lot to bed.

CONSTABLE: All right then. And try and keep folk quiet. I know you've got to buy 'em drink and that—but . . . *you* know—easy?

MUSGRAVE: Aye, aye, easy. We know the trends. Don't you worry: *we* stand for law-and-order too, don't we?

CONSTABLE: Well, I hope so—

He goes to the door and calls into the street.

I said home, no loitering, go on, go on, or I'll run you in!

He comes back to MUSGRAVE *in a confidential conspiratorial sort of way.*

It's a sort of curfew you see. I told His Worship: "If there's trouble at night, you can't hold *me* responsible. I've done my best," I said—I told him frank . . . Oh, and while we're on about His Worship, Serjeant, I might as well take occasion to discuss some names with you. There's a few like I could tell you as'd look very convenient on a regimental muster.

MUSGRAVE *(coldly):* I'm here for volunteers only, you know.

CONSTABLE *(insinuatingly):* Ah, well, what's a volunteer? You, you, and you—the old Army custom—eh, Serjeant? Mrs. Hitchcock! A couple o' pints o' taddy for me and the Serjeant.

MRS. HITCHCOCK: We're closed.

CONSTABLE *(broad-mindedly):* That's all right, missus. Serve to the Serjeant: hotel-resident. All above the board.

MRS. HITCHCOCK *(to* ANNIE*):* So take 'em their drinks. Queen as pays.

She pours herself out another cup of tea. ANNIE *prepares the drinks and brings them to* MUSGRAVE *and the* CONSTABLE, *who get into a huddle over a list the latter produces.*

SPARKY *(to the other two* SOLDIERS*):* Very commodious Queen. I say, a very commodious Queen, ha ha, if she'd drank all she paid for tonight, heh, Sponge By Appointment, they could swab out the Windsor Castle Guardhouse, ha ha, who'd be a Coldstream! I say, they could swab out—

ATTERCLIFFE: Oh shut up, man, for God's sake. We've had all we can take of your stinking patter.

SPARKY *(aggrieved):* Ey-ey, matey—ey-ey.

He withdraws, hurt.

HURST *(to* ATTERCLIFFE*)*: Shut up yourself—what's got into you?
ATTERCLIFFE: Why, *you* were making enough carry-on earlier,
   weren't you? Are you so daft or so drunk you didn't see
   what just happened?
HURST: There was nowt happened. Couple o' pitmen three parts
   pissed? What's the matter wi' that? You were near as bad
   yourself—don't tell *me. You* were on about your *wife!*
ATTERCLIFFE: There was all but a man killed. We've come to
   stop it, not to start it—go on, sing to us.

He sings, with savage emphasis.

> Who'll give a penny to the poor blind man
> Holds out his hand with an old tin can.

—'Cos that's all you are and it curdles up my bowels. I'm
   going to the coach-house.
HURST: The coach-house! What for?
ATTERCLIFFE: Where there's a man to talk to who don't talk
   like a fool.

He goes out of the door behind the bar.

SPARKY: Here, what d'you think to *him?* What sort o' talk does
   he reckon he'll get.
HURST: Keep your mind off that!
SPARKY *(wildly)*: Rattling, clattering, old bones in a box? Billy
   used to sing, d'you think he'll have a sing-song?
HURST: I don't understand you. This don't make *me* laugh. It
   fair makes me sick.
SPARKY *(jeeringly)*: Sick and bloody scared. Hey-ey, that's you,
   that's you truly.
HURST: Well, I've got things on my mind. If you can call it
   scared—
SPARKY: You and me, we're a pair, boy.
HURST *(savagely)*: All right. But you'll learn. All *right.*

He turns abruptly away, and broods.

SPARKY *(beckoning* ANNIE, *who comes unenthusiastically)*: I say
Annie—oh I'll tell you what, Annie, I don't know what I'm
doing here.

She looks at him questioningly; he waves the point aside.

Aha, for that . . . Look, we've made us our beds up in the
stables—ha, loose-box for every man, but the serjeant in
the house.

ANNIE: Aye, I know.

SPARKY: We call it the Discipline, y'see. Yes-sarnt-no-sarnt, three-
bags-full-sarnt—that's our merry lives. Ha ha. Third box
from the end tonight, the fastest racehorse of 'em all.
Oaks, Derby, I carry 'em away, boy: but I'm best at a
steeple-chase—*hup* and *hover,* hedge and ditch, dear, and
not by soldiers' numbers neither . . . Come for a gallop.

It is clear from the tone of the last phrase he is not joking.

ANNIE *(unemotionally)*: Not tonight.

SPARKY: Oh . . . Go on, tonight.

ANNIE *(with something of a sneer)*: Maybe next I will. I can't
tell from day to day.

SPARKY: No more can I. You know, you've not yet give me one
little laugh . . . But I'll contrive it: now y'see, there was a
butcher, a baker, and a cats'-meat-man, all on the edge of
the river. And down this river comes this dead dog, floating.

HURST *(whose head has drooped, suddenly jerks himself up
again)*: God, I was near asleep! I started a bad dream and
it woke me.

MUSGRAVE *(to the* CONSTABLE*)*: No, mister, it won't wash. We
can't play pressgangs these days. If a man gets drunk and
then signs, all right: but otherwise—

CONSTABLE *(vexed)*: You're not over-co-operative, are you?

MUSGRAVE: I'm sorry. Oh, I'll see what I can do: but I won't promise more. Besides, agitators is agitators, in or out the Army. I'm not sure we want 'em. But I'll think. Good night.

He goes with the CONSTABLE *to the street door.*

CONSTABLE: Good night. Good night, missus.

Exit the CONSTABLE. MUSGRAVE *comes down to the* SOLDIERS.

MUSGRAVE *(calling* ANNIE*)*: Lassie.

ANNIE: Hello.

MUSGRAVE: These are my men. They're here with their work to do. You will not distract them.

ANNIE: I won't?

MUSGRAVE: No. Because *they* know, whether you know it or not, that there's work is for women and there's work is for men: and let the two get mixed, you've anarchy.

ANNIE *(rather taken aback)*: Oh? And what's anarchy? You, you clever grinder—words and three stripes—

MUSGRAVE: Look, lassie, anarchy: now, we're soldiers. Our work isn't easy, no and it's not soft: it's got a strong name—duty. And it's drawn out straight and black for us, a clear plan. But if you come to us with what you call your life or love —*I'd* call it your indulgence—and you scribble all over that plan, you make it crooked, dirty, idle, untidy, *bad—there's* anarchy. I'm a religious man. I know words, and I know deeds, and I know how to be strong. So do these men. You will not stand between them and their strength! Go on now: take yourself off.

ANNIE: A little bit of wind and a little bit of water—

MRS. HITCHCOCK: Annie—

ANNIE: But it drowned three score of sailors, and the King of Norway's daughter. *(She smiles for the first time in the play.)*

She sings:

> O mother O mother
> It hurts me so sore

> Sing dody-eye-dodo
> Then ye daft little bitch
> Ye should do it no more
> For you've never left off
> Since we sailed from the shore.

MRS. HITCHCOCK *(sharply)*: Annie, get to bed.

MUSGRAVE *(to the* SOLDIERS*)*: You two, get to bed. And pay heed to what I say.

ANNIE *goes out behind the bar, with a satirical curtsy.* MUSGRAVE *goes out by the street door.* HURST *makes a move as though to speak to him, but is too late. He stands reflective.*

SPARKY:

> To bed to bed says Sleepy-head
> Tarry a while says Slow
> Open the book, says the wise old Rook
> We'll have prayers before we go.

He sways a little tipsily, and laughs.

Scene Two

A street. Night.

The PUGNACIOUS *and* SLOW COLLIERS *enter, drunk and marching, the* BARGEE *drilling them. (This is a kind of "Fred Karno" sequence which must be kept completely under control. At each command each of the three carries out, smartly, a drill-movement; but each drill movement is different for each man, and none of them performs the movement shouted. They must not be so drunk that they cannot appear erect and alertly jerking. The effect should be, not so much of three incompetents pretending to be soldiers, but of three trained soldiers gone mad.) The* COLLIERS *carry pickhefts as rifles, and the* BARGEE *an oar.*

MUSGRAVE *enters, and stands quietly watching.*

BARGEE: Right turn. Forward march. Left right left right left right left.

PUGNACIOUS COLLIER: To the front present. Halt.

BARGEE: About turn.

SLOW COLLIER: One two three four.

BARGEE: Order arms.

PUGNACIOUS COLLIER: Present and correct. By the right, number.

SLOW COLLIER: One two three four.

> *They are now at attention, together.*

PUGNACIOUS COLLIER: Present and correct.

BARGEE *(this order is properly obeyed)*: Stand-at-ease. Easy . . .

PUGNACIOUS COLLIER *(breaking the spell)*: I'll tell you what, we're bloody good.

BARGEE *(with enthusiasm)* : Eh. Lordy, mucker—good! By, I've never seen the like—y'know, if you signed on they'd excuse you three weeks' drill on the spot. You make that serjeant look like Old-Mother-Bunch-in-the-Popshop, alongside o' you—love you, mucker, you're *born* to it!

PUGNACIOUS COLLIER: Well, why didn't I think on it afore?

SLOW COLLIER *(still on parade)*: One two three four.

PUGNACIOUS COLLIER: I'd not ha' got wed if I'd known!

SLOW COLLIER *(suddenly coming to attention and starting off)*: Quick march. One two three—

> *He bumps up against* WALSH, *who has just entered.*

Arh and be damned.

WALSH: Where the hell are you going to?

MUSGRAVE *starts to go out. He passes* WALSH, *who stops him with a hand on his chest.*

WALSH: So we was mistook, eh? You're not here for no riots after all, but catching up men: that's it, isn't it? Guineas?

MUSGRAVE: Sovereigns.

PUGNACIOUS COLLIER *(suddenly indicating* MUSGRAVE *to* WALSH*)*: Here. This one: three stripes, but he's a man.

WALSH: Aye? And hat are you? Drunk on *his* money: marching and drilling like a pack o' nit-headed kids at a barrack-gate!

PUGNACIOUS COLLIER: Better nor bloody starve for no coal-owners, any road!

WALSH *(with passion)*: I'll tell you, I'm that ashamed, I could spew.

MUSGRAVE *(gripping* WALSH *by the lapel and drawing him away)*: Now listen here. I can see you, and see *you* what you are. I wasn't given these—*(he touches his stripes)*—for not knowing men from ninepins. Now I'm telling you one word and I'm telling you two, and that's all. *(He lowers his voice.)* You and me is brothers—

WALSH *(in high irony)*: Eh begod! A Radical Socialist! Careful, soldier, careful. D'ye want to be hanged?

MUSGRAVE *(very seriously)*: No jokes. I mean this. I mean it. Brothers in God—

WALSH *(even more scornful)*: Oh, hoho, *that*—

MUSGRAVE:—And brothers in truth. So watch. And wait. I said, *wait.*

WALSH *(jeering)*: Brothers in God.

> Gentle Jesus send us rest
> Surely the bosses knows what's best!

Get along with yer—

MUSGRAVE *(calmly)*: Well: I said, wait. You'll see.

Exit MUSGRAVE.

SLOW COLLIER (*who has been marking time since his collision, now mutters*):

> One two three four
> Where's the man as lives next door?
> Five six seven eight
> Come on in, he's working late.

WALSH (*looking at him in disgust*): Holy God, I'd never ha' dreamt it.

SLOW COLLIER (*his muttering rising in volume*):

> Nine ten eleven twelve
> Take his place and help yourself,
> Thirteen fourteen fifteen sixteen—

PUGNACIOUS COLLIER (*with a stupid laugh*): He's talking about my wife.

SLOW COLLIER (*annoyed at being interrupted*):

> Thirteen fourteen fifteen sixteen
> Into the bed and there we'll fix him!

PUGNACIOUS COLLIER (*in rising rage*): I couldn't do it to the soldiers, I couldn't do it to the Peeler, but by, I'll do it to you! I'll break your bloody head.

He goes for SLOW COLLIER, *who hits him in the belly, lets off a yell and runs out.* PUGNACIOUS COLLIER *follows with a roar.*

BARGEE (*calling after them in glee*): Watch out for the Constable! Heh heh heh.

WALSH: Holy God! My mates! My brothers!

BARGEE (*kindly*): Ah well, they're drunk.

WALSH: I know they're drunk, and I know who's helped 'em to it.

BARGEE: I could help *you* to summat, and all.

WALSH: What's that?

BARGEE: They won't stay drunk all week. Oh the soldiers gives 'em sport, they *need* a bit o' sport, cold, hungry ... When you want 'em, they'll be there. Crooked Joe, he's *here*.

WALSH: Aye?

BARGEE: Could you shoot a Gatling gun?

WALSH (*looking at him sideways*): I don't know.

BARGEE: If you really want a riot, why don't you go at it proper?
Come on, I'll tell you . . . (*He hops out, whistling "Michael
Finnegan" and looking back invitingly.*)

WALSH (*considering*): Aye, aye? Crooked, clever, keelman, eh?
. . . Well—all right—then *tell* me!

He hurries after him.

Scene Three

Interior of the pub (stable and bedroom).

*Night. The stage is divided into two distinct acting-areas. The
downstage area represents the stable, and is supposed to be
divided into three loose boxes. If it is not practicable for the
partitions between these to be built, it should be sufficient to
suggest them by the three mattresses which are laid parallel, feet
to the audience. The actors must not appear to be able to see
each other from box to box. The forestage represents the central
passage of the stable and is the only access to the boxes. Entry
to the forestage can be from both wings (one side leads to the
house, the other to the yard and coach-house).*

*The upstage area, raised up at least a couple of feet, represents
a bedroom in the house. It is only large enough to contain a
brass-knobbed bedstead with a small table or other support for
a candle. The two areas must be treated as completely separate.
Access to the bedroom area should be from the rear, and the
audience must not be allowed to think that the actors can see
from one area to the other (except as regards the light in the
window, which is supposed to be seen as if from across the yard).*

MUSGRAVE, *in shirt and trousers, is sitting on the bed, reading by candlelight. His tunic etc. lies folded beside the bed.*

HURST *and* SPARKY *come into the stable from the house carrying palliasses and blankets. They proceed to make up their beds (in the two end boxes, leaving the middle one empty.* SPARKY *is at the house end,* HURST *next to the yard). They also undress to their shirts (of grey flannel) and their (long woolen) underpants and socks. Their clothes are laid out neatly beside the beds.*

SPARKY *(as he prepares for bed)*: I say . . . I say, can you hear me?

HURST *(uninterested)*: I can.

SPARKY: You know, I'll tell you: I'm a bit pissed tonight.

HURST: Uh. What of it?

SPARKY: What's that?

HURST: I said what of it? We all are, aren't we? *I* want an hour or two's sleep, I don't know about *you,* so let's have less o' your gab.

SPARKY: I say, there's a light on still in Black Jack's window.

HURST *grunts.*

MUSGRAVE *has now lain down on top of his blanket, but has not taken off his trousers, or put out his candle.*

SPARKY: Aye, aye. God's awake. Ha, ha! Not only God neither. Y'know, I think there might be some of us mortal, even yet . . . I said God's awake!

HURST: I *heard* you, and be damned.

A pause.

SPARKY: Hour or two's sleep . . . What do you want to *sleep* for, and a fine fat tart all promised and ready!

HURST *(who has got undressed and under his blanket)*: That'll do. Now shut your row, can't ye, when you're asked! I said I wanted to sleep, so let me.

SPARKY: Why it's you she's promised, y'see—*you*, not me—wake up, mucker, wake up. She'll soon be here, y'see. She'll soon be here! (*He blows "reveille" with his lips, then gets under his blanket.*) You, boy, *you*, not me! ... Shall I sing you a song?

HURST (*almost asleep, and woken again*): Eh, what? Are you going to shut up, or aren't you!

SPARKY: Well, are *you* going to shut up or aren't you, when she comes? It's all right the best-looker loving the girl, but his two mates along the row wi' nowt but a bit o' wainscot atween—hey-ey-ey, it'll be agony for *us* tonight, y'know—so keep it quiet.

A pause.

(*He starts to sing, softly*):

> She came to me at midnight
> With the moonshine on her arms
> And I told her not to make no noise
> Nor cause no wild alarms.
> But her savage husband he awoke
> And up the stairs did climb
> To catch her in her very deed:
> So fell my fatal crime ...

While he is singing, ANNIE *enters from the house, carrying a candle. She goes gently to* HURST'S *box and stands looking down at him. When she speaks, he sticks his head out of the bedclothes and looks at her.*
In the bedroom, MUSGRAVE *sits up, blows out his light, and goes to sleep.*

ANNIE (*with tender humour*): Here I come. Hello. I'm cold. I'm a blue ghost come to haunt you. Brr. Come on, boy, warm me up. You'll not catch cold off *me*.

HURST (*getting up*): No ... I daresay not ...

They put their arms round each other.

But what about the morning?

ANNIE: Ah, the morning's different, ent it? I'll not say nowt about mornings, 'cos then we'll *all* be cold. Cold and alone. Like, stand in a crowd but every one alone. One thousand men makes a regiment, you'd say?

HURST: Near enough.

ANNIE: But for all that, when you're with them, you're still alone. Ent that right? So huggle me into the warm, boy, now. Keep out the wind. It's late. Dark.

HURST (*suddenly breaking away from her*): No, I won't. I don't care what I said afore, it's all done, ended, capped—get away. Go on. Leave me be.

ANNIE (*astonished and hurt*): What is it? What's the matter? Lovey—

HURST (*with violence*): Go on. As far as *my* mind goes, it's morning already. Every one alone—that's all. You want me to lose my life inside of you—

ANNIE: No. No. But just for five hours, boy, six—

HURST: You heard Black Jack say what's right. Straight, clear, dark strokes, no scrawling. I was wrong afore. I didn't trust him. He talked about God, so I thought he wor just nowt. But what he said about *you*: there, that was truth. He's going to be *strong*!

ANNIE (*scornfully*): So *you* take note of Black Jack, do you?

HURST: Aye, and I do. It's too late tonight for anything else. He's got to be trusted, got to be strong, we've got no alternative!

ANNIE (*standing a little away from him*): My Christ then, they *have* found him a brother! It was only this evening, warn't it, *I* saw you, down by the canal, all alone and wretched—

She sings with fierce emphasis:

All round his hat he wore the green willow—!

HURST: All right.

ANNIE (*not letting him off*) : But it can't have been you, can it? 'Cos now you're just the same as the rest of 'em—the Hungry Army! You eat and you drink and you go. Though *you* won't even eat when it's offered, will you? So *sprawl* yourself on the straw without me, get up to your work tomorrow, drum 'em in and write 'em down, infect 'em all and bury 'em! I don't care.

HURST: What are you on about, what's the matter, why don't you go when you're told? Godsake, Godsake, leave a man to his sleep!

ANNIE: You know what they call me?

HURST: I'd call you a bloody whoor—

ANNIE (*savagely ironical*) : Oh, not just a whoor—*I'm* a whoor-to-the-soldiers—it's a class by itself.

ATTERCLIFFE *has entered from the yard with his bedding. They do not notice him yet.* ANNIE *turns to pleading again.*

ANNIE: Christ, let me stay with you. He called me life and love, boy, just you think on *that* a little.

HURST *pushes her away with a cry. She falls against* ATTERCLIFFE.

ATTERCLIFFE (*holding her up*) : Life and love, is it? I'm an old soldier, girly, a dirty old bastard, me, and *I've* seen it all. Here.

He grips her and kisses her violently all over face and neck. He sneers at HURST.

Hey-up there, son, get in your manger and sleep, and leave this to the men.

HURST: All right . . . and you're welcome.

He goes to his box and lies down again, huffily, trying to sleep.

ATTERCLIFFE (*still holding* ANNIE, *with a sort of tenderness*) : Now then, what'll I do to you, eh? How d'you reckon you're going to quench *me*? Good strong girly with a heart like a horsecollar, open it up and let 'em all in. And it still wouldn't do no good.

ANNIE (*hard and hostile*) : Wouldn't it? Try.

ATTERCLIFFE: Ah, no. Not tonight. What would *you* know of soldiers?

ANNIE: More'n you'd think I'd know, maybe.

ATTERCLIFFE: I doubt it. Our Black Jack'd say it's not material. He'd say there's blood on these two hands. (*He looks at his hands with distaste.*) You can wipe 'em as often as you want on a bit o' yellow hair, but it still comes blood the next time so why bother, *he'd* say. And *I'd* say it too. Here. (*He kisses her again and lets her go.*) There you are, girly: I've given you all you should get from a soldier. Say "Thank you, boy," and that's that.

ANNIE (*still hard*) : Thank you, boy . . . You know it, don't you? All I should get. All I ever have got. Why should I want more? You stand up honest, you do, and it's a good thing too, 'cos you're old enough.

ATTERCLIFFE (*with a wry smile*) : H'm. I am and all. Good night.

He starts making up his bed and undressing. SPARKY *has sat up and is listening. As* ANNIE *is standing still,* ATTERCLIFFE *starts talking to her again.*

ATTERCLIFFE: Girly. When I was a young lad I got married to a wife. And she slept with a greengrocer. He was the best looker (like *he's* the best looker) — (*he points towards* HURST's *box*) —or any road that's what *she* said. *I* saw him four foot ten inch tall and he looked like a rat grinning through a brush; but he sold good green apples and he fed the people and he fed my wife. I didn't do neither. So now I'm a dirty old bastard in a red coat and blue breeches and that's all about it. Blood, y'see: killing. Good night.

He has now undressed and lies down to sleep immediately.

ANNIE *stands for a minute, then subsides to a crouching position, in tears.*
SPARKY *creeps out of his box.*

SPARKY: Tst tst tst, Annie. Stop crying: come here.

ANNIE: Don't talk to me, go to bed, I can't bear wi' no more of you.

SPARKY: Annie, Annie, look now, I want to talk. I'm not deaf, y'know, and I'm not that drunk, I mean I've been drunker, I mean I can stand, ha ha, one foot and all, I'm a stork, look at me— (*He tries to balance on one foot*). Him at the far end—don't you worry for *him*, Annie—why, he's not mortal any more, he's like God, ent he? And God— (*He looks towards* MUSGRAVE'S *light*) —hello, God's asleep.

ANNIE: God?

SPARKY: He's put his light out. Look.

ANNIE: That's where the Serjeant is.

SPARKY: That's right. I never thought he'd sleep. *I* can't sleep . . . what have you got against me?

ANNIE (*surprised*): Nowt that I know.

SPARKY: But you didn't come to me, did you? I mean, you asked *him* and he said no, I asked *you* and you said no. That's all wrong. I mean, you know what the Black Musgrave'd call that, don't you—*he'd* say anarchy!

ANNIE: *He'd* say? He?

MUSGRAVE *groans in his bed.*

Every one of you swaggering lobsters, that serjeant squats in your gobs like an old wife stuck in a fireplace. What's the matter with you all!

SPARKY: Ssh ssh, keep it quiet. Come down here . . .

He leads her as far as possible from the other two.

Listen.

ANNIE: What for?

SPARKY: Snoring. Him? Him? Good, two snorings. They're asleep

. . . I told you in the bar, y'know, they call me Sparky—
name and nature—Sparky has his laugh. . . . A man can
laugh, because or else he might well howl—and howling's
not for men but for dogs, wolves, seagulls—like o' that,
ent it?

ANNIE: You mean that you're frightened?

SPARKY (*with a sort of nervous self-realisation*): Aye, begod,
d'you know: I am. God's not here, he's put his light out: so
I can tell you, love: I *am*. Hey, not of the war, bullets in the
far Empire, that's not the reason, don't think it. They even
give me a medal, silver, to prove so. But I'll tell you, I'm—
here, kiss me, will you, quickly, I oughtn't to be talking . . .
I think I've gone daft.

ANNIE (*who is looking at him curiously, but fascinated*): All
right, I will . . .

She kisses him, and he holds her.

MUSGRAVE (*in clear categorical tones, though in his sleep*):
Twenty-five men. Nine women. Twenty-five men. No children. No.

ANNIE (*in a sudden uprush*): Look, boy, there was a time *I* had
a soldier, he made jokes, he sang songs and all—ah, *he* lived
yes-sarnt no-sarnt three-bags-full-serjeant, but he called it
one damned joke. God damn you, he was killed! Aye, and
in your desert Empire—so what did *that* make?

SPARKY: I don't know . . .

ANNIE: It made a twisted little dead thing that nobody laughed
at. A little withered clover—three in one it made. There was
me, and there was him: and a baby in the ground. Bad
shape. Dead.

*She can say nothing more and he comforts her silently a
moment.*

SPARKY (*his mind working*): Why, Annie . . . Annie . . . you as
well: another one not paid for . . . O, I wish *I* could pay.

Say, I suppose I paid for yours; why, maybe you could pay for mine.

ANNIE: I don't understand.

SPARKY (*following his thought in great disturbance of mind*): It *wouldn't* be anarchy, you know; he can't be right there! All it would be, is: *you* live and *I* live—we don't need his duty, we don't need his Word—a dead man's a dead man! We could call it *all* paid for! Your life and my life—make our *own* road, we don't follow nobody.

ANNIE: What are you talking about?

SPARKY (*relapsing into his despair again*): Oh God, I don't know. God's gone to sleep, but when he wakes up again—

ANNIE (*bewildered but compassionate*): Oh quiet, boy, be quiet, easy, easy.

She stoops over him, where he has crumpled into a corner, and they embrace again with passion.

MUSGRAVE (*now shouting in his sleep*): Fire, fire! Fire, fire, London's burning, London's burning!

MRS. HITCHCOCK, *in a nightdress and robe, and carrying a tumbler, hurries into his bedroom.*

MRS. HITCHCOCK: What's the matter?

She lights his candle.

MUSGRAVE (*sitting up and talking very clearly as if it made sense*): Burning. Burning. One minute from now, and you carry out your orders—get *that* one! *Get* her! Who says she's a child! We've got her in the book, she's old enough to kill! You will carry out your orders. Thirty seconds. Count the time. (*He is looking at his watch.*) Twenty-six . . . twenty-three . . .

MRS. HITCHCOCK (*very alarmed*): Serjeant—Serjeant—

MUSGRAVE: Be quiet. Twenty . . . Eighteen . . . I'm on duty,

woman. I'm timing the end of the world. Ten more seconds,
sir . . . Five . . . three . . . two . . . *one.*

He lets out a great cry of agony and falls back on the bed.
All in the stable hear and take notice. ATTERCLIFFE *turns*
over again to sleep. HURST *sits up in alarm.* ANNIE *and*
SPARKY *stand apart from each other in surprise.*

ANNIE: Sparky, it's your God. He's hurt.

SPARKY *sits staring and gasping, till* ANNIE *pulls him to her*
again.

MRS. HITCHCOCK: What are you playing at—you'll wake up the
town!

MUSGRAVE *shivers and moans.*

MRS. HITCHCOCK (*shaking him gently*): Come on—it's a night-
mare. Wake up and let's get rid of it. Come on, come on.
MUSGRAVE: Leave me alone. I wasn't asleep.
MRS. HITCHCOCK: You warn't awake, any road.
MUSGRAVE: Mind your own business.
MRS. HITCHCOCK: I thought you might be poorly.
MUSGRAVE: No . . . No . . . (*Suddenly*) But it *will* come, won't
it?
MRS. HITCHCOCK: What will?
MUSGRAVE: The end of the world? You tell me it's not material, but if you could come to it, in control; I mean,
numbers and order, like so many ranks this side, so many
that, properly dressed, steadiness on parade, so that whether
you knew you was right, or you knew you was wrong—you'd
know it, and you'd stand. (*He shivers.*) Get me summat to
eat.
MRS. HITCHCOCK: I got you a hot grog. Here. (*She gives him a*
tumbler.)
MUSGRAVE: What—what . . . ?

MRS. HITCHCOCK: I take it at nights for me bad back. I heard you calling so I brought it in. Have a biscuit.

She gives him a biscuit from her dressing gown pocket.

MUSGRAVE: Aye, I will . . . (*He eats and drinks.*) That's better . . . you *do* understand me, don't you? Look, if you're the right-marker to the Company and you're marching to the right, you can't see the others, so you follow the orders you can hear and hope you hear them true. When I was a recruit I found myself once half across the square alone—*they'd* marched the other way and I'd never heard the word!

MRS. HITCHCOCK: You ought to lie down. You *are* poorly, I can tell. Easy, Serjeant, easy.

MUSGRAVE (*relaxing again*): Easy . . . easy . . .

She draws the blanket over him and sits soothing him to sleep.

SPARKY (*with a sudden access of resolution*): Annie, I don't care. Let him wake when he wants to. All I'll do this time is to stand and *really* laugh. Listen to this one, because here's what I'll be laughing at. There was these four lads, y'see, and they made it out they'd have a strong night all night in the town, each boozer in turn, pay-day. And the first one in the first boozer, he says: "Each man drinks my choice," he says. "One sup of arsenic to every man's glass"—and *that's* what they've to drink. Well, one of them, he drinks and he dies, next man drinks and *he* dies, what about the third? Has he to drink to that rule? 'Cos they'd *made* it a rule— each man to the first man's choice.

HURST *has left his box and crept up and is now listening to this.*

ANNIE: I don't know—

SPARKY: Neither do I. But I can tell you what *I'd* do.

ANNIE: What?

SPARKY (*with a switch to hard seriousness*): I'd get out of it, quick. Aye, and with you. Look, love, it's snowing, we can't leave the town now. But you could bed me down some-where's, I mean, like, hide; bide hid *with* me while it's all over, and then get me some clothes and we'd go—I mean, like, go to London? What about London? You've never been to London?

ANNIE: Bide hid while *what's* all over? What's going to happen?

SPARKY: Eh, that's the question. I wish I could tell you. It's Black Jack's work, not mine.

ANNIE: Bad work, likely?

SPARKY: Likely . . . I don't know. D'you know, I never *asked*! You see, he's like God, and it's as if *we* were like angels—*angels*, ha, ha! But that's no joke no more for me. This is funnier nor *I* can laugh at, Annie, and if I bide longer here, I'm *really* wild-wood mad. So get me out of it, quick!

ANNIE (*decisively*): I will. I'm frightened. Pull your clothes on, Sparky, I'll hide you.

SPARKY: Good love, good—

ANNIE: But you'll not leave me behind?

He has started dressing, very confusedly, putting his tunic on first.

SPARKY: No.

ANNIE: Swear it.

He has his trousers ready to step into. He lets them fall while he takes her for a moment in his arms.

SPARKY: Sworn.

HURST *nips in and seizes the trousers.*

(*Releasing* ANNIE.) Now then, sharp. Hey, where's me trousers?

HURST: Here!

SPARKY: What's the goddamn—give 'em back, you dirty—

HURST (*triumphantly*): Come and get 'em, Sparky! Heh, you'll be the grand deserter, won't you, running bare-arsed over the moor in six-foot drifts of snow!

SPARKY: Give me them!

He grabs one end of the trousers and a farcical tug-o'-war begins.

HURST (*in high malice*): A man and a soldier! Jump, natter, twitch, like a clockwork puppet for three parts of the night, but the last night of all, you *run!* You little closhy coward.

ATTERCLIFFE *has woken and tries to intervene.*

ATTERCLIFFE: What the hell's the row—easy, easy, *hold* it!

SPARKY: He's got my bloody trousers!

He gives a great tug on the trousers and pulls them away, HURST *falling down.*

HURST: I'm going to *do* you, Sparky.

His hand falls on SPARKY'S *belt, with bayonet scabbard attached, which is lying on the floor. He gets up, drawing the bayonet.*

ANNIE: No, no, stop him!

ATTERCLIFFE: Drop that bayonet!

ANNIE *mixes in, seizing* HURST'S *wrist and biting it. The bayonet drops to the floor.* ATTERCLIFFE *snatches it and* HURST *jumps upon him. Together they fall against* SPARKY *and all three crash to the floor.* SPARKY *gives a terrifying, choking cry.*

MUSGRAVE *leaps up in the bedroom. Those on the forestage all draw back, appalled, from* SPARKY'S *dead body.*

MUSGRAVE (*to* MRS. HITCHCOCK) : Stay where you are.

He leaves the bedroom.

HURST: He's dead. He's dead. *I* didn't do it. Not me. No.
ATTERCLIFFE: Dead?
HURST: Of course he's dead. He's stuck in the gut. That's you.
Your hand. You killed him.
ATTERCLIFFE: I can't have.
HURST: You did.
ATTERCLIFFE (*stupidly*) : I've got the bayonet.
HURST: Aye, and you've killed him.
ATTERCLIFFE: O Holy God!

MUSGRAVE *enters from the house.* MRS. HITCHCOCK *has left
the bedroom.*

MUSGRAVE: What going on?
HURST: Sparky's been killed.
MUSGRAVE: *What!* How?
HURST: His own bayonet. He was deserting. I tried to stop him.
Then *he—*

He points to ATTERCLIFFE.

MUSGRAVE (*to* ATTERCLIFFE) : Well?
ATTERCLIFFE (*hopelessly*) : Here's the bayonet. I got holding it,
Serjeant. I did. It's always me. You can call it an accident.
But *I* know what that means, it means that it—
MUSGRAVE: Shut up. You said deserting?

HURST *nods.*

What's *she* doing here? Was she with him?

HURST *nods.*

Aye, aye . . . Desertion. Fornication. It's not material. He's dead. Hide him away.

HURST: Where?

MUSGRAVE: In the midden at back of the yard. And don't show no lights while you're doing it. Hurry.

HURST (*to* ATTERCLIFFE): Come on.

ATTERCLIFFE: Holy God, Holy God!

They carry the body out.

MUSGRAVE (*to* ANNIE, *unpleasantly*): Oh, you can shake, you can quiver, you can open your mouth like a quicksand and all —blubbering and trouble—but *I've* got to think, and *I've* got to do.

MRS. HITCHCOCK *enters from the house. She is carrying* MUSGRAVE'S *tunic, hat, and boots, which she puts down.*

Missus, come here. There's things going wrong, but don't ask me what. Will you trust me?

She looks at him searchingly and gives a short nod.

Get hold of this lassie, take her upstairs, lock her in a cup-board, and keep quiet about it. I've got a right reason: you'll know it in good time. Do as I tell you and you won't take no harm.

MRS. HITCHCOCK: The end of the world, already.

MUSGRAVE: What's that? D'ye hear what I say?

MRS. HITCHCOCK: Oh aye, I heard you.

She takes the shuddering ANNIE *by the hand, and then looks sharply at her fingers.*

Hey-ey-ey, this here, it's blood.

MUSGRAVE: I know. I repeat it: don't ask me.

ANNIE *looks at* MUSGRAVE *and at* MRS. HITCHCOCK, *then licks her hand, laughing in a childish fashion.*

MRS. HITCHCOCK: Come away in, Annie . . . Aye, I'll go and lock her up . . . It might be the best thing. I've got to trust you, haven't I? I've always praised religion.

She takes ANNIE *away, into the house.* MUSGRAVE *sits down suddenly, with his head in his hands. The* BARGEE *creeps in from the yard and sits beside him, in a similar attitude.*

BARGEE *(singing softly)* :

> Here we set like birds in the wilderness,
>   birds in the—

MUSGRAVE *sits up, looks at him, realises who it is, and grabs him by the throat.*

BARGEE *(struggling free)* : It's all right, bully, it's only Old Joe.
MUSGRAVE *(relaxing, but still menacing)* : Oh, it is, is it. Well?
BARGEE *(significantly)* : I was thinking, like, if I wor you, *I* wouldn't just set down in a stable, not now I wouldn't, no.
MUSGRAVE: Why not?
BARGEE: *I* see your jolly muckers, over there, mucking in the muck-pile, eh? But if they turned theirselves around and looked at the coach-house—

MUSGRAVE *leaps up in alarm.*

MUSGRAVE: What about the coach-house?
BARGEE: There's bars at its windows: and there's a crowbar at the bars—listen!

A crash of glass offstage from the yard.

That's the glass gone now! If you're quick, you can catch 'em!

MUSGRAVE *has run to the yard side of the stage.*

MUSGRAVE *(calling to offstage)* : Get to the coach-house, get round the back! Quick! Quick!

He runs off in great excitement.
More crashes of glass, shouting and banging.
The BARGEE *watches what is happening in the yard, leaping up and down in high delight.*

BARGEE: Go on, catch 'em, two to the back and the serjeant to the door, open the padlock, swing back the wicket—one little laddie, he's trapped in the window—head in, feet out— pull him down, Serjeant, pull him down, soldiers—boot up, fist down, tie him in a bundle—oh me pretty roses, oh me blood-red flowers o' beauty!

The two SOLDIERS *hurry back, with* WALSH *frogmarched between them, his hands bunched up and tied behind his back.* MUSGRAVE *follows. All are panting. They throw* WALSH *down.*

MUSGRAVE: What about the others?
HURST: Run away, Serjeant.
ATTERCLIFFE: Nigh on a dozen of 'em.
HURST: Ran down the alley.
MUSGRAVE: Let's have a look at this one! Oho, so it's *you*! What were you after?
WALSH *(grinning)* : What d'you think, lobster?
MUSGRAVE: Our little Gatling? Isn't that right?
WALSH: That's right, boy, you're sharp.
MUSGRAVE *(quieter)* : But *you're* not sharp, brother, and I'm going to tell you why.

Shouting and shrill whistles, off.

HURST: It's that Constable's out, and his Specials and all—listen! hey, we'd better get dressed.

He starts huddling on his tunic and trousers.

MUSGRAVE (*to* WALSH): Chasing your friends. He'll be coming here, shortly.

Whistles again.

CONSTABLE (*offstage, in the house*): Open up, Mrs. Hitchcock, open up—name of the Law!

MUSGRAVE: Ah, here he is. Now he asked me this evening to kidnap you for the Army. But *I* told you we was brothers, didn't I? So watch while I prove it. (*To* HURST.) Take him out and hide him.

HURST (*taken aback*): Him in the midden too?

MUSGRAVE: Don't be a fool. Do as you're told.

WALSH: Wait—wait a minute.

MUSGRAVE (*furiously*): Go with him, you damned nignog. Would ye rather trust the Constable?

WALSH (*very puzzled*): What are you on, for God's sake?

MUSGRAVE: Don't waste time! (*He pushes* WALSH *and barks at* HURST.) Get him in that woodshed. God, what a shower o' tortoises!

HURST *hustles* WALSH *out to the yard.* MUSGRAVE *turns on* ATTERCLIFFE.

You get your trousers on.

ATTERCLIFFE *obeys.* MRS. HITCHCOCK *comes in, very agitated.*

MRS. HITCHCOCK: The Constable's here, he's running through the house.

MUSGRAVE: Then send him to me! It's in control, in control, woman. I *know* all about it!

MRS. HITCHCOCK *goes back into the house.*

ATTERCLIFFE: Musgrave, what are you doing?

MUSGRAVE: I'm doing what comes next and that's all I've got time for.

ATTERCLIFFE (*in a gush of despair*): But he was killed, you see, killed. Musgrave, don't you see, that wipes the whole thing out, wiped out, washed out, finished.

MUSGRAVE: *No!*

MRS. HITCHCOCK *and the* CONSTABLE *hurry in from the house.*

CONSTABLE: Ah, Serjeant, what's happened? Saw a gang breaking in at the back of this coach-house. What's kept in the coach-house? (*To* MRS. HITCHCOCK.)

MRS. HITCHCOCK: The Serjeant's got his—

MUSGRAVE: I've got my gear.

MRS. HITCHCOCK: Hello, here's the Parson.

The PARSON *hurries in from the house.*

PARSON: Constable, what's going on?

CONSTABLE: I think it's beginning, sir. I think it's the riots.

PARSON: At this hour of the morning?

CONSTABLE: I've sent word to the Mayor.

He starts making a rapid report to the PARSON. *The* BARGEE *sidles up to* MUSGRAVE.

BARGEE: Don't forget Old Joe. I brought the warning. Let me in on a share of it, go on, there's a bully.

MUSGRAVE: Get out, or you'll get hurt!

The MAYOR *hurries in from the house.*

MAYOR: This is bad, it's bloody bad. How did it start? Never mind that now. What steps have you taken?

CONSTABLE: Me Deputy-Specials all around the streets, but I've not got enough of 'em and they're frightened—that's frank. I *warned* you, Your Worship.

MAYOR: Question is this: can you hold the town safe while twelve o'clock mid-day?

CONSTABLE: Nay I don't know.

MAYOR: The telegraph's working.

MUSGRAVE: The telegraph!

MAYOR: Aye, there's a thaw begun. Thank God for that: they've mended the broken wire on top of the moor. So I sent word for the Dragoons. They'll come as fast as they can, but not afore twelve I shouldn't think, so we've *got* to hold this town!

MUSGRAVE: Six hours, thereabouts. Keep 'em quiet now, they may bide. Mr. Mayor, I'll do it for you.

MAYOR: How?

MUSGRAVE: I'll do what I'm paid for: start a recruiting-meeting. Look, we had 'em last night as merry as Christmas in here, why not this morning? Flags, drums, shillings, sovereigns— hey, start the drum! Top o' the market-place, make a jolly speech to 'em!

MAYOR: Me?

HURST *begins beating the drum outside in the yard.*

MUSGRAVE: You! You, Parson, too. Mrs. Hitchcock, free beer to the crowd!

PARSON: No!

MAYOR (*catching the idea*): *Aye,* missus, bring it! *I'll* pay for it and all!

MUSGRAVE (*to the* BARGEE): *You,* if you want to help, you can carry a flag. (*To* ATTERCLIFFE.) Get him a flag!

Exit ATTERCLIFFE. *Enter* HURST, *drumming furiously.*

We'll *all* carry flags. Fetch me me tunic.

MRS. HITCHCOCK: Here it is. I brought it.

MUSGRAVE (*quite wild with excitement*): Flags, ribbons, bunches o' ribbons, glamourise 'em, glory!

ATTERCLIFFE *hurries in from the yard, with his arms full of colours. He hands these out all round.*

BARGEE: Rosebuds of Old England!
MAYOR: Loyal hearts and true!
PARSON: The Lord mighty in battle!
MUSGRAVE: GOD SAVE THE QUEEN!

General noise, bustle and confusion.

ACT THREE

Scene One

The market-place.
Early morning. In the centre of the stage is a practicable feature—the centre-piece of the market-place. It is a sort of Victorian clock-tower-cum-lamppost-cum-market-cross, and stands on a raised plinth. There is a ladder leaning against it. On the plinth are the soldiers' boxes and a coil of rope. The front of the plinth is draped with bunting, and other colours are leaning against the centre-piece in an impressive disposition.
When the scene opens, the stage is filled with noise and movement. HURST *is beating his drum, the* MAYOR, *the* PARSON *and* MUSGRAVE *are mounting the plinth, and* ATTERCLIFFE *is up already, making the last arrangements. The* CONSTABLE *takes up his stand beside the centre-piece, as does* HURST. *The* BARGEE *is hopping about on the forestage.*
The SOLDIERS *are all now properly dressed, the* MAYOR *has put on his cocked hat and red robe and chain, and the* PARSON *his gown and bands, and carries a Bible. They are all wearing bright cockades.*
The role of the BARGEE *in this scene is important. As there is no crowd, the speeches are delivered straight out to the audience, and the* BARGEE *acts as a kind of fugleman to create the crowd-reactions. Noises-off indicated in the dialogue are rather un-realistic—as it were, token-noises only.*
At one side of the stage there is an upper-storey window.

BARGEE (*casting his cap*):

> Hip hip hooroar
> Hark hark the drums do bark

> The Hungry Army's coming to town
> Lead 'em in with a Holy Book
> A golden chain and a scarlet gown.

Here they are on a winter's morning, you've got six kids at home crying out for bread, you've got a sour cold wife and no fire and no breakfast: and you're too damn miserable even to fight—if there's owt else at all to take your mind off it—so here you are, you lucky people, in your own old marketplace, a real live lovely circus, with real live golden sovereigns in somebody's pocket and real live taddy ale to be doled out to the bunch of you!

MRS. HITCHCOCK *enters, trundling a beer-barrel.*

Oh, it's for free, you can be certain o' that, there's no strings to this packet—let's lend you a hand wi' that, missus!

He helps her roll the barrel to one side of the centre-piece, where she chocks it level and sits down on it. She also has a handbasket full of tankards. The BARGEE *comes back downstage.*

There we are, then. And here *you* are, the streets is filling, roll up, roll up, and wallow in the lot! I'll tell you the word when to cheer.

The platform party is now all in place. The drum gives a final roll. The MAYOR *steps forward.*

CONSTABLE: Silence for the Mayor!
BARGEE: Long live His Worship, who gives us food and clothing and never spares to meet the people with a smile! Hooroar!

Three boos, off.

Boo, boo, boo? Don't be so previous, now; he'll surprise us all yet, boys. Benevolence and responsibility. Silence for the Mayor!

MAYOR: All right. Now then. It's been a hard winter. I know there's a bit of a thaw this morning, but it's not over yet, there may be worse to come. Although you might not think it, I'm as keen and eager as any o' you to get the pits working again, so we can all settle down in peace to a good roast and baked 'taters and a good pudding and the rest of it. But I'm not here to talk strikes today.

A noise off.

BARGEE (*interpreting*): He says: "Who says strikes, it's a bloody lockout."

CONSTABLE: Silence for the Mayor!

BARGEE: Silence for His Worship!

MAYOR: I said I'm not up here to talk on that today. Serjeant Musgrave, on my right, has come to town to find men for the Queen. Now that's a good opportunity—it's a *grand* opportunity. It's up to you to take it. By God, if I was a young lad in a town without work, you'd not catch me thinking twice—

BARGEE: He says: "There's only one man drives the work away in this town."

The CONSTABLE *steps forward, but the* BARGEE *forestalls him.*

Silence for the Mayor!

MAYOR: All right. You think I'm playing it crooked all the time —*I* know.

A cheer off.

But listen at this: (*He holds up a jingling money-bag*). Here's real gold. It rings true to me, it rings true to you, and there's one o' these for every lad as volunteers. That's straight. It's from the shoulder. It pulls no punches. Take it or throw it away—I'm set up here and waiting. (Parson, tell 'em *your* piece now.) And keep quiet while the Rector's at you: he talks good sense and you need it. If you can't give *me* credit, at least you can give *him* some, for considering what's best for the community. Go on, Parson: tell 'em.

He retires and the PARSON *steps forward.*

PARSON: "And Jesus said, I come not to bring peace but a sword." I know very well that the times are difficult. As your minister of religion, and as a magistrate, it is my business to be aware of these matters. But we must remember that this town is only one very small locality in our great country.

BARGEE: Very true, very true.

Two cheers, off.

PARSON: And if our country is great, and I for one am sure that it *is* great, it is great because of the greatness of its responsibilities. They are world wide. They are noble. They are the responsibilities of a first-class power.

BARGEE: Keep 'em there, Reverend! First-class for ever! Give a cheer, you boys!

Three cheers, very perfunctory.

And the crowd roars! Every hat in the air, you've struck 'em in the running nerve, hooroar!

PARSON: Therefore, I say, therefore: when called to shoulder our country's burdens we should do it with a glancing eye and a leaping heart, to draw the sword with gladness, thinking nothing of our petty differences and grievances—but all united under one brave flag, going forth in Christian resolution, and showing a manly spirit! The Empire calls! Greatness is at hand! Serjeant Musgrave will take down the names of any men willing, if you'll file on to the platform in an orderly fashion, in the name of the Father, the Son and mumble mumble mumble . . .

He retires. There is a pause.

MUSGRAVE: Perhaps, Mr. Mayor, before we start enrolling names, it might be as well if I was to say a few words first, like, outlining the type of service the lads is likely to find, overseas, and so forth?

The SLOW COLLIER *slouches in, and up to the base of the plinth.*

SLOW COLLIER: Have you got my name down?

MUSGRAVE: No. Not yet.

SLOW COLLIER: Are you sure of that?

MUSGRAVE: Aye, I'm sure. D'you want me to take it?

SLOW COLLIER: Some of us was a bit full, like, last night in the boozer.

MUSGRAVE: A man's pleasuring, friend, that's all. No harm in that?

SLOW COLLIER (*thrusting forward his hat with the cockade in it*) : Then what's this? Eh? Someone gave me this.

MUSGRAVE (*laughs*) : Oh I'll tell you what that means: you drank along of me—that's all that it means—and you promised you'd come and hear me this morning. Well, here you are.

SLOW COLLIER: Ah. Provisional. Aye. I thought that's what it was. Provisional.

The PUGNACIOUS COLLIER *slouches in.*

PUGNACIOUS COLLIER: Provisional or not, we're not signing nowt without we've heard more. So go on then, soldier, tell us. Prove it's better to be shot nor starve, *we'll* listen to you, man, 'cos we're ready to believe. And more of us and all.

CRIES OFF: Aye. Aye. Aye. Tell us.

BARGEE: Go on, Serjeant, tell us. It's a long strong tale, quiet while he tells it—quiet!

MUSGRAVE: Now there's more tales than one about the Army, and a lot of funny jokers to run around and spread 'em, too. Aye, aye, we've all heard of 'em, we know all about 'em, and it's not my job this morning to swear to you what's true and what's not true. O' *course* you'll find there's an RSM here or a Provost-sarnt there what makes you cut the grass wi' nail-scissors, or dust the parade-ground with a toothbrush. It's all the bull, it's all in the game—but it's not what sends me here and it's not what put *these* on my arm, and it's nowt at all to do with *my* life, or these two with me, or any o' yours. So easy, me boys, don't think it. (*To the* COLLIERS.) There was another lad wi' *you*, in and out last night. He ought to be here. (*To the* BARGEE.) Go and fetch him, will you? You know where he is.

BARGEE (*finger to nose*) : Ah. Ha ha. Aye aye.

He slips out conspiratorially.

MUSGRAVE (*continues his speech*) : I said, easy me boys, and don't think it. Because there's *work* in the Army, and bull's not right work, you can believe me on that—it's just foolery —any smart squaddy can carry it away like a tuppenny-ha'penny jam jar. So I'll tell you what the *work* is—open it up!

ATTERCLIFFE *flings open one of the boxes. It is packed with rifles. He takes one out and tosses it to* MUSGRAVE.

MUSGRAVE: Now this is the rifle. This is what we term the butt of the rifle. This is the barrel. This here's the magazine. And this— (*he indicates the trigger*) —you should know what *this* is, you should know what it does . . . Well, the rifle's a good weapon, it's new, quick, accurate. This is the bayonet — (*he fixes his bayonet*) —it kills men smart, it's good and it's beautiful. But I've more to show than a rifle. Open it up!

AFTERCLIFFE *opens a second case. It contains a Gatling gun and tripod mounting.*

This is the newest, this is the smartest, call it the most beautiful. It's a Gatling gun, this. Watch how it works!

ATTERCLIFFE *secures the gun to its mounting.*

ATTERCLIFFE: The rounds are fed to the chambers, which are arranged in a radial fashion, by means of a hopper-shaped aperture, *here.* Now pay attention while I go through the preliminary process of loading.

He goes through the preliminary process of loading.

MUSGRAVE (*his urgency increasing all the time*) : The point being that here we've got a gun that doesn't shoot like: *Bang,* rattle-click-up-the-spout-what're-we-waiting-for, *bang!* But: Bang-bang-bang-bang-bang-bang-bang-bang-*bang*—and there's not a man alive in the whole of this marketplace. Modern times. Progress. Three hundred and fifty rounds in one minute—*flat!*

The BARGEE *re-enters, soft-footed.*

MUSGRAVE (*quickly to him*) : Is he coming?

The BARGEE *nods, finger to lips.*

ATTERCLIFFE: Now then, you see, the gun's loaded.
MUSGRAVE: It didn't take long, you see.
ATTERCLIFFE: No.

HURST *gives a roll on the drums.*
ATTERCLIFFE *swivels the gun to face out into the audience.*
MUSGRAVE *loads his rifle with a clip of cartridges.*

MUSGRAVE (*his voice very taut and hard*) : The question remains as to the *use* of these weapons! (*He pushes his rifle-bolt home.*) You'll ask me: what's their purpose? Seeing we've beat the Russians in the Crimea, there's no war with France (there *may* be, but there isn't yet) , and Germany's our friend, who do we have to fight? *Well,* the Reverend answered *that* for you, in his good short words. Me and my three lads—two lads, I'd say rather—we belong to a regiment is a few thousand miles from here, in a little country without much importance except from the point of view that there's a Union Jack flies over it and the people of that country can write British Subject after their names. And that makes us proud!

ATTERCLIFFE: I tell you it makes us proud!

HURST: We live in tattered tents in the rain, we eat rotten food, there's knives in the dark streets and blood on the floors of the hospitals, but we stand tall and proud: because of why we are there.

ATTERCLIFFE: Because we're there to serve our duty.

MUSGRAVE: A soldier's duty is a soldier's life.

WALSH *enters at the extreme rear of the stage and walks slowly up behind the others and listens.*
A roll on the drum.

MUSGRAVE: A soldier's life is to lay it down, against the enemies of his Queen,

A roll on the drum.

against the invaders of his home,

A roll on the drum.

against slavery, cruelty, tyrants.

A roll on the drum.

HURST: You put on the uniform and you give your life away, and who do you give it to?

ATTERCLIFFE: You give it to your duty.

MUSGRAVE: And you give it to your people, for peace, and for honesty.

A roll on the drum.

MUSGRAVE: That's *my* book. (*He turns on the* MAYOR.) What's *yours?*

MAYOR (*very taken aback*): Eh? What? Me? I'm not a reading man, but it *sounds* all right . . . strong. Strong . . .

MUSGRAVE (*to the* PARSON): What about *yours?*

PARSON (*dubiously*): You speak with enthusiasm, yes. I hope you'll be listened to.

MUSGRAVE (*at the top of his passion*): By God, I hope I am! D'ye hear me, d'ye hear me, d'ye hear me—I'm the Queen of England's man, and I'm wearing her coat and I know her Book backwards. I'm Black Jack Musgrave, me, the hardest serjeant of the line—I work my life to bugle and drum, for eighteen years I fought for one flag only, salute it in the morning, can you haul it down at dark? The Last Post of a living life? Look—I'll show it to you all. And I'll *dance* for you beneath it—hoist up the flag, boy—up, up, *up!*

ATTERCLIFFE *has nipped up the ladder, holding the rope. He loops the rope over the cross-bar of the lamp-bracket, drops to the plinth again, flings open the lid of the big box, and hauls on the rope.*

HURST *beats frantically on his drum. The rope is attached to the contents of the box, and these are jerked up to the cross-bar and reveal themselves as an articulated skeleton dressed in a soldier's tunic and trousers, the rope noosed round the neck. The* PEOPLE *draw back in horror.* MUSGRAVE *begins to dance, waving his rifle, his face contorted with demoniac fury.*

MUSGRAVE (*as he dances, sings, with mounting emphasis*):

> Up he goes and no one knows
> How to bring him downwards
> Dead man's feet
> Over the street
> Riding the roofs
> And crying down your chimneys
> Up he goes and no one knows
> Who it was that rose him

> But white and red
> He waves his head
> He sits on your back
> And you'll never never lose him
> Up he goes and no one knows
> How to bring him downwards.

He breaks off at the climax of the song, and stands panting. The drum stops.

That'll do. That'll do for *that*. (*He beckons gently to the* PEOPLE.) You can come back. Come back. Come back. We're all quiet now. But nobody move out of this market-place. You saw the gun loaded. Well, it's on a very quick swivel and the man behind it's well trained. (*He gestures with his rifle towards the platform party.*) And *I've* won a regimental cup four year running for small-arms marksmanship. So be good, and be gentle, *all* of you.

That checks the BARGEE, *who made a move. The* MAYOR *seems to be about to speak.*

Right, Mr. Mayor—I'll explain the whole business.

PARSON (*in a smaller voice than usual*): Business? What business, sir? Do you intend to imply you are *threatening* us with these weapons?

MAYOR: The man's gone balmy. Constable, do summat, grab him, quick!

The CONSTABLE *makes an indecisive move.*

MUSGRAVE: Be *quiet*. I shan't warn agen. (*To the* MAYOR *and the* PARSON.) You two. Get down there! Constable, *there*!

He gestures peremptorily and the three of them obey him, moving downstage to stand facing the platform and covered by the gun.

Now I said I'll explain. So listen. (*He points to the skeleton.*) This, up here, was a comrade of mine—of ours. At least, he was till a few months since. He was killed, being there for his duty, in the country I was telling you about, where the regiment is stationed. It's not right a colony, you know, it's a sort of Protectorate, but British, y'know, British. This, up here, he was walking down a street latesh at night, he'd been to the opera—*you've* got a choral society in this town, I daresay—well, he was only a soldier, but North Country, he was full of music, so he goes to the opera. And on his way again to camp he was shot in the back. And it's not surprising, neither: there was patriots abroad, anti-British, subversive; like they didn't dare to shoot him to his face. He was daft to be out alone, wasn't he? Out of bounds, after curfew.

ATTERCLIFFE (*with suppressed frenzy*): Get on to the words as matter, Serjeant!

MUSGRAVE (*turning on him fiercely*): *I'm* talking now; you wait your turn! . . . So we *come* to the words as matter. He was the third to be shot that week. He was the fifteenth that month. In the back and all. Add to which he was young, he was liked, he sang songs, they say, and he joked and he laughed—he was a good soldier, too, else *I'd* not have bothered (we'll leave out his sliding off to the opera WOL, but by and large good, and I've got standards). So at twelve o'clock at night they beat up the drums and sounded the calls and called out the guard and the guard calls us *all* out, and the road is red and slippery, and every soldier in the camp no longer in the camp but in the streets of that city, rifle-butts, bayonets, every street cut off for eight blocks north and west the opera-house. And that's how it began.

HURST (*the frenzy rising*): The streets is empty, but the houses is full. He says, "No undue measures, minimum violence," he says. "But bring in the killers."

ATTERCLIFFE: The killers are gone, they've gone miles off in that time—*sporting* away, right up in the mountains, I told you at the time.

MUSGRAVE: That's not material, there's one man is dead, but there's *everyone's* responsible.

HURST: So bring the *lot* in! It's easy, they're all in bed, kick the front doors down, knock 'em on the head, boys, chuck 'em in the wagons.

ATTERCLIFFE: I didn't know she was only a little kid, there was scores of 'em on that staircase, pitch-dark, trampling, screaming, they're all of 'em screaming, what are we to do?

HURST: Knock 'em on the head, boy, chuck 'em in the wagons.

ATTERCLIFFE: How was I to tell she was only a little kid?

MUSGRAVE (*bringing it to an end*): THAT'S NOT MATERIAL! You were told to bring 'em in. If you killed her, you killed her! She was just one, and who cares a damn for that! Stay in your place and keep your hands on that Gatling. We've got to have order here, whatever there was *there;* and I can tell you it wasn't order ... (*To* HURST.) You, take a rifle. Leave your drum down.

HURST *jumps up on the plinth, takes a rifle and loads.*

We've *got* to have order. So I'll just tell you quietly how many there were was put down as injured—that's badly hurt, hospital, we don't count knocks and bruises, any o' that. Twenty-five men. Nine women. *No* children, whatever *he* says. She was a fully grown girl, and she had a known record as an associate of terrorists. That was her. Then four men, one of them elderly, turned out to have died too. Making five. Not so very many. Dark streets. Natural surge of rage.

HURST: We didn't find the killers.

MUSGRAVE: Of course we didn't find 'em. Not *then* we didn't, any road. We didn't even know 'em. But *I* know 'em, now.

(*He turns on* WALSH.) So what's *your* opinion?

MAYOR: He's not balmy, he's mad, he's stark off his nut.

PARSON: Why doesn't somebody do something, Constable?

Noises off.

MUSGRAVE (*indicates* WALSH) : I'm talking to *him*.

CONSTABLE (*very shakily*): I shall have to ask you to—to come down off this platform, Sarnt Musgrave. It looks to me like your—your meeting's got out of hand.

HURST (*covering the* CONSTABLE) : Aye, it has.

MUSGRAVE (*to* WALSH) : Go on, brother. Tell us.

WALSH *climbs up at the back of the plinth.*

WALSH (*with a certain levity*) : *My* opinion, eh? I don't know why you need it. You've got *him*, haven't you? (*He waggles the skeleton's foot familiarly.*) What more d'you want? (*He comes forward and sits on the front of the plinth, looking at the other two* COLLIERS.) Aye, or you two, with your natty little nosegays dandled in your hatbands. Take 'em out, sharp! He's learnt you the truth, hasn't he?

They remove their cockades, shamefacedly.

PUGNACIOUS COLLIER: All right, *that'll* do.

WALSH: Will it, matey, will it? If it helps you to remember what we've been fighting for, I daresay it will. Trade Unions aren't formed, you know, so we can all have beer-ups on the Army.

SLOW COLLIER: He said that'll do. I'm sick and bloody tired— I don't know *what* it's all about.

WALSH (*drops down to the forestage*) : Come home and I'll tell you. The circus is over. Come on.

MUSGRAVE: Oh no it's not. Just bide still a while. There's more to be said yet. When I asked you your opinion I meant about them we was talking about—them as did *this*, up here.

WALSH: Well, *what* about them—brother? Clear enough to me. You go for a soldier, you find yourself in someone else's country, you deserve all you get. *I'd* say it stands to reason.

MUSGRAVE: And that's *all* you would say? I'd thought better of you.

WALSH (*irritated*) : Now look, look here, what *are* you trying to get? You come to this place all hollering for sympathy, oh you've been beating and murdering and following your trade boo-hoo: but we're not bloody interested! You mend your own heartache and leave us to sort with ours—we've enough and to spare!

MUSGRAVE (*very intensely*) : This *is* for your heart. Take another look at *him*. (*Points to skeleton.*) Go on, man, both eyes, and carefully. Because you all used to know him: or most of you did. Private Billy Hicks, late of this parish, welcome him back from the wars, he's bronzed and he's fit, with many a tall tale of distant campaigning to spin round the fireside—ah, *you* used to know him, *didn't* you, Mrs. Hitchcock!

MRS. HITCHCOCK *has risen in great alarm.*

SLOW COLLIER: That's never Billy Hicks, ye dirty liar.

PUGNACIOUS COLLIER: He wor my putter for two year, when I hewed coal in number five—he hewed there hisself for nigh on a year alongside o' my brother.

SLOW COLLIER: He left his clogs to me when he went to join up —that's never our Billy.

NOISES OFF: Never Billy. Never Billy.

BARGEE: "Never Billy Hicks"—"Never Billy Hicks"—they don't dare believe it. You've knocked 'em to the root, boy. Oh the white faces!

MRS. HITCHCOCK: She ought to be told. She's got a right to know.

MUSGRAVE: Go along then and tell her.

HURST (*to* MUSGRAVE) : You letting her go?

MUSGRAVE: Yes.

HURST: But—

MUSGRAVE (*curtly*) : Attend to your orders.

MRS. HITCHCOCK *goes out.*

When I say it's Billy Hicks, you can believe me it's true.

WALSH: Aye, I'll believe you. And you know what I think—it's downright indecent!

MUSGRAVE: Aye, aye? But wait. Because here is the reason. I'm a religious man, and I see the causes of the Almighty in every human work.

PARSON: That is absolute blasphemy!

MAYOR: This won't do you a pennorth o' good, you know.

MUSGRAVE: Not to me, no. But maybe to you? Now as I understand the workings of God, through greed and the world, this man didn't die because he went alone to the opera, he was killed because he had to be—it being decided; that now the people in that city was worked right up to killing soldiers, then more and more soldiers should be sent for them to kill, and the soldiers in turn should kill the people in that city, more and more, always—that's what I said to you: four men, one girl, then the twenty-five and the nine— *and* it'll go on, there or elsewhere, and it can't be stopped neither, except there's someone finds out Logic and brings the wheel round. You see, the Queen's Book, which eighteen years I've lived, it's turned inside out for *me*. There used to be my duty: now there's a disease—

HURST: Wild-wood mad.

MUSGRAVE: Wild-wood mad we are; and so we've fetched it home. You've had Moses and the Prophets—that's *him*— (*He points at* WALSH.) —'cos he told you. But you were all for enlisting, it'd still have gone on. Moses and the Prophets, what good did they do?

He sits down and broods. There is a pause.

WALSH (*awkwardly*): There's no one from this town be over keen to join up now. You've preached your little gospel: I daresay we can go home?

MUSGRAVE *makes no reply. The* SOLDIERS *look at one another doubtfully.*

HURST: What do we do now?

ATTERCLIFFE: Wait.

HURST: Serjeant—

ATTERCLIFFE (*shushing him*): Ssh-ssh!

A pause. Restive noises, off.

HURST: Serjeant—

ATTERCLIFFE: Serjeant—they've heard your message, they'll none of them forget it. Haven't we done what we came for?

HURST (*astonished, to* ATTERCLIFFE): Done what we came for?

ATTERCLIFFE *shushes him again as* MUSGRAVE *stirs.*

MUSGRAVE (*as though to himself*): One man, and for him five. Therefore, for five of them we multiply out, *and* we find it five-and-twenty. . . . So, as I understand Logic and Logic to me is the mechanism of God—that means that today there's twenty-five persons will have to be—

ATTERCLIFFE *jumps up in horror.* ANNIE *and* MRS. HITCHCOCK *appear at the upper window. When she sees the skeleton* ANNIE *gasps and seems about to scream.*

MUSGRAVE (*cutting her short*): It's true. It's him. You don't need to cry out; you knew it when he left you.

ANNIE: Take him down. Let me have him. I'll come down for him now.

BARGEE: Away down, me strong Annie. I'll carry you a golden staircase—aha, she's the royal champion, stand by as she comes down.

As he speaks he jumps on to the plinth, takes away the ladder, nips across the stage and props it under the window.

MUSGRAVE: No! Let her wait up there. I said: wait! . . . Now then, who's with me! Twenty-five to die and the Logic is worked out. Who'll help me? You? (*He points to* WALSH.) I made sure that you would: you're a man like the Black Musgrave, you: you have purposes, and you can lead. Join along with my madness, friend. I brought it back to England but I've brought the cure too—to turn it on to them that sent it out of this country—way-out-ay they sent it, where they hoped that only soldiers could catch it and rave! Well here's three redcoat ravers on their own kitchen hearthstone! Who do we start with? These? (*He turns on the* MAYOR.) "Loyal hearts and true, every man jack of us." (*To the* PARSON.) "Draw the sword with gladness." Why, *swords* is for honour, carry 'em on church parade, a *sword'll* never offer you three hundred and fifty bullets in a minute—and it was no bright sword neither finished *his* life in a back street! (*He points to* BILLY, *and then at the* CONSTABLE.) Or what about the Peeler? If we'd left it to *him, you'd* ha' been boxed away to barracks six or eight hours ago! Come on now, let's have you, you know I'm telling you the truth!

WALSH: Nay: it won't do.

HURST: It won't do? Why not?

WALSH: I'm not over clear why not. Last night there was me and some others tried to whip away that Gatling. And we'd ha' used it and all: by God, there was need. But that's one thing, y'see, and this is another—ent it, you tell me?

He appeals to the COLLIERS.

PUGNACIOUS COLLIER: Nay, I don't know.

SLOW COLLIER: I think they're all balmy, the whole damn capful's arse-over-tip—

WALSH: No it's not. *I'm* not. And it comes to this wi' me: *he's* still in uniform, and he's still got his Book. He's doing his duty. Well, I take no duties from no bloody lobsters. This town lives by collieries. That's coal-owners and it's pitmen —aye, and they battle, and the pitmen'll win. But not wi' no soldier-boys to order our fight for us. Remember their trade: you give 'em one smell of a broken town, you'll never get 'em out!

MUSGRAVE (*with growing desperation*): But you don't understand me—all of you, listen! I told you we could *cure*—

ATTERCLIFFE: I don't think you can.

MUSGRAVE (*flabbergasted*): Eh? What's that? Stay by your weapon!

ATTERCLIFFE: No. (*He stands away from the gun.*)

HURST *rapidly takes his place.*

HURST (*to the crowd*): Keep still, the lot of you!

ATTERCLIFFE: It won't do, Black Jack. You swore there'd be no killing.

MUSGRAVE: No I did not.

ATTERCLIFFE: You gave us to believe. We've done what we came for, and it's there we should have ended. *I've* ended. No killing.

He deliberately gets down from the platform, and squats on the ground. MUSGRAVE *looks around him, appealing and appalled.*

BARGEE: I'm with you, general!

MUSGRAVE: You?

BARGEE: Nobody else! I'll serve you a lovely gun! Rapine and riot! (*He scrambles on to the plinth, picks up a rifle from the box and loads it.*) When do we start breaking open the boozers? Or the pawnshops and all—who's for a loot?

MUSGRAVE: None of you at all? Come on, come on, why, he was your Billy, wasn't he? That you knew and you worked with —don't you want to revenge him?

ANNIE: Somebody hold the ladder. I'm going to come down.

The SLOW COLLIER *does so.*

MUSGRAVE (*urgently, to her*): Billy Hicks, lassie: here: he used to be yours! Tell them what they've got to do: tell them the truth!

ANNIE *has started to come down the ladder. When she is down, the* COLLIER *lowers it to the ground.*

HURST: Wait a minute, Serjeant, leave me to talk to them! We've not got time bothering wi' no squalling tarts.

MUSGRAVE: Keep you your place.

HURST (*furiously*): I'm in my bloody place! And I'll tell you

this straight, if we lose this crowd now, we've lost all
the work, for ever! And remember summat else. There's
Dragoons on the road!

General sensation. Shouts off: "Dragoons."

HURST (*to the crowd*) : So you've just got five minutes to make
up your minds.

He grabs his rifle up, and motions the BARGEE *violently to
the Gatling. The* BARGEE *takes over, and* HURST *leaps off the
plinth and talks straight into the* COLLIERS' *faces and at the
audience.*

We've earned our living by beating and killing folk like
yourselves in the streets of their own city. Well, it's drove us
mad—and so we come back here to tell you how and to
show you what it's like. The ones we want to deal with
aren't, for a change, you and your mates, but a bit higher
up. The ones as never get hurt. (*He points at the* MAYOR,
PARSON *and* CONSTABLE.) Him. Him. Him. You hurt them
hard, and they'll not hurt you again. And they'll not send
us to hurt you neither. But if you let 'em be, then us three'll
be killed—aye and worse, we'll be forgotten—and the whole
bloody lot'll start all over again!

He climbs back and takes over the gun.

MUSGRAVE: For God's sake stand with us. We've *got* to be re-
membered!
SLOW COLLIER: We ought to, you know. He might be right.
WALSH: I don't know. I don't trust it.
PUGNACIOUS COLLIER: Ahr and be damned, these are just like
the same as us. Why don't we stand with 'em?
WALSH (*obstinately*) : I've not yet got this clear.
ANNIE: To me it's quite clear. He asked me to tell you the truth.
My truth's an easy tale, it's old true-love gone twisted, like
they called it "malformed"—they put part in the ground,

and hang the rest on a pillar here, and expect me to sit
under it making up song-ballads. All right.

> My true love is a scarecrow
> Of rotted rag and bone
> Ask him: where are the birds, Billy?
> Where have they all gone?

He says: Unbutton my jacket, and they'll all fly out of the
ribs—oh, oh, I'm not mad, though you told us that *you*
were—let's have that bundle!

MRS. HITCHCOCK *throws down a bundle.* ANNIE *shakes it out,
revealing* SPARKY'S *tunic.*

Take a sight o' this, you hearty colliers: see what they've
brought you. You can match it up with Billy's. Last night
there were four o' these walking, weren't there? Well, this
morning there's three. They buried the other one in Ma
Hitchcock's midden. Go on, ask 'em why!

HURST: He's a deserter, is why!

ANNIE (*holding up the tunic*): Hey, here's the little hole where
they let in the bayonet. Eee, aie, easily in. His blood's on
my tongue, so hear what it says. A bayonet is a raven's beak.
This tunic's a collier's jacket. That scarecrow's a birdcage.
What more do you want!

WALSH: Is this what she says true? Where *is* he, the fourth of
you?

MUSGRAVE: He was killed, and that's all. By an accident killed.
It's barely materi—

ATTERCLIFFE: Oh, it's material. And no goddamned accident.
I said it to you, Musgrave, it washes it all out.

WALSH: It bloody does and all, as far as I go. (*He turns to the
other* COLLIERS.) If you want to stand by 'em when they've
done for their own mucker and not one of the bastards can
tell ye the same tale, well, you're at your damned liberty
and take it and go!

The COLLIERS *murmur dubiously.*

HURST (*frantic*) : I'm going to start shooting!

General reaction of fear: he clearly means it. He spits at MUSGRAVE.

You and your everlasting Word—you've pulled your own roof down! But *I'll* prop your timber for you—I'll give a One, Two, and a Three: and I'm opening fire!

ATTERCLIFFE: No.

He jumps up and stands on the step of the plinth, below the gun and facing it, with his arms spread out so that the muzzle is against his breast.

HURST (*distorted with rage*) : Get down! Get down off it, you old cuckold, I don't care who you are. I'll put the first one through you! I *swear* it, I will! One! Two! . . .

MAYOR (*to the* CONSTABLE) : Go for that gun.

The CONSTABLE *is making a cautious move towards the gun, but he is forestalled by* MUSGRAVE, *who flings himself at* HURST *and knocks him away from the breech. There is a moment's tense struggle behind the gun.*

MUSGRAVE (*as he struggles*) : The wrong way. The wrong way. You're trying to do it without Logic.

Then HURST *gives way and falls back down the steps of the plinth. He recovers himself.*

HURST (*panting with excitement*) : All right then, Black Jack. All right, it's finished. The lot. You've lost it. I'm off!

MUSGRAVE (*stunned*) : Come back here. You'll come back, you'll obey orders.

HURST *makes a grab forward, snatches his rifle from the platform and jumps back clear.*

HURST (*to the crowd*): Get out o' my road!

At the very instant he turns towards the wings to run away, a shot is fired offstage. His quick turn changes into a grotesque leap as the bullet hits him, and he collapses on the stage. A bugle blares from offstage.

VOICES OFF: Dragoons!

Orders shouted and general noise of cavalry coming to a halt and dismounting.

MAYOR: ⎫ (*one after another, rapidly.*)
CONSTABLE: ⎬ The Dragoons! The Dragoons!
PARSON: ⎭ Saved! Saved! Saved!
VOICES OFF: Saved! Saved! Saved!

MUSGRAVE *is standing beside the gun, temporarily at a loss.* ATTERCLIFFE *has jumped down beside* HURST *and lifted his head. Everyone else stands amazed.*
Suddenly MUSGRAVE *swings the gun to point towards the Dragoons. The* BARGEE *ups with his rifle and sticks it into* MUSGRAVE'S *back.*

BARGEE: Serjeant, put your hands up!

MUSGRAVE *is pushed forward by the rifle, but he does not obey. The* TROOPER *enters, clicking the bolt of his smoking carbine, and shouting.*

TROOPER: Everybody stand where you are! You, put your hands up!

MUSGRAVE *does so.*

BARGEE: I've got him, soldier! I've got him! Crooked Joe's got him, Mr. Mayor.

The OFFICER *strides in, drawing his sabre.*

Give a cheer—hooroar!

Cheers off.
The OFFICER *comes to attention before the* MAYOR *and salutes with his sabre.*

OFFICER: Mr. Mayor, are we in time?
MAYOR: Aye, you're in time. You're *just* in bloody time.
OFFICER (*seeing* MUSGRAVE): 22128480 Serjeant Musgrave, J.?
MUSGRAVE: My name.
OFFICER: We heard word you'd come here. You are under arrest. Robbery and desertion. There were *three* who came with you.
ATTERCLIFFE (*getting up from* HURST, *whose head falls back*): You can count me for one of them. One other's dead already. Here's the third.
OFFICER: You're under arrest.
CONSTABLE: Hold out your hands.

He takes out two pairs of handcuffs and fetters them.

OFFICER: Mr. Mayor, my troopers are at your disposal. What do you require of us?
MAYOR: Well, I'd say it was about all over by now, young man— wouldn't you?
OFFICER: Law and order is established?
PARSON: Wiser counsels have prevailed, Captain.
BARGEE: *I* caught him, *I* caught him, *I* used me strategy!
OFFICER: My congratulations, all.
WALSH (*with great bitterness*): The community's been saved. Peace and prosperity rules. We're all friends and neighbours for the rest of today. We're all sorted out. We're back where we were. So what do we do?
BARGEE:
Free beer. It's still here.

No more thinking. Easy drinking.
End of a bad bad dream. Gush forth the foaming stream.

*He takes the bung out of the barrel and starts filling
tankards.*

OFFICER: The winter's broken up. Let normal life begin again.
BARGEE: Aye, aye, *begin* again!

*He is handing the mugs to the people. He starts singing,
and they all join in, by degrees.*

> There was an old man called Michael Finnegan
> He had whiskers on his chin-egan.
> The wind came out and blew them in agen
> Poor old Michael Finnegan—
> Begin agen—
>
> There was an old man etcetera . . .

He gives out mugs in the following order: the MAYOR, *the*
PARSON, *the* SLOW COLLIER, *the* PUGNACIOUS COLLIER, *the* CON-
STABLE. *Each man takes his drink, swigs a large gulp, then
links wrists with the previous one, until all are dancing
round the centre-piece in a chain, singing.*
ANNIE *has climbed the plinth and lowers the skeleton. She
sits with it on her knees. The* DRAGOONS *remain standing at
the side of the stage.* MUSGRAVE *and* ATTERCLIFFE *come slowly
downstage. The* BARGEE *fills the last two tankards and hands
one to* WALSH, *who turns his back angrily. The* BARGEE
*empties one mug, and joins the tail of the dance, still hold-
ing the other. After one more round he again beckons*
WALSH. *This time the latter thinks for a moment, then bit-
terly throws his hat on the ground, snarls into the impassive face of the* DRAGOON, *and joins in the dance, taking the
beer.*
The scene closes, leaving MUSGRAVE *and* ATTERCLIFFE *on the
forestage.* MRS. HITCHCOCK *retires from the window.*

Scene Two

A prison cell.
This scene is achieved by a barred wall descending in front of
the dancers of the previous scene. After a while the sound dies
away, and the lights change so that we can no longer see past
the bars.
    MUSGRAVE *remains standing, looking into the distance with*
his back to the audience. ATTERCLIFFE *sighs and sits down gin-*
gerly on the floor.

ATTERCLIFFE: Sit down and rest yourself, serjeant. That's all
    there is left . . . Go on, man, sit down . . . Then stand and
    the devil take you! It's *your* legs, not mine. It's my *hands* is
    what matters. They finished Sparky and that finished me,
    and Sparky finished you. Holy God save us, why warn't I a
    greengrocer, then I'd never ha' been cuckolded, never gone
    for no soldier, never no dead Sparky, and never none of this.
    Go on, Serjeant, talk to me. I'm an old old stupid bastard
    and I've nowt to do now but fret out the runs of the conse-
    quence; and the whole croaking work it's finished and done.
    Go on, serjeant, talk.

    MUSGRAVE *does not move.*
    A pause.
    MRS. HITCHCOCK *enters, carrying a glass.*

MRS. HITCHCOCK (*to* MUSGRAVE): It's port with a bit o' lemon.
    I often take it of a morning; like it settles me stummick
    for the day. The officer said I could see you, if I warn't
    no more nor five minutes. Sit down and I'll give it to your
    mouth—them wrist-irons makes it difficult, I daresay.
MUSGRAVE (*without looking at her*): Give it to him. I don't
    want it.

MRS. HITCHCOCK: He can have half of it. You take a sup first.

MUSGRAVE *shakes his head.*

All right. How you like.

She goes to ATTERCLIFFE *and puts the glass to his mouth.*

ATTERCLIFFE: I'm obliged to you, missus.

MRS. HITCHCOCK: It's on the house, this one. Change from the Queen, ent it?

MUSGRAVE: Numbers and order. According to Logic. I had worked it out for months.

He swings round to MRS. HITCHCOCK.

What made it break down!

MRS. HITCHCOCK: Ah, there's the moral of it. You ask our Annie.

MUSGRAVE (*furiously*): He was killed by pure accident! It had nothing to do—

ATTERCLIFFE: Oh by God, it had.

MRS. HITCHCOCK: The noisy one, warn't he? Pack o' cards and all the patter. You asked me to trust you— (*her voice rises with rage and emotion*) —he was only a young lad, for gracious goodness Christ, he'd a voice like a sawmill—what did you want to do it for, you gormless great gawk!

ATTERCLIFFE: *He* didn't do it.

MRS. HITCHCOCK: He did, oh he did! And he broke his own neck.

MUSGRAVE: What's the matter with you, woman!

MRS. HITCHCOCK: All wrong, you poured it out all wrong! I could ha' told you last night if only I'd known—the end of the world and you thought you could call a parade. In con-trol—*you!*

MUSGRAVE (*very agitated*): Don't talk like that. You're talking about my duty. Good order and the discipline: it's the only road I know. Why can't you see it?

MRS. HITCHCOCK: All I can see is Crooked Joe Bludgeon having

his dance out in the middle of fifty Dragoons! It's time you
learnt your life, you big proud serjeant. Listen: last evening
you told all about this anarchy and where it came from—
like, scribble all over with life or love, and that makes
anarchy. Right?

MUSGRAVE: Go on.

MRS. HITCHCOCK: Then *use* your Logic—if you can. Look at it
this road: here we are, and we'd got life and love. Then *you*
came in and you did your scribbling where nobody asked
you. Aye, it's arsy-versey to what you said, but it's still an
anarchy, isn't it? And it's all your work.

MUSGRAVE: Don't tell me there was life or love in this town.

MRS. HITCHCOCK: There was. There was hungry men, too—fighting for their food. But *you* brought in a different war.

MUSGRAVE: I brought it in to end it.

ATTERCLIFFE: To end it by its own rules: no bloody good. She's
right, you're wrong. You can't cure the pox by further
whoring. Sparky died of those damned rules. And so did the
other one.

MUSGRAVE: That's not the truth. (*He looks at them both in
appeal, but they nod.*) That's not the truth. God was with
me . . . God . . . (*He makes a strange animal noise of
despair, a sort of sob that is choked off suddenly, before it
can develop into a full howl.*)—and all they dancing—all
of them—there.

MRS. HITCHCOCK: Ah, not for long. And it's not a dance of joy.
Those men are hungry, so they've got no time for *you*. One
day they'll be full, though, and the Dragoons'll be gone,
and then they'll remember.

MUSGRAVE (*shaking his head*): No.

MRS. HITCHCOCK: Let's hope it, any road. Eh?

*She presents the glass to his lips. This time he accepts it and
drinks, and remains silent.*

ATTERCLIFFE (*melancholy but quiet*): That running tyke of a
Sparky, he reckoned he wor the only bastard in the barracks
had a voice. Well, he warn't. There's other men can sing
when he's not here. So listen at this.

He sings.

> I plucked a blood-red rose-flower down
> And gave it to my dear.
> I set my foot out across the sea
> And she never wept a tear.
>
> I came back home as gay as a bird
> I sought her out and in:
> And I found her at last in a little attic room
> With a napkin round her chin.

At her dinner, you see. Very neat and convenient.

He sings.

> Oh are you eating meat, I said,
> Or are you eating fish?
> I'm eating an apple was given me today,
> The sweetest I could wish.

So I asked her where she got it, and by God the tune changed then. Listen at what she told me.

He sings to a more heavily accented version of the tune.

> Your blood-red rose is withered and gone
> And fallen on the floor:
> And he who brought the apple down
> Shall be my darling dear.
> For the apple holds a seed will grow
> In live and lengthy joy
> To raise a flourishing tree of fruit
> For ever and a day.
> With fal-la-la-the-dee, toor-a-ley,
> For ever and a day.

They're going to hang us up a length higher nor most apple-trees grow, Serjeant. D'you reckon we can start an orchard?

The end.

ONE WAY

PENDULUM

A Farce in a New Dimension

N. F. Simpson

ONE WAY PENDULUM was first presented at the Theatre Royal, Brighton, on 14 December 1959 by the English Stage Company. It was directed by William Gaskill, with decor by Stephen Doncaster, music arranged by Dudley Moore, and with the following cast:

KIRBY GROOMKIRBY	Roddy Maude-Roxby
ROBERT BARNES	John Horsley
MABEL GROOMKIRBY	Alison Leggatt
SYLVIA GROOMKIRBY	Patsy Rowlands
AUNT MILDRED	Patsy Byrne
MYRA GANTRY	Gwen Nelson
ARTHUR GROOMKIRBY	George Benson
STAN HONEYBLOCK	Douglas Livingstone
JUDGE	Douglas Wilmer
POLICEMAN	Alan Gibson
USHER	Jeremy Longhurst
CLERK OF THE COURT	Robert Levis
PROSECUTING COUNSEL	Graham Crowden
DEFENDING COUNSEL	Graham Armitage

CHARACTERS

KIRBY GROOMKIRBY

has the gauche ungainliness of the self-absorbed introvert.
Takes himself very seriously. Only with his weighing ma-
chines is he at all relaxed, and remains even then slightly
grotesque. Uneasy and querulous in his rare encounters
with people. Dressed entirely in black.

ROBERT BARNES

a well-built man in his middle thirties. Has a friendly,
casual, confident manner—a police sergeant, perhaps, off-
duty. Wears a sports jacket and grey trousers. On neigh-
bourly terms both with the Groomkirbys and the audience.
Throws out remarks in an informative, conversational way.

MABEL GROOMKIRBY

a woman of about forty-five. Mother of Kirby Groomkirby.
Takes in her stride most of what happens indoors, and is
only marginally concerned with anything that may happen
elsewhere. Moves briskly and would rather get things done
herself than wait for other people to do them.

SYLVIA GROOMKIRBY

daughter of Mabel Groomkirby. Not yet nineteen, but with
a permanent air of premature disillusionment about her.
Her clothes are casual—neither conventional nor exception-
ally bizarre.

AUNT MILDRED

sister of Mabel Groomkirby. A little older than her sister.
Her hair and her clothes, which are nondescript, combine to
suggest something remote and fey about her in a down-to-
earth way. But she is not overtly eccentric.

MYRA GANTRY

enormously fat through incessant eating in a vocational capacity. She gives her services professionally, but has acquired a somewhat special status in the Groomkirby household through the regularity of her visits.

ARTHUR GROOMKIRBY

husband of Mabel Groomkirby. He is an ineffectually self-important man in his middle forties, who sets far greater store by being master in his own house than he would if he were. Takes for granted the overriding importance of everything he himself is engaged on.

STANLEY HONEYBLOCK

looks like a sensible, well-balanced practical young man. A skilled technician of some kind, probably, in a reasonably well-paid job which enables him to dress in a neat and appropriately conventional way, when he comes to take Sylvia out. Good-natured, unpretentious.

IN THE LAW COURT:

JUDGE

A taller man than Arthur Groomkirby, and slightly older. He is unhurried, sure of himself, and with the instincts—sublimated by his profession—of a stoat.

PROSECUTING COUNSEL

thrusting, relentless, slightly sadistic—but using as a weapon an elaborate pretence of casual, supercilious indifference.

DEFENDING COUNSEL

seedy, bumbling, sentimental, well-meaning. Older than the prosecuting counsel, but conscious of being less effectual —hence very determined.

USHER   CLERK OF THE COURT   POLICEMAN

ACT ONE

The GROOMKIRBY'S living-room.
A door back opens inwards. Part of a kitchen can be seen through it.
A door right opens inwards giving a view of the hall, and part of the staircase.
Against the wall right, and right of this door, stands a cash register, covered and so unrecognizable.
Leading inconspicuously up the wall from the cash register is a tube which disappears into the ceiling.
The fireplace is on the left. On the mantelpiece above it, almost lost among other oddments, stands a small replica of a skull, where a clock might normally be.
A table, with a chair by it, is covered with papers and large black books. These also are to be seen filling a bookshelf, and scattered about the room. There is the usual furniture in addition, including an armchair, a sideboard downstage left, and a wall mirror.
When the curtain rises the stage is in darkness. The light comes slowly up on three centrally placed weighing machines.
NUMBER ONE, in the middle, is large and eye-catching and flamboyantly ugly. On it is an enormous weight.
NUMBER TWO, on the right, and NUMBER THREE, on the left, are identically small, modest, unpretentious. On them are correspondingly smaller weights.
Pause.
KIRBY enters with a music stand which he places centrally opposite NUMBER ONE. He adjusts its height. There is no music on it.
As KIRBY takes up his baton and adopts an appropriate stance, the light contracts to isolate NUMBER ONE.

KIRBY (*on one note*): Mi mi mi mi mi mi mi mi mi mi mi mi mi.

He listens coaxingly. Silence. He tries again.
Pause.

NUMBER ONE (*metallic, mechanical voice*): Mi mi mi mi mi mi mi mi mi mi mi mi mi.

KIRBY *repeats the sound a tone higher.*
Short pause.
NUMBER ONE *repeats it as before.*
KIRBY *raises the sound another tone.*

NUMBER ONE (*imitating*): Mi mi mi mi . . . (*pause*) . . . Fifteen stone ten pounds.

KIRBY *makes an impatient gesture and repeats the sound on the same note as before.*
Pause.

NUMBER ONE: Fifteen stone ten pounds.

Dismissively KIRBY *taps the music stand and beckons to* NUMBER TWO.
Light comes up on NUMBER TWO *and goes down on* NUMBER ONE.

KIRBY (*baton raised; confident*): Doh me soh doh[1] soh.
NUMBER TWO (*sweet soprano*): Doh me soh doh[1] soh.

This is repeated antiphonally several times, acquiring a kind of jaunty, flirtatious rhythm until, suddenly recollecting himself, KIRBY *pulls it up short by two sharp taps on the music stand. At this signal the light comes up on* NUMBER THREE, *leaving* NUMBER ONE *visible but in shadow.*

KIRBY: Doh me soh doh[1] soh.

He beckons to NUMBER TWO.

KIRBY: } *(an octave higher)*
NUMBER TWO: } Doh me soh doh¹ soh.

He beckons NUMBER THREE *with the baton.*

KIRBY: }
NUMBER TWO: } (NUMBER THREE *sings in a fruity baritone, an*
NUMBER THREE: } *octave lower than* KIRBY) Doh me soh doh¹ soh.

This is repeated firmly twice. KIRBY *now fixes his attention sternly on* NUMBER ONE. *Light contracts to isolate* NUMBER ONE *which is very strongly lit.*

KIRBY *(leaning forward; forcefully)* : Mi mi mi mi mi mi mi mi mi mi mi mi mi.

Silence. KIRBY *repeats this twice, trying each time to coax a response but without success. He drops his arms to his side and walks a few steps away from the music stand in despair. The light begins to fade on* NUMBER ONE.

NUMBER ONE *(just before becoming obliterated)* : Fifteen stone ten pounds.

BARNES *materializes downstage right and stands looking on. With sudden decision* KIRBY *returns to the music stand and gives two sharp taps. Light comes up on* NUMBER TWO *and* NUMBER THREE.

BARNES: Works like a slave on this. Every night. As soon as he gets in.
KIRBY *(baton poised)*: Doh¹. *(Very rapidly.)* Doh¹ doh¹ doh¹ doh¹ doh¹ doh¹ doh¹ doh¹ doh¹. Doh¹
NUMBER TWO: } Doh¹ me soh doh¹ soh la doh¹ soh fa me doh
NUMBER THREE: } doh ti doh.

Pause.

BARNES: It's a form of escape, of course. Escapism.

Projected on to a screen behind are about a score of weighing machines in two rows. These swell the density of the sound but the volume is reduced. All except NUMBER ONE *sing.*

ALL (*at a signal from* KIRBY; *muted*): Doh me soh doh[1] soh la doh[1] soh: fa me doh doh ti doh.

Pause.

BARNES: He's got big ideas eventually. Massed choirs and that sort of thing.

KIRBY *taps more peremptorily on the music stand. Two more rows of weighing machines appear. They launch, full-throatedly, into the Hallelujah Chorus.* KIRBY *rises magnificently to the occasion and conducts them with splendid panache.*

CHOIR: Ha . . . llelujah!

Six more rows of weighing machines appear.

CHOIR: Ha . . . llelujah!

Another dozen rows.

CHOIR: Hallelujah. Hallelujah.

Countless weighing machines as far as the eye can see.

CHOIR (*a glorious avalanche of sound*): Ha . . . a . . . llelu . . . u . . . jah!

KIRBY, *after the sound has died away and as the vista fades, stands transfixed in triumphant ecstasy with arms outstretched.*

BARNES (*nonchalantly*) : Delusions of grandeur they call it, don't they?

The vision fades, the light contracts and at last only NUMBER ONE *is visible.*

NUMBER ONE (*metallic and mechanical as ever*) : Fifteen stone ten pounds.

KIRBY *deflates slowly but perceptibly. Fade out. Isolated in two pools of light are* BARNES, *who is still downstage right, and* MRS. GROOMKIRBY, *who is at the open drawer of the sideboard downstage left.*

BARNES (*on Fade out*) : Good long way to go yet.
MRS. G. (*looking sharply round*) : What?
BARNES (*gesturing upwards*) : Hallo, Mrs. Groomkirby. I was just talking about Kirby up there.
MRS. G. (*reverting to the drawer*) : Oh, it's you, Mr. Barnes. I wondered who it was.
BARNES: Won't have to worry about hiring the Wembley Stadium, just yet awhile.
MRS. G. (*without looking round*) : Still having trouble with Brother Gormless up there, is he?
BARNES: Running his head up against a brick wall there, if you ask me.
MRS. G.: The whole thing's ridiculous. Why he can't use records . . .
BARNES: The lazy man's way, Mrs. Groomkirby. Besides—*you* don't know what's behind it.
MRS. G. (*closing drawer and opening another*) : No. Neither does anybody else. I don't think he knows himself.

BARNES: Wait till he's got all five hundred of them up to concert pitch!

MRS. G.: Well, as far as that goes, if we've got to *have* five hundred weighing machines in the house, I'd just as soon they did sing. Especially if they've got nothing more to say for themselves than Gormless.

BARNES: True enough.

MRS. G.: "Fifteen stone ten" all day long—it gets a bit monotonous after a time.

BARNES: I should imagine it does. (*Pause*) Is it all right if we come in, by the way?

MRS. G. (*looking sharply at* BARNES *and then suspiciously into the Auditorium*) : If who come in?

BARNES: Unless you'd rather we went off and came back later?

MRS. GROOMKIRBY *gives* BARNES *a meaningful glance and, closing the drawer, starts tidying things on top of the sideboard.*

MRS. G.: Like living on the pavement!

Pause.

BARNES: I'll bring them in, then, shall I, Mrs. Groomkirby?

MRS. G.: Yes. I suppose they'd better come in if they're coming.

As MRS. GROOMKIRBY *briskly passes into the room the light follows her and comes up over the whole room. She picks up papers and other oddments in her passage towards the door into the kitchen. As the light comes up the phone rings in the hall.*

MRS. G.: There's the phone, Sylvia. (*To* BARNES *without looking round.*) They'll have to take it as they find it. I haven't got time to go round scrubbing and polishing for them. (*She goes out into the kitchen leaving the door open.*)

BARNES: Oh, no, they won't expect anything like that.

SYLVIA *has been sitting languidly in the armchair reading a magazine. She gets up with a marked lack of enthusiasm and crosses to the door into the hall. As she opens it* KIRBY'S *voice can be heard singing "Mi mi mi mi . . . ," and this is repeated in metallic tones.* SYLVIA *goes out leaving the door slightly open.*

SYLVIA *(off; in a bored, disenchanted voice)* : Yes?

BARNES *(gently closing the door on the inside behind* SYLVIA *and at the same time cutting off the sound. With a nod upwards)* : Still at it. *(Moving casually towards the table in the middle of the room.)* He's just above here. He's got the room over this one.

He approaches the table, which is littered with books and papers, and in a mildly inquisitive way begins glancing at titles.

BARNES *(as an afterthought)* : This is the living-room, of course. *(More loudly.)* Where's Arthur this evening, Mrs. Groomkirby?

MRS. G. *(off)* : Need you ask?

BARNES: Across at the library again, I suppose?

MRS. G. *(off)* : I wonder he doesn't take his bed there and have done with it.

BARNES *(to audience; informatively)* : Mr. Groomkirby. He makes a bit of a hobby of the law. Gets a lot of books out of the library and one thing and another. They're all legal books —all this lot. *(Reading out titles.)* "Every Man His Own Lawyer." "Legal Procedure for the Layman." *(He drifts across to the bookshelf.)* Actually he's an insurance agent or something, I believe, when he's working. There's some more of them over here. This is his great hobby at the moment.

MRS. G. *(entering to put something in a drawer)* : Hobby. I don't know about a hobby. (*Going out.*) He spends more time on that than he does on anything else.

BARNES (*taking down a book that has caught his eye and thumbing through it*) : Gets a bit single-minded about it at times, doesn't he?

MRS. G. (*off*) : Cluttering the place up. What with Kirby upstairs and him down. Never speaking to each other from one week's end to the next.

BARNES (*putting the book back and running his finger along the titles*) : "Perjury for Pleasure." "Out and About on Circuit." "Teach Yourself Torts." (*He stops short at a title.*) *Cabinet* making? (*He looks in an intensely puzzled way in the vague direction of the audience and then back at the shelf.*) What does *he* want with a book on cabinet making? "The Complete Cabinet Maker and Joiner." "Do's and Don't's for Dovetailers." "Ways With Wood." What's going on? (*Loudly.*) He's not taking up carpentry now, is he? As well?

MRS. G. (*appearing at door*) : Who?

BARNES: Arthur. He's got enough books here on it. There's another one down here—"Noah's Ark: The Supreme Achievement in Wood." What's he up to, Mrs. Groomkirby?

MRS. G. (*going*) : Don't ask me. Something else for me to dust, I expect, whatever it is.

BARNES (*moving downstage left*) : Well, if he's got ideas about building Noah's Ark in a room this size, he'll find he's bitten off a bit more than he can chew.

MRS. G. (*off*) : As long as we won't have to be knee-deep in shavings while he's finding out.

BARNES: I shouldn't worry too much. It probably doesn't amount to anything, Mrs. Groomkirby. I just happened to see them there. He's probably had them for years.

MRS. G. (*entering with wheelchair as* SYLVIA *enters from hall, letting in the sound momentarily of* KIRBY'S *singing lesson, which is cut off abruptly as she closes door again*) : He's seen them lying about somewhere and picked them up thinking he'd got hold of something else. He doesn't know what day it is half the time.

MRS. GROOMKIRBY *places the wheelchair downstage left in the position it quite clearly occupies regularly. In it is* AUNT MILDRED. *She sits placidly gazing at the floor some ten feet in front of her.* MRS. GROOMKIRBY *settles* AUNT MILDRED *in an impersonal, businesslike way, and then crosses the room to get a large coloured travel brochure to bring to* AUNT MILDRED. SYLVIA *has crossed without a word to the armchair and thrown herself down in it to look again at her magazine.*

BARNES (*leaning against the edge of the seat quite close to* AUNT MILDRED. *Aside to audience with nod towards* AUNT MILDRED): Aunt Mildred. (*Pause.*) Never think they were sisters, would you?

MRS. GROOMKIRBY *returns with the travel brochure and puts it on* AUNT MILDRED'S *lap unceremoniously in passing like a waitress putting a menu on a table.*

BARNES (*with a nod*): Travel brochure.
MRS. G. (*going briskly out to kitchen; without looking at* SYLVIA): Who was that?
SYLVIA (*without looking up*): Stan.

Pause.

BARNES (*half to himself, half to audience; shaking his head dubiously*): Noah's Ark in *there*! I hope he knows what he's doing.

Pause. He begins to move off left.

AUNT M. (*quoting indignantly from brochure*): "By rail to Outer Space!" And here I am sitting here.

BARNES *checks.*

BARNES (*with a sly glance at the audience; very slightly humour-*

ing her) : Perhaps you got on the wrong train, Aunt Mildred.

AUNT M.: Of course I was on the wrong train. I knew the moment I heard the man say Outer Hebrides that I was on the wrong train.

BARNES: She's got this bug about transport. Wants us all moving about. Don't you, Aunt Mildred? Plenty of destinations— so we can feel as if we're getting somewhere. She's probably right. Nothing like a good old destination for giving you a sense of purpose. Till you get there, of course. Then you have to start looking round for another one. That's why you need plenty *of* them. Can't have too many, can you, Aunt Mildred? (*No reply.*) Too wrapped up in her brochure. (*Moving off left.*) Just want to slip upstairs for a moment. I'll be back in a minute.

> BARNES *goes off.*
> *Pause.*
> MRS. GROOMKIRBY *enters briefly to put something away.*

MRS. G. (*without looking at* SYLVIA) : I thought you weren't seeing Stan any more.

SYLVIA (*without looking up*) : I didn't say I *was* seeing him.

MRS. G. (*disappearing through the door*) : As long as you don't expect *me* to be all over him when he comes.

> *Pause.* MRS. GROOMKIRBY *enters with a tray on which a snack is laid out.*

MRS. G. (*putting the tray down*) : Here you are, Sylvia. If you're not doing anything you can take this upstairs to Kirby.

> SYLVIA *looks momentarily up and goes back to the magazine.*
> MRS. GROOMKIRBY *begins clearing* MR. GROOMKIRBY's *books and papers off the table.*
> *Short pause.*

SYLVIA: Can't he come down for it himself?
MRS. G.: You know very well he's busy up there.

MRS. GROOMKIRBY *briskly completes the clearing of the table with no respect at all for the books or papers, which she puts unceremoniously in a corner, and goes out to the kitchen.*

MRS. G. (*going and indicating tray*): Don't let that get cold, Sylvia.
SYLVIA (*stirring herself reluctantly*): Why can't he get records or something and play those—like anybody else? Instead of this everlasting mi mi mi mi all the damn time.

SYLVIA *takes up the tray and makes for the door into the hall.*

SYLVIA: I suppose that's something else that's against his principles. He'd rather go through all this pantomime. (*Opening door. Sound of singing lesson.*) Listen to it!
MRS. G. (*off*): It's only until he gets them all trained properly, Sylvia.
SYLVIA (*closing the door behind her and cutting off the sound*): Gets them trained! I can't wait! (*Reopening door.*) Then, I suppose, we shall have Handel's Messiah driving us all up the wall every time there's anything on the telly. (*She closes door.*) MRS. GROOMKIRBY *comes in and out during the following dialogue to put food on the table. She lays a place for one but the food is enough for ten.*

Pause.
MRS. GROOMKIRBY *enters briefly.*

AUNT M.: What's happened to my tricycle, Mabel?
MRS. G. (*going out*): You know perfectly well it hasn't come yet, Aunt Mildred.

Pause.

AUNT M.: I shall be too old to ride it if it doesn't come soon.

Pause.

AUNT M. (*loudly to* MRS. GROOMKIRBY): Do you remember the trouble Maud had with that tricycle of hers, Mabel?

Pause. MRS. GROOMKIRBY *enters.*

AUNT M.: She went by bus in the end.

Pause.

AUNT M.: It didn't take her long to change from one to the other. She never stuck to anything for any length of time. Wheelbarrows, roller skates, rickshaws—I think she's tried practically everything at one time or another.

MRS. GROOMKIRBY *goes out.*

AUNT M.: I can remember when it was camels. (*Loudly.*) Do you remember that, Mabel? I can remember the time when she wouldn't go anywhere without her camel. If she wasn't up on top of it she was walking along beside it.

Pause.

AUNT M.: She rode to hounds on it more than once.

Pause.

AUNT M.: Until it threw her. Then she went on to roller skates.

Pause.

AUNT M.: Now it's buses. She wouldn't hear a word at one time against that camel. "My ship of the desert" she used to say. But not any longer. Not since it threw her.

Pause.

AUNT M.: I told her they were treacherous. But she wouldn't listen.

Pause.

AUNT M.: She was perfectly all right till the police stopped her that time with Dr. Picklock's ambulance.

Pause.

AUNT M.: Do you remember that, Mabel? In the middle of the night.

MRS. G. (*speaking as she crosses the kitchen past the open door but without looking in*): She was committing a nuisance with it, Aunt Mildred.

Pause.

AUNT M.: It was only through the kindness of Dr. Picklock that she had an ambulance to commit a nuisance with.

Pause. MRS. GROOMKIRBY *crosses back.*

AUNT M.: In any case it was empty.

MRS. GROOMKIRBY *enters, speaking impatiently but without looking at* AUNT MILDRED.

MRS. G.: We know it was empty, Aunt Mildred. But she knocked down Dr. Picklock with it.

Pause. MRS. GROOMKIRBY *busies herself with the table.*

AUNT M. (*as* MRS. GROOMKIRBY *is about to go out*): Knocked down a doctor? With an ambulance? How could she? It's a contradiction in terms!

MRS. G. (*checking and turning to look for the first time straight at* AUNT MILDRED's *back. In angry impatience*) : He was six weeks in *plaster*, Aunt Mildred!

As MRS. GROOMKIRBY *turns and goes out*, SYLVIA *enters from the hall. Brief sound of singing lesson.* MRS. GROOMKIRBY *checks momentarily and then continues out.*

SYLVIA (*closing door and crossing to armchair*) : Listen to it out there! It's going to drive me up the wall before long.

MRS. G. (*off*) : For goodness' sake don't *you* start, Sylvia.

SYLVIA (*sitting with magazine*) : Mi mi mi mi-ing all over the place. He's been on it now since I don't know when and he still isn't any further.

MRS. G. (*off*) : He's got to go at the pace of the slowest. You know that, Sylvia, as well as I do.

SYLVIA: He's got four hundred and ninety-nine others for goodness' sake! He doesn't have to hold everything up just for the sake of Gormless! If he goes at the pace of Gormless he'll still be mi mi mi-ing in six months' time.

MRS. G. (*off*) : That's Kirby's affair, Sylvia. I've got quite enough to do down here moving your father's stuff about all over the place before I can get on with anything—without bothering about what Kirby's doing or isn't doing. (*Pause.*) If *you* gave a hand now and again it might be a help. (*Pause.*) What with you moaning and Aunt Mildred on all the time.

SYLVIA: Why? What's wrong with her?

MRS. G. (*off*) : Nothing. Don't for heaven's sake start her off.

Pause.

SYLVIA: I don't know what she's doing there in the first place.

MRS. G. (*entering with food*) : You know perfectly well she got on the wrong train, Sylvia.

SYLVIA: Cluttering up the place.

MRS. G.: We're not getting rid of her. If that's what you're leading up to. We've been over this before.

SYLVIA: Great old-fashioned thing in the living-room.

MRS. G.: Yes. Well, she's staying where she is. (*Pause. Going out to kitchen.*) Did you ring Kirby's bell when you came down? Because I didn't hear it if you did.

SYLVIA *throws down the magazine in exasperation and getting up crosses to the cash register.*

SYLVIA: I don't know what he wants a bell rung every time for.

MRS. G. (*off*): You know he won't start eating till he's heard it.

SYLVIA (*uncovering the cash register*): What happens when this thing wears out? That's what I want to know. (*Pausing with fingers poised over the keys.*) What is it—No Sale?

MRS. G. (*off*): Surely you know by now, Sylvia. Yes.

SYLVIA: Starve to death, I suppose. (*Ringing up No Sale.*) He was perfectly all right till he heard about Pavlov and those stupid dogs. (*Covering the cash register and returning to armchair, but checking on passing the table as though noticing it for the first time.*) What's all this for, mum, for goodness' sake? Not Mrs. Gantry again?

MRS. G. (*off*): Somebody's got to eat the food up, Sylvia.

SYLVIA (*sitting*): Oh, no! Not her *again*!

MRS. G. (*off*): It's no use leaving it to mount up. I've only got the one larder, Sylvia.

SYLVIA: Couldn't she have come some other night? She would have to be here on the one night I've got Stan coming.

MRS. G. (*appearing at the door and looking pointedly in* SYLVIA's *direction for a moment before speaking*): I thought you weren't seeing Stan.

SYLVIA: Trust her to choose tonight of all nights!

MRS. GROOMKIRBY *says nothing. She goes back into the kitchen.*
Pause.

SYLVIA: What time's she going to be here?

MRS. G. (*entering with food*): I don't know, Sylvia.

SYLVIA: It's eight o'clock now gone. Stan's supposed to be coming at quarter past nine.

MRS. G.: You haven't got to both sit there and watch her, have you?

SYLVIA: What are we supposed to do then?

MRS. G.: If you were to do your proper share of the eating between you, instead of leaving it all to me, I shouldn't have to have Mrs. Gantry in anything like so often. (*Pause.*) Paying out good money all the time. (*Pause.*) If it weren't for your father's parking meters we just shouldn't be able to run to it. Then we should *have* to get it eaten ourselves.

AUNT M.: Twenty-five years since I left St. Pancras . . .

MRS. G.: Be quiet, Aunt Mildred!

AUNT M.: . . . and here I am still sitting here.

MRS. G.: It's all very well for you, Sylvia, to sit there carrying on. It's your father who has to stand out there hour after hour in all weathers to try and get enough together to pay the bills with. (*Pause.*) If you don't want to stay in, there's nothing to stop you going out, is there? You're not going to sit there saying nothing all the evening, both of you, are you?

SYLVIA: I don't know what we're going to do yet. If she's coming we haven't got much choice. I can't take him upstairs with the Mastersingers going full blast up there, can I?

MRS. G. (*checking*): No, you certainly can't, Sylvia! And while we're about it let's get one thing clear. I don't mind Stan coming here. As long as he's not under *my* feet all the time. But we can get one thing settled here and now—he's not being taken upstairs. That's quite definite.

AUNT M.: It isn't at all how I envisaged it, Mabel.

MRS. G. (*reverting to table*): That's one thing I do draw the line at. (*Pause.*) (*Going out to kitchen with a glance in passing at the mantelpiece.*) If that's yours on the mantelpiece, Sylvia, you might put it away somewhere before Mrs. Gantry gets here.

SYLVIA *glances up momentarily and goes on reading.*
Pause.

AUNT M.: Not even a luggage rack for my things, Mabel.

SYLVIA: She's off again, mum.

MRS. G. (*off*): For goodness' sake leave her alone. I can hear she is.

Pause.

AUNT M.: It hardly seems like travelling. (*Pause.*) I wouldn't mind if I could feel I were moving towards something.

MRS. G. (*entering and answering the earlier point about luggage racks*): You can hardly *expect* to have a luggage rack in the Outer Hebrides, Aunt Mildred.

SYLVIA: Pity she can't *be* in the Outer Hebrides.

Pause.
A series of regular thuds as of someone rolling a heavy angular weight across the floor overhead is heard.
MRS. GROOMKIRBY *looks up, then across at* SYLVIA, *who does not react in any way at all, then briefly up again before reverting with a resigned sigh to what she was doing before.*
Pause.

MRS. G. (*going*): You haven't done anything about that yet, have you, Sylvia? It isn't exactly an ornament to have about the place.

SYLVIA: Why? What's wrong with it? It's only a death's head.

MRS. G. (*off*): A dirty old skull on the mantelpiece. (*Pause.*) (*Entering.*) I should have thought you could have found something better to do with your money than spend it on a thing like that.

SYLVIA: As a matter of fact, it's a memento mori, if you really want to know.

MRS. G.: Oh? And what's a memento mori for heaven's sake?

SYLVIA: Stan bought it for me. You carry it round with you.

MRS. G.: It looks like it. Stuck up there.

SYLVIA: You don't *have* to carry it round. As long as it's somewhere where you can see it. It's supposed to remind you of death.

There is an eloquent pause.

MRS. G.: And does it?

SYLVIA *(looking up)* : Does it what?

MRS. G. *(without looking round)* : I thought it was supposed to remind you of death.

SYLVIA *(shrugging)*: Oh. *(Glancing at skull and going back to magazine.)* Not all that much.

Pause.

MRS. G. *(going out into kitchen)* : I think you'd better tell Stan he's been done over that, then, Sylvia.

SYLVIA *affects indifference and goes on reading.*
Pause.
A second series of thuds, slightly louder and slightly slower, as though the weight this time were a heavier one.
Pause.

AUNT M.: If only I could feel I had a proper destination!
(Pause.) And proper transport to take me there.

SYLVIA: Oh for goodness' sake shut her up, mum!

MRS. G. *(off)* : Be quiet and leave her alone, Sylvia!

Pause.
MRS. GROOMKIRBY *enters briefly.*

AUNT M.: We should be a very static lot without any transport to take us from one destination to another.

MRS. G. *(in desperation)* : We don't have to be obsessed with it, Aunt Mildred! (MRS. GROOMKIRBY *goes out into the kitchen.*)

Long pause.
A third series of thuds, louder and slower, is heard.

MRS. G. (*appearing at kitchen door*) : What's he up to?

SYLVIA: For goodness' sake stop fussing! He's only moving his weights about.

MRS. G. (*crossing to door into hall*) : He'll be rupturing himself up there.

MRS. GROOMKIRBY *opens the door. As she does so the lights in the room go down and* MRS. GROOMKIRBY *is seen by the light from the hall outside, standing in the doorway and looking up the stairs. The thuds have become slightly louder through the open door.*

MRS. G. (*calling*) : Are you all right, Kirby?

The light in the hall quickly fades out. At the same time KIRBY *appears downstage left. He crosses from left to right rolling a heavy angular weight as large as himself over and over and goes off.*

MRS. G. (*heard off*) : I suppose he's all right.

As the weight disappears off stage a final louder thud is heard.
Short pause.
The sound of a small, male voice choir is heard rather self-consciously singing Rock-a-Bye Baby. KIRBY *reappears downstage right and retreats backward from right to left conducting imaginary singers with his baton. He disappears offstage on the words "Down Will Come Baby and Cradle and All."*
Short pause. A reverberating crash.
Short pause.

NUMBER ONE (*off; in the familiar tones*) : Fifteen stone ten pounds.

Light up on living-room.
MRS. GROOMKIRBY *has appeared, alarmed and uncertain for the moment, at the kitchen door.*

MRS. G. (*suddenly recollecting herself, seizing a cloth and wiping her hands with it as she crosses to the door into the hall*): Don't just sit there, Sylvia!

SYLVIA: He's only knocked his weights down.

Short pause.

SYLVIA (*as* MRS. GROOMKIRBY *is going out into the hall*): Or tripped over them or something.

MRS. GROOMKIRBY *checks and turns back into the room.*

MRS. G.: He's probably waiting up there to fall back unconscious.

She goes to the cash register, tears off the cover and throws it down, and rings up No Sale.
A sharp single thud is heard.

MRS. G. (*rushing out and upstairs*): I thought as much.

NUMBER ONE (*off*): Fifteen stone ten pounds.

Long pause.

AUNT M.: Four hundred and seventy-nine destinations and not so much as a tricycle to take me to one of them!

Long pause.
BARNES *reappears* (*casually*) *downstage left.*

BARNES: Everything under control? (*Noticing the door into the hall is open.*) What's happened to the music?

MRS. GROOMKIRBY *comes downstairs and into the room, closing the door behind her.*

MRS. G. (*crossing to kitchen*): He's lying there stunned.

BARNES *tries, puzzled, to pick up the lost threads.*

MRS. G. (*off*) : It won't hurt him to stay there for a little while. The rest might do him good.

Sound of doorbell. Very short pause.
MRS. GROOMKIRBY *enters and crosses briskly to the door into the hall.*

MRS. G. (*with heavy sarcasm*) : Don't bother to answer it, Sylvia, will you?

SYLVIA (*as* MRS. GROOMKIRBY *goes out, leaving the door open*) : If that's Mrs. Gantry, mum, I shall be out here washing some things through.

She goes languidly out into the kitchen, closing the door.
BARNES *reacts strongly to the name* GANTRY. *He turns to take down an outdoor coat from a hook offstage.*

BARNES (*confidentially*) : I think perhaps this is where we'll quietly scarper. Before we get caught. (*Getting into outdoor coat.*) We'll go outside and have a breather for a minute or two . . .

MRS. G. (*off*) : Hello, Myra.

MRS. GANTRY (*off*) : I hope I'm not too early, Mabel?

MRS. G. (*off*) : Of course not, Myra. Let me hang that up here for you.

BARNES (*crossing rapidly from left to right*) : Come on. (*As he passes in front of* AUNT MILDRED.) Excuse us, Aunt Mildred. We're leaving you to it for a little while.

MRS. G. (*at door*) : I've got everything set out ready for you.

BARNES (*checking; he is off the set downstage right*) : Here she is. The fifteen stone wonder.

MRS. GANTRY *comes in followed by* MRS. GROOMKIRBY.

MRS. G. (*pushing back, as she passes it, the drawer of the cash register, which she previously left open*) : We're just waiting for the kettle.

NUMBER ONE (*off; as though in response to the slight ping from the cash register*) : Fifteen stone ten pounds.

> MRS. GANTRY *checks in surprise which has begun to turn to indignation when the lights quickly fade and go up again on a street scene drop showing a corner house.*

BARNES: I stand corrected.

Pause.
Barnes begins rolling a cigarette.

BARNES: I should have told you about the cash register. Communicates with Kirby's room up there. (*He gestures vaguely towards one of the upper windows.*) Don't ask me why. They've got some crack-brained ideas in that house. He has to have a bell rung before he can eat anything. He's trained himself. Conditioned reflex or something. Why it has to be a cash register God only knows. Anything with a bell on it would have done just as well as long as he's got something he can respond to. Doorbell as far as that goes. All it wants is for someone to run a lead up to his room—wouldn't take more than a few minutes. I'd suggest doing it myself only they're a bit funny about letting anybody in on it from outside. They generally keep it covered up actually. I'm surprised it wasn't covered just now. . . .

> BARNES *breaks off, cigarette poised half-way to his lips, and stares in amazement as a small handcart comes on from left. It is stacked precariously with oak panelling.*
> BARNES *watches it well on to the stage in its progress across from left to right.*
> *Pushing it is* MR. GROOMKIRBY.

BARNES: Hold it! (*He darts forward to steady the load.*)
MR. G. (*peering round the load and seeing* BARNES) : Oh, it's you, Bob, is it? Wondered who it was.

BARNES: What's it all in aid of?

MR. G.: I've been an hour and a half with this lot. (*He starts pushing again.*) Getting it up here. Traffic lights and what not.

BARNES: Wait! (*He retrieves a piece of panelling.*) You've got about twice as much on here as you can manage. (*Pause.*) There. Try that.

MR. G. (*moving off*): Oak. Good, solid stuff.

BARNES (*watching him off*): You're not thinking of trying to get that whatever it is set up indoors, are you, by any chance?

MR. G.: Why not?

BARNES: Good God! She'll have a fit!

He shakes his head after MR. GROOMKIRBY *despairingly.*

BARNES (*calling*): Look out! (*Pause.*) You nearly lost the lot then.

MR. G. (*off*): It's all right. I've only got to get it round the back now.

BARNES: You should have made two journeys with it.

MR. G. (*off*): No, I didn't want to do that. I just made the one journey and went the long way round. It's as broad as it's long.

As BARNES *crosses to the right the drop quickly rises on the living-room where* MRS. GROOMKIRBY *and* MRS. GANTRY *are in conversation.*

MRS. GANTRY *is sitting at the table where her ravages are already apparent.* MRS. GROOMKIRBY *is ironing.*

MRS. G. (*as drop rises*): They go round in circles with it.

MRS. GANTRY: Of course they do.

BARNES *cautiously backs out of their line of vision.*
Pause.

MRS. G.: It's the same with his parking meters.

MRS. GANTRY: Like Mr. Gantry with his.

BARNES (*aside*) : I think I'll just go round and see what's going on out at the back. (*Withdrawing, with a gesture into the room.*) Good luck to you! (*He goes.*)

MRS. G.: Five of them altogether he's got out there, in different places. Round the lawn and up by the rockery. But once he's put his sixpence in there's no budging him. He'll stand there like a statue till his hour's up.

MRS. GANTRY: Mr. Gantry generally takes a book out there with him.

MRS. G.: Instead of going away after he's stood there for ten minutes or so and having sixpenn'orth in front of one of the others. What's the good of *having* five? And the consequence is, of course, that when he goes round to empty them all at the end of the month he's got practically nothing to show for hours of waiting. And he's out in all weathers.

MRS. GANTRY: It's the only way they can save anything.

MRS. G.: He's afraid of anything that's got the least suggestion of overcharging about it. Unless he gets his full hour once he's put his sixpence in he feels he's been done in some way. He's frightened he'll end up losing his own custom.

MRS. GANTRY: If you don't speculate you don't accumulate.

MRS. G.: I tell him, by the time it came to losing his own custom—if it ever did—he could have made enough overcharging himself to pay somebody to stand in front of them twenty-four hours a day. And make his fortune practically. But he can't seem to see it.

MRS. GANTRY: They don't, Mabel. Once they get an idea in their heads. (*Pause.*) You've still got your Aunt Mildred, I see.

MRS. G.: She's in the Outer Hebrides. Waiting for a train back to St. Pancras.

Pause.

MRS. GANTRY: She lives for her transport, doesn't she?

MRS. G.: We're trying to get a tricycle for her—but they don't seem to make them side-saddle any more.

Long pause.

MRS. GANTRY: You heard about Mr. Gridlake?
MRS. G.: No?
MRS. GANTRY: I thought you might have heard. Had an accident on his skis.
MRS. G.: Serious?
MRS. GANTRY: Killed himself.
MRS. G.: No!
MRS. GANTRY: Straight into the jaws of death, so Mrs. Honeyblock was saying.

Pause.

MRS. G.: What on earth did he expect to find in there, for goodness' sake?
MRS. GANTRY: Showing off, I suppose.

Pause.

MRS. G.: You'd think he'd have had more sense.

Pause.

MRS. GANTRY: He hadn't intended staying there, of course.

Pause.

MRS. G.: In one side and out the other, I suppose.
MRS. GANTRY: That's why he had his skis on sideways, according to Mrs. Honeyblock.

Pause.

MRS. G.: I can't think what possessed him.
MRS. GANTRY: Trying to take death in by putting his skis on the wrong way round!

Pause.

MRS. GANTRY: I feel sorry for Mrs. Gridlake.

MRS. G.: What actually happened in there? Missed his footing, I suppose?

MRS. GANTRY: I'll tell you what *I* think happened, Mabel.

MRS. G.: Too confident.

MRS. GANTRY: No. What I think happened was that he went in all right and then caught his head a glancing blow as he was coming out. (*Pause.*) It's easily done. Especially a tall man.

MRS. G.: Stunned himself.

MRS. GANTRY: Stunned himself, and then of course it was too late.

Pause.

MRS. G.: Instead of *allowing* for his height.

MRS. GANTRY: Allow for it? I don't suppose he even knew what it was.

MRS. G. (*in remonstrance*): Oh! But he must have done! I can't believe he didn't know his own height, Myra.

MRS. GANTRY: Mr. Gantry doesn't.

MRS. G.: Do you mean to say he doesn't know how tall he is?

MRS. GANTRY: He's not all that certain how short he is, Mabel, if it comes to that.

MRS. G.: It's about time you made him have himself measured, Myra.

MRS. GANTRY: The same with his weight. He has to work it out every time.

Pause. MRS. GROOMKIRBY *maintains a silence of disapprobation.*

MRS. GANTRY: I didn't tell you about the summer before last, did I? When he went over the edge at Scarborough?

MRS. G.: No?

MRS. GANTRY: Yes—he fell off one of the cliffs playing dominoes with the children.

MRS. G.: I never knew that.

MRS. GANTRY: How long do you think it took him to get to the bottom?

MRS. GROOMKIRBY *looks inquiringly.*

MRS. GANTRY: Three hours!

MRS. G.: No!

MRS. GANTRY: All but five minutes.

MRS. G.: But what was he *doing*?

MRS. GANTRY: Working out his weight, if you please.

MRS. G.: Not on the way down!

MRS. GANTRY: On the way down, Mabel. He'd left his diary, with his weight and everything in it, back at the caravan.

MRS. G.: Wouldn't it have done when he got home?

MRS. GANTRY: It was a question of knowing how hard to fall, Mabel. He needed to know his weight before he could work it out. (*Pause.*) And then after all that he found he'd fallen harder than he need have done. Made a mistake with one of the figures or something.

MRS. G.: It's easily done.

Pause.

MRS. GANTRY: Any other man would have known his weight, of course.

MRS. G.: You should make him carry his diary about with him, Myra.

Pause.

BARNES (*off*): Where do you want this?

Light fades rapidly on living-room and comes up down-stage right where BARNES *can be seen in his shirtsleeves. He has a panel in his hands and is facing offstage.*

MR. G. (*off*): What is it?

BARNES: Front panel. Top left.

MR. G. (*off*) : That goes over here. Give it to me.

MR. GROOMKIRBY *appears, takes the panel and disappears.*

BARNES: We'd better start taking some of this round, hadn't we? What about these side panels? Are they ready to go?

MR. G. (*off*) : Yes. And the bolts. They can all go round. We shall have to assemble them properly when we've got them inside.

BARNES: Right. (*He begins to cross from right to left with a large panel.*) Where do you want this? Outside the kitchen window?

MR. G. (*off*) : That'll do.

STANLEY HONEYBLOCK *enters from left and crosses to right.*

BARNES (*over the top of the panel*) : Hallo, Stan. I shouldn't go that way round, if I were you.

STAN: Why? What's going on?

BARNES: Have a look. (*Going.*) Round the corner. Don't let him see you, that's all. Unless you want to get roped in. Noah's Ark isn't in it.

STAN (*looking at disappearing panel*) : What's that? A coffin he's building himself?

BARNES (*off*) : He'll need one before he's finished, the way he's going.

STAN *shrugs and continues across.*

STAN (*over his shoulder to* BARNES) : Haven't seen anything of Sylvia, I suppose?

BARNES (*off*) : She's around somewhere, Stan.

STAN (*going off*) : Be another hour I expect before she's ready.

Light comes up in living-room. SYLVIA *is going out into the kitchen, having come in to fetch something. She leaves the door open.* MRS. GROOMKIRBY *and* MRS. GANTRY *are as before.*

MRS. G.: I wish I'd known sooner. I could have told Kirby.

MRS. GANTRY: Sooner?

MRS. G.: About Mr. Gridlake. He's always glad of an excuse to go into mourning.

MRS. GANTRY: Kirby likes his black, doesn't he?

MRS. G.: He's never out of it, Myra. That reminds me. Sylvia— if you're going upstairs in a minute you might just look in and see if Kirby's all right.

SYLVIA (*off*): Why can't you stop fussing about him all the time, mum? He's perfectly all right.

MRS. G. (*to* MRS. GANTRY): Knocked himself out up there.

MRS. GANTRY: Oh, dear.

MRS. G.: With his weights. He may want a ping if he's ready to come round. He does everything to the bell these days.

SYLVIA (*off*): It'll do him good to lie there unconscious for a bit. Give his brain a rest.

MRS. G.: It wouldn't hurt you to look in and see, Sylvia.

SYLVIA: You know yourself what he's like, mum, if anybody interferes with him when he's unconscious.

Pause.

MRS. G. (*indicating the cash register*): That thing over there's been more trouble than it's worth ever since he came home with it.

MRS. GANTRY: I can't think why you don't have an ordinary bell rigged up for him, Mabel.

MRS. G.: No, he's got attached to that now. He bought it originally so he could have something to offer in part exchange if he ever wanted a typewriter—and now we seem to be stuck with it.

MRS. GANTRY: That must have been when he was working on his book.

MRS. G.: It was. When he was learning how to make the paper.

MRS. GANTRY: What happened about that, Mabel? Did he ever get any further with it?

MRS. G.: Oh, yes. He made enough paper to last us till kingdom come. Stacked up out there in bales—you can't move for it.

Pause.

MRS. GANTRY: As long as he managed to get the book finished.

MRS. G.: He didn't seem to get much further with that, Myra. By the time he'd made the paper and got the ingredients together for his ink he'd lost the thread of his story.

Pause.

MRS. GANTRY: Pity. He could have written a nice book if he hadn't lost the thread.

Pause.

MRS. G. (*with a nod towards the cash register*): So then of course it became an egg-timer—and now he uses it for everything practically. Every time he wants a ping.

Pause.

MRS. GANTRY: Rather novel.

MRS. G.: What?

MRS. GANTRY: Using it as an egg-timer.

MRS. G.: He won't trust his stop-watch. That's the real reason.

MRS. GANTRY: Oh?

MRS. G.: He's had it ever since he was ten, but he can't bring himself to trust it.

MRS. GANTRY: Fancy.

Pause.

MRS. G.: At least, he'll trust it for the minutes if he's in the mood, but . . .

MRS. GANTRY: . . . not for the seconds.

MRS. G.: He's afraid of being led up the garden.

MRS. GANTRY: I wonder why that is.

MRS. G.: I don't know, Myra, I'm sure. He's always been the same. (*Pause.*) Just the seconds.

Pause.

MRS. GANTRY: Perhaps he thinks he can check up better on the minutes and see that he's not being led up the garden.

MRS. G.: It may be that. He's certainly quite decided about it whatever it is. As far as the seconds are concerned.

Pause.

MRS. GANTRY: It's not so easy to keep check with the seconds. Unless you've got another stop-watch.

MRS. G.: He probably wouldn't trust that any more than he does his own, Myra.

MRS. GANTRY: They like to know where they are with things, don't they? Everything cut and dried and that.

Pause.

MRS. G.: So of course there was nothing for it but to use the cash register and time his eggs with that. And the telephone, of course.

MRS. GANTRY: They're not worth eating unless they're done just right, are they?

MRS. G.: He won't touch them, Myra.

SYLVIA *enters from the kitchen and makes her way languidly and erratically to the door into the hall.*

MRS. G.: Sylvia—what was the name of that man with the dogs Kirby always used to be on about?

SYLVIA: Oh—I keep *telling* you, mum, who he was.

MRS. G. (*to* MRS. GANTRY): He used to ring a bell to make their mouths water.

SYLVIA: Pavlov.

MRS. G.: That's right. So of course next thing we knew he was giving himself a ping on the cash register every time he sat down to a meal. Now he can't do a thing without it.

MRS. GANTRY: Dependent on it.

MRS. G.: You know he wanted to *be* one of that man's dogs at one time?

SYLVIA (*going out*) : Oh—for goodness' sake, mum! (*She closes the door impatiently behind her.*)

MRS. G.: As a matter of fact I think that's what's at the bottom of half Kirby's trouble.

MRS. GANTRY: I must say I've never really visualized him as a dog, Mabel.

MRS. G.: He keeps on about being born too late and into the wrong species. I think it preys on him.

MRS. GANTRY: It's silly to hold it against himself.

MRS. G.: The same with his black. He won't wear his black now unless he's got somebody to go into mourning for.

MRS. GANTRY: Been killing people, I suppose?

MRS. G.: Not so far as I know, Myra. We don't say too much about it to him because it only drives him in on himself—but he thinks a lot too much about death to be good for him.

MRS. GANTRY: Perhaps now he's got his music it might take his mind off it a bit.

MRS. G.: Arthur's as bad really—although he's more taken up with the legal side of it, of course. Books all over the place. Look at them. They're all law books of one kind or another. I've never finished moving them about from one place to another.

MRS. GANTRY: They get very tied up in it, don't they?

MRS. G.: I spend half my time one way and another between the two of them, tidying up and this, that and the other.

MRS. GANTRY: I think they're all the same, Mabel.

Pause.

MRS. G.: What I'm dreading is the day he brings the Old Bailey home for us all to fall over.

MRS. GANTRY: He's too wrapped up in his books, Mabel.

MRS. G.: I wouldn't be so sure, Myra. I've got a sort of sixth sense about these things.

MR. GROOMKIRBY *appears downstage right. He crosses labori-*
ously with a faint suggestion of sternly repressed stealth
from right to left in front of the living-room set.
He is carrying the front end of a very long, very high oak
panel which completely masks the living-room set as it passes
across.
On the panel are the words "THIS WAY UP." They are
stencilled upside down at the bottom.
MR. GROOMKIRBY *disappears off left but the panel continues*
to pass across. On it, as a kind of trade mark, is the figure
of Justice—blindfolded and with sword and scales—also up-
side down. Above it, upside down, are the words: BUILD-
IT-YOURSELF. SERIES NINE—FAMOUS INSTITU-
TIONS. NUMBER SEVEN: OLD BAILEY.
When the other end of the panel comes into view it is seen
to be carried by STAN.
He looks less neat than he did, has obviously been working
hard, and looks very much like a forced volunteer.
When the panel has passed across MRS. GANTRY *is preparing*
to go.

MRS. GANTRY: I think that's more or less everything, Mabel.
(*Rising.*) I haven't touched the gherkins, but I can attend
to those when I come in in the morning.

MRS. G.: Oh, don't worry about those, Myra. (*She goes to the*
mantelpiece.) It's the other things *I* can't manage. You've
no idea what a difference it makes just having you come
once or twice a week. What did I do with your envelope?

MRS. GANTRY: And you want me first thing in the morning, Mabel
—is that right?

MRS. G.: If you could manage it, Myra.

AUNT M.: There's no alternative, Mabel. I shall have to go by
sedan chair.

MRS. G.: Here it is. (*Handing a small brown envelope to* MRS.
GANTRY.) That's for tonight and last Friday, Myra. I think
you'll find it's all there.

MRS. GANTRY: Last Friday?

MRS. G.: When you came in to give us a hand with the leftovers.

MRS. GANTRY (*putting the envelope just the same into her hand-bag*): Oh, good heavens, Mabel—that was only a few bits and pieces. You shouldn't have bothered.

MRS. G. (*indicating* AUNT MILDRED): I wondered when the sedan chair was coming up. We always get that when it's time for her to be going off to bed.

MRS. GANTRY: She'd be better off on a tricycle.

MRS. G. (*moving towards the door*): It never seems to occur to her that a sedan chair would be far too heavy for her.

MRS. GANTRY: It needs two in any case.

MRS. G.: Of course it does.

MRS. GANTRY: One at the front and one at the back.

MRS. G.: She couldn't be in both places at once.

MRS. GANTRY (*going*): And inside.

MRS. G.: And inside as well. (*Following* MRS. GANTRY *out.*) It's too much for one person.

> MRS. GROOMKIRBY *closes the door behind her.*
> *Light fades out on living-room.*
> STAN *appears downstage right and is about to cross to left. He has the air of someone who feels he is being imposed on.*

STAN: She does know I'm here, I suppose?

MRS. G. (*off*): What?

STAN (*checking*): Sylvia. She's not waiting for me in there or anything, is she?

MR. G. (*off*): No. She'll be down when she's ready.

> STAN *continues across.*

MR. G. (*off*): It's in among the straw there somewhere. Rolled up—with a rubber band round it. I can't get on till I've got it. It'll be there if you look. Marked "blueprint." In with the straw the brass fittings were packed in.

> STAN *goes off.*
> AUNT MILDRED *is isolated in a strong light.*

AUNT M.: If Maud Banquet were here now I could have taken
her out to look at the aurora borealis. (*Pause.*) Or she
could have stood on a chair and seen it through the window
in the station-master's office. (*Pause.*) You can get a wonderful view from the window in the station-master's office
if you stand on a chair. (*Pause.*) The last time I took Maud
Banquet to see the aurora borealis she thought it was the
signals. (*Pause.*) Look, Mildred, she said. If it isn't those
dreadful men in the signal boxes—they've been carousing
again!

Pause.

MRS. G. (*opening door from hall and calling upstairs*): Are you
up there for good, Sylvia? You'll have Stan here presently.
I'm not entertaining him.

*The opening of the door is the signal for the light to come
up over the whole living-room.*
As it does so, and while MRS. GROOMKIRBY *is still at the door
looking upstairs,* MR. GROOMKIRBY *is making his way out into
the kitchen having apparently set up a witness box in the
living-room.*
MRS. GROOMKIRBY *closes the door, crosses briskly to* AUNT
MILDRED, *checks on seeing the witness box, looks at it for
several seconds with incredulous hostility, turns away tight-
lipped, and going up to* AUNT MILDRED *unceremoniously
takes her travel brochure and puts it back on its shelf on
the other side of the room.*

AUNT M.: Maud wanted to call it the northern lights, but I said
No. (*Pause.*) Either we call it the aurora borealis, I said,
or we don't call it anything at all. (*Pause.*) In the end we
took it in turns.

Pause.
MRS. GROOMKIRBY *has returned and is folding up* AUNT
MILDRED's *rug.*

AUNT M.: Some days she'd call it the northern lights while I called it the aurora borealis. Some days it was the other way round.

Pause. MRS. GROOMKIRBY *goes behind the wheelchair and begins to turn it in the direction of the kitchen door.*

AUNT M.: She'd call it the aurora borealis while I called it the northern lights.

Pause. MRS. GROOMKIRBY *wheels her briskly out past the witness box, which involves a slight detour.*

AUNT M. (*as she goes through the door*): We got on very well together.

BARNES *appears downstage left. He takes down his jacket from a peg just out of sight and moves just to the edge of the set where he can see the witness box. Having satisfied himself about this, he puts his jacket over his arm and turns to the audience.*

BARNES (*looking at his hands*): Go up and try and get some of this off.

He crosses to right, pausing on the way for another look at the witness box and to size up the room.

BARNES: I hope he knows what he's doing, that's all.

MRS. GROOMKIRBY *enters from hall.*

MRS. G. (*seeing* BARNES): Now what's he letting us all in for? (*She indicates witness box.*)

BARNES (*anxious to extricate himself as soon as possible*): Hallo, Mrs. Groomkirby.

MRS. G.: What is it? A pulpit or something? Stuck right where we can fall over it?

BARNES (*edging off*) : I think it's just a witness box.

MRS. G. (*going to cupboard*) : Doesn't he think I've got enough to do moving his books from one place to another?

BARNES: I shouldn't worry too much, Mrs. Groomkirby.

MRS. G. (*going out to the kitchen*) : It was bad enough when he brought Stonehenge home and we had it stuck in here for weeks.

BARNES: It probably won't come to anything.

> BARNES *makes good his escape while he can with a brief explanatory glance at the audience.*
>
> MRS. GROOMKIRBY *addresses remarks from time to time to* BARNES, *whom she thinks to be still within earshot.*

MRS. G. (*off*) : Everybody calling us Druids behind our backs. (*Pause.*) This time we shall have a lot of jury men tramping all over the carpet every time we want to sit down to a meal, as well. (*Longer pause.*) What does he think we're going to do? (*Glancing in at the witness box as she crosses past the open door.*) Walk round *that* every time we want to go from one side of the room to the other? (*Pause.*) Next thing we know we shall have the entire Old Bailey or something in here. Collecting the dust. I wouldn't put anything past him—once he gets an idea in his head. Before we know where we are we shall be having walls knocked out to make room for it and one thing and another. (*Pause.*) (*Crossing back without looking in.*) And the ceiling raised. (*Pause.*) (*Off.*) Putting our hands in our pockets all the time for chandeliers and cornices and goodness knows what. (*Pause.*) And flunkeys. Under our feet. (*Pause.*) A room the size he'll need for the Old Bailey. We shan't know where we are. Upper class, lower class, Tom, Dick or Harry or what. We shall be on the phone half the time trying to find out. (*Pause.*) What else has he got out there to bring in? (*Pause.*) (*Appearing at the door.*) Is he bringing anything else in?

> MRS. GROOMKIRBY *looks around for* BARNES, *registers his absence and turns to go out again.*

The door from the hall opens and SYLVIA *enters. She is wearing slightly more formal clothes and carries an outdoor coat which she flings over a chair.*
MRS. GROOMKIRBY *glances round and continues out.*

MRS. G.: I thought you'd gone, Sylvia.

SYLVIA *holds her arms straight by her sides and tries to see the effect in the mirror. This involves standing on a chair.*

SYLVIA: How can I go out with my arms like this? Look at them!

MRS. GROOMKIRBY *enters to put something away and checks to glance at* SYLVIA's *arms.*

MRS. G.: What's the matter with your arms?
SYLVIA: You can see what's the matter with them. You've only got to look at them.

MRS. GROOMKIRBY *continues across the room and then turns to go out.*

MRS. G.: You've been out with them like that often enough before. I can't see anything wrong with them.
SYLVIA: They're absolutely ridiculous!
MRS. G. (*checking*): Turn round and let me see. Hold them naturally! They look just the same to me as they always do.
SYLVIA: That doesn't make them any better. (*Turning back to the mirror.*) Look where they reach to!
MRS. G. (*making for the kitchen door*): I'm looking, Sylvia. They're perfectly all right. It's the proper length for them. Mine are exactly the same. So are your father's.
SYLVIA (*getting impatiently down*): Oh for goodness' sake, mum!

MRS. GROOMKIRBY *goes out into the kitchen.*
Pause.

MRS. G. (*off*): What time's Stan supposed to be coming?

SYLVIA (*fuming*) : Quarter of an hour ago!

Pause.

SYLVIA (*getting up again to look in the mirror*) : If they started lower down it would be something.

MRS. G. (*crossing past open door without looking in*) : What difference would that make?

Pause.

SYLVIA (*getting down and going to kitchen door*) : Look where they reach to! Just look at that gap.

MRS. G. (*appearing at door*) : What gap?

SYLVIA: There!

MRS. G.: I don't know what you're talking about, Sylvia. I can't see any gap.

SYLVIA *gives up and goes across to the armchair.* MRS. GROOM-KIRBY *raises her eyes and goes off.* SYLVIA *throws herself moodily down in the chair.*
Pause.

SYLVIA: If they didn't *start* so blessed high up I might be able to reach my knees with them!

Pause.

MRS. G. (*off*) : It's beyond me, Sylvia, why you should want to reach your knees with them!

SYLVIA *reacts impatiently but says nothing.*

MRS. G. (*off*) : In any case you can bend down and do it, can't you?

SYLVIA: I don't *want* to have to bend down! That's the whole point!

Pause.

MRS. G. (*off*) : I suppose it's Stan we've got to thank for this.
SYLVIA: Oh—Stan, Stan, Stan! I wish you wouldn't keep on about *Stan* all the time! It's got nothing to do with Stan.

Pause.

MRS. G. (*off*) : In any case there isn't anything we can do about it now. (*Crossing past the open door without looking in.*) You should have thought of all this before you were born.
SYLVIA: For goodness' sake, mum! How *could* I have?

> MRS. GROOMKIRBY *enters and begins clearing away the remnants left by* MRS. GANTRY.

MRS. G.: We're not turning you into some monstrosity or other just to satisfy one of your whims, Sylvia.
SYLVIA (*scornfully*) : Whim!
MRS. G. (*going out to kitchen*) : Making you look like an ape.

> MR. GROOMKIRBY *enters from the kitchen at the same time. He carries a toolbag.*
> MRS. GROOMKIRBY *checks and watches him into the room.*
> MR. GROOMKIRBY *goes to the witness box, sets down the toolbag, and taking out a screwdriver and screws, begins to screw down the witness box by means of metal brackets fixed to the bottom.*

MRS. G.: That's a sensible place for a witness box, I must say.

> MR. GROOMKIRBY *remains silent in the manner of one who has moved on from words to action.*
> MRS. GROOMKIRBY *goes out in eloquent silence.*
> *Pause.*

SYLVIA: At least apes can reach their knees without bending.

MRS. G. (*reappearing and looking curiously at* SYLVIA) : Apes are bending all the time, Sylvia. (*After continuing to look at* SYLVIA *for a moment, she goes off.*) As you well know.

Pause.

SYLVIA: Not all that much.

Pause.

MR. G. (*without in any way diverting his attention from the job*) : You'd need a complete new set of glands, Sylvia. We couldn't run to it.

MRS. G. (*off*) : She's spending too much time at the Zoo.

Pause.

SYLVIA: I don't know what it is you've both got against apes as far as that goes.

MRS. G. (*off*) : We've got nothing against apes, Sylvia. As such. (*Long pause.*) I thought we were leading up to something like this when you started on about your arms in the first place.

SYLVIA (*starting up*) : Oh!

MRS. G. (*off*) : It's only since you've been going to the Zoo with Stan two or three times a week that we've had all this.

SYLVIA (*checking on her way to the door to the hall*) : For the last time will you shut *up* about Stan, mum? For God's *sake!* It's got nothing to do with Stan! (*She makes for the door and opens it.*) Or the Zoo either as far as that goes. (*She goes out and closes the door behind her.*)

MRS. G. (*off*) : What with that and the Natural History Museum every weekend. I'm not surprised she gets hold of all these idiotic ideas. (*Pause.*) Spending all her time amongst a lot of mastodons and pterodactyls. (*Pause.*) (*Appearing at the door and addressing* MR. GROOMKIRBY.) *I* blame Stan for all this, you know.

MR. GROOMKIRBY *says nothing.*

MRS. G. (*indicating skull*) : Look at that thing! Supposed to remind you of death. It's never worked since he gave it to her.

MR. G. (*without looking up as* MRS. GROOMKIRBY *is about to go back into the kitchen*) : You don't have to keep on at her all the time, Mabel.

> MRS. GROOMKIRBY *gives him a tight-lipped look and goes back into the kitchen. She reappears with a tray and in silence goes to the table to clear the remains of the meal on to it.*

MRS. G. (*after a pause*) : I notice you soon had something to say when you thought you might have to dip in your pocket for her for new glands.

> *Pause.* MRS. GROOMKIRBY *takes up the full tray and goes out with it.*

(*As she goes through the door.*) It won't last five minutes when she gets them. (*Pause.*) (*Off.*) Look at the mastodon. How long did that last?

> *Pause.*

MR. G. (*without looking up*) : She might have made a go of the mastodon if you hadn't been on at her all the time, Mabel.

> MRS. GROOMKIRBY *appears with a tray on which a snack has been laid out.*

MRS. G. (*crossing with tray to door into hall*) : In any case what man in his right senses is going to look twice at an ape?

> *Short pause.*

MR. G.: Stan, for one.

MRS. G. (*opening the door*) : Stan!

At this moment SYLVIA *is entering by the same door. Simultaneously* STAN *comes in from the kitchen.*

MRS. G. (*going out and leaving* SYLVIA *to close the door*) : This is a fine time to be going out anywhere, I must say!

Instead of closing the door, SYLVIA *stands stock-still in dumbfounded horror. She is staring at* STAN, *who is framed in the kitchen doorway. He is dirty, dishevelled, and covered in straw.*

STAN: Don't tell me you're ready, Sylvia. At last.

MR. G. (*looking up*) : Did you find it, Stan?

STAN (*puzzled by* SYLVIA's *scrutiny*): What's the matter?

(*He moves to the mirror.*)

MR. G. (*straightening up; irritably*) : Wasn't it there?

SYLVIA (*as* STAN *sees himself in the mirror*) : What on earth do you think you look like?

MR. G.: He's been trying to find something, Sylvia. For me. (*Moving to the hall door.*) I think I know where I might have left it.

STAN: Lend me a clothes brush. (*Going out into the kitchen.*) Where do you keep it? Won't take a minute.

Pause. SYLVIA *is breathing heavily.*

MR. G. (*going out into hall*) : It's all right, Stan. Don't worry. I'll find it.

STAN (*off*) : It's coming off. It's only a bit of straw.

SYLVIA: Is that *all*?

STAN (*appearing with brush*) : What do you mean? You don't imagine I *came* here like this, do you? (*Going.*) I thought I was doing someone a good turn.

SYLVIA: Not me, by any chance?

STAN (*off*) : If you'd been ready at the proper time I wouldn't have been let in for this in the first place. (*Appearing at the door more or less free from straw and with the brush in his hand.*) How's that? (*He is still dishevelled.*)

SYLVIA: Are you trying to make out it's *my* fault? You've got a nerve! Covered in a lot of old straw and muck!

STAN: If it's any interest to you, Sylvia, I've been helping your father.

SYLVIA: Oh, *have* you? (*Turning on her heel and going out.*) Well, you'd better go and ask him if he's got any more jobs for you, hadn't you? (*She slams the door.*)

STAN (*with an impulsive move towards the closing door*) : Look, for God's sake, Sylvia! I can get home and change in ten minutes!

STAN *turns away in furious frustration. The door immediately opens again.* STAN *wheels expectantly.* MR. GROOMKIRBY *enters, brandishing the rolled-up blueprint and leaving the door open.*

MR. G.: Now perhaps we shall be able to see where we are.

STAN *looks venomously at* MR. GROOMKIRBY *for a moment.* MR. GROOMKIRBY *spreads out the plan on the table and bends over it.* STAN *suddenly turns and vents his fury on the nearest object, which is the cash register. He brings his fist down and rings up No Sale. After the slightest of pauses a massed choir launches full-throatedly into the Hallelujah Chorus.* STAN *is momentarily electrified and then begins moving stealthily towards the door. Once at it he disappears with singleminded alacrity out into the hall. The front door is heard to shut.*
Simultaneously the music is cut off and the set blacked out. STAN *appears downstage right crossing purposefully.* KIRBY *appears on forestage. He appears dazed.*

KIRBY: I might have been dreaming for all he knew!

Louder as STAN *passes him without turning.*

Might have stopped me stone dead in the middle of an orgasm!

STAN (*going off*) : Go to hell!

Fade out on KIRBY.

BARNES, *in an outdoor coat, comes on casually where* STAN *went off.*

BARNES: That, I rather fancy, might be carrying coals to New-castle—but never mind. (*Looking at his watch.*) Fifteen minutes? And then back here.

BARNES *continues across to go off right, checks, changes his mind and quickly goes off the way he came as the houselights go up.*

End of Act One.

ACT TWO

The living-room. Furniture has been crowded to one side by the courtroom which dominates. Part of one wall has had to go in order to make room for it. Access to various parts of the room, and to cupboards, involves squeezing with difficulty round some part of the Court. Table, with two chairs, is now downstage.

Even so, the Court is incomplete. There is a bench for the JUDGE, *a witness box to the* JUDGE's *left, and benches for Counsel to his right.*

Downstage right is a small control panel for the Court.

When the curtain rises MRS. GANTRY *is seen sitting at the table.*

MRS. GROOMKIRBY *has almost finished pressing a pair of black trousers. The jacket is hanging on a hanger nearby.*

MRS. GANTRY (*rising as at exit in Act One*): I think that's more or less everything, Mabel.

MRS. G. (*switching off the iron and hanging up the trousers on the hanger with the jacket*): Finished, Myra? I'll get your envelope.

MRS. GANTRY: I haven't touched the asparagus, but I can attend to that first thing in the morning.

MRS. G. (*she leaves the suit hanging from a peg*): Don't worry about the asparagus, Myra. I can see to that. It's those great packets of cereals they send us. (*She finds the envelope.*) I think you'll find that's right, Myra.

AUNT M. (*off*): It's all the same, Mabel. Roller-skates, round-abouts, rickshaws. As long as it's getting us somewhere.

MRS. GANTRY: You've had to move her, then.

MRS. G. (*indicating Court*): We can't get her in here for this great white elephant. (*To* AUNT MILDRED.) You'd never be able to pull a rickshaw, Aunt Mildred. (*To* MRS. GANTRY *as they go out together.*) She wants something she can go over Niagara Falls in.

MRS. GANTRY (*at door*) : She'd be better off with a barrel, Mabel.

MRS. G. (*following* MRS. GANTRY *out and closing the door*) : Of course she would.

Short pause.
SYLVIA *enters from the hall in outdoor clothes.*

SYLVIA: Come on. I thought you were supposed to be ready.

STAN *appears from behind the control panel looking at his watch.*

STAN: You know we were going to be there by quarter to, don't you? It's now ten past.

SYLVIA: Well come on then.

STAN *makes a final adjustment to something behind the panel and then switches it on as though to test it briefly for sound.*

MRS. G. (*entering as* SYLVIA *is about to go out*) : This is a fine time to be going somewhere, I must say! (*She catches sight of* STAN *in passing on her way to the kitchen.*) The pair of you. (*She goes out.*)

SYLVIA (*at door; impatiently*) : Oh come on, for goodness' sake, and leave it.

JUDGE'S VOICE: . . . and even your own counsel has to admit that not only were you as drunk as a wheelbarrow, but that you were quite incapable of so much as falling flat on your face when asked to do so. Moreover . . .

STAN (*switching off and following* SYLVIA *out*) : I wonder if he knows how much current this thing's going to eat up.

(*Calling.*) Good night, Mrs. Groomkirby. (*He goes out, closing the door behind him.*)

MRS. G. (*entering with large tray*) : Back goodness knows when, I suppose.

AUNT M. (*off*) : Things seem to have been happening, Mabel.

Pause. MRS. GROOMKIRBY *begins clearing everything from the table on to the tray.*

AUNT M.: They've put me where I can see through the window. (*Pause.*) I think I must be in the station-master's office, Mabel. (*Pause.*) I can see out through the window. (*Pause.*) Did you know there were two Red Setters at the end of the garden, Mabel? (*Pause.*) I can see them from where I'm sitting.

Pause. MRS. GROOMKIRBY *takes up the full tray and moves downstage with it on her way to the kitchen as* MR. GROOM-KIRBY *enters from the hall.*
He is wearing outdoor clothes and carries a large brown paper bag. He switches on the set from the control panel in passing, and puts the brown paper bag on a chair.

MRS. G.: A Mr. Justice called. (*Going off.*) Something about being on circuit.

MR. GROOMKIRBY *takes off his hat and coat, opens the bag, and takes out a Judge's robe and wig. He begins trying these on, but they are too large for him.*

MRS. G. (*off*) : To do with the mains, I expect. They've probably been looking at our electricity bills. (*Pause.*) What it's going to be like when it's *all* there eating up the current, goodness only knows!

The JUDGE *materializes from out of the Court and advances upon* MR. GROOMKIRBY *who is at first unaware of him.*

AUNT M. (*off*) : Look at those two Red Setters, Mabel. I can see them from here at the end of the garden. (*Pause.*) They must be blue with cold out there, Mabel.

MRS. G. (*off; irritably*) : Red Setters are *red*, Aunt Mildred!

The JUDGE *now confronts* MR. GROOMKIRBY.

JUDGE: Your wig? Or mine, Mr. Groomkirby?

MR. GROOMKIRBY, *overawed, removes the wig.*

MR. G.: Oh. Perhaps I've got hold of the wrong one. I thought . . .
JUDGE: It's an easy mistake to make, Mr. Groomkirby.
MR. G.: Yes—I'm sorry.

MR. GROOMKIRBY *removes the robe and puts it on the* JUDGE.

MR. G.: Rather silly of me. (*He adjusts the robe and fetches the wig.*) I thought it didn't seem quite right. (*He puts the wig on the* JUDGE.)
JUDGE (*as he turns to go*) : You'll in all probability be needed as a witness, Mr. Groomkirby. So be on hand. It saves wasting the time of the Court.

As the JUDGE *disappears the Court begins gradually to assemble. A* POLICEMAN, *in uniform but without helmet, approaches* MR. GROOMKIRBY *with a sheet of paper.*

POLICEMAN: Mr. Groomkirby?
MR. G.: Yes?
POLICEMAN: Through the door over there, please.

The POLICEMAN *looks round for someone else.*

MR. G.: What's this for?
POLICEMAN (*turning back to* MR. GROOMKIRBY *and jabbing with his finger toward the kitchen door*) : Out there. With the

other witnesses. (*Calling more respectfully.*) Detective-Sergeant Barnes?

BARNES *appears downstage left.* MR. GROOMKIRBY *goes resentfully out into the kitchen.*

BARNES: Yes?

POLICEMAN: I think there's a strong possibility you may be wanted, sir, a bit later on.

BARNES: Right. (*Looking round the room.*) Been letting himself go a bit, hasn't he?

POLICEMAN: Beg your pardon, sir?

BARNES (*with an offhand gesture towards the Court*): This lot. Plenty of it for a living-room.

POLICEMAN: Don't know where to stop, do they, some of them.

BARNES (*going to door*): In here?

POLICEMAN: That's right, sir.

BARNES *and* POLICEMAN *go off.*
The Court is now assembled and awaiting the JUDGE. *The* CLERK *calls for the Court to rise. The* JUDGE *enters, bows to the Court, sits.* PROSECUTING COUNSEL *rises.*

PROS. COUN.: M'lord. (*Addressing* JURY.) The facts you have heard so far in this case, members of the jury, have been simple enough and I do not propose . . .

JUDGE (*intervening*): I see no sign of the jury. Are they here?

PROS. COUN.: I understand they are, m'lord.

USHER (*intervening*): There is no jury box, m'lord. As yet.

JUDGE: And no jury either apparently.

USHER: They are here in spirit, m'lord.

JUDGE: I see. (*He ponders momentarily.*) As long as they are here in one form or another. (*He nods to* COUNSEL.)

PROS. COUN.: The facts to which I am now going to direct your attention, members of the jury, and upon which it will be necessary for you to exercise your judgment in due course, concern the activities of the accused on a day last summer when he was allegedly . . .

JUDGE (*intervening*) : Where is the accused? Is he in the Court?
PROS. COUN.: He is in the dock, m'lord.
JUDGE (*looking at it*) : I see no dock.
USHER: The dock has not yet arrived, m'lord.
JUDGE: Where is it?
USHER: I understand it is on its way, m'lord.

   Pause.

JUDGE: With the accused in it.
USHER: Yes, m'lord.

   DEFENDING COUNSEL *rises.*

DEF. COUN.: There have been certain delays, m'lord.
JUDGE: Traffic lights, I suppose.
DEF. COUN.: That and other untoward occurrences, m'lord.
JUDGE: He should be here. I have already disorganized my personal arrangements pretty considerably in order to accommodate the Court by being present, and I do not propose to put myself to further inconvenience by having this case running overtime. If the accused is not here, the hearing will have to go on without him.
DEF. COUN.: As your lordship pleases.

   DEFENDING COUNSEL *sits.* PROSECUTING COUNSEL *rises.*

PROS. COUN.: The whereabouts of the accused, members of the jury, on that vital day when he was allegedly elsewhere, tally in every single particular with the whereabouts of the only other person who so far as we know was on the spot at the time, and who is in the Court at this moment. The whereabouts of this other person are therefore of paramount importance, and I should like to call him to the witness box now. (*To* USHER.) Mr. Groomkirby, please.

   The USHER *goes off.*
   MRS. GROOMKIRBY *appears from the kitchen carrying a hot water bottle. She crosses to the door into the hall.*

MRS. G.: I'm going up, Arthur. (*She opens door.*) You might notice what time Sylvia gets back. (*She goes out and closes door.*)

The USHER *returns, approaches the* CLERK *and whispers to him. The* CLERK *stands and turns to enter into a whispered discussion with the* JUDGE *while the* USHER *withdraws respectfully.*

JUDGE (*looking across to* USHER *and addressing him*) : Is this an objection to swearing per se?

USHER: Only to swearing on the unexpurgated Bible, m'lord. I understand there are certain passages he takes exception to, m'lord. On moral grounds.

JUDGE (*after a pause for reflection*) : Is he prepared to swear on anything?

USHER: I understand he has no objection to swearing on "Uncle Tom's Cabin," m'lord.

JUDGE: On what?

USHER: "Uncle Tom's Cabin," m'lord.

JUDGE (*to* CLERK) : I thought the issue of slavery on the American plantations had been settled by Abraham Lincoln?

CLERK (*looking for confirmation to* USHER) : I gather he has been informed of this, m'lord.

USHER: Yes, m'lord.

JUDGE: What did he say?

USHER: He said "Not in my world it isn't." Those were his words, m'lord.

JUDGE (*to* CLERK) : Which world is he referring to?

CLERK: I understand he has one of his own, m'lord.

JUDGE: Then why isn't he in it?

CLERK: He says he was told to come here, m'lord.

Pause. The JUDGE *considers.*

JUDGE: If it's a genuinely conscientious objection, I suppose I shall have to allow it. Has he got this work with him in Court?

USHER: He has a copy, yes, m'lord.
JUDGE: Tell him to bring it to the witness box.

The USHER *goes out behind the Court.* COUNSEL FOR THE DEFENCE *rises.*

DEF. COUN.: With very great respect, m'lord.
JUDGE: Yes?
DEF. COUN.: I have discussed this with my learned friend, m'lord, and if your lordship has no objection I should be most obliged if your lordship would consider dispensing with the oath altogether in respect of this witness, m'lord. I understand that if the oath is administered there is a strong possibility of prevarication, m'lord.
JUDGE: You mean he's a liar?
DEF. COUN.: Only when on oath, m'lord. I am told he looks on the oath in the light of a challenge, m'lord.
JUDGE: That's entirely a matter for him. If he's lying I shall direct the jury accordingly.
DEF. COUN.: As your lordship pleases.

PROSECUTING COUNSEL *rises.* DEFENDING COUNSEL *sits.*

PROS. COUN.: Might I, m'lord, with your lordship's permission, suggest to my learned friend that evidence from this source be accepted by the defence in the spirit in which it is given?
JUDGE: I suppose there's no objection. It would certainly save the time of the Court.

PROSECUTING COUNSEL *sits.* DEFENDING COUNSEL *rises.*

DEF. COUN.: Thank you, m'lord. My learned friend has suggested a way out of the difficulty and this is entirely acceptable to the defence, m'lord.

The JUDGE *nods briefly.*
The USHER *enters followed by* MR. GROOMKIRBY, *whom he directs into the witness box.* MR. GROOMKIRBY *takes the oath.*

MR. G. (*holding up a copy of "Uncle Tom's Cabin"*) : I swear, by Harriet Beecher Stowe, that the evidence I shall give shall be the truth, the whole truth, and nothing but the truth.

JUDGE: You understand, do you, that you are now on oath?

MR. G.: I do, m'lord.

JUDGE: You understand what being on oath means?

MR. G.: Yes, m'lord.

JUDGE: It means that you have undertaken in the sight—in your case—of Harriet Beecher Stowe, to give honest answers, as honest and truthful as you can make them, in reply to questions which are shortly going to be put to you by learned counsel.

MR. G.: I understand that, m'lord.

JUDGE: Anything you are unsure about, or anything you have no direct knowledge of, you must not try to fill out in any way by the use of your imagination. You are here simply and solely to give the Court the facts as you know them. Anything more or less than this is not, and can never be, the truth. You must therefore in your answers avoid anything which is not to the best of your knowledge factually true. This is what the solemn undertaking you have given to the Court means.

MR. G.: I understand that, m'lord.

JUDGE: And you intend therefore to be bound by this undertaking?

MR. G.: No, m'lord.

JUDGE: You mean, in other words, that you intend to lie to the Court.

MR. G.: That is so, m'lord, yes.

JUDGE: A frank and honest reply.

DEFENDING COUNSEL *rises.*

DEF. COUN.: With respect, m'lord.

JUDGE: Yes?

DEF. COUN.: This is a point for your lordship, but it would be of the greatest possible assistance to my friend and me, m'lord, and possibly to the jury later, if your lordship would give a ruling on this point of the witness's intended perjury at this stage, m'lord. The witness says he is lying, m'lord, but we have every reason to believe that in saying this he is lying.

JUDGE: And that he is, in fact, telling the truth?

DEF. COUN.: That is the dilemma we are in, m'lord.

JUDGE: No very great dilemma. This is clearly a witness of candid integrity upon whom it would be perfectly proper to place the utmost reliance.

DEF. COUN. (*sitting*) : As your lordship pleases.

PROSECUTING COUNSEL *rises.*

PROS. COUN. (*addressing* MR. GROOMKIRBY) : Are you Arthur Rudge Groomkirby?

MR. G. (*full of a confidence verging on truculence*) : That's right, sir.

PROS. COUN.: And you live now—have been living since 1949—at 93 Chundragore Street.

MR. G.: Yes, sir. I had it done out back and front three years ago.

PROS. COUN.: By whom, Mr. Groomkirby?

MR. G.: By the deceased, sir.

JUDGE (*intervening*) : He was not, I take it, deceased at the time?

MR. G. (*slightly patronizingly*) : No, m'lord. He was alive when he did it.

PROS. COUN.: Mr. Groomkirby—I want you to cast your mind back a little way to the summer of last year. To the twenty-third of August. Do you happen to remember where you were, or what you were doing, on that day?

MR. G.: Yes, sir. I was in Chester-le-Street.

PROS. COUN.: What happened in Chester-le-Street on that day to cause you to remember it so clearly?

MR. G.: I interviewed someone there. About a life insurance.

PROS. COUN.: I take it you don't often go so far afield to interview people.

MR. G.: That's why I particularly remember it.

PROS. COUN.: I see. (*Pause.*) And this interview, you say, took place in Chester-le-Street on the twenty-third of August last year?

MR. G.: Yes, sir. It was a Tuesday.

PROS. COUN.: At what time on the Tuesday?

MR. G.: Three-fifteen, sir.

PROS. COUN.: At three-fifteen on Tuesday the twenty-third of August last year you were in Chester-le-Street interviewing this man about a life insurance policy.

JUDGE (*testily*) : He's already said he was.

PROS. COUN.: As your lordship pleases.

MR. G. (*smugly*) : It was a woman I interviewed. By the name of Myra Penelope Straightpiece Gantry.

PROS. COUN.: How certain are you, Mr. Groomkirby, of the exact time?

MR. G.: There was a clock striking the quarter just outside the window when I put my first question to her.

PROS. COUN.: And what was this first question, Mr. Groomkirby?

MR. G.: I asked her if there was anything she would like to add, sir.

JUDGE (*intervening*) : What was her reply?

MR. G.: It was in the form of a sentence, m'lord.

JUDGE: We know it must have been in the form of a sentence, but what form did the sentence take?

MR. G. (*feeling in his pocket and bringing out a notebook*) : I made a note of it at the time, m'lord. (*Reads from notebook.*) She said she had a string of pearls in the form of a necklace but she wore it round her waist for the tightness.

PROS. COUN.: She wore it round her waist for the tightness. Didn't this strike you as being a rather extraordinary remark for her to make?

MR. G.: I didn't take much notice of it at the time, sir.

PROS. COUN.: You didn't think it at all remarkable. But you made a note of it.

MR. G. (*smugly*) : I was interviewing her, sir.

Pause.

MR. GROOMKIRBY *has passed from semi-truculence to a sort*

of cocky assurance, but this is from now on broken down, at first by imperceptible degrees and then more and more rapidly.

PROS. COUN.: Would you agree, Mr. Groomkirby, that there were at the time possibly several thousand other inhabitants of Chester-le-Street equally eligible for interview, by you or someone else, on the subject of life insurance?

MR. G.: I dare say there would have been, yes, sir.

PROS. COUN.: But out of several thousand eligible people, the one person to be interviewed that afternoon happened, by a curious coincidence no doubt, to have been this woman, Myra Gantry?

MR. G.: If you put it like that, yes, I suppose that would be true.

PROS. COUN.: Even though the chances against it were several thousand to one?

MR. G.: I hadn't really thought of it in the light of a coincidence.

PROS. COUN.: Would you also agree, Mr. Groomkirby, that— confining ourselves to these islands alone—something of the order of fifty million people could, if the need had arisen, have gone to Chester-le-Street and interviewed this woman that afternoon?

MR. G.: I should think probably something of that order, yes, sir.

PROS. COUN.: The chances, in fact, were almost fifty million to one against its being you who did so?

MR. G.: I remember doing so, sir. I made a note of it at the time.

PROS. COUN.: Very well. And the time of this interview was three-fifteen. A clock, you told us, was striking outside.

MR. G.: That's right, sir. I could hear it from where I was standing.

PROS. COUN.: And precisely at that very moment, when not one but both hands of the clock were at virtually the same point on the dial—at the figure three—precisely at the moment when the clock was striking the quarter, you put your first question to Myra Gantry.

MR. G. (*defiantly*): Yes, sir.

PROS. COUN.: Perhaps you hadn't thought of that as a coincidence either, Mr. Groomkirby?

MR. G.: That was what happened, sir.

PROS. COUN.: You see, Mr. Groomkirby, this statement seems to be based upon a whole chain of these—to say the least of it —extraordinary coincidences. This question you put to Myra Gantry. You say it was your first. But in the course of an interview of this kind you might well have put twenty or thirty questions to her. This one, which happened—so we are asked to believe—to have been the first, could equally well it seems to me have been the seventh or the third or the twenty-ninth.

MR. G.: No, sir. It was the first.

PROS. COUN.: And this answer she is supposed to have given you. Goodness knows the words alone in the English language must be enough in all their various forms virtually to defy computation—the possible ways of combining them must be infinite. And yet it was precisely *this* combination she hit on.

MR. G.: I made a note of it, sir.

PROS. COUN.: I know you did, Mr. Groomkirby. She said I have a string of pearls in the form of a necklace but I wear it round my waist for the tightness.

JUDGE (*intervening*): For the what?

PROS. COUN.: For the tightness, m'lord.

MR. G.: That's what she said, sir.

> Pause. PROSECUTING COUNSEL *sighs*.

PROS. COUN.: Coincidence after coincidence. (*Lazily flicking through his papers.*) For instance you say all this took place on a Tuesday.

MR. G.: Tuesday the twenty-third of August, sir.

PROS. COUN.: You see, Mr. Groomkirby, I have here a calendar for last year and for a number of years prior to that. And I find that since 1950 there has been only one year in which the twenty-third of August has fallen on a Tuesday.

MR. G.: It fell on a Tuesday last year, sir.

PROS. COUN. (*lazily delivering the coup de grâce*): The very year, in fact, when it so happened that Tuesday the twenty-third

of August was the day you were in Chester-le-Street interviewing Myra Gantry.

MR. G. (*dogged now, rather than cocky*) : That's where I was, sir.

Long pause. PROSECUTING COUNSEL *flicks through his papers
preparatory to changing course.*

PROS. COUN. (*in a quiet, bored voice*) : There must have been
quite a number of places from which you absented yourself
on that rather vital twenty-third of August, Mr. Groomkirby, in order to be in Chester-le-Street?

MR. G.: I dare say that would be so, yes, sir.

PROS. COUN.: You were not, for instance, in London?

MR. G.: No, sir.

PROS. COUN.: Or Paris?

MR. G.: No, sir.

PROS. COUN.: Or Rome?

MR. G.: No, I wasn't there, sir.

PROS. COUN.: You were not, I imagine, in Reykjavik either?

MR. G.: I couldn't say for sure where that is, sir.

PROS. COUN.: Yet you absented yourself from it?

MR. G.: As far as I know, I did, yes.

PROS. COUN.: *And* from Kostroma.

MR. G.: I suppose I must have done.

PROS. COUN.: And Chengtu, and Farafangana, and Pocatello.

MR. G.: I'm afraid I'm not all that much good at geography.

PROS. COUN.: Not much good at geography, Mr. Groomkirby, yet
you want the Court to believe that in order to be present
at Chester-le-Street you absented yourself from a whole host
of places which only an expert geographer could possibly be
expected to have heard of.

MR. G. (*beginning to flag*) : That's where I thought I was, sir.

Pause.

PROS. COUN. (*changing course again*) : It is a good many months
since all this happened, is it not, Mr. Groomkirby?

MR. G.: Several months, yes, sir.

PROS. COUN.: You have no doubt in your mind, all the same, that this person who interviewed Myra Gantry last August was the person I am addressing now?

MR. G.: It was me, sir.

PROS. COUN.: It was you. (*Pause.*) Mr. Groomkirby—do you know what happens to the body in sleep?

MR. G.: It recuperates its energies, sir.

PROS. COUN.: Certain chemical and other changes take place, do they not?

MR. G.: I understand they sometimes do, yes, sir.

PROS. COUN.: You must have spent a good many hours in sleep since last August?

MR. G.: I dare say that would be true, sir.

The JUDGE *begins to look at* MR. GROOMKIRBY *with suspicion and curiosity from time to time.*

PROS. COUN.: You must have eaten a good many meals, and absorbed a fair amount of food?

MR. G.: Yes, sir.

PROS. COUN.: It would be true to say, would it not, that the normal processes of what is known sometimes as metabolism, whereby body tissue is constantly being built up or broken down, have been going on unceasingly since the twenty-third of August last year?

MR. G.: I couldn't say, sir.

The JUDGE *looks up and continues to stare intently at* MR. GROOMKIRBY *with the same curiosity and suspicion as before.*

PROS. COUN.: I suggest to you, Mr. Groomkirby, that in view of these changes the man you say was in Chester-le-Street last year is not the man who is standing in the witness box at this moment.

JUDGE (*intervening*): Are you suggesting he's someone else?

PROS. COUN.: It is the contention of the prosecution, m'lord, that he has been gradually replaced in the intervening period by the man who is now before the court.

JUDGE (*to* MR. GROOMKIRBY, *accusingly*) : Is this so?

MR. G.: It's difficult to say, sir.

JUDGE: Do you mean you're not *sure*?

MR. G.: Not to say sure, no, m'lord.

The JUDGE *looks intently at* MR. GROOMKIRBY *for a moment longer and then nods to* COUNSEL.

PROS. COUN.: Where were you, Mr. Groomkirby, before you came here today?

MR. G.: I was living in a world of my own, sir.

PROS. COUN.: Where, roughly, would this world be in relation to, say, Chester-le-Street?

MR. G.: Quite some way away.

PROS. COUN.: Your presence there, in other words, entailed travelling some distance.

MR. G.: Quite some distance, yes.

PROS. COUN.: Do you enjoy travelling, Mr. Groomkirby?

MR. G.: On the contrary, sir.

JUDGE (*intervening*) : You mean you actively dislike it?

MR. G.: Actively dislike it, m'lord.

PROS. COUN.: You actively dislike travelling and yet you made this lengthy journey to Chester-le-Street?

MR. GROOMKIRBY'S *answers are beginning to be made wildly at random in an attempt to satisfy the Court and so escape from it.*

MR. G.: I was a masochist at the time, sir.

JUDGE (*intervening*) : A what?

PROS. COUN.: A masochist, m'lord. A term employed in certain quarters to denote an addiction to pain as a source of pleasure.

JUDGE (*to* MR. GROOMKIRBY) : Where does the pain come into it?

MR. G. (*wildly*) : I had myself tattooed on the way, m'lord.

JUDGE: Where?

MR. G.: On the train, m'lord, between Boreham Wood and . . .

JUDGE: Whereabouts on the body?

MR. G.: I had one done on my left arm, m'lord, and a Crown and Anchor on my right hip as we came into Watford.

JUDGE: Were there any others?

MR. G.: There was a butterfly design between my shoulder blades, m'lord.

JUDGE: Was this put on after the others?

MR. G.: Before, m'lord.

The JUDGE *intensifies his look of suspicion.*

MR. G.: In a tunnel outside Leeds.

JUDGE: How was it done?

MR. G. *(relaxing momentarily on what seems safe ground)* : It was done with a needle, m'lord.

JUDGE: We know it must have been done with a needle, but how well was it done?

MR. G. *(nonplussed again)* : Do you mean in my own opinion, m'lord?

JUDGE: In anyone's opinion!

MR. G.: I think it was up to standard, m'lord.

The JUDGE *continues to stare for a moment at* MR. GROOM-KIRBY *and then with the air of a man whose mind is made up nods to* COUNSEL.

PROS. COUN.: You say you were a masochist, Mr. Groomkirby. Are you a masochist now?

MR. G. *(fervently)* : No, sir.

PROS. COUN.: When did you cease your masochism?

MR. G.: A month or two ago, sir.

PROS. COUN.: And what made you give it up?

MR. G.: It was taking up too much of my time.

JUDGE *(intervening)* : Too much of your time? And how long had you been a masochist when you suddenly decided that your time was so valuable that you could no longer spare any of it for your masochism?

MR. G.: For something like three or four years, m'lord.

PROS. COUN.: What was it that made you take it up in the first place?

MR. G.: I was at a loose end at the time, sir.

The JUDGE *looks sharply up.*

PROS. COUN.: You were at a loose end. Would you tell the court, Mr. Groomkirby, as clearly as you can in your own words, exactly how loose this end was?

MR. G.: It was worn right down, sir.

JUDGE (*intervening*): Worn right down. That tells us very little. Was it swinging loose? Was it rattling about?

COUNSEL, *with a barely perceptible sigh and the briefest of glances toward* COUNSEL FOR THE DEFENCE, *sits down.*

MR. G.: It was practically hanging off, m'lord.

JUDGE: And this is the end you say you were *at*? This loose end that in your own words was practically hanging off?

MR. G.: I was pretty nearly at it, m'lord.

JUDGE: You told the Court a moment ago you were at it. Now you say "pretty nearly at it." Which of these assertions is the true one?

MR. G.: It was touch and go, sir.

JUDGE: What was?

MR. G.: Whether I fell off, sir.

JUDGE: And what prevented you?

MR. G.: It was that or take up masochism, m'lord.

JUDGE: I see. The facts are beginning to emerge. You took up masochism when you began to realize that unless you did so the end you were at might come away and you with it. And you remained loyal to your masochism just so long as it suited you.

PROS. COUN. (*rising*): With very great respect, m'lord . . .

JUDGE: The moment it was no longer useful to you you abandoned it without the slightest compunction. I can find no possible shred of excuse for behaviour of this kind.

DEF. COUN.: . . . if I might have your indulgence for a moment, m'lord . . .

JUDGE: The law would be moribund if it were unable to deal with a case such as this, and I should be failing in my duty if I were to allow a man of the kind you have shown yourself to be to go at large.

PROS. COUN.: The *accused* will be here at any moment, m'lord.

Pause. PROSECUTING COUNSEL *sits in despair.*

JUDGE: You will be remanded in custody while arrangements are being made to have you sent back to the world you have come from and claim to have been living in, where your activities will be of no concern to anyone but yourself.

Fast fade out lingering for a moment on the JUDGE.
Pause.
Door into hall opens. The light outside in the hall shows MRS. GROOMKIRBY *in a dressing-gown, standing at the door she has half opened fumbling with the switch and then speaking into the darkened room.*

MRS. G.: *Now* what have you done? Fused the lights, I suppose?

There is no reply. She puts her head round the door but, seeing nothing, withdraws it again.

MRS. G.: If you're going to stay down here waiting up for the dawn again, I'll put this light out.

MRS. GROOMKIRBY *waits for a reply. None comes.*

MRS. G. (*Closing door*): And then for goodness' sake come up to bed.

Pause.
The JUDGE *and* MR. GROOMKIRBY *become dimly visible down-stage.*

JUDGE: Well, Mr. Groomkirby. There's rather more here than meets the eye, don't you think?

Pause.

MR. G. *(there is a defensive edge on his voice)* : They've got the blinds down.
JUDGE: Possibly. *(Pause.)* At all events we shall know as soon as it's light enough to see anything.

Pause.

MR. G. *(there is a surly edge on his defensiveness)* : We're not going to see much with the blinds down.

MR. GROOMKIRBY *becomes cowed, sullen, resentful, belligerent by turns.*

JUDGE: You should have brought a torch, Mr. Groomkirby.

Pause.
The JUDGE *approaches the table, which is now downstage and has a chair on either side of it.*

JUDGE *(about to sit at the table where he can see* MR. GROOM-KIRBY*)* : In the meantime *(sitting)* perhaps it would be best if we were to play three-handed whist together.
MR. G.: Just the two of us?

Pause.

JUDGE: How many did you want, Mr. Groomkirby?

MR. GROOMKIRBY *finds himself moving imperceptibly nearer to the* JUDGE.

MR. G.: Three-handed whist isn't a game to play between two people.
JUDGE: I see. And why not, Mr. Groomkirby?

Pause.

MR. G. (*moving still nearer*) : And even if it were, we can't see to play.
JUDGE: Only because there isn't enough light, Mr. Groomkirby. Where are the cards?
MR. G.: I haven't got any cards.
JUDGE: You mean you've lost them?
MR. G.: I never had any.

Pause.

JUDGE: I think it might be as well, Mr. Groomkirby, if you were to go outside and look for some light.

MR. GROOMKIRBY *is seen to hesitate for a moment. Then his resistance crumbles and he moves off.*
Pause.
MR. GROOMKIRBY *returns.*
Pause.

JUDGE: Well?
MR. G.: Not a sound.

Pause.

JUDGE: Oh. (*Pause.*) And the light?

Pause.

JUDGE: What about the light?

MR. G.: I didn't see any.

JUDGE: Where did you look?

MR. G.: I had my eyes shut. (*Pause.*) I don't intend to be blinded suddenly by the sunrise.

Pause.

JUDGE: Or deafened, I suppose—by the dawn chorus. (*Pause.*) What precautions are you taking against that?

Pause.

MR. G. (*reluctantly*) : I wear earplugs.

Pause.

JUDGE: That perhaps is why you weren't able to hear anything out there, Mr. Groomkirby.

MR. G.: There was nothing to hear!

Pause.

JUDGE: You were wearing earplugs, Mr. Groomkirby.

MR. G.: It was silent out there, I tell you!

JUDGE: Faulty earplugs evidently.

Pause.

JUDGE: You could be as sure as you like about it as long as you knew your earplugs to be faulty.

Pause.

JUDGE: But not otherwise, Mr. Groomkirby.

Pause.

JUDGE: *Were* they faulty?

Pause.

JUDGE: I'm asking you a question! Were your earplugs faulty?
MR. G.: What if they were?
JUDGE: I see.

Pause.

MR. G.: What is it to you if I wear faulty earplugs?

Pause.

JUDGE: We'll play three-handed whist, shall we?

The JUDGE *begins shuffling imaginary cards and then deals them on to the table.*

MR. G. *(slowly drawing nearer to the table)*: Who's going to be dummy?
JUDGE: You, Mr. Groomkirby.

Pause.

MR. G. *(sitting)*: I've got my own hand to play.
JUDGE: You can leave that to me.

Pause.

MR. G. *(picking up his cards)*: It's too dark for this sort of thing.

Both go through the motions of playing whist.

MR. G.: If you play my hand, who's going to play yours?
JUDGE: I don't think we need either of us worry too much about that.

Pause. They continue to play in silence.

JUDGE: It's in some ways a pity you forgot to bring the cards, Mr. Groomkirby, but we seem to be managing quite well without them. My trick.

Pause. The game continues.

MR. G.: I feel cold.
JUDGE: You should have taken precautions.

Pause. The game continues.

JUDGE: My trick.
MR. G.: What possible precautions could I have taken?
JUDGE: You could have come here for one thing on a warmer night.
MR. G.: There aren't any warmer nights at this time of the year.
JUDGE: My trick.
MR. G.: You know that as well as I do.
JUDGE (*gathering up the cards*): Go and see whether it's light yet outside. There's a good fellow.

MR. GROOMKIRBY *hesitates, then gets up and goes out as before. He returns and sits down. Pause.*

JUDGE: Well?
MR. G.: Frost.

Pause.

JUDGE: You were right then about its being cold, Mr. Groomkirby.
MR. G.: It's colder in here than it was outside.
JUDGE: You may well be right about that too, Mr. Groomkirby. But is it darker?

Pause.

JUDGE: I said is it darker in here than it was outside?

MR. G.: How the hell can I tell? You know I'm as blind as a bat with my eyes closed!

Pause.

JUDGE: Mr. Groomkirby. I wonder if you'd mind taking out your earplugs for a moment.

MR. GROOMKIRBY *reluctantly takes them out.*

JUDGE: Well?

Pause.

JUDGE: What do you notice?

MR. GROOMKIRBY *makes signs with his hands.*

JUDGE: Do you notice anything?

MR. GROOMKIRBY *begins again making signs and then with a shrug abandons the attempt.*

JUDGE: What's the matter with you?

MR. GROOMKIRBY *sits motionless.*

JUDGE: Cold, blind, deaf—and now dumb! (*Loudly.*) For God's sake, Mr. Groomkirby! Put your earplugs back in!

MR. GROOMKIRBY *begins slowly replacing his earplugs.*

JUDGE: Why do I shout? I dare say he can't hear a word without his crutches.

MR. G.: You think I'm paralysed, don't you?

JUDGE: I don't doubt you'll show us a clean enough pair of heels once your teeth have had proper attention.

Pause.

JUDGE (*savagely*) : Are you dentally fit?

Pause.

JUDGE: No. I thought not.

> *The lights come fully up. The courtroom is empty but for the three weighing machines of ACT ONE which stand, covered up, in the well of the Court.*

MR. G. (*with monumental relief*) : Dawn!
JUDGE (*rising*) : Punctual as ever!

> *At the kitchen door is* SYLVIA. *She is in her stockinged feet and carrying her shoes in her hand. The other hand is on the light switch as the lights go up, but she takes it away in order to signal to someone else out of sight in the kitchen. She retreats and closes the door.*
> *The* JUDGE *looks at his watch as he rises, and then from his watch across to the death's head on the mantelpiece as though at a clock and compares the "time." He then goes up to the death's head, takes it up and shakes it as though starting a clock which has stopped. He puts it to his ear and, satisfied, replaces it.*
> *He turns away and without a glance at* MR. GROOMKIRBY *goes into the courtroom and out of sight.*
> MR. GROOMKIRBY *has the air of a man coming round after a concussion. He has got up and made his way in a dazed manner towards the courtroom.*

MR. G.: God! What a night!

> *He goes, still dazed, to the Clerk's table, where he absent-mindedly gathers up some papers and wanders off out of sight with them.*
> SYLVIA *tentatively opens the kitchen door.*

SYLVIA (*looking in; good-humouredly*): Don't be a fool, Stan. He didn't say any such thing!

STAN (*off*): Ask Tony. He was there.

SYLVIA (*entering*): Come on. It's all clear.

STAN (*off*): Right. Do you know there's some food out here on a tray? And a flask?

SYLVIA (*pirouetting round the room*): Bring it in then. (*As STAN enters with tray.*) I don't believe he said any such thing. What did *she* say?

STAN (*putting the tray down*): I don't know. I didn't stop to listen.

SYLVIA: We could do with some music.

STAN: There probably is some if you open the door. (*Mimicking.*) Doh me soh doh soh.

They both take this up as a sort of comic duet, and then, hotting it up, begin to jive to it.

STAN (*as they approach the cash register*): Let's get the Hallelujah Chorus. (*He clouts the cash register in passing.*)

SYLVIA (*breaking from him*): Don't be such a fool, Stan! You'll have mum down here!

STAN goes to the door into the hall and opens it.

STAN (*listening in mock consternation*): Not a sound.

SYLVIA has crossed to the tray.

SYLVIA: You didn't bring any mustard in.

STAN (*with exaggerated mock gallantry*): Good God! (*Going posthaste into kitchen.*) How *could* I have been so very careless!

SYLVIA turns and looks into the mirror.

STAN (*off*): Where the devil is it, anyway?

SYLVIA *has caught sight in the mirror of something behind her and transfixed with horror does not reply. Instead she spins round and faces the mantelpiece, gives a terrified look in the direction of her skull, and then turning away buries her face in her hands.*

STAN (*off*) : It's all dried up, the only bit I can find out here. You'll have to do without by the look of it.

SYLVIA *has drawn her hands down her face and is looking out front with an expression of bewildered hopelessness.* STAN *enters, sees* SYLVIA, *and checks.*

STAN (*with a kind of dumbfounded solicitude*) : What's the matter, Sylvia?

SYLVIA *looks straight ahead.*

SYLVIA (*flat voice*) : Someone's been messing about with my death's head.

STAN *looks across at the skull and back to* SYLVIA.

SYLVIA (*turning and going out*) : It wasn't working when *you* gave it to me.

STAN *takes a step towards her, stops, watches her out of the room, and then turns to look at the skull.*
He stares at it for a time, then gazes down at the floor several feet in front of him and begins to turn away towards the kitchen door behind him.
On an impulse, and mastering a strong reluctance, he goes instead up to the mantelpiece, takes up the skull, puts it straight into his pocket and turning on his heel goes out through the kitchen.
Pause.
MR. GROOMKIRBY *emerges from the courtroom in a manner*

*suggesting that he has been wandering around behind it all
the time in a kind of trance, and with every sign of exhaus-
tion makes his way slowly to the door into the hall.*
*When he reaches it he switches off the light in the room,
which is now in total darkness.*
*As though at a signal the sound of doh me soh doh soh
comes from upstairs.*
By the light in the hall MR. GROOMKIRBY *can be seen to
check, stiffen, listen, and then quite suddenly on an angry
impulse turn back into the room, slam the door and so cut
off the sound, and with a stride to the control panel violently switch on the Court.*

MRS. G. *(appearing at door)*: What's going on, Arthur?

The Court is assembled.

USHER: Silence.

PROSECUTING COUNSEL *is on his feet addressing the* JUDGE.

PROS. COUN.: The accused is Kirby Groomkirby.
MRS. G. *(crossing to pick up suit)*: Oh, he'll need his suit then.

MRS. GROOMKIRBY *crosses back with suit and goes out, taking*
MR. GROOMKIRBY *with her.*

Come on up, Arthur.
PROS. COUN.: M'lord, the facts, as your lordship is aware, are not
in dispute in this case. The accused, Kirby Groomkirby, has
admitted in the Magistrate's Court that between the first of
August last year and the ninth of April he has been fairly
regularly taking life, and since the case was heard there
three weeks ago has asked for nine other offences in addition to the thirty-four in the original indictment to be taken
into account, making a total altogether of forty-three. On
the last occasion on which he took a life he was warned
by Detective-Sergeant Barnes that complaints had been
lodged and that action would be taken against him if he

failed to conform to the law. It was after this, while he was preparing to repeat the offence, that Detective-Sergeant Barnes arrested him.

JUDGE: This would have been the forty-fourth offence?

PROS. COUN.: Yes, m'lord, but it was never carried out.

JUDGE: Because he was arrested.

PROS. COUN.: Yes, m'lord.

JUDGE (*with heavy sarcasm*): It would be a pity to credit him with the wrong number of offences.

PROS. COUN.: He went before the Magistrate's Court on the third of this month where he pleaded guilty and was remanded for sentence. Since then he has asked for the nine other offences to be taken into account.

JUDGE: Are these nine offences exactly similar?

PROS. COUN.: They are exactly the same, m'lord, except that the victims are different.

JUDGE: Naturally the victims wouldn't be the same. What method has he been using?

PROS. COUN.: He seems to have been using the same technique fairly consistently, m'lord. He tells his victim a joke, waits for him to laugh, and then strikes him with an iron bar.

JUDGE (*after pondering for a second*): Is there any previous record?

PROS. COUN.: No, m'lord.

JUDGE: He's been in no other kind of trouble at all?

PROS. COUN.: None at all, m'lord.

JUDGE: I see.

The JUDGE *writes.* PROSECUTING COUNSEL *sits.*

JUDGE (*to* DEFENDING COUNSEL): Yes?

DEF. COUN. (*rising*): M'lord, I should like to begin by calling Detective-Sergeant Barnes to the witness box.

BARNES *is shown into the witness box by the* USHER *and sworn.*

BARNES: I swear by Almighty God that the evidence I shall give shall be the truth, the whole truth, and nothing but the truth. Detective-Sergeant Barnes, Gamma Division.

DEF. COUN.: Sergeant Barnes, you I believe spoke to the accused and to his parents, shortly before he was arrested?

BARNES: That is so, yes, sir.

DEF. COUN.: Would it be true to say that you found him very communicative and helpful?

BARNES: He was as communicative as I understand he usually is, yes, sir.

DEF. COUN.: And helpful?

BARNES: He was quite helpful, yes, sir.

DEF. COUN.: Whom did you see first, Sergeant Barnes—the accused or his parents?

BARNES: I saw his parents to begin with, sir.

DEF. COUN.: What did you say to them?

BARNES: I put the position to them, sir, and told them that complaints had been received about their son's conduct . . .

DEF. COUN.: Yes—I'm sorry to interrupt you, Sergeant Barnes, but perhaps you can tell the Court what in so many words you said on this first occasion?

BARNES: Yes, I think I can remember what I said, sir. When I went in, the first person I saw was Mr. Groomkirby, so I addressed what I had to say to him. I said, to the best of my recollection, something to the effect that "It's beginning to add up down at the mortuary, Mr. Groomkirby."

JUDGE (*intervening*): Meaning that you were keeping a check of this man's victims?

BARNES: We were rather pressed for space, m'lord.

JUDGE: I know that, Sergeant. What I'm asking you now is whether your remark "It's beginning to add up down at the mortuary" referred to this man's victims only, or to those of other people as well.

BARNES: It was a kind of joke, m'lord. I was trying to keep on friendly terms at that stage and I made the remark in a somewhat humorous manner. I went on to say "We haven't got the Albert Hall, Mr. Groomkirby."

JUDGE: So you weren't giving information?

BARNES: Not what you might call information, no, m'lord.

The JUDGE *returns the ball to* COUNSEL.

DEF. COUN.: What did Mr. Groomkirby say to you, as far as you can remember, Sergeant Barnes, in reply to that remark of yours?

BARNES: It was Mrs. Groomkirby, sir. She said "We shall have to have another word with him, Arthur."

JUDGE (*intervening*) : Who is Arthur?

DEF. COUN.: The father, m'lord.

JUDGE: Arthur Groomkirby.

DEF. COUN.: Yes, m'lord. (*To* BARNES.) Did you get the impression from the conversation you had with the mother and father of the accused, Sergeant Barnes, that they were doing all they could to help their son and take his mind off law-breaking?

BARNES: I got the impression that they were very concerned at the turn things seemed to have been taking, sir.

DEF. COUN.: And genuinely determined to do what they could for their son, to get him to mend his ways?

BARNES: Yes, sir.

DEF. COUN.: And the accused—it would be true to say, wouldn't it, Sergeant Barnes, that he rather confided in you?

BARNES: He told me certain things about himself, yes, sir.

DEF. COUN.: Can you tell his lordship what you were able to gather from this conversation with the accused—and his parents—about his character in general, and what you think may have caused him to act as he did?

BARNES: He seemed to have a strong desire, m'lord, to wear black clothes. He told me he'd had it for as long as he could remember, and his mother, m'lord, told me the same. For the last year or two he's been studying what he calls logical analysis, and this has gradually taken the form of looking for a logical pretext for wearing his black clothes. Prior to that I understand he just wore them without concerning himself about finding a pretext, m'lord.

JUDGE: There's nothing reprehensible in his wanting to be rational about it.

BARNES: No, m'lord. But with the accused it seems to have combined rather adversely with this urge to wear black, m'lord.

JUDGE: In what way?

BARNES: He said he had to have rational grounds for wearing it, m'lord.

JUDGE: Yes?

BARNES: And he hit upon this idea of going into mourning.

JUDGE: For his own victims, I suppose.

BARNES: For his own victims, m'lord.

JUDGE (*after pondering for a second*): Surely there must have been plenty of people dying from natural causes.

BARNES: He wouldn't wear mourning for anyone he didn't know, m'lord. I put that specifically to him. He said he felt it would be a mockery, m'lord.

JUDGE: Was he sincere about this?

BARNES: I think he was, m'lord, yes.

JUDGE *nods imperceptibly to* COUNSEL.

DEF. COUN.: I want you to look now, Sergeant, at the weighing machines there in front of the witness box. (*To* USHER.) Could we have Exhibit Nine uncovered, please.

The covers are removed from the weighing machines.

DEF. COUN.: Have you seen these machines, or machines like them, Sergeant, before?

BARNES: Yes, sir. I have.

DEF. COUN.: Where did you see them?

BARNES: They were upstairs with a good many more, sir, at the house where I interviewed the accused, sir.

DEF. COUN.: Are these the ordinary kind of weighing machines such as anyone going into an amusement arcade or into a chemist's shop might expect to find?

BARNES: They are a fairly common type, yes, sir.

DEF. COUN.: They are, in fact, what are sometimes known as Speak-your-weight machines?

BARNES: Yes, sir.

DEF. COUN.: How many of these machines did you find when you went to the house at which the accused was living?

BARNES: A good many, sir. I didn't count them, but I should say running into several hundred.

DEF. COUN.: Would the number you saw be consistent with there being five hundred of these machines?

BARNES: It would be consistent with that, yes, sir.

DEF. COUN.: Were you able to discover in your conversation with the accused, Sergeant Barnes, any motive he might possibly have for building up this exceptionally large collection of Speak-your-weight machines?

BARNES: He did refer to them, sir. I didn't set much store by what he said because I thought it sounded a bit far-fetched, but I gathered it was more the volume of sound he was concerned about. He wanted them to be heard over a long distance.

DEF. COUN.: By anyone in particular?

BARNES: By as many people as possible, sir.

DEF. COUN.: He was teaching them to sing, wasn't he, Sergeant?

BARNES: That was his intention, sir.

JUDGE: To do *what*?

DEF. COUN.: To sing, m'lord.

JUDGE: I thought we were talking about weighing machines?

DEF. COUN.: These are a special type, m'lord, which speak when subjected to weight and can also be trained to sing. I have had these three brought into the Court for this reason, m'lord. There would be no difficulty in arranging for them to sing a short song, or part of a song, if your lordship would allow.

JUDGE: How long is this going to take?

DEF. COUN.: It would take a matter of minutes, m'lord.

JUDGE (*unenthusiastically*): Yes. I suppose so.

DEF. COUN.: I am very much obliged to your lordship.

DEFENDING COUNSEL *nods to* USHER.

The USHER *lifts a weight on to each of the three weighing machines in turn.*

When all three weights have been placed in position, the USHER *gives middle C on a whistle.*

After a brief pause NUMBERS TWO *and* THREE *launch into the Lizzie Borden song as a duet.* NUMBER ONE *is silent.*

The JUDGE, *in so far as he takes notice of the song at all, remains unimpressed by it.*

The song ends.

Pause.

DEF. COUN. (*rising*) : Thank you, m'lord.

The USHER *removes the weight first from* TWO *and then from* THREE.

DEF. COUN. (*as* USHER *goes to remove the weight from* NUMBER ONE) : One final question, Sergeant Barnes.

NUMBER ONE (*as weight is removed*) : Fifteen stone ten pounds.

There is a pause for one puzzled moment.

DEF. COUN. (*resuming*) : Was anything said to you, Sergeant Barnes, either by the accused or by his parents, that might lead you to believe he was intending eventually to have these weighing machines shipped to the North Pole?

BARNES: Yes, sir. Arrangements were actually in hand for this, sir.

DEF. COUN.: Did he volunteer any information that might explain this action?

BARNES: Only to say that he wanted them to act as sirens, sir.

JUDGE (*intervening*) : Sirens?

BARNES (*in an explanatory manner*) : To lure people to the North Pole, m'lord.

DEF. COUN.: There was a scientific reason for this, Sergeant Barnes, wasn't there?

BARNES: Yes, sir.

DEF. COUN.: Will you try and enlarge on this for his lordship, Sergeant Barnes?

BARNES (*to* JUDGE): I fancy he had some notion, m'lord, that once these people were at the North Pole, if he could get enough of them together in the one place, he would have very little difficulty in persuading them all to jump at the same moment.

JUDGE: And what inscrutable purpose was this manoeuvre calculated to serve?

BARNES: I think he was more concerned with what would happen when they landed again, m'lord. He was hoping it might have the effect of tilting the earth's axis a little more to one side, m'lord.

Pause.

JUDGE: I see.

DEF. COUN.: This would very likely bring about quite far-reaching climatic changes, would it not, Sergeant?

BARNES: I think something of that kind was what he had in mind, sir.

DEF. COUN.: A shifting of the Ice Cap, for instance.

BARNES: Yes, sir.

DEF. COUN.: This might well give rise to a new Ice Age so far as these islands are concerned?

BARNES: In all probability, yes, sir.

DEF. COUN.: Would it be true to say, Sergeant Barnes, that he was hoping in this way to provide himself with a self-perpetuating pretext for wearing black?

BARNES: Yes, sir.

DEF. COUN.: By ensuring that for an indefinite period deaths from various causes connected with the excessive cold would be many and frequent?

BARNES: That was at the back of it, yes, sir.

DEF. COUN.: Thank you, Sergeant Barnes.

BARNES *stands down.*

DEF. COUN.: I would like to call Mrs. Groomkirby now to the witness box. (*To* USHER). Mrs. Groomkirby?

USHER: Mrs. Groomkirby!

POLICEMAN: Mrs. Groomkirby!

MRS. G. (*off*): Give me time to get downstairs. (*Appearing from hall.*) Where do I go?

She is shown into the witness box.

MRS. G.: You feel so public.

In the witness box MRS. GROOMKIRBY *becomes somewhat overawed by her surroundings. She takes the oath.*

DEF. COUN.: You are Mabel Laurentina Groomkirby.

MRS. G.: Yes, sir.

DEF. COUN.: You are the mother of the accused, Mrs. Groomkirby are you not?

MRS. G.: Oh. Well, yes. I suppose if he's on trial I must be. I hadn't realized.

DEF. COUN.: It would be true to say, wouldn't it, Mrs. Groomkirby, that your son likes wearing black?

MRS. G.: He's worn it all his life.

DEF. COUN.: He likes wearing black but he doesn't feel justified in wearing it except at the funeral of someone he knows?

MRS. G.: Well, it's only in the last few years he's come to think like that, really. He always used to just wear it.

DEF. COUN.: His attitude has changed?

MRS. G.: It's been very noticeable over the last year or two.

DEF. COUN.: Can you account for this change in any way, Mrs. Groomkirby?

MRS. G.: Not really—unless his studies have had anything to do with it. He's always been of a very logical turn of mind ever since he was born, but what with all this studying lately he seems to have got a different attitude altogether these last few years.

DEF. COUN.: Your son is a rather ingenious young man, is he not, Mrs. Groomkirby?

MRS. G.: A lot of people say he is, yes, sir.

DEF. COUN.: He has a cash register, I believe.

MRS. G.: That's right.

DEF. COUN.: What exactly is the function of this cash register, Mrs. Groomkirby? What does your son use it for?

MRS. G.: It was an egg-timer to begin with, and then he gradually came to rely on it more and more for other things.

DEF. COUN.: When it was an egg-timer—can you tell his lordship how it worked?

MRS. G.: Well, sir, it was rigged up in the kitchen with the telephone on one side of it and the gas stove on the other. He likes to have his eggs done the exact time—just the four minutes ten seconds—or he won't eat them. He just goes right inside himself. So he rigged up the cash register.

DEF. COUN.: How did it work, Mrs. Groomkirby?

MRS. G.: He'd got a stop-watch but he wouldn't trust that. He'd trust it for the minutes but he wouldn't trust it for the seconds.

DEF. COUN.: And so he used the cash register instead?

MRS. G.: That and the telephone. He had them side by side.

DEF. COUN.: What was the actual procedure he adopted, Mrs. Groomkirby?

MRS. G.: Well, he'd put his egg on to boil, then he'd stand there with his stop-watch.

DEF. COUN.: Go on, Mrs. Groomkirby.

MRS. G.: Well, then the moment it said four minutes exactly on his stop-watch, he'd simply dial TIM, wait for the pips, ring up No Sale on the cash register and take out his egg.

DEF. COUN.: And this was, in fact, the only sequence of actions that took precisely the ten seconds?

MRS. G.: That's right, sir. He wouldn't eat them otherwise.

DEF. COUN.: And he worked this out for himself without any assistance whatever from anyone else?

MRS. G.: Oh, yes. It was entirely his own. And then he started getting dependent on the bell for other things as well. Eating first; and now practically everything he does he has to have a bell rung.

DEF. COUN.: To come back to this question of the black clothes, Mrs. Groomkirby.

MRS. G.: They've as good as told him that if ever he were to part with his cash register it would mean total paralysis for him.

DEF. COUN.: Yes. You say your son, Mrs. Groomkirby, has always liked wearing black. Will you tell his lordship in your own words about this attachment to black clothes?

MRS. G.: Well, sir, all his baby things were black. He had a black shawl and rompers and even down to his bib were all black, and his sheets and pillow-cases. We had everything in black for him as soon as he was born. People used to stop in the street and remark about him. He's never worn anything white. Sometimes when he was in his pram people used to say he looked like a wee undertaker lying there. We got it all planned before he was born that if we had a white baby we were going to dress him in black—or her in black if it had been a girl—and if either of them were black we'd have everything white, so as to make a contrast. But when he came he was white so we had the black.

JUDGE (*intervening*): Is your husband a coloured man, Mrs. Groomkirby?

MRS. G.: He's an insurance agent, sir.

JUDGE: Yes, but is he coloured?

MRS. G.: Well, no, sir. Not so far as I know.

JUDGE: What I'm trying to get from you, Mrs. Groomkirby, is the simple fact of your husband's racial characteristics. Does he, for instance, have any Negro blood?

MRS. G.: Well—he *has* got one or two bottles up in his room, but he doesn't tell me what's *in* them.

The JUDGE *looks blankly at* MRS. GROOMKIRBY *for a moment and then relinquishes the matter.*

DEF. COUN.: There's one more thing I should like to ask you, Mrs. Groomkirby. Each of your son's forty-three victims was

struck with an iron bar after having been told a joke. Would
it be true to say that your son, Mrs. Groomkirby, went to
considerable trouble over these jokes?

MRS. G.: He went to very great trouble indeed, sir. He sat up to
all hours thinking out jokes for them.

DEF. COUN.: Can you tell his lordship why your son went to all
this trouble with every one of his forty-three victims, when
there were a number of far simpler methods he could have
used?

MRS. G.: I think for one thing he rather took to the humorous side
of it. And for another thing he always wanted to do everything he could for these people. He felt very sorry for them.

DEF. COUN.: He wanted to make things as pleasant as possible
for them even at some considerable trouble and inconvenience to himself?

MRS. G.: He didn't mind how much trouble he went to, as long
as they ended on a gay note.

DEF. COUN.: Thank you, Mrs. Groomkirby.

> MRS. GROOMKIRBY *is invited by a sign from the* USHER *to
> stand down and does so with respectful restraint.*
> *Once out of the aura of the Court, and in her own home,
> she resumes a brisker manner and picking up the tray goes
> into the kitchen with it.*
> COUNSEL FOR THE DEFENCE *begins his speech to the* JUDGE.

DEF. COUN.: M'lord, in asking you to take a lenient view of this
case, I am not underestimating the seriousness of the offences
this young man has committed. They are very grave breaches
of the law, and no one realizes this now more than he does
himself. He has made very considerable efforts to find other
ways of satisfying this—in itself quite harmless, indeed laudable—desire for a logical pretext, but so far, unfortunately,
he has met with little success. He has had this scheme in-
volving the weighing machines. We may think this to have
been a somewhat grandiose scheme and that there could be
very little hope of its succeeding, or even indeed of its being

universally acceptable were it possible to adopt it; the important thing is that it has been worked out by this astonishingly resourceful and gifted young man as the result of a determination to avoid by every means in his power any further breach of the law in satisfying this craving he has for black clothes. He has gone to very great trouble and expense in training these weighing machines, m'lord, with the intention not of sitting idly down beside them to listen to and enjoy the fruits of his labours himself, but of keeping himself indirectly from coming into conflict with the law. In my respectful submission, m'lord, this very complex personality with whom we are dealing is not in any ordinary sense of the word a killer; he is, on the contrary, a kindly, rather gentle young man, not given to violence—except in this one respect—and showing himself to be quite exceptionally considerate of others even to the extent of arranging, at considerable personal sacrifice of time and energy, for them to die laughing. I would therefore ask your lordship to pass as light a sentence as, in your lordship's judgment, is warranted in this very exceptional case.

DEFENDING COUNSEL *sits.*
KIRBY *appears, looking for* GORMLESS. *He checks on seeing* GORMLESS *and raises his baton.*
The JUDGE *addresses the accused.*
KIRBY *drops to his knees facing the* JUDGE.

JUDGE: There have been too many crimes of this nature: people killing a number of victims—forty-three in your case—from what appear to be, and indeed often are in themselves, laudable motives. Your counsel has made an eloquent plea for you, and two people have been willing to come into the witness box—one of them the detective who arrested you—and give a favourable account of you. But from your forty-three victims—not a word. Not one of those forty-three has felt under any obligation to come forward and speak for you, notwithstanding the great trouble we are told you went to in furnishing them with laughing matter. And what about the iron bar you used? Was this also chosen and wielded with the well-being of your victims in mind? I think not. Your mother has said that you wear black. This is not surprising. Such a taste seems to me to be in perfect conformity with the career you have chosen to embark upon. I am not greatly influenced by the reasons that have been put forward for your having this apparently irresistible craving— they seem to me to have very little bearing on the matter. It is becoming more and more an accepted feature of cases of this kind that in the course of them the court is subjected to a farrago of psychological poppycock in which every imaginable ailment in the nursery is prayed in aid. As for your desire to find a logical pretext, this is the one redeeming feature I have been able to find in this case. But you could have come by a pretext in any one of a number of quite legitimate ways. I have no doubt at all that at least a score of undertakers could have been found whose advice and assistance you could have had for the asking. Instead you chose another way, a way which has led you straight to this court. You began a few months ago by telling your first joke to your first victim and then striking him with an iron bar. What did you get out of it? The excuse to wear black for a day or two. Was it really worth breaking the law in order to be able to wear black for forty-eight hours? And then a little later on came your second murder, and the opportunity to wear black again for a short time. And so it has gone on: victim after victim, until even you could not have expected the authorities to overlook it any longer. Indeed Detective-Sergeant Barnes warned you quite explicitly what would happen if you broke the law for the forty-fourth time. There seems to me to be not the smallest shred of excuse for these repeated offences. As for this diabolical scheme to send weighing machines to the North Pole, which we have been told is so ingenious, the less said about it the better. If the song we have just had to listen to in this court is in any way typical of the kind of thing we were to have been regaled by from the North Pole, it would be hard to imagine what sort of person would have been enticed there by it—or having got there would want to remain for long within earshot, still less be in any fit state to jump up and down. In deciding upon the sentence I shall impose in this case, I have been influenced by one consideration, and it is this: that in sentencing a man for one crime, we may be putting him beyond the reach of the law in respect of those other crimes of which he might otherwise have become guilty. The law, however, is not to be cheated in this way. I shall therefore discharge you.

MRS. GROOMKIRBY *enters from the hall on the last words of the* JUDGE *and rings up No Sale on the cash register.*
This is the signal for a massed choir to launch into the Hallelujah Chorus, and for blackout of the Court and living-room.
KIRBY *flings out his arms to conduct choir.*
Each alternate Hallelujah is sung by GORMLESS *who is now lit up with the words "I speak your weight" in red.*
GORMLESS *takes over from the massed choir,* KIRBY *in a mood of ungainly gaiety conducts him, and finally, when* GORMLESS *relapses into silence takes out a weight and crossing the forestage with it conducts and accompanies its tiny piping treble in a gay childlike rendering of the same Hallelujah Chorus. He goes off left.*
The light comes up on the living-room.
The Court is empty. MRS. GROOMKIRBY *is dusting it.*
SYLVIA *is sitting as at the beginning of Act One in silence.*

MRS. G. *(with a nod towards the music stand which remains where* KIRBY *placed it)* : What's that doing down here?

Pause.

MRS. G.: You might take it up, Sylvia.
SYLVIA *(looking up)* : Take what up?

MRS. G. (*going out to kitchen*) : That thing whatever it is of Kirby's. It's no business being down here.

SYLVIA: Can't he come and get it himself?

MRS. G. (*off*) : You know very well he's busy up there, Sylvia.

SYLVIA *shrugs, goes on reading for a moment, then puts her magazine down and saunters out with the music stand.*

BARNES *appears from the forestage left. He is getting into his overcoat and calls somewhat defensively to* MRS. GROOM-KIRBY.

BARNES: Thank you, Mrs. Groomkirby.

MRS. GROOMKIRBY *enters from the kitchen with a tray of food which she sets out on the table as for* MRS. GANTRY.

MRS. G.: Just off, are you?

BARNES: Yes—they've had a good look round and . . .

SYLVIA *enters from the hall and sits with magazine.*

MRS. G. (*without looking up from her work*) : Seen all they want, have they?

BARNES: I think they have, yes. More or less. (*Edging off.*)

MRS. G. (*half to herself*) : Day in day out. Gawping. The place isn't your own.

BARNES (*escaping*) : Back tomorrow about half past seven then, Mrs. Groomkirby—if that's all right.

MRS. G.: They won't have to come expecting anything.

BARNES: I'll tell them. Good-bye, Mrs. Groomkirby. Good-bye, Sylvia. (BARNES *goes off.*)

MR. GROOMKIRBY *enters from the hall and crosses the stage slowly with a book open in his hand. He has on the* JUDGE's *wig and robe. Neither seems to be made for him.*

SYLVIA (*without looking up*) : I don't know why they don't all

go and stand outside Buckingham Palace or something
instead.

MR. G. (*trying out what he thinks may be an appropriate voice
and manner as he reads. At large*) : That, members of the
jury, is the evidence before you.

*Dissatisfied, he moves further right and takes up one or two
tentative stances.*

SYLVIA: Or the Taj Mahal or something. And gawp at that,
instead.

MR. G. (*in an undertone*) : That, members of the jury . . .

He abandons it and tries again.

AUNT M.: On roller-skates. By moonlight. To Outer Space!

MR. G. (*he has got it right and addresses* GORMLESS *without recognition as though speaking to the* FOREMAN *of the jury*) :
That, members of the jury, is the evidence before you. (*He
turns to go, delivering his final words in a dismissively offhand manner.*) What weight you give to it is a matter
entirely for you.

GORMLESS (*lighting up*) : Fifteen stone ten pounds.

The sound stops MR. GROOMKIRBY *in his tracks. He turns,
startled, puzzled, deflated in turn. He goes hopelessly off.*

Curtain.

THE CARETAKER

Harold Pinter

THE CARETAKER was first presented by the Arts Theatre Club in association with Michael Codron and David Hall at the Arts Theatre, London, W.C.2, on 27 April 1960.

On 30 May 1960, it was presented by Michael Codron and David Hall at the Duchess Theatre, London, directed by Donald McWhinnie, and with the following cast:

MICK, *a man in his late twenties*	Alan Bates
ASTON, *a man in his early thirties*	Peter Woodthorpe
DAVIES, *an old man*	Donald Pleasence

The action of the play takes place in a house in west London.

ACT I: *A night in winter.*

ACT II: *A few second later.*

ACT III: *A fortnight later.*

A room. A window in the back wall, the bottom half covered by a sack. An iron bed along the left wall. Above it a small cupboard, paint buckets, boxes containing nuts, screws, etc. More boxes, vases, by the side of the bed. A door, up right. To the right of the window, a mound: a kitchen sink, a step-ladder, a coal bucket, a lawn-mower, a shopping trolley, boxes, sideboard drawers. Under this mound an iron bed. In front of it a gas stove. On the gas stove a statue of Buddha. Down right, a fireplace. Around it a couple of suitcases, a rolled carpet, a blow-lamp, a wooden chair on its side, boxes, a number of ornaments, a clothes horse, a few short planks of wood, a small electric fire and a very old electric toaster. Below this a pile of old newspapers. Under ASTON's bed by the left wall, is an electrolux, which is not seen till used. A bucket hangs from the ceiling.

ACT ONE

MICK *is alone in the room, sitting on the bed. He wears a leather jacket.*

Silence.

He slowly looks about the room, looking at each object in turn. He looks up at the ceiling, and stares at the bucket. Ceasing, he sits quite still, expressionless, looking out front.

Silence for thirty seconds.

A door bangs. Muffled voices are heard.

MICK *turns his head. He stands, moves silently to the door, goes out, and closes the door quietly.*

Silence.

Voices are heard again. They draw nearer, and stop. The door opens. ASTON *and* DAVIES *enter,* ASTON *first,* DAVIES *following, shambling, breathing heavily.*

ASTON *wears an old tweed overcoat, and under it a thin shabby dark-blue pinstripe suit, single-breasted, with a pullover and faded shirt and tie.* DAVIES *wears a worn brown overcoat, shapeless trousers, a waistcoat, vest, no shirt, and sandals.* ASTON *puts the key in his pocket and closes the door.* DAVIES *looks about the room.*

ASTON: Sit down.
DAVIES: Thanks. (*Looking about.*) Uuh. . . .
ASTON: Just a minute.

> ASTON *looks around for a chair, sees one lying on its side by the rolled carpet at the fireplace, and starts to get it out.*

DAVIES: Sit down? Huh . . . I haven't had a good sit down . . .

I haven't had a proper sit down . . . well, I couldn't tell you. . . .

ASTON (*placing the chair*): Here you are.

DAVIES: Ten minutes off for tea-break in the middle of the night in that place and I couldn't find a seat, not one. All them Greeks had it, Poles, Greeks, Blacks, the lot of them, all them aliens had it. And they had me working there . . . they had me working. . . .

ASTON *sits on the bed, takes out a tobacco tin and papers, and begins to roll himself a cigarette.* DAVIES *watches him.*

All them Blacks had it, Blacks, Greeks, Poles, the lot of them, that's what, doing me out of a seat, treating me like dirt. When he come at me tonight I told him.

Pause.

ASTON: Take a seat.

DAVIES: Yes, but what I got to do first, you see, what I got to do, I got to loosen myself up, you see what I mean? I could have got done in down there.

DAVIES *exclaims loudly, punches downward with closed fist, turns his back to* ASTON *and stares at the wall.*
Pause. ASTON *lights a cigarette.*

ASTON: You want to roll yourself one of these?

DAVIES (*turning*): What? No, no, I never smoke a cigarette. (*Pause. He comes forward.*) I'll tell you what, though. I'll have a bit of that tobacco there for my pipe, if you like.

ASTON (*handing him the tin*): Yes. Go on. Take some out of that.

DAVIES: That's kind of you, mister. Just enough to fill my pipe, that's all. (*He takes a pipe from his pocket and fills it.*) I had a tin, only . . . only a while ago. But it was knocked off. It was knocked off on the Great West Road. (*He holds out the tin.*) Where shall I put it?

ASTON: I'll take it.

DAVIES (*handing the tin*) : When he come at me tonight I told him. Didn't I? You heard me tell him, didn't you?

ASTON: I saw him have a go at you.

DAVIES: Go at me? You wouldn't grumble. The filthy skate, an old man like me, I've had dinner with the best.

Pause.

ASTON: Yes, I saw him have a go at you.

DAVIES: All them toe-rags, mate, got the manners of pigs. I might have been on the road a few years but you can take it from me I'm clean. I keep myself up. That's why I left my wife. Fortnight after I married her, no, not so much as that, no more than a week, I took the lid off a saucepan, you know what was in it? A pile of her underclothing, unwashed. The pan for vegetables, it was. The vegetable pan. That's when I left her and I haven't seen her since.

DAVIES *turns, shambles across the room, comes face to face with a statue of Buddha standing on the gas stove, looks at it and turns.*

I've eaten my dinner off the best of plates. But I'm not young any more. I remember the days I was as handy as any of them. They didn't take any liberties with me. But I haven't been so well lately. I've had a few attacks.

Pause.

(*Coming closer.*) Did you see what happened with that one?

ASTON: I only got the end of it.

DAVIES: Comes up to me, parks a bucket of rubbish at me, tells me to take it out the back. It's not my job to take out the bucket! They got a boy there for taking out the bucket. I wasn't engaged to take out buckets! My job's cleaning the floor, clearing up the tables, doing a bit of washing-up, nothing to do with taking out buckets!

ASTON: Uh.

He crosses down right, to get the electric toaster.

DAVIES (*following*): Yes, well say I had! Even if I had! Even if
I was supposed to take out the bucket, who was this git to
come up and give me orders? We got the same standing.
He's not my boss. He's nothing superior to me.
ASTON: What was he, a Greek?
DAVIES: Not him, he was a Scotch. He was a Scotchman. (ASTON
*goes back to his bed with the toaster and starts to unscrew
the plug.* DAVIES *follows him.*) You got an eye of him, did
you?
ASTON: Yes.
DAVIES: I told him what to do with his bucket. Didn't I? You
heard. Look here, I said, I'm an old man, I said, where I
was brought up we had some idea how to talk to old people
with the proper respect, we was brought up with the right
ideas, if I had a few years off me I'd . . . I'd break you in
half. That was after the guvnor give me the bullet. Making
too much commotion, he says. Commotion, me! Look here,
I said to him, I got my rights. I told him that. I might have
been on the road but nobody's got more rights than I have.
Let's have a bit of fair play, I said. Anyway, he give me the
bullet. (*He sits in the chair.*) That's the sort of place.

Pause.

If you hadn't come out and stopped that Scotch git I'd be
inside the hospital now. I'd have cracked my head on that
pavement if he'd have landed. I'll get him. One night I'll
get him. When I find myself around that direction.

ASTON *crosses to the plug box to get another plug.*

I wouldn't mind so much but I left all my belongings in
that place, in the back room there. All of them, the lot there
was, you see, in this bag. Every lousy blasted bit of all my

bleeding belongings I left down there now. In the rush of it.
I bet he's having a poke around in it now this very moment.

ASTON: I'll pop down sometime and pick them up for you.

ASTON *goes back to his bed and starts to fix the plug on the
toaster.*

DAVIES: Anyway, I'm obliged to you, letting me . . . letting me
have a bit of a rest, like . . . for a few minutes. (*He looks
about.*) This your room?

ASTON: Yes.

DAVIES: You got a good bit of stuff here.

ASTON: Yes.

DAVIES: Must be worth a few bob, this . . . put it all together.

Pause.

There's enough of it.

ASTON: There's a good bit of it, all right.

DAVIES: You sleep here, do you?

ASTON: Yes.

DAVIES: What, in that?

ASTON: Yes.

DAVIES: Yes, well, you'd be well out of the draught there.

ASTON: You don't get much wind.

DAVIES: You'd be well out of it. It's different when you're kipping
out.

ASTON: Would be.

DAVIES: Nothing but wind then.

Pause.

ASTON: Yes, when the wind gets up it. . . .

Pause.

DAVIES: Yes. . . .

ASTON: Mmnn. . . .

Pause.

DAVIES: Gets very draughty.
ASTON: Ah.
DAVIES: I'm very sensitive to it.
ASTON: Are you?
DAVIES: Always have been.

Pause.

You got more rooms then, have you?
ASTON: Where?
DAVIES: I mean, along the landing here . . . up the landing there.
ASTON: They're out of commission.
DAVIES: Get away.
ASTON: They need a lot of doing to.

Slight pause.

DAVIES: What about downstairs?
ASTON: That's closed up. Needs seeing to. . . . The floors. . . .

Pause.

DAVIES: I was lucky you come into that caff. I might have been done by that Scotch git. I been left for dead more than once.

Pause.

I noticed that there was someone was living in the house next door.
ASTON: What?
DAVIES (*gesturing*): I noticed. . . .
ASTON: Yes. There's people living all along the road.

DAVIES: Yes, I noticed the curtains pulled down there next door as we come along.

ASTON: They're neighbours.

Pause.

DAVIES: This your house then, is it?

Pause.

ASTON: I'm in charge.

DAVIES: You the landlord, are you?

He puts a pipe in his mouth and puffs without lighting it. Yes, I noticed them heavy curtains pulled across next door as we come along. I noticed them heavy big curtains right across the window down there. I thought there must be someone living there.

ASTON: Family of Indians live there.

DAVIES: Blacks?

ASTON: I don't see much of them.

DAVIES: Blacks, eh? (DAVIES *stands and moves about.*) Well, you've got some knick-knacks here all right, I'll say that. I don't like a bare room. (ASTON *joins* DAVIES *upstage centre.*) I'll tell you what, mate, you haven't got a spare pair of shoes?

ASTON: Shoes?

ASTON *moves downstage right.*

DAVIES: Them bastards at the monastery let me down again.

ASTON (*going to his bed*) : Where?

DAVIES: Down at Luton. Monastery down at Luton. . . . I got a mate at Shepherd's Bush, you see. . . .

ASTON (*looking under his bed*) : I might have a pair.

DAVIES: I got this mate at Shepherd's Bush. In the convenience. Well, he was in the convenience. Run about the best convenience they had. (*He watches* ASTON.) Run about the best one. Always slipped me a bit of soap, any time I went in there. Very good soap. They have to have the best soap. I was never without a piece of soap, whenever I happened to be knocking about the Shepherd's Bush area.

ASTON (*emerging from under the bed with shoes*) : Pair of brown.

DAVIES: He's gone now. Went. He was the one who put me on to this monastery. Just the other side of Luton. He'd heard they give away shoes.

ASTON: You've got to have a good pair of shoes.

DAVIES: Shoes? It's life and death to me. I had to go all the way to Luton in these.

ASTON: What happened when you got there, then?

Pause.

DAVIES: I used to know a bootmaker in Acton. He was a good mate to me.

Pause.

DAVIES: You know what that bastard monk said to me?

Pause.

How many more Blacks you got around here then?

ASTON: What?

DAVIES: You got any more Blacks around here?

ASTON (*holding out the shoes*) : See if these are any good.

DAVIES: You know what that bastard monk said to me? (*He looks over to the shoes.*) I think those'd be a bit small.

ASTON: Would they?

DAVIES: No, don't look the right size.

ASTON: Not bad trim.

DAVIES: Can't wear shoes that don't fit. Nothing worse. I said to this monk, here, I said, look here, mister, he opened the door, big door, he opened it, look here, mister, I said, I come all the way down here, look, I said, I showed him these, I said, you haven't got a pair of shoes, have you, a pair of shoes, I said, enough to keep me on my way. Look at these, they're nearly out, I said, they're no good to me. I heard you got a stock of shoes here. Piss off, he said to me. Now look here, I said, I'm an old man, you can't talk to me like that, I don't care who you are. If you don't piss off, he says, I'll kick you all the way to the gate. Now look here, I said, now wait a minute, all I'm asking for is a pair of shoes, you don't want to start taking liberties with me, it's taken me three days to get out here, I said to him, three days without a bite, I'm worth a bite to eat, en I? Get out round the corner to the kitchen, he says, get out round the corner, and when you've had your meal, piss off out of it. I went round to this kitchen, see? Meal they give me! A bird, I tell you, a little bird, a little tiny bird, he could have ate it in under two minutes. Right, they said to me, you've had your meal, get off out of it. Meal? I said, what do you think I am, a dog? Nothing better than a dog. What do you think I am, a wild animal? What about them shoes I come all the way here to get I heard you was giving away? I've a good mind to report you to your mother superior. One of them, an Irish hooligan, come at me. I cleared out. I took a short cut to Watford and picked up a pair there. Got onto the North Circular, just past Hendon, the sole come off, right where I was walking. Lucky I had my old ones wrapped up, still carrying them, otherwise I'd have been finished, man. So I've had to stay with these, you see, they're gone, they're no good, all the good's gone out of them.

ASTON: Try these.

DAVIES *takes the shoes, takes off his sandals and tries them on.*

DAVIES: Not a bad pair of shoes. (*He trudges round the room.*) They're strong, all right. Yes. Not a bad shape of shoe. This leather's hardy, en't? Very hardy. Some bloke tried to flog me some suede the other day. I wouldn't wear them.

Can't beat leather, for wear. Suede goes off, it creases, it stains for life in five minutes. You can't beat leather. Yes. Good shoe this.

ASTON: Good.

DAVIES *waggles his feet.*

DAVIES: Don't fit though.

ASTON: Oh?

DAVIES: No. I got a very broad foot.

ASTON: Mmnn.

DAVIES: These are too pointed, you see.

ASTON: Ah.

DAVIES: They'd cripple me in a week. I mean, these ones I got on, they're no good but at least they're comfortable. Not much cop, but I mean they don't hurt. (*He takes them off and gives them back.*) Thanks anyway, mister.

ASTON: I'll see what I can look out for you.

DAVIES: Good luck. I can't go on like this. Can't get from one place to another. And I'll have to be moving about, you see, try to get fixed up.

ASTON: Where you going to go?

DAVIES: Oh, I got one or two things in mind. I'm waiting for the weather to break.

Pause.

ASTON (*attending to the toaster*): Would . . . would you like to sleep here?

DAVIES: Here?

ASTON: You can sleep here if you like.

DAVIES: Here? Oh, I don't know about that.

Pause.

How long for?

ASTON: Till you . . . get yourself fixed up.

DAVIES (*sitting*) : Ay well, that. . . .
ASTON: Get yourself sorted out. . . .
DAVIES: Oh, I'll be fixed up . . . pretty soon now. . . .

Pause.

Where would I sleep?
ASTON: Here. The other rooms would . . . would be no good
to you.
DAVIES (*rising, looking about*) : Here? Where?
ASTON (*rising, pointing upstage right*) : There's a bed behind
all that.
DAVIES: Oh, I see. Well, that's handy. Well, that's . . . I tell you
what, I might do that . . . just till I get myself sorted out.
You got enough furniture here.
ASTON: I picked it up. Just keeping it here for the time being.
Thought it might come in handy.
DAVIES: This gas stove work, do it?
ASTON: No.
DAVIES: What do you do for a cup of tea?
ASTON: Nothing.
DAVIES: That's a bit rough. (DAVIES *observes the planks.*) You
building something?
ASTON: I might build a shed out the back.
DAVIES: Carpenter, eh? (*He turns to the lawn-mower.*) Got a
lawn?
ASTON: Have a look.

ASTON *lifts the sack at the window. They look out.*

DAVIES: Looks a bit thick.
ASTON: Overgrown.
DAVIES: What's that, a pond?
ASTON: Yes.
DAVIES: What you got, fish?
ASTON: No. There isn't anything in there.

Pause.

DAVIES: Where you going to put your shed?
ASTON (*turning*) : I'll have to clear the garden first.
DAVIES: You'd need a tractor, man.
ASTON: I'll get it done.
DAVIES: Carpentry, eh?
ASTON (*standing still*) : I like . . . working with my hands.

DAVIES *picks up the statue of Buddha.*

DAVIES: What's this?
ASTON (*taking and studying it*) : That's a Buddha.
DAVIES: Get on.
ASTON: Yes. I quite like it. Picked it up in a . . . in a shop.
Looked quite nice to me. Don't know why. What do you
think of these Buddhas?
DAVIES: Oh, they're . . . they're all right, en't they?
ASTON: Yes, I was pleased when I got hold of this one. It's very
well made.

DAVIES *turns and peers under the sink, etc.*

DAVIES: This the bed here, is it?
ASTON (*moving to the bed*) : We'll get rid of all that. The
ladder'll fit under the bed. (*They put the ladder under the
bed.*)
DAVIES (*indicating the sink*) : What about this?
ASTON: I think that'll fit in under here as well.
DAVIES: I'll give you a hand. (*They lift it.*) It's a ton weight,
en't?
ASTON: Under here.
DAVIES: This in use at all, then?
ASTON: No. I'll be getting rid of it. Here.

They place the sink under the bed.

There's a lavatory down the landing. It's got a sink in there.
We can put this stuff over there.

They begin to move the coal bucket, shopping trolley, lawn-mower and sideboard drawers to the right wall.

DAVIES (*stopping*) : You don't share it, do you?
ASTON: What?
DAVIES: I mean you don't share the toilet with them Blacks, do you?
ASTON: They live next door.
DAVIES: They don't come in?

ASTON *puts a drawer against the wall.*

Because, you know . . . I mean . . . fair's fair. . . .

ASTON *goes to the bed, blows dust and shakes a blanket.*

ASTON: You see a blue case?
DAVIES: Blue case? Down here. Look. By the carpet.

ASTON *goes to the case, opens it, takes out a sheet and pillow and puts them on the bed.*

That's a nice sheet.
ASTON: The blanket'll be a bit dusty.
DAVIES: Don't you worry about that.

ASTON *stands upright, takes out his tobacco and begins to roll a cigarette. He goes to his bed and sits.*

ASTON: How are you off for money?
DAVIES: Oh well . . . now, mister, if you want the truth . . . I'm a bit short.

ASTON *takes some coins from his pocket, sorts them, and holds out five shillings.*

ASTON: Here's a few bob.

DAVIES (*taking the coins*) : Thank you, thank you, good luck.
I just happen to find myself a bit short. You see, I got
nothing for all that week's work I did last week. That's the
position, that's what it is.

Pause.

ASTON: I went into a pub the other day. Ordered a Guinness.
They gave it to me in a thick mug. I sat down but I couldn't
drink it. I can't drink Guinness from a thick mug. I only
like it out of a thin glass. I had a few sips but I couldn't
finish it.

ASTON *picks up a screwdriver and plug from the bed and
begins to poke the plug.*

DAVIES (*with great feeling*) : If only the weather would break!
Then I'd be able to get down to Sidcup!
ASTON: Sidcup?
DAVIES: The weather's so blasted bloody awful, how can I get
down to Sidcup in these shoes?
ASTON: Why do you want to get down to Sidcup?
DAVIES: I got my papers there!

Pause.

ASTON: Your what?
DAVIES: I got my papers there!

Pause.

ASTON: What are they doing at Sidcup?
DAVIES: A man I know has got them. I left them with him. You
see? They prove who I am! I can't move without them
papers. They tell you who I am. You see! I'm stuck without
them.
ASTON: Why's that?

DAVIES: You see, what it is, you see, I changed my name! Years ago. I been going around under an assumed name! That's not my real name.

ASTON: What name you been going under?

DAVIES: Jenkins. Bernard Jenkins. That's my name. That's the name I'm known, anyway. But it's no good me going on with that name. I got no rights. I got an insurance card here. (*He takes a card from his pocket.*) Under the name of Jenkins. See? Bernard Jenkins. Look. It's got four stamps on it. Four of them. But I can't go along with these. That's not my real name, they'd find out, they'd have me in the nick. Four stamps. I haven't paid out pennies, I've paid out pounds. I've paid out pounds, not pennies. There's been other stamps, plenty, but they haven't put them on, the nigs, I never had enough time to go into it.

ASTON: They should have stamped your card.

DAVIES: It would have done no good! I'd have got nothing anyway. That's not my real name. If I take that card along I go in the nick.

ASTON: What's your real name, then?

DAVIES: Davies. Mac Davies. That was before I changed my name.

Pause.

ASTON: It looks as though you want to sort all that out.

DAVIES: If only I could get down to Sidcup! I've been waiting for the weather to break. He's got my papers, this man I left them with, it's got it all down there, I could prove everything.

ASTON: How long's he had them?

DAVIES: What?

ASTON: How long's he had them?

DAVIES: Oh, must be . . . it was in the war . . . must be . . . about near on fifteen year ago.

Pause.

ASTON: Sure he's still got them?

DAVIES: He's got them.

ASTON: Might have moved.

DAVIES: I know the house he lives in, I tell you! Once I set foot in Sidcup I could go there blindfold. Can't remember the number though. I've got a good mind to . . . I've got a good mind. . . .

Pause.

ASTON: Well, you ought to try to get down there.

DAVIES: I can't go in these shoes. It's the weather, you see. If only the weather would break.

ASTON: I'll keep my eye on the weather report.

DAVIES: Once I got on the road I'd be there quick enough.

DAVIES *suddenly becomes aware of the bucket and looks up quickly.*

ASTON: Any time you want to . . . get into bed, just get in. Don't worry about me.

DAVIES *(taking off his overcoat)*: Eh, well, I think I will. I'm a bit . . . a bit done in. *(He steps out of his trousers, and holds them out.)* Shall I put these on here?

ASTON: Yes.

DAVIES *puts the coat and trousers on the clothes horse.*

DAVIES: I see you got a bucket up here.

ASTON: Leak.

DAVIES *looks up.*

DAVIES: Well, I'll try your bed then. You getting in?

ASTON: I'm mending this plug.

DAVIES: What's the matter with it?

ASTON: Doesn't work.

Pause.

DAVIES: You getting to the root of the trouble, are you?
ASTON: I've got a suspicion.
DAVIES: You're lucky.

DAVIES *goes towards his bed and stops at the gas stove.*

You . . . you can't move this, eh?
ASTON: Bit heavy.
DAVIES: Yes.

DAVIES *gets into bed. He tests his weight and length.*

Not bad. Not bad. A fair bed. I think I'll sleep in this.
ASTON: I'll have to fix a proper shade on that bulb. The light's
a bit glaring.
DAVIES: Don't you worry about that, mister, don't you worry
about that. (*He turns and puts the cover up.*)

ASTON *sits, poking his plug.*
The LIGHTS FADE OUT. *Darkness.*
LIGHTS UP. *Morning.*
ASTON *is fastening his trousers, standing by the bed. He
straightens his bed. He turns, goes to the centre of the room
and looks at* DAVIES. *He turns, puts his jacket on, turns, goes
towards* DAVIES *and looks down on him.*
He coughs. DAVIES *sits up abruptly.*

DAVIES: What? What's this? What's this?
ASTON: It's all right.
DAVIES (*staring*) : What's this?
ASTON: It's all right.

DAVIES *looks about.*

DAVIES: Oh, yes.

ASTON *goes to his bed, picks up the plug and shakes it.*

ASTON: Sleep well?
DAVIES: Yes. Dead out. Must have been dead out.

ASTON *goes downstage right, collects the toaster and examines it.*

ASTON: You . . . er. . . .
DAVIES: Eh?
ASTON: Were you dreaming or something?
DAVIES: Dreaming?
ASTON: Yes.
DAVIES: I don't dream. I've never dreamed.
ASTON: No, nor have I.
DAVIES: Nor me.

Pause.

Why you ask me that, then?
ASTON: You were making noises.
DAVIES: Who was?
ASTON: You were.

DAVIES *gets out of bed. He wears long underpants.*

DAVIES: Now, wait a minute. Wait a minute, what do you mean?
What kind of noises?
ASTON: You were making groans. You were jabbering.
DAVIES: Jabbering? Me?
ASTON: Yes.
DAVIES: I don't jabber, man. Nobody ever told me that before.

Pause.

What would I be jabbering about?
ASTON: I don't know.

DAVIES: I mean, where's the sense in it?

Pause.

Nobody ever told me that before.

Pause.

You got hold of the wrong bloke, mate.

ASTON (*crossing to the bed with the toaster*) : No. You woke me up. I thought you might have been dreaming.

DAVIES: I wasn't dreaming. I never had a dream in my life.

Pause.

ASTON: Maybe it was the bed.

DAVIES: Nothing wrong with this bed.

ASTON: Might be a bit unfamiliar.

DAVIES: There's nothing unfamiliar about me with beds. I slept in beds. I don't make noises just because I sleep in a bed. I slept in plenty of beds.

Pause.

I tell you what, maybe it were them Blacks.

ASTON: What?

DAVIES: Them noises.

ASTON: What Blacks?

DAVIES: Them you got. Next door. Maybe it were them Blacks making noises, coming up through the walls.

ASTON: Hmmnn.

DAVIES: That's my opinion.

ASTON *puts down the plug and moves to the door.*

Where you going, you going out?

ASTON: Yes.

DAVIES (*seizing the sandals*) : Wait a minute then, just a minute.

ASTON: What you doing?

DAVIES *(putting on the sandals)* : I better come with you.

ASTON: Why?

DAVIES: I mean, I better come out with you, anyway.

ASTON: Why?

DAVIES: Well . . . don't you want me to go out?

ASTON: What for?

DAVIES: I mean . . . when you're out. Don't you want me to get out . . . when you're out?

ASTON: You don't have to go out.

DAVIES: You mean . . . I can stay here?

ASTON: Do what you like. You don't have to come out just because I go out.

DAVIES: You don't mind me staying here?

ASTON: I've got a couple of keys. *(He goes to a box by his bed and finds them.)* This door and the front door. *(He hands them to* DAVIES.*)*

DAVIES: Thanks very much, the best of luck.

Pause. ASTON *stands.*

ASTON: I think I'll take a stroll down the road. A little . . . kind of a shop. Man there'd got a jig saw the other day. I quite liked the look of it.

DAVIES: A jig saw, mate?

ASTON: Yes. Could be very useful.

DAVIES: Yes.

Slight pause.

What's that then, exactly, then?

ASTON *walks up to the window and looks out.*

ASTON: A jig saw? Well, it comes from the same family as the fret saw. But it's an appliance, you see. You have to fix it on to a portable drill.

DAVIES: Ah, that's right. They're very handy.

ASTON: They are, yes.

Pause.

DAVIES: What about a hack-saw?
ASTON: Well, I've got a hack-saw, as a matter of fact.
DAVIES: They're handy.
ASTON: Yes.

Pause.

So's a keyhole saw.
DAVIES: Ah.

Pause.

Yes, there's no getting away from that. I mean, I know that, I know they're very handy. As long as you got the feel how to use it.

Pause.

On the other hand, they wouldn't . . . they wouldn't be as handy as a hack-saw, though, would they?
ASTON (*turning to him*): Wouldn't they?
DAVIES: I mean, I'm only saying that from . . . from what I've come across of them, like.

Slight pause.

ASTON: They're handy.
DAVIES: I know they're handy.
ASTON: But they're limited. There's a lot you can do with a jig saw, you see. Once you've fixed it . . . to this portable drill. You can do a lot with it. It speeds things up.
DAVIES: Yes.

Slight pause.

Eh, look. I been thinking.

ASTON: Uh?

DAVIES: Yes, look here. Look. Maybe it was you who was dreaming.

ASTON: What?

DAVIES: Yes, I mean, maybe you were dreaming you were hearing noises. A lot of people, you see, they dream, you see what I mean, they hear all kinds of things. Maybe it was you who was making them noises and you didn't know it.

ASTON: I don't have dreams.

DAVIES: But that's my meaning, that's what I'm trying to say! I don't either! That's why I thought it might have been you.

Pause.

ASTON: What did you say your name was?

DAVIES: Jenkins. Bernard Jenkins is my assumed one.

Slight pause.

ASTON: You know, I was sitting in a café the other day. I happened to be sitting at the same table as this woman. Well, we started to . . . we started to pick up a bit of a conversation. I don't know . . . about her holiday, it was, where she'd been. She'd been down to the south coast. I can't remember where though. Anyway, we were just sitting there, having this bit of a conversation . . . then suddenly she put her hand over to mine . . . and she said, how would you like me to have a look at your body?

DAVIES: Get out of it.

Pause.

ASTON: Yes. To come out with it just like that, in the middle of this conversation. Struck me as a bit odd.

DAVIES: They've said the same thing to me.

ASTON: Have they?

DAVIES: Women? There's many a time when they've come up to me and asked me more or less the same question.

Pause.

ASTON: No, your other name, your real name, what's that?
DAVIES: Davies. Mac Davies. That's my real name.
ASTON: Welsh, are you?
DAVIES: Eh?
ASTON: You Welsh?

Pause.

DAVIES: Well, I been around, you know . . . what I mean . . . I been about. . . .
ASTON: Where were you born then?
DAVIES (*darkly*) : What do you mean?
ASTON: Where were you born?
DAVIES: I was . . . uh . . . oh, it's a bit hard, like, to set your mind back . . . see what I mean . . . going back . . . a good way . . . lose a bit of track, like . . . you know. . . .
ASTON (*going to below the fireplace*) : See this plug? Switch it on here, if you like. This little fire.
DAVIES: Right, mister.
ASTON: Just plug in here.
DAVIES: Right, mister.

ASTON *goes towards the door.*

(*Anxiously.*) What do I do?
ASTON: Just switch it on, that's all. The fire'll come on.
DAVIES: I tell you what. I won't bother about it.
ASTON: No trouble.
DAVIES: No, I don't go in for them things much.
ASTON: Should work. (*Turning.*) Right.
DAVIES: Eh, I was going to ask you, mister, what about this stove? I mean, do you think it's going to be letting out any . . . what do you think?

ASTON: It's not connected.

DAVIES: You see, the trouble is, it's right on top of my bed, you see . . . What I got to watch is nudging . . . one of them gas taps with my elbow when I get up, you get my meaning?

(He goes round to the other side of stove and examines it.)

ASTON: There's nothing to worry about.

DAVIES: Now look here, don't you worry about it. All I'll do, I'll keep an eye on these taps every now and again, like, you see. See they're switched off. You leave it to me.

ASTON: I don't think. . . .

DAVIES *(coming round)*: Eh, mister, just one thing . . . eh . . . you couldn't slip me a couple of bob, for a cup of tea, just, you know?

ASTON: I gave you a few bob last night.

DAVIES: Eh, so you did. So you did. I forgot. Went clean out of my mind. That's right. Thank you, mister. Listen. You're sure now, you're sure you don't mind me staying here? I mean, I'm not the sort of man who wants to take any liberties.

ASTON: No, that's all right.

DAVIES: I might get down to Wembley later on in the day.

ASTON: Uh-uh.

DAVIES: There's a caff down there, you see, might be able to get fixed up there. I was there, see? I know they were a bit short-handed. They might be in the need of a bit of staff.

ASTON: When was that?

DAVIES: Eh? Oh, well, that was . . . near on . . . that'll be . . . that'll be a little while ago now. But of course what it is, they can't find the right kind of people in these places. What they want to do, they're trying to do away with these foreigners, you see, in catering. I mean, that's what they're aiming at. That's one thing I know for a fact.

ASTON: Hmmn.

DAVIES: See, I was thinking, once I got down there, I might have a look in at the stadium, at Wembley Stadium. For all the big matches, get my meaning? They need people down there to run the ground, see, to keep the ground. Or another thing I could do, I could go along down there to Kennington Oval. All these big sports grounds, it stands to reason, they need people, to keep the ground, that's what they want, that's what they're crying out for. It's only common sense, en't? Oh, I got all that under way . . . that's . . . uh . . . that's . . . what I'll be doing.

Pause.

If only I could get down there.
ASTON: Mmnn. (ASTON *moves to the door.*) Well, I'll be seeing you then.
DAVIES: Yes. Right.

ASTON *goes out and closes the door.*
DAVIES *stands still. He waits a few seconds, then goes to the door, opens it, looks out, closes it, stands with his back to it, turns swiftly, opens it, looks out, comes back, closes the door, finds the keys in his pocket, tries one, tries the other, locks the door. He looks about the room. He then goes quickly to* ASTON'S *bed, bends and brings out the pair of shoes. He takes off his sandals and puts his shoes on, then walks up and down, shaking his feet and swinging his legs. He presses the leather against his toes.*

Not a bad pair of shoes. Bit pointed.

He takes the shoes off and puts them back under the bed. He examines the area by ASTON'S *bed, picks up a vase and looks into it, then picks up a box and shakes it.*

Screws!

He sees paint buckets at the top of the bed, goes to them, and examines them.

Paint. What's he going to paint?

He puts the bucket down, comes to the centre of the room, looks up at bucket, and grimaces.

I'll have to find out about that. (*He crosses right, and picks up a blow-lamp.*) He's got some stuff in here. (*He picks up the Buddha and looks at it.*) Full of stuff. Look at all this.

He stands, looking. A key turns in the door, very softly. The door opens. DAVIES *moves forward and stubs his toe on a box. He cries out, clutches his toe, and half turns. The door is pulled to, swiftly, but not closed.* DAVIES *puts the Buddha into a sideboard drawer and massages his toe.*

Bugger it! Bloody box! (*His eye falls on the piles of papers.*) What's he got all those papers for? Damn pile of papers.

He goes to a pile and touches it. The pile wobbles. He steadies it.

Hold it, hold it!

He holds the pile and pushes the papers back into place. The door opens.
MICK *comes in, puts the key in his pocket, and closes the door silently. He stands at the door and watches* DAVIES.

What's he got all these papers for? (DAVIES *climbs over the rolled carpet to the blue case.*) Had a sheet and pillow ready in here. (*He opens the case.*) Nothing. (*He shuts the case.*) Still, I had a sleep though. I don't make no noises. (*He looks at the window.*) He could close that window. That sack's no good. I'll tell him. What's this?

He picks up another case and tries to open it. MICK *moves upstage, silently.*

Locked. (*He puts it down and moves downstage.*) Must be something in it. (*He picks up a sideboard drawer, rummages in the contents, then puts it down.*)

MICK *slides across the room.*
DAVIES *half turns,* MICK *seizes his arm and forces it up his back.* DAVIES *screams.*

Uuuuuuuhhh! Uuuuuuuhhh! What! What! What! Uuuuuuuhhhh!

MICK *swiftly forces him to the floor, with* DAVIES *struggling, grimacing, whimpering and staring.*
MICK *holds his arm, puts his other hand to his lips, then puts his hand to* DAVIES' *lips.* DAVIES *quietens.* MICK *lets him go.* DAVIES *writhes.* MICK *holds out a warning finger. He then squats down to regard* DAVIES. *He regards him, then stands looking down on him.* DAVIES *massages his arm, watching* MICK. MICK *turns slowly to look at the room. He goes to* DAVIES' *bed and uncovers it. He turns, goes to the clothes horse and picks up* DAVIES' *trousers.* DAVIES *starts to rise.* MICK *presses him down with his foot and stands over him. Finally he removes his foot. He examines the trousers and throws them back.* DAVIES *remains on the floor, crouched.* MICK *slowly goes to the chair, sits, and watches* DAVIES, *expressionless.*
Silence.

MICK: What's the game?

Curtain.

ACT TWO

A few seconds later.
     MICK *is seated,* DAVIES *on the floor, half seated, crouched.*
Silence.

MICK: Well?
DAVIES: Nothing, nothing. Nothing.

     A drip sounds in the bucket overhead. They look up. MICK
     looks back to DAVIES.

MICK: What's your name?
DAVIES: I don't know you. I don't know who you are.

     Pause.

MICK: Eh?
DAVIES: Jenkins.
MICK: Jenkins?
DAVIES: Yes.
MICK: Jen . . . kins.

     Pause.

You sleep here last night?
DAVIES: Yes.
MICK: Sleep well?
DAVIES: Yes.
MICK: I'm awfully glad. It's awfully nice to meet you.

     Pause.

What did you say your name was?
DAVIES: Jenkins.
MICK: I beg your pardon?
DAVIES: Jenkins!

Pause.

MICK: Jen . . . kins.

A drip sounds in the bucket. DAVIES *looks up.*

You remind me of my uncle's brother. He was always on the
move, that man. Never without his passport. Had an eye for
the girls. Very much your build. Bit of an athlete. Long-
jump specialist. He had a habit of demonstrating different
run-ups in the drawing-room round about Christmas time.
Had a penchant for nuts. That's what it was. Nothing else
but a penchant. Couldn't eat enough of them. Peanuts,
walnuts, brazil nuts, monkey nuts, wouldn't touch a piece of
fruit cake. Had a marvellous stop-watch. Picked it up in
Hong Kong. The day after they chucked him out of the
Salvation Army. Used to go in number four for Beckenham
Reserves. That was before he got his Gold Medal. Had
a funny habit of carrying his fiddle on his back. Like a
papoose. I think there was a bit of the Red Indian in him.
To be honest, I've never made out how he came to be my
uncle's brother. I've often thought that maybe it was the
other way round. I mean that my uncle was his brother and
he was my uncle. But I never called him uncle. As a matter
of fact I called him Sid. My mother called him Sid too.
It was a funny business. Your spitting image he was. Married a Chinaman and went to Jamaica.

Pause.

I hope you slept well last night.
DAVIES: Listen! I don't know who you are!

MICK: What bed you sleep in?

DAVIES: Now look here—

MICK: Eh?

DAVIES: That one.

MICK: Not the other one?

DAVIES: No.

MICK: Choosy.

Pause.

How do you like my room?

DAVIES: Your room?

MICK: Yes.

DAVIES: This ain't your room. I don't know who you are. I ain't never seen you before.

MICK: You know, believe it or not, you've got a funny kind of resemblance to a bloke I once knew in Shoreditch. Actually he lived in Aldgate. I was staying with a cousin in Camden Town. This chap, he used to have a pitch in Finsbury Park, just by the bus depot. When I got to know him I found out he was brought up in Putney. That didn't make any difference to me. I know quite a few people who were born in Putney. Even if they weren't born in Putney they were born in Fulham. The only trouble was, he wasn't born in Putney, he was only brought up in Putney. It turned out he was born in the Caledonian Road, just before you get to the Nag's Head. His old mum was still living at the Angel. All the buses passed right by the door. She could get a 38, 581, 30 or 38A, take her down the Essex Road to Dalston Junction in next to no time. Well, of course, if she got the 30 he'd take her up Upper Street way, round by Highbury Corner and down to St. Paul's Church, but she'd get to Dalston Junction just the same in the end. I used to leave my bike in her garden on my way to work. Yes, it was a curious affair. Dead spit of you he was. Bit bigger round the nose but there was nothing in it.

Pause.

Did you sleep here last night?
DAVIES: Yes.
MICK: Sleep well?
DAVIES: Yes!
MICK: Did you have to get up in the night?
DAVIES: No!

Pause.

MICK: What's your name?
DAVIES *(shifting, about to rise)* : Now look here!
MICK: What?
DAVIES: Jenkins!
MICK: Jen . . . kins.

DAVIES *makes a sudden movement to rise. A violent bellow
from* MICK *sends him back.*

(A shout.) Sleep here last night?
DAVIES: Yes. . . .
MICK *(continuing at a great pace)* : How'd you sleep?
DAVIES: I slept——
MICK: Sleep well?
DAVIES: Now look—
MICK: What bed?
DAVIES: That—
MICK: Not the other?
DAVIES: No!
MICK: Choosy.

Pause.

(Quietly.) Choosy.

Pause.

(Again amiable.) What sort of sleep did you have in that
bed?

DAVIES (*banging the floor*) : All right!
MICK: You weren't uncomfortable?
DAVIES (*groaning*) : All right!

MICK *stands, and moves to him.*

MICK: You a foreigner?
DAVIES: No.
MICK: Born and bred in the British Isles?
DAVIES: I was!
MICK: What did they teach you?

Pause.

How did you like my bed?

Pause.

That's my bed. You want to mind you don't catch a draught.
DAVIES: From the bed?
MICK: No, now, up your arse.

DAVIES *stares warily at* MICK, *who turns.* DAVIES *scrambles to the clothes horse and seizes his trousers.* MICK *turns swiftly and grabs them.* DAVIES *lunges for them.* MICK *holds out a hand, warningly.*

You intending to settle down here?
DAVIES: Give me my trousers then.
MICK: You settling down for a long stay?
DAVIES: Give me my bloody trousers!
MICK: Why, where you going?
DAVIES: Give me and I'm going, I'm going to Sidcup!

MICK *flicks the trousers in* DAVIES' *face several times.*
DAVIES *retreats.*
Pause.

MICK: You know, you remind me of a bloke I bumped into once, just the other side of the Guildford by-pass—
DAVIES: I was brought here!

Pause.

MICK: Pardon?
DAVIES: I was brought here! I was brought here!
MICK: Brought here? Who brought you here?
DAVIES: Man who lives here . . . he. . . .

Pause.

MICK: Fibber.
DAVIES: I was brought here, last night . . . met him in a caff . . . I was working . . . I got the bullet . . . I was working there . . . bloke saved me from a punch up, brought me here, brought me right here.

Pause.

MICK: I'm afraid you're a born fibber, en't you? You're speaking to the owner. This is my room. You're standing in my house.
DAVIES: It's his . . . he seen me all right . . . he. . . .
MICK (*pointing to* DAVIES' *bed*) : That's my bed.
DAVIES: What about that, then?
MICK: That's my mother's bed.
DAVIES: Well she wasn't in it last night!
MICK (*moving to him*): Now don't get perky, son, don't get perky. Keep your hands off my old mum.
DAVIES: I ain't . . . I haven't. . . .
MICK: Don't get out of your depth, friend, don't start taking liberties with my old mother, let's have a bit of respect.
DAVIES: I got respect, you won't find anyone with more respect.
MICK: Well, stop telling me all these fibs.
DAVIES: Now listen to me, I never seen you before, have I?
MICK: Never seen my mother before either, I suppose?

Pause.

I think I'm coming to the conclusion that you're an old
rogue. You're nothing but an old scoundrel.

DAVIES: Now wait—

MICK: Listen, son. Listen, sonny. You stink.

DAVIES: You ain't got no right to—

MICK: You're stinking the place out. You're an old robber,
there's no getting away from it. You're an old skate. You
don't belong in a nice place like this. You're an old barbarian. Honest. You got no business wandering about in an
unfurnished flat. I could charge seven quid a week for this
if I wanted to. Get a taker tomorrow. Three hundred and
fifty a year exclusive. No argument. I mean, if that sort of
money's in your range don't be afraid to say so. Here you
are. Furniture and fittings, I'll take four hundred or the
nearest offer. Rateable value ninety quid for the annum.
You can reckon water, heating and lighting at close on fifty.
That'll cost you eight hundred and ninety if you're all that
keen. Say the word and I'll have my solicitors draft you out
a contract. Otherwise I've got the van outside, I can run you
to the police station in five minutes, have you in for tres-
passing, loitering with intent, daylight robbery, filching,
thieving and stinking the place out. What do you say?
Unless you're really keen on a straightforward purchase. Of
course, I'll get my brother to decorate it up for you first.
I've got a brother who's a number one decorator. He'll decorate it up for you. If you want more space, there's four
more rooms along the landing ready to go. Bathroom, living-
room, bedroom and nursery. You can have this as your study.
This brother I mentioned, he's just about to start on the
other rooms. Yes, just about to start. So what do you say?
Eight hundred odd for this room or three thousand down
for the whole upper storey. On the other hand, if you prefer
to approach it in the long-term way I know an insurance
firm in West Ham'll be pleased to handle the deal for you.
No strings attached, open and above board, untarnished

record; twenty per cent interest, fifty per cent deposit; down payments, back payments, family allowances, bonus schemes, remission of term for good behaviour, six months lease, yearly examination of the relevant archives, tea laid on, disposal of shares, benefit extension, compensation on cessation, comprehensive indemnity against Riot, Civil Commotion, Labour Disturbances, Storm, Tempest, Thunderbolt, Larceny or Cattle all subject to a daily check and double check. Of course we'd need a signed declaration from your personal medical attendant as assurance that you possess the requisite fitness to carry the can, won't we? Who do you bank with?

Pause.

Who do you bank with?

The door opens. ASTON *comes in.* MICK *turns and drops the trousers.* DAVIES *picks them up and puts them on.* ASTON, *after a glance at the other two, goes to his bed, places a bag which he is carrying on it, sits down and resumes fixing the toaster.* DAVIES *retreats to his corner.* MICK *sits in the chair. Silence.*
A drip sounds in the bucket. They all look up.
Silence.

You still got that leak.
ASTON: Yes.

Pause.

It's coming from the roof.
MICK: From the roof, eh?
ASTON: Yes.

Pause.

I'll have to tar it over.

MICK: You're going to tar it over?
ASTON: Yes.
MICK: What?
ASTON: The cracks.

Pause.

MICK: You'll be tarring over the cracks on the roof.
ASTON: Yes.

Pause.

MICK: Think that'll do it?
ASTON: It'll do it, for the time being.
MICK: Uh.

Pause.

DAVIES (*abruptly*) : What do you do—?

They both look at him.

What do you do . . . when that bucket's full?

Pause.

ASTON: Empty it.

Pause.

MICK: I was telling my friend you were about to start decorating
the other rooms.
ASTON: Yes.

Pause.

(*To* DAVIES.) I got your bag.

DAVIES: Oh. (*Crossing to him and taking it.*) Oh thanks, mister, thanks. Give it to you, did they?

DAVIES *crosses back with the bag.*
MICK *rises and snatches it.*

MICK: What's this?
DAVIES: Give us it, that's my bag!
MICK (*warding him off*) : I've seen this bag before.
DAVIES: That's my bag!
MICK (*eluding him*) : This bag's very familiar.
DAVIES: What do you mean?
MICK: Where'd you get it?
ASTON (*rising, to them*) : Scrub it.
DAVIES: That's mine.
MICK: Whose?
DAVIES: It's mine! Tell him it's mine!
MICK: This your bag?
DAVIES: Give me it!
ASTON: Give it to him.
MICK: What? Give him what?
DAVIES: That bloody bag!
MICK (*slipping it behind the gas stove*) : What bag? (*To* DAVIES.) What bag?
DAVIES (*moving*) : Look here!
MICK (*facing him*) : Where you going?
DAVIES: I'm going to get . . . my old . . .
MICK: Watch your step, sonny! You're knocking at the door when no one's at home. Don't push it too hard. You come busting into a private house, laying your hands on anything you can lay your hands on. Don't overstep the mark, son.

ASTON *picks up the bag.*

DAVIES: You thieving bastard . . . you thieving skate . . . let me get my——
ASTON: Here you are. (ASTON *offers the bag to* DAVIES.)

MICK *grabs it.* ASTON *takes it.*
MICK *grabs it.* DAVIES *reaches for it.*
ASTON *takes it.* MICK *reaches for it.*
ASTON *gives it to* DAVIES. MICK *grabs it.*
Pause.
ASTON *takes it.* DAVIES *takes it.* MICK *takes it.* DAVIES *reaches for it.* ASTON *takes it.*
Pause.
ASTON *gives it to* MICK. MICK *gives it to* DAVIES.
DAVIES *grasps it to him.*
Pause.
MICK *looks at* ASTON. DAVIES *moves away with the bag. He drops it.*
Pause.
They watch him. He picks it up. Goes to his bed, and sits. ASTON *goes to his bed, sits, and begins to roll a cigarette.* MICK *stands still.*
Pause.
A drip sounds in the bucket. They all look up.
Pause.

How did you get on at Wembley?
DAVIES: Well, I didn't get down there.

Pause.

No. I couldn't make it.

MICK *goes to the door and exits.*

ASTON: I had a bit of bad luck with that jig saw. When I got there it had gone.

Pause.

DAVIES: Who was that feller?
ASTON: He's my brother.

DAVIES: Is he? He's a bit of a joker, en' he?
ASTON: Uh.
DAVIES: Yes . . . he's a real joker.
ASTON: He's got a sense of humour.
DAVIES: Yes, I noticed.

Pause.

He's a real joker, that lad, you can see that.

Pause.

ASTON: Yes, he tends . . . he tends to see the funny side of things.
DAVIES: Well, he's got a sense of humour, en' he?
ASTON: Yes.
DAVIES: Yes, you could tell that.

Pause.

I could tell the first time I saw him he had his own way of
looking at things.

ASTON *stands, goes to the sideboard drawer, right, picks up
the statue of Buddha, and puts it on the gas stove.*

ASTON: I'm supposed to be doing up the upper part of the house
for him.
DAVIES: What . . . you mean . . . you mean it's his house?
ASTON: Yes. I'm supposed to be decorating this landing for him.
Make a flat out of it.
DAVIES: What does he do, then?
ASTON: He's in the building trade. He's got his own van.
DAVIES: He don't live here, do he?
ASTON: Once I get that shed up outside . . . I'll be able to give a
bit more thought to the flat, you see. Perhaps I can knock
up one or two things for it. (*He walks to the window.*)

I can work with my hands, you see. That's one thing I can do. I never knew I could. But I can do all sorts of things now, with my hands. You know, manual things. When I get that shed up out there . . . I'll have a workshop, you see. I . . . could do a bit of woodwork. Simple woodwork, to start. Working with . . . good wood.

Pause.

Of course, there's a lot to be done to this place. What I think, though, I think I'll put in a partition . . . in one of the rooms along the landing. I think it'll take it. You know . . . they've got these screens . . . you know . . . Oriental. They break up a room with them. Make it into two parts. I could either do that or I could have a partition. I could knock them up, you see, if I had a workshop.

Pause.

Anyway, I think I've decided on the partition.

Pause.

DAVIES: Eh, look here, I been thinking. This ain't my bag.
ASTON: Oh. No.
DAVIES: No, this ain't my bag. My bag, it was another kind of bag altogether, you see. I know what they've done. What they done, they kept my bag, and they given you another one altogether.
ASTON: No . . . what happened was, someone had gone off with your bag.
DAVIES (*rising*): That's what I said!
ASTON: Anyway, I picked that bag up somewhere else. It's got a few . . . pieces of clothes in it too. He let me have the whole lot cheap.
DAVIES (*opening the bag*): Any shoes?

DAVIES *takes two check shirts, bright red and bright green, from the bag. He holds them up.*

Check.

ASTON: Yes.

DAVIES: Yes . . . well, I know about these sort of shirts, you see. Shirts like these, they don't go far in the wintertime. I mean, that's one thing I know for a fact. No, what I need, is a kind of a shirt with stripes, a good solid shirt, with stripes going down. That's what I want. (*He takes from the bag a deep-red velvet smoking-jacket.*) What's this?

ASTON: It's a smoking-jacket.

DAVIES: A smoking-jacket? (*He feels it.*) This ain't a bad piece of cloth. I'll see how it fits.

He tries it on.

You ain't got a mirror here, have you?

ASTON: I don't think I have.

DAVIES: Well, it don't fit too bad. How do you think it looks?

ASTON: Looks all right.

DAVIES: Well, I won't say no to this, then.

ASTON *picks up the plug and examines it.*

No, I wouldn't say no to this.

Pause.

ASTON: You could be . . . caretaker here, if you liked.

DAVIES: What?

ASTON: You could . . . look after the place, if you liked . . . you know, the stairs and the landing, the front steps, keep an eye on it. Polish the bells.

DAVIES: Bells?

ASTON: I'll be fixing a few, down by the front door. Brass.

DAVIES: Caretaking, eh?

ASTON: Yes.

DAVIES: Well, I . . . I never done caretaking before, you know . . . I mean to say . . . I never . . . what I mean to say is . . . I never been a caretaker before.

Pause.

ASTON: How do you feel about being one, then?

DAVIES: Well, I reckon . . . Well, I'd have to know . . . you know. . . .

ASTON: What sort of. . . .

DAVIES: Yes, what sort of . . . you know. . . .

Pause.

ASTON: Well, I mean. . . .

DAVIES: I mean, I'd have to . . . I'd have to. . . .

ASTON: Well, I could tell you. . . .

DAVIES: That's . . . that's it . . . you see . . . you get my meaning?

ASTON: When the time comes. . . .

DAVIES: I mean, that's what I'm getting at, you see. . . .

ASTON: More or less exactly what you. . . .

DAVIES: You see, what I mean to say . . . what I'm getting at is . . . I mean, what sort of jobs. . . .

Pause.

ASTON: Well, there's things like the stairs . . . and the . . . the bells. . . .

DAVIES: But it'd be a matter . . . wouldn't it . . . it'd be a matter of a broom . . . isn't it?

ASTON: You could have a duster. . . .

DAVIES: Oh, I know I could have that . . . but I couldn't manage without a . . . without a broom . . . could I?

ASTON: You'd have to have a broom. . . .

DAVIES: That's it . . . that's just what I was thinking. . . .

ASTON: I'd be able to pick one up for you, without much trouble
. . . and of course, you'd . . . you'd need a few brushes. . . .

DAVIES: You'd need implements . . . you see . . . you'd need a
good few implements. . . .

ASTON: I could teach you how to use the electrolux, if you
. . . wanted to learn. . . .

DAVIES: Ah, that'd be. . . .

ASTON *takes a white overall from a nail over his bed, and*
shows it to DAVIES.

ASTON: You could wear this, if you liked.

DAVIES: Well . . . that's nice, en't?

ASTON: It'd keep the dust off.

DAVIES (*putting it on*): Yes, this'd keep the dust off, all right.
Well off. Thanks very much, mister.

ASTON: You see, what we could do, we could . . . I could fit a
bell at the bottom, outside the front door, with "Caretaker"
on it. And you could answer any queries.

DAVIES: Oh, I don't know about that.

ASTON: Why not?

DAVIES: Well, I mean, you don't know who might come up them
front steps, do you? I got to be a bit careful.

ASTON: Why, someone after you?

DAVIES: After me? Well, I could have that Scotch git coming
looking after me, couldn't I? All I'd do, I'd hear the bell. I'd
go down there, open the door, who might be there, any
Harry might be there. I could be buggered as easy as that,
man. They might be there after my card, I mean look at it,
here I am, I only got four stamps, on this card, here it is,
look, four stamps, that's all I got, I ain't got any more, that's
all I got, they ring the bell called Caretaker, they'd have
me in, that's what they'd do, I wouldn't stand a chance. Of
course I got plenty of other cards lying about, but they
don't know that, and I can't tell them, can I, because then
they'd find out I was going about under an assumed name.
You see, the name I call myself now, that's not my real
name. My real name's not the one I'm using, you see. It's

different. You see, the name I go under now ain't my real
one. It's assumed.

Silence.
THE LIGHTS FADE TO BLACKOUT.
THEN UP TO DIM LIGHT THROUGH THE WINDOW.
A door bangs.
Sound of a key in the door of the room.
DAVIES *enters, closes the door, and tries the light switch, on,*
off, on, off.

DAVIES *(muttering)*: What's this? *(He switches on and off.)*
What's the matter with this damn light? *(He switches on
and off.)* Aaah. Don't tell me the damn light's gone now.

Pause.

What'll I do? Damn light's gone now. Can't see a thing.

Pause.

What'll I do now? *(He moves, stumbles.)* Ah God, what's
that? Give me a light. Wait a minute.

*He feels for matches in his pocket, takes out a box and
lights one. The match goes out. The box falls.*

Aah! Where is it? *(Stooping.)* Where's the bloody box?

The box is kicked.

What's that? What? Who's that? What's that?

Pause. He moves.

Where's my box? It was down here. Who's this? Who's
moving it?

Silence.

Come on. Who's this? Who's this got my box?

Pause.

Who's in here!

Pause.

I got a knife here. I'm ready. Come on then, who are you?

He moves, stumbles, falls and cries out.
Silence.
A faint whimper from DAVIES. *He gets up.*

All right!

He stands. Heavy breathing.
Suddenly the electrolux starts to hum. A figure moves with it, guiding it. The nozzle moves along the floor after DAVIES, *who skips, dives away from it and falls, breathlessly.*

Ah, ah, ah, ah, ah, ah! Get away-y-y-y-y!

The electrolux stops. The figure jumps on ASTON's *bed.*

I'm ready for you! I'm . . . I'm . . . I'm here!

The figure takes out the electrolux plug from the light socket and fits the bulb. The light goes on. DAVIES *flattens himself against right wall, knife in hand.* MICK *stands on the bed, holding the plug.*

MICK: I was just doing some spring cleaning. (*He gets down.*)
There used to be a wall plug for this electrolux. But it
doesn't work. I had to fit it in the light socket. (*He puts the*

electrolux under ASTON's *bed.*) How do you think the place is looking? I gave it a good going over.

Pause.

We take it in turns, once a fortnight, my brother and me, to give the place a thorough going over. I was working late tonight, I only just got here. But I thought I better get on with it, as it's my turn.

Pause.

It's not that I actually live here. I don't. As a matter of fact I live somewhere else. But after all, I'm responsible for the upkeep of the premises, en' I? Can't help being house-proud.

He moves towards DAVIES *and indicates the knife.*

What are you waving that about for?

DAVIES: You come near me. . . .

MICK: I'm sorry if I gave you a start. But I had you in mind too, you know. I mean, my brother's guest. We got to think of your comfort, en't we? Don't want the dust to get up your nose. How long you thinking of staying here, by the way? As a matter of fact, I was going to suggest that we'd lower your rent, make it just a nominal sum, I mean until you get fixed up. Just nominal, that's all.

Pause.

Still, if you're going to be spiky, I'll have to reconsider the whole proposition.

DAVIES *goes slowly to his bed.*

MICK, *turning, watches.* DAVIES *sits, with his knife.*

Eh, you're not thinking of doing any violence on me, are you? You're not the violent sort, are you?

DAVIES (*vehemently*): I keep myself to myself, mate. But if anyone starts with me though, they know what they got coming.

MICK: I can believe that.

DAVIES: You do. I been all over, see? You understand my meaning? I don't mind a bit of a joke now and then, but anyone'll tell you . . . that no one starts anything with me.

MICK: I get what you mean, yes.

DAVIES: I can be pushed so far . . . but. . . .

MICK: No further.

DAVIES: That's it.

MICK *sits on the head of* DAVIES' *bed.*

What you doing?

MICK: No, I just want to say that . . . I'm very impressed by that.

DAVIES: Eh?

MICK: I'm very impressed by what you've just said.

Pause.

Yes, that's impressive, that is.

Pause.

I'm impressed, anyway.

DAVIES: You know what I'm talking about, then?

MICK: Yes, I know. I think we understand one another.

DAVIES: Uh? Well . . . I'll tell you . . . I'd . . . I'd like to think that. You been playing me about, you know. I don't know why. I never done you no harm.

MICK: No, you know what it was? We just got off on the wrong foot. That's all it was.

DAVIES: Ay, we did.

MICK: Like a sandwich?

DAVIES: What?

MICK (*taking a sandwich from his pocket*) : Have one of these.

DAVIES: Don't you pull anything.

MICK: No, you're still not understanding me. I can't help being interested in any friend of my brother's. I mean, you're my brother's friend, aren't you?

DAVIES: Well, I . . . I wouldn't put it as far as that.

MICK: Don't you find him friendly, then?

DAVIES: Well, I wouldn't say we was all that friends. I mean, he done me no harm, but I wouldn't say he was any particular friend of mine. What's in that sandwich, then?

MICK: Cheese.

DAVIES: That'll do me.

MICK: Take one.

DAVIES: Thank you, mister.

MICK: I'm sorry to hear my brother's not very friendly.

DAVIES: He's friendly, he's friendly, I didn't say he wasn't. . . .

MICK (*taking a salt-cellar from his pocket*) : Salt?

DAVIES: No thanks. (*He munches the sandwich.*) I just can't exactly . . . make him out.

MICK (*feeling in his pocket*) : I forgot the pepper.

DAVIES: Just can't get the hang of him, that's all.

MICK: I had a bit of beetroot somewhere. Must have mislaid it.

Pause.

DAVIES *chews the sandwich.* MICK *watches him eat. He then rises and strolls downstage.*

Uuh . . . listen . . . can I ask your advice? I mean, you're a man of the world. Can I ask your advice about something?

DAVIES: You go right ahead.

MICK: Well, what it is, you see, I'm . . . I'm a bit worried about my brother.

DAVIES: Your brother?

MICK: Yes . . . you see, his trouble is. . . .

DAVIES: What?

MICK: Well, it's not a very nice thing to say. . . .

DAVIES (*rising, coming downstage*): Go on now, you say it.

MICK *looks at him.*

MICK: He doesn't like work.

Pause.

DAVIES: Go on!

MICK: No, he just doesn't like work, that's his trouble.

DAVIES: Is that a fact?

MICK: It's a terrible thing to have to say about your own brother.

DAVIES: Ay.

MICK: He's just shy of it. Very shy of it.

DAVIES: I know that sort.

MICK: You know the type?

DAVIES: I've met them.

MICK: I mean, I want to get him going in the world.

DAVIES: Stands to reason, man.

MICK: If you got an older brother you want to push him on, you want to see him make his way. Can't have him idle, he's only doing himself harm. That's what I say.

DAVIES: Yes.

MICK: But he won't buckle down to the job.

DAVIES: He don't like work.

MICK: Work shy.

DAVIES: Sounds like it to me.

MICK: You've met the type, have you?

DAVIES: Me? I know that sort.

MICK: Yes.

DAVIES: I know that sort. I've met them.

MICK: Causing me great anxiety. You see, I'm a working man, I'm a tradesman. I've got my own van.

DAVIES: Is that a fact?

MICK: He's supposed to be doing a little job for me . . . I keep him here to do a little job . . . but I don't know . . . I'm coming to the conclusion he's a slow worker.

Pause.

What would your advice be?
DAVIES: Well . . . he's a funny bloke, your brother.
MICK: What?
DAVIES: I was saying, he's . . . he's a bit of a funny bloke, your
brother.

MICK *stares at him.*

MICK: Funny? Why?
DAVIES: Well . . . he's funny. . . .
MICK: What's funny about him?

Pause.

DAVIES: Not liking work.
MICK: What's funny about that?
DAVIES: Nothing.

Pause.

MICK: I don't call it funny.
DAVIES: Nor me.
MICK: You don't want to start getting hypercritical.
DAVIES: No, no, I wasn't that, I wasn't . . . I was only saying. . . .
MICK: Don't get too glib.
DAVIES: Look, all I meant was—
MICK: Cut it! (*Briskly.*) Look! I got a proposition to make to
you. I'm thinking of taking over the running of this place,
you see? I think it could be run a bit more efficiently. I got
a lot of ideas, a lot of plans. (*He eyes* DAVIES.) How would
you like to stay on here, as caretaker?
DAVIES: What?
MICK: I'll be quite open with you. I could rely on a man like
you around the place, keeping an eye on things.
DAVIES: Well now . . . wait a minute . . . I . . . I ain't never done
no caretaking before, you know. . . .

MICK: Doesn't matter about that. It's just that you look a capable sort of man to me.

DAVIES: I am a capable sort of man. I mean to say, I've had plenty offers in my time, you know, there's no getting away from that.

MICK: Well, I could see before, when you took out that knife, that you wouldn't let anyone mess you about.

DAVIES: No one messes me about, man.

MICK: I mean, you've been in the services, haven't you?

DAVIES: The what?

MICK: You been in the services. You can tell by your stance.

DAVIES: Oh . . . yes. Spent half my life there, man. Overseas . . . like . . . serving . . . I was.

MICK: In the colonies, weren't you?

DAVIES: I was over there. I was one of the first over there.

MICK: That's it. You're just the man I been looking for.

DAVIES: What for?

MICK: Caretaker.

DAVIES: Yes, well . . . look . . . listen . . . who's the landlord here, him or you?

MICK: Me. I am. I got deeds to prove it.

DAVIES: Ah . . . (*Decisively.*) Well listen, I don't mind doing a bit of caretaking, I wouldn't mind looking after the place for you.

MICK: Of course, we'd come to a small financial agreement, mutually beneficial.

DAVIES: I leave you to reckon that out, like.

MICK: Thanks. There's only one thing.

DAVIES: What's that?

MICK: Can you give me any references?

DAVIES: Eh?

MICK: Just to satisfy my solicitor.

DAVIES: I got plenty of references. All I got to do is to go down to Sidcup tomorrow. I got all the references I want down there.

MICK: Where's that?

DAVIES: Sidcup. He ain't only got my references down there, he got all my papers down there. I know that place like the back of my hand. If I got down there I wouldn't just get my references, I'd get all my papers. I'm going down there anyway, see what I mean, I got to get down there, or I'm done.

MICK: So we can always get hold of these references if we want them.

DAVIES: I'll be down there any day, I tell you. I was going down today, but I'm . . . I'm waiting for the weather to break.

MICK: Ah.

DAVIES: Listen. You can't pick me up a pair of good shoes, can you? I got a bad need for a good pair of shoes. I can't get anywhere without a pair of good shoes, see? Do you think there's any chance of you being able to pick me up a pair?

THE LIGHTS FADE TO BLACKOUT.
LIGHTS UP. *Morning.*
ASTON *is pulling on his trousers over long underwear. A slight grimace. He looks around at the head of his bed, takes a towel from the rail and waves it about. He puts it down, goes to* DAVIES *and wakes him.* DAVIES *sits up abruptly.*

ASTON: You said you wanted me to get you up.

DAVIES: What for?

ASTON: You said you were thinking of going to Sidcup.

DAVIES: Ay, that'd be a good thing, if I got there.

ASTON: Doesn't look much of a day.

DAVIES: Ay, well, that's shot it, en't it?

ASTON: I . . . I didn't have a very good night again.

DAVIES: I slept terrible.

Pause.

ASTON: You were making. . . .

DAVIES: Terrible. Had a bit of rain in the night, didn't it?

ASTON: Just a bit.

He goes to his bed, picks up a small plank and begins to sandpaper it.

DAVIES: Thought so. Come in on my head.

Pause.

Draught's blowing right in on my head, anyway.

Pause.

Can't you close that window behind that sack?
ASTON: You could.
DAVIES: Well then, what about it, then? The rain's coming right in on my head.
ASTON: Got to have a bit of air.

DAVIES *gets out of bed. He is wearing his trousers, waistcoat and vest.*

DAVIES (*putting on his sandals*): Listen. I've lived all my life in the air, boy. You don't have to tell me about air. What I'm saying is, there's too much air coming in that window when I'm asleep.
ASTON: Gets very stuffy in here without that window open.

ASTON *crosses to the chair, puts the plank on it, and continues sandpapering.*

DAVIES: Yes, but listen, you don't know what I'm telling you. That bloody rain, man, come right in on my head. Spoils my sleep. I could catch my death of cold with it, with that draught. That's all I'm saying. Just shut that window and no one's going to catch any colds, that's all I'm saying.

Pause.

ASTON: I couldn't sleep in here without that window open.

DAVIES: Yes, but what about me? What . . . what you got to say about my position?

ASTON: Why don't you sleep the other way round?

DAVIES: What do you mean?

ASTON: Sleep with your feet to the window.

DAVIES: What good would that do?

ASTON: The rain wouldn't come in on your head.

DAVIES: No, I couldn't do that. I couldn't do that.

Pause.

I mean, I got used to sleeping this way. It isn't me has to change, it's that window. You see, it's raining now. Look at it. It's coming down now.

Pause.

Look at that roof, see? Look at that roof where the draught's coming through. It's coming through up there.

ASTON: Yes. There's no proper ceiling. (ASTON *crosses back to the bed with the plank.*)

DAVIES: No, I mean, you can tell that. There's no proper ceiling. That's why the wind's pouring through.

Slight pause.

ASTON: I think I'll have a walk down to Goldhawk Road. I got talking to a man there. He had a saw bench. It looked in pretty good condition to me. Don't think it's much good to him.

Pause.

Have a walk down there, I think.

DAVIES: No, you see, what I mean about this window, it's not just coming in on my head, it'll be coming in on my pillow. The wind blows right on it, you see. That pillow, it'll . . . it'll be like a piece of sponge in the morning.

ASTON: You want to sleep the other way round.
DAVIES: What do you mean?
ASTON: With your feet to the window.
DAVIES: I don't see what good that would do.
ASTON: The rain wouldn't come in on your head.
DAVIES: That may be so, that may be so.

Pause.

It'd come in on my feet, wouldn't it? It'd crawl up my body, wouldn't it? I'd be worse off still. As it is, it's only my head.

DAVIES *roams about the room.*

Listen to that. That's done my trip to Sidcup. Eh, what about closing that window now? It'll be coming in here.
ASTON: Close it for the time being.

DAVIES *closes the window and looks out.*

DAVIES: What's all that under that tarpaulin out there?
ASTON: Wood.
DAVIES: What for?
ASTON: To build my shed.

DAVIES *sits on his bed.*

DAVIES: You haven't come across that pair of shoes you was going to look out for me, have you?
ASTON: Oh. No. I'll see if I can pick some up today.
DAVIES: I can't go out in this with these, can I? I can't even go out and get a cup of tea.
ASTON: There's a café just along the road.
DAVIES: There may be, mate.

During ASTON'S *speech the room grows darker.*
By the close of the speech only ASTON *can be seen clearly.*
DAVIES *and all the objects are in the shadow.*

ASTON: I used to go there quite a bit. Oh, years ago now. But I
stopped. I used to like that place. Spent quite a bit of time
in there. That was before I went away. Just before. I think
that . . . place had a lot to do with it. They were all . . . a
good bit older than me. But they always used to listen. I
thought . . . they understood what I said. I mean I used to
talk to them. I talked too much. That was my mistake. The
same in the factory. Standing there, or in the breaks, I used
to . . . talk about things. But it all seemed all right. I mean,
some of these men, from the café, we used to knock about
together sometimes, I used to tag along on some of their
evenings. It was all right. And they used to listen, whenever
I . . . had anything to say. The trouble was, I used to have
kind of hallucinations. They weren't hallucinations, they
. . . I used to get the feeling I could see things . . . very
clearly . . . everything . . . was so clear . . . everything
used . . . everything used to get very quiet . . . everything
got very quiet . . . all this . . . quiet . . . and . . . this clear
sight . . . it was . . . but maybe I was wrong. Anyway, someone must have said something. I didn't know anything
about it. And . . . some kind of lie must have got around.
And this lie went round. I thought people started being
funny. In that café. The factory. I couldn't understand it.
Then one day they took me to a hospital, right outside
London. They . . . got me there. I didn't want to go. Anyway . . . I tried to get out, quite a few times. But . . . it
wasn't very easy. They asked me questions, in there. Got
me in and asked me all sorts of questions. Well, I told
them . . . anyone who asked . . . they all used to stand
round . . . I told them, when they wanted to know . . .
what my thoughts were. Hmmnn. Then one day . . . this
man . . . doctor, I suppose . . . the head one . . . he was
quite a man of . . . distinction . . . although I wasn't so
sure about that. He called me in. He said . . . he told me
I had something. He said they'd concluded their examination. That's what he said. And he showed me a pile of
papers and he said that I'd got something, some complaint. You see, I wish I could remember what it was. . . .

I've tried to remember. He said . . . he just said that, you see. You've got . . . this thing. That's your complaint. And we've decided, he said, that in your interests there's only one course we can take. He said . . . but I can't . . . exactly remember . . . how he put it . . . he said, we're going to do something to your brain. He said . . . if we don't, you'll be in here for the rest of your life, but if we do, you stand a chance. You can go out, he said, and live like the others. What do you want to do to my brain, I said to him. But he just repeated what he'd said. Well, I wasn't a fool. I knew I was a minor. I knew he couldn't do anything to me without getting permission. I knew he had to get permission from my mother. So I wrote to her and told her what they were trying to do. But she signed their form, you see, giving them permission. I know that because he showed me her signature when I brought it up. Well, that night I tried to escape, that night. I spent five hours sawing at one of the bars on the window in this ward. Right throughout the dark. They used to shine a torch over the beds every half hour. So I timed it just right. And then it was nearly done, and a man had a . . . he had a fit, right next to me. And they caught me, anyway. About a week later they started to come round and do this thing to the brain. We were all supposed to have it done, in this ward. And they came round and did it one at a time. One a night. I was one of the last. And I could see quite clearly what they did to the others. They used to come round with these . . . I don't know what they were . . . they looked like big pincers, with wires on, the wires were attached to a little machine. It was electric. They used to hold the man down, and this chief . . . the chief doctor, used to fit the pincers, something like earphones, he used to fit them on either side of the man's skull. There was a man holding the machine, you see, and he'd . . . he'd do something . . . I can't remember now whether he pressed a switch or turned something, just a matter of switching the current . . . I suppose it was, and the chief would just press these pincers on either side of the skull and keep them there. Then he'd take them off. They'd cover the man up . . . and they wouldn't touch him again until later on. Some used to put up a fight, but most of them didn't. They just lay there. Well, they were coming round to me, and the night they came I got up and stood against the wall. They told me to get on the bed, and I knew they had to get me on the bed because if they did it while I was standing up they might break my spine. So I stood up and then one or two of them came for me, well, I was younger then, I was much stronger than I am now, I was quite strong then, I laid one of them out and I had another one round the throat, and then suddenly this chief had these pincers on my skull and I knew he wasn't supposed to do it while I was standing up, that's why I . . . . . . anyway, he did it. So I did get out. I got out of the place. . . . but I couldn't walk very well. I don't think my spine was damaged. That was perfectly all right. The trouble was . . . my thoughts . . . had become very slow . . . I couldn't think at all . . . I . . . I couldn't . . . get . . . my thoughts . . . together . . . uuuhh . . . I could . . . never quite get it . . . together. The trouble was, I couldn't hear what people were saying. I couldn't look to the right or the left, I had to look straight in front of me, because if I turned my head round . . . I couldn't keep . . . upright. And I had these headaches. Then I went along to people, but they wanted to take me in, but I wasn't going to go in . . . anywhere. So I couldn't do any work, because I . . . I couldn't write any more, you see. I couldn't write my name. I used to sit in my room. That was when I lived with my mother. And my brother. He was younger than me. And I laid everything out, in order, in my room, all the things I knew were mine, but I didn't die. I never had those hallucinations any more. And I never spoke to anyone any more. The funny thing is, I can't remember much . . . about what I said, what I thought . . . I mean before I went into that place. The thing is, I should have been dead. I should have died. And then, anyway, after a time, I got a bit better, and I started to do things with my hands, and then about two years ago I came here, because my brother had got this house, and so I decided to have a go at decorating it, so I came into this room, and I started to collect wood, for my shed, and all these bits and pieces, that I thought might come in handy for the flat, or around the house, sometime. I feel much better now. But I don't talk to people now. I steer clear of places like that café. I never go into them now. I don't talk to anyone . . . like that. I've often thought of going back and trying to find the man who did that to me. But I want to do something first. I want to build that shed out in the garden.

Curtain.

ACT THREE

Two weeks later.
MICK *is lying on the floor, down left, his head resting on the*
rolled carpet, looking up at the ceiling.
DAVIES *is sitting in the chair, holding his pipe. He is wearing*
the smoking-jacket. It is afternoon.
Silence.

DAVIES: I got a feeling he's done something to them cracks.

Pause.

See, there's been plenty of rain in the last week, but it ain't
been dripping into the bucket.

Pause.

He must have tarred it over up there.

Pause.

There was someone walking about on the roof the other
night. It must have been him.

Pause.

I mean, that was dangerous, that bucket. It might have come
down on my head, any time of the day, whenever I happened to be standing there. I don't know as he's emptied it
now, do I?

Pause.

But I got a feeling he's tarred it over on the roof up there. Ain't said a word to me about it. Don't say a word to me.

Pause.

He don't answer me when I talk to him.

He lights a match, holds it to his pipe, and blows it.

He don't give me no knife!

Pause.

He don't give me no knife to cut my bread.

Pause.

How can I cut a loaf of bread without no knife?

Pause.

It's an impossibility.

Pause.

MICK: You've got a knife.
DAVIES: What?
MICK: You've got a knife.
DAVIES: I got a knife, sure I got a knife, but how do you expect me to cut a good loaf of bread with that? That's not a bread-knife. It's nothing to do with cutting bread. I picked it up somewhere. I don't know where it's been, do I? No, what I want—
MICK: I know what you want.

Pause. DAVIES *rises and goes to the gas stove.*

DAVIES: What about this gas stove? He tells me it's not connected. How do I know it's not connected? Here I am, I'm
sleeping right with it, I wake up in the middle of the night,
I'm looking right into the oven, man! It's right next to my
face, how do I know, I could be lying there in bed, it might
blow up, it might do me harm!

Pause.

But he don't seem to take any notice of what I say to him.
I told him the other day, see, I told him about them Blacks,
about them Blacks coming up from next door, and using the
lavatory. I told him, it was all dirty in there, all the banis-
ters were dirty, they were black, all the lavatory was black.
But what did he do? He's supposed to be in charge of it
here, he had nothing to say, he hadn't got a word to say.

Pause.

I mean, look at it, you and me, we got ideas for this place,
en't we? We could get going here. I'd be your caretaker,
we'd get things going. But he . . . he don't care about that,
he . . . he don't care about getting the place going. Couple
of week ago . . . he sat there, he give me a long chat . . .
about a couple of week ago. A long chat he give me. Since
then he ain't said hardly a word. He went on talking there
. . . I don't know what he was . . . he wasn't looking at
me, he wasn't talking to me, he don't care about me. He was
talking to himself! That's all he worries about. I mean, you
come up to me, you ask my advice, he wouldn't never do a
thing like that. I mean, we don't have any conversation,
you see? You can't live in the same room with someone
who . . . who don't have any conversation with you.

Pause.

I just can't get the hang of him.

Pause.

You and me, we could get this place going.

MICK (*ruminatively*): Yes, you're quite right. Look what I could do with this place.

Pause.

I could turn this place into a penthouse. For instance . . . this room. This room you could have as the kitchen. Right size, nice window, sun comes in. I'd have . . . I'd have teal-blue, copper and parchment linoleum squares. I'd have those colours re-echoed in the walls. I'd offset the kitchen units with charcoal-grey worktops. Plenty of room for cupboards for the crockery. We'd have a small wall cupboard, a large wall cupboard, a corner wall cupboard with revolving shelves. You wouldn't be short of cupboards. You could put the dining-room across the landing, see? Yes. Venetian blinds, venetian blinds on the window, cork floor, cork tiles. You could have an off-white pile linen rug, a table in . . . in afromosia teak veneer, sideboard with matt black drawers, curved chairs with cushioned seats, armchairs in oatmeal tweed, beech frame settee with woven sea-grass seat, white-topped heat-resistant coffee table, white tile surround. Yes. Then the bedroom. What's a bedroom? It's a retreat. It's a place to go for rest and peace. So you want quiet decoration. The lighting functional. Furniture . . . mahogany and rose-wood. Deep azure-blue carpet, unglazed blue and white curtains, a bedspread with a pattern of small blue roses on a white ground, dressing-table with a lift-up top containing a plastic tray, table lamp of white raffia . . . (MICK *sits up*) it wouldn't be a flat it'd be a palace.

DAVIES: I'd say it would, man.

MICK: A palace.

DAVIES: Who would live there?

MICK: I would. My brother and me.

Pause.

DAVIES: What about me?

MICK (*quietly*): All this junk here, it's no good to anyone. It's just a lot of old iron, that's all. Clobber. You couldn't make a home out of this. There's no way you could arrange it. It's junk. He could never sell it, either, he wouldn't get tuppence for it.

Pause.

Junk.

Pause.

But he doesn't seem to be interested in what I got in mind, that's the trouble. Why don't you have a chat with him, see if he's interested?

DAVIES: Me?

MICK: Yes. You're a friend of his.

DAVIES: He's no friend of mine.

MICK: You're living in the same room with him, en't you?

DAVIES: He's no friend of mine. You don't know where you are with him. I mean, with a bloke like you, you know where you are.

MICK *looks at him.*

I mean, you got your own ways, I'm not saying you ain't got your own ways, anyone can see that. You may have some funny ways, but that's the same with all of us, but with him it's different, see? I mean at least with you, the thing with you is you're . . .

MICK: Straightforward.

DAVIES: That's it, you're straightforward.

MICK: Yes.

DAVIES: But with him, you don't know what he's up to half the time!

MICK: Uh.

DAVIES: He's got no feelings!

Pause.

See, what I need is a clock! I need a clock to tell the time! How can I tell the time without a clock? I can't do it! I said to him, I said, look here, what about getting in a clock, so's I can tell what time it is? I mean, if you can't tell what time you're at you don't know where you are, you understand my meaning? See, what I got to do now, if I'm walking about outside, I got to get my eye on a clock, and keep the time in my head for when I come in. But that's no good, I mean I'm not in here five minutes and I forgotten it. I forgotten what time it was!

DAVIES *walks up and down the room.*

Look at it this way. If I don't feel well I have a bit of a lay down, then, when I wake up, I don't know what time it is to go and have a cup of tea! You see, it's not so bad when I'm coming in. I can see the clock on the corner, the moment I'm stepping into the house I know what the time is, but when I'm *in*! It's when I'm *in* . . . that I haven't the foggiest idea what time it is!

Pause.

No, what I need is a clock in here, in this room, and then I stand a bit of a chance. But he don't give me one.

DAVIES *sits in the chair.*

He wakes me up! He wakes me up in the middle of the night! Tells me I'm making noises! I tell you I've half a mind to give him a mouthful one of these days.
MICK: He don't let you sleep?
DAVIES: He don't let me sleep! He wakes me up!
MICK: That's terrible.
DAVIES: I been plenty of other places. They always let me sleep. It's the same the whole world over. Except here.

MICK: Sleep's essential. I've always said that.

DAVIES: You're right, it's essential. I get up in the morning, I'm worn out! I got business to see to. I got to move myself, I got to sort myself out, I got to get fixed up. But when I wake up in the morning I ain't got no energy in me. And on top of that I ain't got no clock.

MICK: Yes.

DAVIES (*standing, moving*) : He goes out, I don't know where he goes to, where's he go, he never tells me. We used to have a bit of a chat, not any more. I never see him, he goes out, he comes in late, next thing I know he's shoving me about in the middle of the night.

Pause.

Listen! I wake up in the morning . . . I wake up in the morning and he's smiling at me! He's standing there, look-ing at me, smiling! I can see him, you see, I can see him through the blanket. He puts on his coat, he turns himself round, he looks down at my bed, there's a smile on his face! What the hell's he smiling at? What he don't know is that I'm watching him through that blanket. He don't know that! He don't know I can see him, he thinks I'm asleep, but I got my eye on him all the time through that blanket, see? But he don't know that! He just looks at me and he smiles, but he don't know that I can see him doing it!

Pause.

(*Bending, close to* MICK.) No, what you want to do, you want to speak to him, see? I got . . . I got that worked out. You want to tell him . . . that we got ideas for his place, we could build it up, we could get it started. You see, I could decorate it out for you, I could give you a hand in doing it . . . between us.

Pause.

Where do you live now, then?

MICK: Me? Oh, I've got a little place. Not bad. Everything laid on. You must come up and have a drink some time. Listen to some music.

DAVIES: No, you see, you're the bloke who wants to talk to him. I mean, you're his brother.

Pause.

MICK: Yes . . . maybe I will.

A door bangs.
MICK *rises, goes to the door and exits.*

DAVIES: Where you going? This is him!

Silence.
DAVIES *stands, then goes to the window and looks out.*
ASTON *enters. He is carrying a paper bag. He takes off his overcoat, opens the bag and takes out a pair of shoes.*

ASTON: Pair of shoes.
DAVIES (*turning*): What?
ASTON: I picked them up. Try them.
DAVIES: Shoes? What sort?
ASTON: They might do you.

DAVIES *comes downstage, takes off his sandals and tries the shoes on. He walks about, waggling his feet, bends, and presses the leather.*

DAVIES: No, they're not right.
ASTON: Aren't they?
DAVIES: No, they don't fit.
ASTON: Mmnn.

Pause.

DAVIES: Well, I'll tell you what, they might do . . . until I get another pair.

Pause.

Where's the laces?

ASTON: No laces.

DAVIES: I can't wear them without laces.

ASTON: I just got the shoes.

DAVIES: Well now, look, that puts the tin lid on it, don't it? I mean, you couldn't keep these shoes on right without a pair of laces. The only way to keep a pair of shoes on, if you haven't got no laces, is to tighten the foot, see? Walk about with a tight foot, see? Well, that's no good for the foot. Puts a bad strain on the foot. If you can do the shoes up proper there's less chance of you getting a strain.

ASTON *goes round to the top of his bed.*

ASTON: I might have some somewhere.

DAVIES: You see what I'm getting at?

Pause.

ASTON: Here's some. (*He hands them to* DAVIES.)

DAVIES: These are brown.

ASTON: That's all I got.

DAVIES: These shoes are black.

ASTON *does not answer.*

Well, they can do, anyway, until I get another pair.

DAVIES *sits in the chair and begins to lace his shoes.*

Maybe they'll get me down to Sidcup tomorrow. If I get down there I'll be able to sort myself out.

Pause.

I've been offered a good job. Man has offered it to me, he's
. . . he's got plenty of ideas. He's got a bit of a future. But
they want my papers, you see, they want my references. I'd
have to get down to Sidcup before I could get hold of them.
That's where they are, see. Trouble is, getting there. That's
my problem. The weather's dead against it.

ASTON *quietly exits, unnoticed.*

Don't know as these shoes'll be much good. It's a hard road,
I been down there before. Coming the other way, like. Last
time I left there, it was . . . last time . . . getting on a
while back . . . the road was bad, the rain was coming
down, lucky I didn't die there on the road, but I got here, I
kept going, all along . . . yes . . . I kept going all along.
But all the same, I can't go on like this, what I got to do, I
got to get back there, find this man—

He turns and looks about the room.

Christ! That bastard, he ain't even listening to me!

BLACKOUT.
DIM LIGHT THROUGH THE WINDOW.
It is night. ASTON *and* DAVIES *are in bed,* DAVIES *groaning.*
ASTON *sits up, gets out of bed, switches on the light, goes
over to* DAVIES *and shakes him.*

ASTON: Hey, stop it, will you? I can't sleep.
DAVIES: What? What? What's going on?
ASTON: You're making noises.
DAVIES: I'm an old man, what do you expect me to do, stop
    breathing?
ASTON: You're making noises.

DAVIES: What do you expect me to do, stop breathing?

ASTON *goes to his bed, and puts on his trousers.*

ASTON: I'll get a bit of air.

DAVIES: What do you expect me to do? I tell you, mate, I'm not surprised they took you in. Waking an old man up in the middle of the night, you must be off your nut! Giving me bad dreams, who's responsible, then, for me having bad dreams? If you wouldn't keep mucking me about I wouldn't make no noises! How do you expect me to sleep peaceful when you keep poking me all the time? What do you want me to do, stop breathing?

He throws the cover off and gets out of bed, wearing his vest, waistcoat and trousers.

It's getting so freezing in here I have to keep my trousers on to go to bed. I never done that before in my life. But that's what I got to do here. Just because you won't put in any bleeding heating! I've had just about enough with you mucking me about. I've seen better days than you have, man. Nobody ever got me inside one of them places, anyway. I'm a sane man! So don't you start mucking me about. I'll be all right as long as you keep your place. Just you keep your place, that's all. Because I can tell you, your brother's got his eye on you. He knows all about you. I got a friend there, don't you worry about that. I got a true pal there. Treating me like dirt! Why'd you invite me in here in the first place if you was going to treat me like this? You think you're better than me you got another think coming. I know enough. They had you inside one of them places before, they can have you inside again. Your brother's got his eye on you! They can put them pincers on your head again, man! They can have them on again! Any time. All they got to do is get the word. They'd carry you in there, boy. They'd come here and pick you up and carry you in! They'd keep you fixed! They'd put them pincers on your head, they'd have you fixed! They'd take one look at all this junk I got to sleep with they'd know you were a creamer. That was the greatest mistake they made, you take my tip, letting you get out of that place. Nobody knows what you're at, you go out you come in, nobody knows what you're at! Well, nobody messes me about for long. You think I'm going to do your dirty work? Haaaaahhhhh! You better think again! You want me to do all the dirty work all up and down them stairs, just so I can sleep in this lousy filthy hole every night? Not me, boy. Not for you, boy. You don't know what you're doing half the time. You're up the creek! You're half off! You can tell it by looking at you. Who ever saw you slip me a few bob? Creeping in creeping out. Your brother's got his sights on you, man. He's got ideas for this place, he's going to set it up. And one thing you want to understand is I got as much rights as you have. If only the weather'd break I'd be able to lay my hands on more references than you've seen in a week! Treating me like a bloody animal! I never been inside a nuthouse!

ASTON *makes a slight move towards him.* DAVIES *takes his knife from his back pocket.*

Don't come nothing with me, mate. I got this here. I used it. I used it. Don't come it with me.

A pause. They stare at each other.

Mind what you do now.

Pause.

Don't you try anything with me.

Pause.

ASTON: I . . . I think it's about time you found somewhere else. I don't think we're hitting it off.

DAVIES: Find somewhere else?

ASTON: Yes.

DAVIES: Me? You talking to me? Not me, man! You!

ASTON: What?

DAVIES: You! You better find somewhere else!

ASTON: I live here. You don't.

DAVIES: Don't I? Well, I live here. I been offered a job here.

ASTON: Yes . . . well, I don't think you're really suitable. I don't think you'd like it here.

DAVIES: I like it here all right! It's you playing me about I don't like!

ASTON: You . . . better go. We don't hit it off.

DAVIES: Not suitable, eh? Well, I can tell you, there's someone here thinks I am suitable. And I'll tell you. I'm staying on here. I'm staying on here as caretaker! Get it! Your brother, he's told me, see, he's told me the job is mine. Mine! So that's where I am. I'm going to be his caretaker.

ASTON: My brother?

DAVIES: He's staying, he's going to run this place, he's going to make some changes here, and I'm staying with him, so . . . so there's not going to be any room for you!

ASTON: I live here.

DAVIES: Not for long! I know where I stand. Chuck me out, eh? Give me a lousy dirty pair of shoes and chuck me out! You got hold of the wrong end of the stick, boy.

ASTON: Look. If I give you . . . a few bob you can get down to Sidcup.

DAVIES: You build your shed first! A few bob! When I can earn a steady wage here! You build your stinking shed first! That's what!

ASTON *stares at him.*

ASTON: That's not a stinking shed.

Silence.
ASTON *moves to him.*

It's clean. It's all good wood. I'll get it up. No trouble.
DAVIES: Don't come too near!
ASTON: You've no reason to call that shed stinking.

DAVIES *points the knife.*

You stink.
DAVIES: What!
ASTON: You've been stinking the place out.
DAVIES: Christ, you say that to me!
ASTON: For days. That's one reason I can't sleep.
DAVIES: You call me that! You call me stinking!
ASTON: You better go.
DAVIES: I'LL STINK YOU!

He thrusts his arm out, the arm trembling, the knife point-
ing at ASTON's *stomach.* ASTON *does not move. Silence.*
DAVIES' *arm moves no further. They stand.*

I'll stink you. . . .

Pause.

ASTON: Get your stuff.

DAVIES *draws the knife in to his chest, breathing heavily.*
ASTON *goes to* DAVIES' *bed, collects his bag and puts a few*
of DAVIES' *things into it.*

DAVIES: You ain't . . . you ain't got the right . . . Leave that
alone, that's mine!

DAVIES *takes the bag and presses the contents down.*

All right . . . I been offered a job here . . . you wait . . .
(*He puts on his smoking-jacket.*) . . . you wait . . . your
brother . . . he'll sort you out . . . you call me that . . .
you call me that . . . no one's ever called me that . . .
(*He puts on his overcoat.*) You'll be sorry you called me
that . . . you ain't heard the last of this . . . (*He picks up his
bag and goes to the door.*) You'll be sorry you called me
that. . . .

He opens the door, ASTON *watching him.*

Now I know who I can trust.

DAVIES *goes out.* ASTON *stands.*
BLACKOUT.
LIGHTS UP. *Early evening.*
MICK *is sitting in the chair.*
DAVIES *moves about the room.*

DAVIES: Stink! You hear that! Me! I told you what he said,
didn't I? Stink! You hear that? That's what he said to me!
MICK: Tch, tch, tch.
DAVIES: That's what he said to me.
MICK: You don't stink.
DAVIES: No, sir!
MICK: If you stank I'd be the first one to tell you.
DAVIES: I told him, I told him he . . . I said to him, you ain't
heard the last of this man! I said, don't you forget your
brother. I told him you'd be coming along to sort him out.
He don't know what he's started, doing that. Doing that to
me. I said to him, I said to him, he'll be along, your
brother'll be along, he's got sense, not like you—
MICK: What do you mean?
DAVIES: Eh?
MICK: You saying my brother hasn't got any sense?
DAVIES: What? What I'm saying is, you got ideas for this place,
all this . . . all this decorating, see? I mean, he's got no

right to order me about. I take orders from you, I do my
caretaking for you, I mean, you look upon me . . . you
don't treat me like a lump of dirt . . . we can both . . .
we can both see him for what he is.

Pause.

MICK: What did he say then, when you told him I'd offered you
the job as caretaker?

DAVIES: He . . . he said . . . he said . . . something about . . .
he lived here.

MICK: Yes, he's got a point, en he?

DAVIES: A point! This is your house, en't? You let him live here!

MICK: Yes . . . it's my house. I got it cheap . . . and I let him
live here.

DAVIES: That's what I'm saying. You own the place.

MICK: Yes, but he does live here, doesn't he? I could tell him
to go. . . .

DAVIES: That's what I'm saying.

MICK: I could tell him to go, I suppose. I mean, I'm the landlord. On the other hand, he's the sitting tenant. Giving him
notice, you see, what it is, it's a technical matter, that's what
it is. It depends how you regard this room. I mean it
depends whether you regard this room as furnished or unfurnished. See what I mean?

DAVIES: No, I don't.

MICK: All this furniture, you see, in here, it's all his, except the
beds, of course. So what it is, it's a fine legal point, that's
what it is.

Pause.

DAVIES: I tell you he should go back where he come from!

MICK (*turning to look at him*): Come from?

DAVIES: Yes.

MICK: Where did he come from?

DAVIES: Well . . . he . . . he . . . .

MICK: You get a bit out of your depth sometimes, don't you?

Pause.

(*Rising, briskly.*) Well, anyway, as things stand, I don't mind having a go at doing up the place. . . .

DAVIES: That's what I wanted to hear!

MICK: No, I don't mind.

He turns to face DAVIES.

But you better be as good as you say you are.

DAVIES: What do you mean?

MICK: Well, you say you're an interior decorator, you'd better be a good one.

DAVIES: A what?

MICK: What do you mean, a what? A decorator. An interior decorator.

DAVIES: Me? What do you mean? I touched that. I never been that.

MICK: You've never what?

DAVIES: No, no, not me, man. I'm not an interior decorator. I been too busy. Too many other things to do, you see. But I . . . but I could always turn my hand to most things . . . give me . . . give me a bit of time to pick it up.

MICK: I don't want you to pick it up. I want a first-class experienced interior decorator. I thought you were one.

DAVIES: Me? Now wait a minute—wait a minute—you got the wrong man.

MICK: How could I have the wrong man? You're the only man I've spoken to. You're the only man I've told, about my dreams, about my deepest wishes, you're the only one I've told, and I only told you because I understood you were an experienced first-class professional interior and exterior decorator.

DAVIES: Now look here—

MICK: You mean you wouldn't know how to fit teal-blue, copper and parchment linoleum squares and have those colours re-echoed in the walls?

DAVIES: Now, look here, where'd you get—?

MICK: You wouldn't be able to decorate out a table in afromosia teak veneer, an armchair in oatmeal tweed and a beech frame settee with a woven sea-grass seat?

DAVIES: I never said that!

MICK: Christ! I must have been under a false impression!

DAVIES: I never said it!

MICK: You're a bloody impostor, mate!

DAVIES: Now you don't want to say that sort of thing to me. You took me on here as caretaker. I was going to give you a helping hand, that's all, for a small . . . for a small wage, I never said nothing about that . . . you start calling me names—

MICK: What is your name?

DAVIES: Don't start that—

MICK: No, what's your real name?

DAVIES: My real name's Davies.

MICK: What's the name you go under?

DAVIES: Jenkins!

MICK: You got two names. What about the rest? Eh? Now come on, why did you tell me all this dirt about you being an interior decorator?

DAVIES: I didn't tell you nothing! Won't you listen to what I'm saying?

Pause.

It was him who told you. It was your brother who must have told you. He's nutty! He'd tell you anything, out of spite, he's nutty, he's halfway gone, it was him who told you.

MICK *walks slowly to him.*

MICK: What did you call my brother?

DAVIES: When?

MICK: He's what?

DAVIES: I . . . now get this straight. . . .

MICK: Nutty? Who's nutty?

Pause.

Did you call my brother nutty? My brother. That's a bit of
. . . that's a bit of an impertinent thing to say, isn't it?

DAVIES: But he says so himself!

MICK *walks slowly round* DAVIES' *figure, regarding him, once.
He circles him, once.*

MICK: What a strange man you are. Aren't you? You're really
strange. Ever since you come into this house there's been
nothing but trouble. Honest. I can take nothing you say at
face value. Every word you speak is open to any number of
different interpretations. Most of what you say is lies. You're
violent, you're erratic, you're just completely unpredictable.
You're nothing else but a wild animal, when you come down
to it. You're a barbarian. And to put the old tin lid on it,
you stink from arse-hole to breakfast time. Look at it. You
come here recommending yourself as an interior decorator,
whereupon I take you on, and what happens? You make a
long speech about all the references you've got down at
Sidcup, and what happens? I haven't noticed you go down
to Sidcup to obtain them. It's all most regrettable but it
looks as though I'm compelled to pay you off for your caretaking work. Here's half a dollar.

He feels in his pocket, takes out a half-crown and tosses it at
DAVIES' *feet.* DAVIES *stands still.* MICK *walks to the gas stove
and picks up the Buddha.*

DAVIES (*slowly*): All right then . . . you do that . . . you do it
. . . if that's what you want. . . .

MICK: THAT'S WHAT I WANT!

He hurls the Buddha against the gas stove. It breaks.

(*To himself, slowly, broodingly.*) Anyone would think this house was all I got to worry about. I got plenty of other things I can worry about. I've got other things. I've got plenty of other interests. I've got my own business to build up, haven't I? I got to think about expanding . . . in all directions. I don't stand still. I'm moving about, all the time. I'm moving . . . all the time. I've got to think about the future. I'm not worried about this house. I'm not interested. My brother can worry about it. He can do it up, he can decorate it, he can do what he likes with it. I'm not bothered. I thought I was doing him a favour, letting him live here. He's got his own ideas. Let him have them. I'm going to chuck it in.

Pause.

DAVIES: What about me?

Silence. MICK *does not look at him.*
A door bangs.
Silence. They do not move.
ASTON *comes in. He closes the door, moves into the room and faces* MICK. *They look at each other. Both are smiling, faintly.* MICK *begins to speak, stops, goes to the door and exits.* ASTON *leaves the door open, crosses behind* DAVIES, *sees the broken Buddha, and looks at the pieces for a moment. He then goes to his bed, takes off his overcoat, sits, takes the screwdriver and plug and pokes the plug.*

I just come back for my pipe.
ASTON: Oh yes.
DAVIES: I got out and . . . halfway down I . . . I suddenly . . .
found out . . . you see . . . that I hadn't got my pipe. So I
come back to get it. . . . So I . . . I thought I'd . . . nip
back, like.

ASTON: Did you find it?

DAVIES: Yes. Yes, I found it all right.

Pause.

That ain't the same plug, is it, you been . . . ?

ASTON: Yes.

DAVIES *moves to the centre of the room.*

DAVIES: Still can't get anywhere with it, eh?

ASTON: There's something the matter with it. I'm trying to find out what.

DAVIES: Well, if you . . . persevere, in my opinion, you'll probably find out.

ASTON: I think I've got a pretty good idea.

DAVIES *moves a little closer.*

DAVIES: I . . . don't know much about them, see . . . otherwise I might be able to give you . . . some advice on it. Still, I expect you'll get to the bottom of it.

Pause.

Listen. . . .

Pause.

You didn't mean that, did you, about me stinking, did you?

Pause.

Did you? You been a good friend to me. You took me in. You took me in, you didn't ask me no questions, you give me a bed, you been a mate to me. Listen. I been thinking, why I made all them noises, it was because of the draught, see, that draught was on me as I was sleeping, made me make noises, without me knowing it, so I been thinking, what I mean to say, if you was to give me your bed, and you have my bed, there's not all that difference between them, they're the same sort of bed, if I was to have yourn, you sleep, wherever bed you're in, so you have mine, I have yourn, and that'll be all right, I'll be out of the draught, see, I mean, you don't mind a bit of wind, you need a bit of air, I can understand that, you being in that place that time, with all them doctors and all they done, closed up, I know them places, too hot, you see, they're always too hot, I had a peep in one once, nearly suffocated me, so I reckon that'd be the best way out of it, we swap beds, and then we could get down to what we was saying, I'd look after the place for you, I'd keep an eye on it for you, for you, like, not for the other . . . not for . . . for your brother, you see, not for him, for you, I'll be your man, you say the word, just say the word. . . .

Pause.

What do you think of this I'm saying?

Pause.

ASTON: No, I like sleeping in this bed.
DAVIES: But you don't understand my meaning!
ASTON: Anyway, that one's my brother's bed.
DAVIES: Your brother?
ASTON: Any time he stays here. This is my bed. It's the only bed I can sleep in.
DAVIES: But your brother's gone! He's gone!

Pause.

ASTON. No. I couldn't change beds.
DAVIES: But you don't understand my meaning!
ASTON (*rising and going to the window*): Anyway, I'm going to

be busy. I've got that shed to get up. If I don't get it up
now it'll never go up. Until it's up I can't get started.
DAVIES: I'll give you a hand to put up your shed, that's what
I'll do!

Pause.

Can't you see what I'm getting at? I'll give you a hand!
We'll both put up that shed together! See? Get it done in
next to no time! Do you see what I'm saying?

Pause.

ASTON: No. I can get it up myself.
DAVIES: But listen. I'm with you, I'll be here, I'll do it for you,
we'll do it together, and I'll take care of the place for you,
I'll keep an eye on the place for you, at the same time,
I'll caretake for you.

Pause.

ASTON: No.
DAVIES: Why not?
ASTON: I don't sleep well at night.
DAVIES: But damn it I've told you we'll change beds! Christ!
We'll change beds! That'll do it. Can't you see the sense in
what I'm saying?

ASTON *remains with his back to* DAVIES, *at the window.*

You mean you're throwing me out? You can't do that.
Listen man, listen man, I don't mind, you see, I don't mind,
I'll stay, I don't mind, I'll tell you what, if you don't want
to change beds, we'll keep it as it is, I'll stay in the same bed,
maybe if I can get a stronger piece of sacking, like, to go
over the window, keep out the draught, that'll do it, what
do you say, we'll keep it as it is?

Pause.

ASTON: No.
DAVIES: Why . . . not?

ASTON *turns to look at him.*

ASTON: You make too much noise.
DAVIES: But . . . but . . . look . . . listen . . . listen here . . . I
mean. . . .

ASTON *turns back to the window.*

What am I going to do?

Pause.

What shall I do?

Pause.

Where am I going to go?

Pause.

I could stay here. We could put up your shed.

Pause.

If you want me to go . . . I'll go. You just say the word.

Pause.

I'll tell you what though . . . them shoes . . . them shoes
you give me . . . they're working out all right . . . they're
all right. Maybe I could . . . get down. . . .

ASTON *remains still, his back to him, at the window.*

Listen . . . if I . . . got down . . . if I was to . . . get my papers . . . would you . . . would you let . . . would you . . . if I got down . . . and got my. . . .

Long silence.

Curtain.

NOTES ON
THE THEATER
BY DIRECTORS
AND PLAYWRIGHTS

PLAYS FOR THE PEOPLE

Joan Littlewood

AT THE BEGINNING of this century, the comfortable traditions of
nineteenth-century theatre were being shaken to their founda-
tions. At the end of the first World War the old conventions
were completely shattered and experiment, criticism, genius
and anarchy gave rise to the "New Movement in the Theatre" of
the twenties, whose influence was strongly felt in every European country. The theories of the brilliant technical innovators
Appia, Craig, Laban, Stanislavsky inspired new concepts of acting, architecture, lighting, decor, stage movement and choreog-
raphy which have since then stimulated every worthwhile experiment in theatrecraft.

The two great Puritans, Shaw and Brecht, went further. For
them, the technique and content of their art must be directed
towards the reform of society itself. Their theatre was to help
to bring about a finer relationship between man and his fellows.
Their shock treatment, arguments, wit and their superb theatrecraft created the finest didactic theatre of all times.

As in Ben Jonson's day, some artists in every country came
to believe that a play production must have beneath its entertainment value, a great moral purpose. The concept was re-
born of an ensemble working together, to perfect, technically
and artistically, a style which could reflect the tempo of their
time, and so we get the great companies of Copeau, Brecht, the
Habimah, the Moscow Arts Theatre.

In England unfortunately during the first half of this century
the theatre was firmly in the hands of the philistines, and in

spite of Shaw the majority of plays mounted were of such banality that it is difficult to imagine where they found an audience, even in the barren reaches of the "upper" classes, so-called. Even the great English classics were produced and acted as if they had been conceived by Edwardian old ladies seated at their embroidery.

The only director in England who seemed to have any knowledge of the European movement was Terence Gray, an Irishman, who after six years of experimental work in Cambridge gave up and fled to France. This new movement in the theatre, brilliant and inspiring as it was and is, nevertheless could not be called popular. It was to some extent eclectic and it came from rebels who were bred in the bourgeois society which they attempted to devastate. Even the "left wing," using all the bright new techniques for its own purpose failed thereby to win a really wide public for its work. Great feats of organisation were achieved, notably by the Volksbuhne, later by the Théâtre Nationale Populaire in France and once, in Roosevelt's America, by the Federal Theatre Project. In many countries working-class support was heavily canvassed; sometimes, as in the case of our own performances to unemployed workers in the thirties, such audiences were attracted to the theatre for a time—but today the stream of life has left most of these projects far behind, and the signs of any important popular theatre are few and far between. But what do we mean by "popular" theatre?

In the Soviet Union, for example, the theatres are full, and the plays are defunct. It is a "popular" theatre but without an active function, its only purpose the enjoyment of witnessing the art and problems of the past. If the theatre is to fulfill its social purpose it is contemporary and vital material which must make up the dramaturgy, and its themes must be important to the audience. Theatre must be in the present tense.

Today, everywhere, from Moscow to New York, young artists and critics get together to complain about the state of the theatre and the lack of plays. The need for a popular theatre is recognized, but the talk is pessimistic and it seldom falls into a discussion on new forms. For all the new forms, the critiques and theories of the first half of the century have fallen, so it seems, on barren soil. Where is the great popular theatre that the "new movement" was to usher in?

"It is impossible," "it's no use" they tell you; the arts councils and even some of the "artists" in the "communist" countries all talk the same way. It is difficult to find out how they know these things for one finds little evidence of persistent and inspired activity related to the problem.

In actual fact, most of the talk is "hot air." Frankly, most of these "artists" are contemptuous of the "uneducated masses." They believe that their great problems are too subtle, too personal and too intellectual to be aired, or appreciated, by the vulgar, so they shun the people whose ribaldry and cynical criticism is fearful to them. To such artists of course a Brendan Behan must be a mere vulgarian. It is interesting to note that Behan's writing is sprinkled with phrases lifted from the daily aphorisms of his people, not doggerel, great lines. It is also interesting that such artists prefer to spend their time away from the beaten track of artistic and literary discussion —and even enjoy the unnatural pleasure of laughter, and that dull working-class quality, optimism. Really can such people have any intellectual stimulus to offer us?

Well I'm sure there will always be a place for art for the artist, art expressing the problem of the esoteric or the refugee from life who sees the world through the distorting mirror of his own isolation. Unfortunately there seems to be too large a place for such art at the moment; and for those who must face life's problems, who cannot escape into the cloud cuckoo land of fear and contempt and self-examination, such art offers little sustenance.

For too long now the theatre has been only a retreat for the abnormal. There are an incredible number of themes which could make great theatre; they remain untouched while the plays produced in the old convention go on exploring a dwindling world of so-called intellectual activity.

Great popular theatre supplies a fundamental human need, it is a communion, it gives understanding, it bestows on man a sense of identity, it rationalizes fear and hate. The need for such theatre is creating the supply.

In England the infantile, snobbish theatre which we have had for so long is showing obvious signs of decay and now the doors are opening to new talent. The talent was always there, but in the England of ascendant imperialism, it was kept strictly in the workhouse.

At last you can hear the real English language in the theatre and the people on the stage move like human beings, neither producer's puppets nor sexless mannequins, but people arguing and living.

The building of a popular theatre is a question of opening new doors. With new material and actors of wit and invention working on it, it is only a matter of time now before we have an extensive new dramaturgy. It must come from actor-writers working together this time, the work is waiting to be done. Already the drama produced in this way in England has brought into theatre a new public, a young audience. But it is a drama which shuns the lack of variety and inaction of the old psychological, introspective theatre. We must use more swift moving techniques, poetry, living music and song, dance, and above all understanding; actors and actresses who are artists not puppets, and theatres freed of the bed bugs—the businessmen and agents who batten off the theatre and have nothing to give it in return.

This future great theatre will, and can, arise everywhere, its achievement requires only work and patience.

THE RIGHT TO FAIL

George Devine

I DON'T BELIEVE THAT it matters *how* you achieve what you
achieve so long as what finally appears on the stage is theatri-
cally valid. You can take any moral or aesthetic attitudes you
like, provided that something exciting and true is created. If
you have a director who says that every actor has to stand on
his head for half an hour every morning before he starts to
rehearse, and the director and his actors actually *get something*
out of that, then—fair enough—that works, for the moment.
But there are basically two kinds of direction. There's the
kind that imposes a strong personal stamp on the play, the
stamp of brilliant people like Joan Littlewood and Tony
Guthrie and Peter Brook. I think that in one way we suffer
from the lack of that stamp at the Royal Court. If I did all the
productions and said *"Right, THIS is the way we produce plays,"*
then we might do better at the box office. But I don't believe
that this kind of direction is very fertile for the dramatist, and
what we're trying to do here is to practise the other kind—
which attempts to get the best out of each particular element
in a production and make them work together in realizing the
play. This place is a sort of *school*, after all, with different talents
and points of view—as different as Tony Richardson, Bill Gaskill, John Dexter and Lindsay Anderson. But they do share a
certain attitude towards the author.

No, I wouldn't say that the director is the author's *servant*.
That's too strong. I don't think that an author really knows
what he's written, in theatrical terms, when it comes to inter-
pretation on the stage. It all seems so obvious to him that he

can't understand why the actors shouldn't see it at once. It's usually there in the lines, of course, but somebody has to discover that and interpret it to a group of people, while being completely faithful to what the author basically felt. That somebody is the director. He has to induce all the people concerned to make their own individual, personal contributions inside the framework, while he is responsible primarily to the source material. He has to make the actors feel, finally, that it's *their* show, because from the first night onwards he isn't there. He's got to let them take it away. There was a period about five years ago when I was working at Stratford and the Vic and other places when I found that the reliance of actors on the director was much too great, for my money. They expected you to tell them absolutely everything about the characters they were playing. But that, I think, is work the actor must do for himself. Nowadays, I always say to actors here: "I'm not going to do your job for you. I will help you in every way I possibly can. I will guide you, select for you, tell you what I think the play is about and what the relationships are *between* the characters, because I have an overall view. But it's up to *you* to discover what is inside the character." When you do that the actor makes a much bigger contribution than if you marshal him, and I think the young actor prefers it—especially as in general he's much more *serious* than the young actor of thirty years ago, when I started in the theatre. He talks far more about the theatre in general and the world outside it, for one thing. In my day young actors talked about Money or Billing. And he has a more serious attitude to his work. He's less willing to sell himself as an article worth so many pounds a week, to be shoved around by a clever director who will Do Something with him, in any kind of play.

Just to be a director by itself, producing one play here and one play there, isn't enough. You should try to create conditions of work, perhaps even by starting your own company or running your own theatre. We're the only people in the theatre whose temperaments fit us for that kind of job. You can't expect an author or an actor to do it, as a rule. I feel that part of my job of creating conditions is to train directors here. I have two or three at a time, working three months as assistants to me, then spending a month in the office and a month in the work-shops. They have to learn stage management, and they have to know all about business. I think a director ought to have been an actor, too, if possible, because then he'll have a better idea of what the actors' problems are. Some people who want to be directors think of him as a sort of superior being who has wonderful Ideas. But *anybody* can have ideas: the point is what you do with them, how you turn them into theatre fact. This is where the fight comes in. I also encourage these assistants to learn about the other arts. None of us—dramatists or directors or actors—*know* enough. I urge them to keep in touch with the other movements, and not just to live inside the theatre. We can't afford to be so absorbed in our own little world of the stage. We've got to participate, we've got to read, we've got to know what's going on.

I feel that the first statement of the Court has now been made, and all sorts of people are looking to me and saying, "What are we going to do next?" It's terribly difficult to know for sure because there are so many things to do, so many fields which are quite unexplored. There's the job, for instance, of developing and opening out the possibilities of what the theatre itself can be, and architecture—of course—has a lot to do with that. Our old playhouses—beautiful as some of them are —are like remnants of the old court or *haut bourgeois* theatre. A theatre is a great man's house, with all the old images— chandeliers, red plush, liveried servants—that don't have any meaning for people today. People like the Court, they like pageantry, but if the theatre is not just a place you go to for special treats, if it is to be part of your life, then it ought to be quite a different *kind* of place. I'd like to rip out the inside of this one and create a playhouse with a very different feeling. I'd like a bigger theatre—with more seats at cheap prices— which would be a very free and open place, and the old feeling of freedom that there used to be in the music hall. It could be a really popular theatre, and you could do plays there just as serious in intention as those we do today in our little worried boxes. Then there's the field of the audience. There's a whole audience that we just don't speak to at all—not only among the working class but the professional classes, among the people between twenty and thirty in industry and commerce who are earning good wages and who would sooner think of flying to the moon than coming here to see, say, a play by Shelagh Delaney. And there's the *young* audience missing from the theatre. I've just started here—and it's a very long-term thing—to make contact with the schools. In the last few weeks we've had two groups of older children from different schools at the theatre. They come here for a whole week without a teacher. They meet a young director, an actor, an author. They're taken to other theatres, to a designer's studio, to an acting school, to the workshop. They see a rehearsal at the beginning of the week and then again at the end. They have a complete week of theatre. Most of them seem to have been thrilled, and some have written to tell us that it's given them a totally different idea of what the theatre means. One boy said that it had not only affected his feelings about the theatre, but about life in general, to see a group of people working together in this dedicated way . . . .

This started from a long talk I had a few months ago with Helene Weigel. Now I'm going to try to organize one visit a week. If we could get five hundred of them round the theatre in a year, that would eventually build up into something quite formidable. What we ought to do is to send a team round the schools to show them how theatre works and what it is, but we've got too much on our plate here as it is. Yet the theatre must explore this field. Middle-aged playgoers come to a play if it's successful, or if they think they're going to get a kick out of it. But if you're going to make the theatre a part of your life—if you're going to be demanding, to take an attitude, to be critical —then you need *formation* and that, I think, ought to start in schooldays.

Then, of course, there's the development of the actor. Take somebody like Albert Finney. He's a wonderful actor, and he can sing and dance and mime and be an acrobat; if only you could build up a group of artists like that, and put them to work in a really popular theatre. That could transform the whole situation. It's not a *new* idea, of course, but what the hell? It may have been done before, but it needs to be done again right now. As far as this theatre is concerned I'm going to make a big effort this year to start collecting a permanent company. If I can find the money, I want to persuade them to work on a kind of part-time contract. I had that idea from the start, but I couldn't put it into practice, though I've had a nucleus of players working here on and off.

It's part of a director's job, I believe, to be aware of all these things—and not least of the need for sheer *education,* of authors and actors and directors and audiences. One of the good signs for the 1960's, I think, is that more new work is being performed all over the country. The quality may be dubious here and there, but the quantity has increased and the field is open. You cannot say today that a new play with merit won't get a hearing somewhere. The dramatists ought to be all right for a bit, and their attitude to form will take its own natural course. I think John Osborne's *Luther* will create as much of an impact as *Look Back in Anger* did, but in a very different way, and already—even before that—you have Wesker planning to write a play about Jesus, and Delaney thinking of a play about Derby in the fifteenth century. There's a movement away from modern dress naturalism. To begin with, they had to write what was close to them, from their own experience. Now they're starting to explore a much wider territory. . . .

Somebody asked me at a meeting in America, "What would you say in four words was the most important thing you have established at the Royal Court?" I'd asked Tony Richardson that very same question: what had we *really* established? He said, "I'll tell you what: *the right to fail.*" And that's the answer I gave in America.

LET BATTLE COMMENCE!

Arnold Wesker

AFTER MANY YEARS of writing I have written something which has been accepted. After burrowing in the dark I emerge and look around. It was a play I wrote, I am in the theatre. It could have been a volume of poetry, a novel, a book of short stories or a film script, but it seems I was destined to say best what I wanted to say in a play. For the moment, at least, I am a playwright.

I have arrived knowing exactly what I want to do, but how I am to do it, or whether I can, is the challenge my art presents. The "what" and the "how" and indeed the "why" are the purpose of this article.

I want to write about people in a way that will somehow give them an insight to an aspect of life which they may not have had before; and further, I want to impart to them some of the enthusiasm I have for that life. I want to teach.

I want to write my plays not only for the class of people who acknowledge plays to be a legitimate form of expression, but for those to whom the phrase "form of expression" may mean nothing whatsoever. It is the bus driver, the housewife, the miner and the Teddy Boy to whom I should like to address myself.

There we have three statements which, when I think about them from one point of view, seem pretty outrageous. But do not let us assume a cynical air too soon, let us think about them. I was brought up in an atmosphere where the bus driver, the housewife, the miner and the Teddy Boy were the people that mattered. Later on, as I came to meet others whose education and social background separated them from the people I'm talking about, I was regarded as a romantic—the ineffectual angel type, you know. But what was worse I was accused of audacity! For consider, who was *I* to teach the man in the street, and what the hell was there to teach him anyway? Was he unhappy, did he need teaching, or did he want me to poke my nose into his life?—which is one way of looking at any art: an intrusion of the artist's personality into your life. How dare I assume that what I believed was life was any better than what they believed was life. So I paused and considered this, and felt duly ashamed of my pomposity.

There was Mr. Smith. He was married, he had children, a home and a good job. He went to pictures once a week, to the pub twice a week, a football match, a whist drive or a darts tournament. He had his friends, he could laugh and make people laugh, and in the summer he had a good three weeks' holiday at the seaside or in a caravan. What more could I give him, what more did I want of him? I did not then, nor do I now, consider any of those activities lamentable, unworthy or a waste of time. This was human activity, Mr. Smith was happy. Why should I want him to be interested in politics, history, music, art or literature?

And then I left school and found that I was working and living among them. (God! I wish one did not have to talk about "them" and "us.") And I discovered that there were aspects of character beyond the cockney's humour and the farm-labourer's phlegmatic contentment. One day, Mr. Smith had a row with his wife, something was going wrong with married life and he could not understand. All he could do was shout abuse and accusations at her. He was not equipped to handle the situation. Then there was a dispute at work and he was asked out on strike, he went but was not sure why. Suddenly one of his children did something wrong and was taken to court; Mr. Smith woke up to find a human being who was part of him by all that was natural but yet, who was this human being? Why had his child done this? He could not understand it. Shortly afterwards he found himself unemployed, there was a slump, the papers raved about an economic crisis; he did not know what this was or how it came about. But then these things were not to be understood by the likes of him. When the war came he was called up and his son was killed. Now who was responsible for this? Oh well it's all over, home again. But home wasn't the same. Everything was broken up. Funny how things changed. There were his friends, the pubs, the holidays—but he was bored more easily now, quick to take offence and row with his wife. The jolly things were a little stale—but then that was life, stale and depressing. The new generation don't think so though—still, we never could teach them anything. Mustn't grumble—make the best of it—any sort of best. And so he died, not having had a glimpse of anything that might have told him what it was all about, not having understood much. At each crisis in his life, somehow, he had found he was not equipped to handle it—and not only that, he had never understood the nature of that crisis. It was not simply that no one had given him tools for living, but no one had told him he *needed* any tools beyond a job that would earn him money to fulfill responsibilities.

"Tools," perhaps, is the key word. I think that is how I look upon art—as a tool, equipment for the enjoyment of living, for its better understanding. And it is with this definition that I shall approach my writing.

But equip him to deal with life? Surely that is the job of education? Right! It is! But one of the fundamental concepts in art is that all great art is a product of its own time. Now, I feel that our time is one where education is not merely scant and inadequate but is bankrupt of any values; therefore the art we must produce is one that struggles to fill that gap in education, that struggles to rouse interest in the world and persuade one to have faith in life. An art, in fact, that establishes values. After all, what is valued today, what is sacred? The Queen? A football coupon? Even the home and family is dying of nervous strain. Life certainly is not valued, the last war numbed the senses of us all. The function of art changes—when education is doing what it should then we shall write about other things and in a different way. *So we are agreed that there is a general malaise.*

Perhaps Osborne, Tynan, Anderson or Logue want to do it and are not capable—but somebody must be. Is John Berger the man, with his programmes on Independent Television talking about Léger and workers on a building site? Perhaps it needs the *Daily Mirror* to sponsor a "Public meet your artist" programme on the television screen. I'm not sure. But it must surely be obvious that it is not enough simply to write our little bit and trust to luck it will reach someone, somewhere. We must pick up our poems, our plays and films, tuck them under our arms and go out to the public and do battle with them. It should not be necessary, I know, but it is, these are our sort of times. Perhaps it is our bad luck—it is also our challenge.

Now let us go a little deeper. Here is a long extract from a letter from a writer friend, Dai Vaughan. Apart from the fact that he has written better prose than I have done he seems to me to have stated the issue so well as to need no further embellishment from me:

"Just look into your own experience," he tells me, "and I think you will agree that one of the easiest ways of arousing someone's hostility is to try—from the most selfless motives imaginable—to introduce him to some experience from which you have derived great enjoyment. Talk to a concertgoer about the pleasures of jazz, or to a jazz lover about the pleasures of concert music, and you will meet not with gratitude or even with 'enlightened interest' but with a tremendous barrier of resentment. Why is this? It is because our cultural tastes are an expression—almost the most public expression—of our fundamental values; and such values are expressed not only in what we like but also in what we choose to reject. If a man dislikes jazz, this is not some accident which has befallen him; it is something essential to his coming to terms with life in the way he has chosen. Let us be clear about the use of the word 'enrichment': it is quite O.K. for me to speak of the arts enriching my experience (since they do so in so far as I have accepted them); but to speak of my enriching someone *else's* experience *through* art is false, since what I am doing is to attack the very roots of his being.

"So let's be honest about it. Let's not regard ourselves as

scattering grain to chicken, but admit instead that what we want to do is to undermine people's existing values and impose our own upon them. (If we believe in our own values we will accept this as a responsibility—as part of the struggle for survival, conducted on a new plane.) Let's drop the air of philanthropy and the talk about 'broadening people's horizons.' If we respect men, then we must respect them enough to be willing to fight them and not be upset if they don't come to heel at the cry of 'enrichment.' And if this thought intimidates us then for God's sake let's admit that what we really want is an esoteric culture."

And then further on in the letter: "But with the working class you encounter people who have learned through a couple of hundred years of bourgeois culture to equate all thought and intellectualism with the ivory tower. You face the man who says, 'I don't understand long words' and implies thereby that long words are irrelevant. There is no mental defect here. The same man will have the clearest understanding of the permutations necessary for filling in a football coupon (a thing no one has ever succeeded in making intelligible to me), and he would understand long words soon enough if you could convince him that they *weren't* irrelevant. But this is just the problem. And it is not just a case of confronting a class which mistrusts the intellectual. You are confronting a multitude of individuals for each of whom anti-intellectualism is an inextricable element in his adjustment to life, so that what you are attempting for each of these people is something of the magnitude of a religious conversion."

I agree. It is rather frightening when put like that—a religious conversion. Yet are not the values an artist holds his religion? Surely each work of art is an attempt to convert anyway? Ought we not to acknowledge this? But even so this is only a beginning. What now is to be our action?

Looking at it personally I see two problems. First, how is this to affect my actual writing; second, how do I attempt to establish this kind of contact with my audience? Let us look at the first problem. My play, *Chicken Soup with Barley*, is about a family who, all except the mother, lose faith in an ideal. It is also about the relationships between the people of that family. The family relations part of the play will be easily understood, but with the question of ideals it is a case of convincing the audience that to be concerned about disillusionment *is to be concerned about anything worthwhile anyway.* I accept that the language has to be a language they understand—and because it is art it has to be ordinary in a way that is poetic and not banal. But beyond that it has not merely to assume values which are foreign to them but to assume values in a way which suggests that values are worth assuming *at all.* I must not use the arguments of a bourgeois society but the facile, blind arguments, the platitudinous phrases which are the barricades of the man in the street to anything new, and break these down one by one first of all. In other words, I cannot simply *write* plays, I have to write them in such a way as to suggest a play is worthwhile writing for something more than telling a tale. Consider half a dozen words like irony, satire, enrichment, commitment, fulfilment, cultural bankruptcy. These are fields in which we wander at ease. But writing in the way I want to write means that I cannot assume the power of these words, I have to explain them somehow. It is as basic as that. And at the same time it has to be art. I do not say I have succeeded in my first play, but I have learned in time for my next one. And so we come to the second problem.

Having tucked my plays under my arm and stepped out— where do I go? Well, we are in the midst of a new movement, ideas are stirring and the artist is beginning to realise that the man in the street affects his life so he must affect theirs. I know there are always new movements, that they fade out and that new ones appear. I do not take this as a sign of the fickleness of the intellectual or as a sign of the inherent thick skin of the ordinary man. Rather I take it as a sign of inevitable human activity. There will always be problems to solve, but it is when there are no new movements to meet the problems that I shall be sick, for then we shall have stagnated and poisoned ourselves. Where then is the new movement and what has it produced?

It has produced the Universities and Left Review Club, Free

Cinema, the Royal Court Theatre, our Civic theatre, *Encore* magazine and various resistance groups up and down the country. In addition to this we have the diverse products of our own industrial and commercial society. Namely: television, the co-op societies, blocks of council flats with community centres *and* committees of those communities, trade unions and the *Daily Mirror*. Frankly, I despise the *Mirror*. It claims to be a paper of the people and yet, apart from shouting loudly in a language everyone can understand—which is all right, don't misunderstand me—yet it doesn't shout about things which can benefit the life of any one member of the public. Nevertheless it claims to be a paper of the people, for and by the people. We could call its bluff. Let us challenge it to spend its money on sponsoring a film by Lindsay Anderson or a play at the Royal Court Theatre for its own readers. Let it open its pages to the Royal Court writers' group or the new and young politicians of the Universities and Left Review Club. It can get together its own Deb's ball, let it call youth together on a conference about problems concerning themselves. Well, why not? We have called the *New Statesman* to account, why not the *Mirror*?

Next we have the trade unions—rich and powerful. Primarily the purpose of the union is to protect and further the interests of its members. But what can be the virtues of protecting the interests of people who are apathetic to living because no one involves them in living? Could not Universities and Left Review send its speakers to union members in order to discuss industrial problems? Or could not the Royal Court suggest to the Amalgamated Engineering Union that it sponsor a play for its members? Why not a film about them? Ford does it, and Shell, and Schweppes have financed a play. And what of the communities of people living in blocks of flats? Who will approach the London County Council to help organise a series of film shows or one-act plays in the community halls where the artist can go and talk and discuss his art with the people? What about those bastions of working-class people in the co-op societies? Here exist groups waiting for us. Discussion groups, film societies, drama and literary circles; we could be using them, we should be using them. And last, there is television—well, if we can be exciting enough, television might have us, and there is our public, so hungry that it cannot wait to switch on its set.

There, has it sounded like high-class snobbery? But why should it? There is nothing wrong with rock 'n' roll, there is only something wrong with it every day; three cheers for the whist drive and the football game, but God help the man who cannot enjoy something more—just as the man who likes the classics only and closes his ears to all other music is a bore and is only half alive. Have I made it sound easy? Of course it is not. The greatest problem, even when the principle is agreed upon, is the one of organisation. Who can do it? Are we capable? And having set my vision I may not be big enough for it. I do not know. I shall learn as I go along. It means starting from scratch, and breaking our hearts again and again, but at least something would be happening. And England would know that its community was alive and kicking and critical and eager.

WRITING FOR THE THEATRE

Harold Pinter

I'M NOT A THEORIST. I'm not an authoritative or reliable commentator on the dramatic scene, the social scene, any scene. I write plays, when I can manage it, and that's all. That's the sum of it. So I'm speaking with some reluctance, knowing that there are at least twenty-four possible aspects of any single statement, depending on where you're standing at the time or on what the weather's like. A categorical statement, I find, will never stay where it is and be finite. It will immediately be subject to modification by the other twenty-three possibilities of it. No statement I make, therefore, should be interpreted as final and definitive. One or two of them may sound final and definitive, they may even be *almost* final and definitive, but I won't regard them as such tomorrow, and I wouldn't like you to do so today.

I've had two full-length plays produced in London. The first ran a week and the second ran a year. Of course, there are differences between the two plays. In *The Birthday Party* I employed a certain amount of dashes in the text, between phrases. In *The Caretaker* I cut out the dashes and used dots instead. So that instead of, say: "Look, dash, who, dash, I, dash, dash, dash," the text would read: "Look, dot, dot, dot, who, dot, dot, dot, I, dot, dot, dot, dot." So it's possible to deduce from this that dots are more popular than dashes and that's why *The Caretaker* had a longer run than *The Birthday Party*. The fact that in neither case could you hear the dots and dashes in performance is beside the point. You can't fool the critics for long.

They can tell a dot from a dash a mile off, even if they can hear neither.

It took me quite a while to grow used to the fact that critical and public response in the theatre follows a very erratic temperature chart. And the danger for a writer is where he becomes easy prey for the old bugs of apprehension and expectation in this connection. But I think Düsseldorf cleared the air for me. In Düsseldorf about two years ago I took, as is the Continental custom, a bow with a German cast of *The Caretaker* at the end of the play on the first night. I was at once booed violently by what must have been the finest collection of booers in the world. I thought they were using megaphones, but it was pure mouth. The cast was as dogged as the audience, however, and we took thirty-four curtain calls, all to boos. By the thirty-fourth there were only two people left in the house, still booing. I was strangely warmed by all this, and now, whenever I sense a tremor of the old apprehension or expectation, I remember Düsseldorf, and am cured.

The theatre is a large, energetic, public activity. Writing is, for me, a completely private activity, a poem or a play, no difference. These facts are not easy to reconcile. The professional theatre, whatever the virtues it undoubtedly possesses, is a world of false climaxes, calculated tensions, some hysteria, and a good deal of inefficiency. And the alarms of this world which I suppose I work in become steadily more widespread and intrusive. But basically my position has remained the same. What I write has no obligation to anything other than to itself. My responsibility is not to audiences, critics, producers, directors, actors or to my fellow men in general, but to the play in hand, simply. I warned you about definitive statements but it looks as though I've just made one.

I have usually begun a play in quite a simple manner; found a couple of characters in a particular context, thrown them together and listened to what they said, keeping my nose to the ground. The context has always been, for me, concrete and particular, and the characters concrete also. I've never started a play from any kind of abstract idea or theory and never envisaged my own characters as messengers of death, doom, heaven or the milky way or, in other words, as allegorical representations of any particular force, whatever that may mean. When a character cannot be comfortably defined or understood in terms of the familiar, the tendency is to perch him on a symbolic shelf, out of harm's way. Once there, he can be talked about but need not be lived with. In this way, it is easy to put up a pretty efficient smoke screen, on the part of the critics or the audience, against recognition, against an active and willing participation.

We don't carry labels on our chests, and even though they are continually fixed to us by others, they convince nobody. The desire for verification on the part of all of us, with regard to our own experience and the experience of others, is understandable but cannot always be satisfied. I suggest there can be no hard distinctions between what is real and what is unreal, nor between what is true and what is false. A thing is not necessarily either true or false; it can be both true and false. A character on the stage who can present no convincing argument or information as to his past experience, his present behaviour or his aspirations, nor give a comprehensive analysis of his motives is as legitimate and as worthy of attention as one who, alarmingly, can do all these things. The more acute the experience the less articulate its expression.

Apart from any other consideration, we are faced with the immense difficulty, if not the impossibility, of verifying the past. I don't mean merely years ago, but yesterday, this morning. What took place, what was the nature of what took place, what happened? If one can speak of the difficulty of knowing what in fact took place yesterday, one can I think treat the present in the same way. What's happening now? We won't know until tomorrow or in six months' time, and we won't know then, we'll have forgotten, or our imagination will have attributed quite false characteristics to today. A moment is sucked away and distorted, often even at the time of its birth. We will all interpret a common experience quite differently, though we prefer to subscribe to the view that there's a shared common ground, a known ground. I think there's a shared common ground all right, but that it's more like a quicksand. Because "reality" is quite a strong firm word we tend to think, or to hope, that the state to which it refers is equally firm, settled and unequivocal. It doesn't seem to be, and in my opinion, it's no worse or better for that.

A play is not an essay, nor should a playwright under any exhortation damage the consistency of his characters by injecting a remedy or apology for their actions into the last act, simply because we have been brought up to expect, rain or sunshine, the last act "resolution." To supply an explicit moral tag to an evolving and compulsive dramatic image seems to be facile, impertinent and dishonest. Where this takes place it is not theatre but a crossword puzzle. The audience holds the paper. The play fills in the blanks. Everyone's happy.

There is a considerable body of people just now who are asking for some kind of clear and sensible engagement to be evidently disclosed in contemporary plays. They want the playwright to be a prophet. There is certainly a good deal of prophecy indulged in by playwrights these days, in their plays and out of them. Warnings, sermons, admonitions, ideological exhortations, moral judgements, defined problems with built-in solutions; all can camp under the banner of prophecy. The attitude behind this sort of thing might be summed up in one phrase: *"I'm* telling *you!"*

It takes all sorts of playwrights to make a world, and as far as I'm concerned "X" can follow any course he chooses without my acting as his censor. To propagate a phoney war between hypothetical schools of playwrights doesn't seem to me a very productive pastime and it certainly isn't my intention. But I can't but feel that we have a marked tendency to stress, so glibly, our empty preferences. The preference for "Life" with a capital L, which is held up to be very different to life with a small l, I mean the life we in fact live. The preference for goodwill, for charity, for benevolence, how facile they've become, these deliverances.

If I were to state any moral precept it might be: Beware of the writer who puts forward his concern for you to embrace, who leaves you in no doubt of his worthiness, his usefulness, his altruism, who declares that his heart is in the right place, and ensures that it can be seen in full view, a pulsating mass where his characters ought to be. What is presented, so much of the time, as a body of active and positive thought is in fact a body lost in a prison of empty definition and cliché.

This kind of writer clearly trusts words absolutely. I have mixed feelings about words myself. Moving among them, sorting them out, watching them appear on the page, from this I derive a considerable pleasure. But at the same time I have another strong feeling about words which amounts to nothing less than nausea. Such a weight of words confronts us day in, day out, words spoken in a context such as this, words written by me and by others, the bulk of it a stale dead terminology; ideas endlessly repeated and permutated become platitudinous, trite, meaningless. Given this nausea, it's very easy to be overcome by it and step back into paralysis. I imagine most writers know something of this kind of paralysis. But if it is possible to confront this nausea, to follow it to its hilt, to move through it and out of it, then it is possible to say that something has occurred, that something has even been achieved.

Language, under these conditions, is a highly ambiguous business. So often, below the word spoken, is the thing known and unspoken. My characters tell me so much and no more, with reference to their experience, their aspirations, their motives, their history. Between my lack of biographical data about them and the ambiguity of what they say lies a territory which is not only worthy of exploration but which it is compulsory to explore. You and I, the characters which grow on a page, most of the time we're inexpressive, giving little away, unreliable, elusive, evasive, obstructive, unwilling. But it's out of these attributes that a language arises. A language, I repeat, where under what is said, another thing is being said.

Given characters who possess a momentum of their own, my job is not to impose upon them, not to subject them to a false articulation, by which I mean forcing a character to speak where he could not speak, making him speak in a way he could not speak, of making him speak of what he could never speak. The relationship between author and characters should be a highly respectful one, both ways. And if it's possible to talk of gaining a kind of freedom from writing, it doesn't come by leading one's characters into fixed and calculated postures, but by allowing them to carry their own can, by giving them a legitimate elbowroom. This can be extremely painful. It's much easier, much less pain, not to let them live.

I'd like to make quite clear at the same time that I don't regard my own characters as uncontrolled, or anarchic. They're not. The function of selection and arrangement is mine. I do all the donkeywork, in fact, and I think I can say I pay meticulous attention to the shape of things, from the shape of a sentence to the overall structure of the play. This shaping, to put it mildly, is of the first importance. But I think a double thing happens. You arrange *and* you listen, following the clues you leave for yourself, through the characters. And sometimes a balance is found, where image can freely engender image and where at the same time you are able to keep your sights on the place where the characters are silent and in hiding. It is in the silence that they are most evident to me.

There are two silences. One when no word is spoken. The other when perhaps a torrent of language is being employed. This speech is speaking of a language locked beneath it. That is its continual reference. The speech we hear is an indication of that which we don't hear. It is a necessary avoidance, a violent, sly, anguished or mocking smoke screen which keeps the other in its place. When true silence falls we are still left with echo but are nearer nakedness. One way of looking at speech is to say that it is a constant stratagem to cover nakedness.

We have heard many times that tired, grimy phrase: "Failure of communication"... and this phrase has been fixed to my work quite consistently. I believe the contrary. I think that we communicate only too well, in our silence, in what is unsaid, and that what takes place is a continual evasion, desperate rear guard attempts to keep ourselves to ourselves. Communication is too alarming. To enter into someone else's life is too frightening. To disclose to others the poverty within us is too fearsome a possibility.

I am not suggesting that no character in a play can ever say what he in fact means. Not at all. I have found that there invariably does come a moment when this happens, when he says something, perhaps, which he has never said before. And where this happens, what he says is irrevocable, and can never be taken back.

A blank page is both an exciting and a frightening thing. It's what you start from. There follow two further periods in the progress of a play. The rehearsal period and the performance. A dramatist will absorb a great many things of value from an active and intense experience in the theatre, throughout these two periods. But finally he is again left looking at the blank page. In that page is something or nothing. You don't know until you've covered it. And there's no guarantee that you will know then. But it always remains a chance worth taking.

I've written nine plays, for various mediums, and at the moment I haven't the slightest idea how I've managed to do it. Each play was, for me, "a different kind of failure." And that fact, I suppose, sent me on to write the next one.

And if I find writing plays an extremely difficult task, while still understanding it as a kind of celebration, how much more difficult it is to attempt to rationalise the process, and how much more abortive, as I think I've clearly demonstrated to you this morning.

Samuel Beckett says, at the beginning of his novel *The Unnamable*, "The fact would seem to be, if in my situation one may speak of facts, not only that I shall have to speak of things of which I cannot speak, but also, which is even more interesting, but also that I, which is if possible even more interesting, that I shall have to, I forget, no matter."

BUILDING THE PLAY

an interview with
John Arden

Is PLAYWRITING THE ONLY form of literature that interests you?

ARDEN: The major form. Once or twice when I was a bit younger I tried writing short stories, and never managed to finish one. I find it a very difficult form. I have always preferred to write in terms of the theatre rather than anything else. I don't know why. It's just that I like to see the play acted . . . you know? I began to write plays when I was about sixteen. I never actually finished them either but I used to start one periodically, fill up a couple of exercise books, then it would get left. They were mostly prose plays, set in an historical period, and the prose tended to be a bit Wardour Street. I had a fascination for the Middle Ages in those days, and was always writing plays about the Crusades and things. I wrote a lot of peculiar plays— one (when I was a schoolboy) was based on the death of Hitler written in the style of *Sweeney Agonistes*. I have always been interested in different experiments with verse and prose—I think that the assumption that a play must be exclusively one or the other is a very limiting one.

Why plays? You had never seen much theatre, had you?

ARDEN: No. I used to go occasionally to see the rep. at Sheffield or something like that, and we did plays at school, of course— I played Hamlet once. But the professional theatre—in the best sense of the word—was more or less unobtainable in the North. But if you are interested in literature, you read plays and feel a sort of urge to know a bit more about it. At my prep. school they started us on Shakespeare when I was about nine.

Where were you educated?

ARDEN: I went to a Public School. Prep. school first, and before that a couple of years at a Barnsley Elementary School, so I had a bit of both. The school was Sedbergh, in Yorkshire. I personally think it is a very good one, with less nonsense about it than most of the Public Schools I've heard about. There was a good deal of sensible work on the arts.

How was it that you went to both sorts of school?

ARDEN: I was being educated in Barnsley where we lived at the beginning of the war, and my parents thought I ought to be sent away from an industrial town in case there was bombing so I went to a boarding school, and ended up at a Public School, where I did English and languages.

Did you decide to take up architecture at that time?

ARDEN: Well, yes, I was interested in it, and did quite a lot of art generally at school—there was a very good art teacher there.

Ever since the age of sixteen or seventeen you saw yourself as a writer?

ARDEN: Yes, I did.

Yet you still took up architecture?

ARDEN: Well, I don't know any *way* of becoming a writer. Some people at school seemed to think that I ought to go to the University to read English, but I didn't see why that would help me to be a writer any more than anything else, and I was interested in architecture. Also, to be a writer is a fairly chancy

thing because there is no recognised period of training for it—
you either are or you aren't, and you don't know at the age of
eighteen. You can't be certain whether you are going to carry
on with it. Architecture was a professional training which I
found interesting in itself, and which I could drop if I found my
writing developing. Then again, the disagreeable thing about
studying literature is that you have to read a lot of things you
don't like. This is necessary as a sort of grounding—even if you
don't like the Augustans, for instance, it is as well you should
know what sort of poetry they wrote. But I had a feeling that to
a creative writer the sort of academic study that is done at university was not particularly necessary.

Did you do any dramatic work at Cambridge?

ARDEN: No. I used to write plays but they were never very
much. I studied architecture there for three years, then did my
last two years at the College of Art in Edinburgh. At Edinburgh
I had a play done by the College of Art theatre group—my first
stage play to be performed. A period comedy, very much in
the style of John Whiting's *A Penny for a Song,* which came out
at almost the same time. There was no connection between the
two—it was just the *Zeitgeist.* A Victorian piece, about the building of a railway, called *All Fall Down.* It hasn't been published.
I have a script somewhere, but it's rather embarrassing to bring
out. This was the first play which anybody saw fit to do. I had
previously finished a pseudo-Elizabethan tragedy on the Gun-
powder Plot, which was very bad, a sort of academic play in verse,
an unsatisfactory mixture of the Elizabethans and T. S. Eliot.

Before I could be completely qualified as an architect I had
to work for a year in an office which I did in London and then
qualified—a large private office which was putting up a lot of
these nasty office blocks that one sees: not a very ethical office,
but a pleasant place to work as I liked the people, and it gave
me some insight into how architecture should not be organised.

Has your architecture had any bearing on your work as a
dramatist?

ARDEN: It is difficult to say, except that it has made me very conscious of the stage designer's work in presenting a play. I think I find a definite relation between planning a building and planning a play—but that, of course, would apply to almost anything—creative structure in any sense. If you plan a building, someone gives you a schedule of accommodation. He wants two living rooms, three bedrooms, kitchen, bathroom and so forth; you are given a site, then you have to put it together to ensure that it works on the inside—all the rooms open out of each other at the right place—and at the same time it looks attractive on the outside. Planning a play is rather similar. You start, perhaps, with a story that divides itself naturally into half-a-dozen scenes (the rooms of the house) which you have to put together so that they work one from the other, and at the same time the thing has to add up to a complete whole.

Is this perhaps why many people said that *Serjeant Musgrave's Dance* was slow, that the early scenes didn't carry the play forward, whereas they are, in fact, cornerstones which you must have?

ARDEN: Well, I think the thing about the early scenes in *Musgrave* is that it is a play which started in my mind with the last act. When I wrote it, I was roughly aware of what the climax was to be—the soldiers staging a public meeting, apparently a recruiting meeting, which would turn into a protest. In order to make this credible, it was necessary to lay out a number of scenes in which the soldiers showed themselves for what they were, and at the same time all the people in the town revealed enough of their personality to illustrate their attitude towards war. I think what I was doing in *Musgrave* was using two acts for what is commonly done in one, in most three-act plays. I don't see that this is necessarily wrong.

Were you writing all the time you worked in the architect's office?

ARDEN: Yes, I was. I stayed for another year after qualifying and during this time *The Waters of Babylon,* which I wrote specifically for the *Observer* competition where it finished in the last short list, was done at the Royal Court Theatre. *Live Like Pigs* was almost finished and when the Court commissioned it, I quit the office for good. Just before the Court took *Waters of Babylon,* I had won a prize on the B.B.C. North of England network, which actually got me in at the Court. It was called *The Life of Man,* a sort of seafaring thing: not a bad play, but I wouldn't write it now. It has a little too much of *Moby Dick* in it. It won a prize. At that time the English Stage Company had just set itself up, and George Devine was busy writing round the country to anybody whose name appeared in connection with playwriting prizes. The first play I sent them, they rejected: another historical play, on the Arthurian legend. I should like to return to it one day, because I thought it had something, but I can see why they rejected it. The central theme was very inconclusively stated. Some of the ideas in it I worked into *Musgrave* anyway, although there was a jump of some hundreds of years.

Was *The Waters of Babylon* pure invention?

ARDEN: One of the characters was drawn from life but the story of the play was invention. It was partly, of course, a satire on Macmillan's Premium Bond Scheme which came in at that time. *Live Like Pigs* was based on something which happened in Barnsley some years before, when a council house was given to a family of squatters. I didn't find out too many actual details, because I didn't want to be stuck too closely to a documentary form, but it was a similar situation, and certainly ended up like *Live Like Pigs,* with the house being besieged by the neighbours. I had actually written my first television play, *Soldier, Soldier* before *Live Like Pigs,* but it wasn't produced until later.

Soldier, Soldier was not, in fact, done until after *Serjeant Musgrave's Dance?*

ARDEN: No. The B.B.C. were a bit hesitant about it until *Serjeant Musgrave* was produced, and then I think they saw the connection, and thought if they put it on it might take some of the interest that *Serjeant Musgrave* may have aroused.

Was there any connection between *Soldier, Soldier* and *Serjeant Musgrave?*

ARDEN: Oh, there was, yes. There's a definite follow-through of the same story idea. *Soldier, Soldier* was a sixty minute comedy, and it had exactly the same situation as *Serjeant Musgrave.* That is, the same setting, a colliery town and the arrival of a soldier—different periods, certainly, one being contemporary and the other not. In the case of *Musgrave,* being a longer play the number was stepped up to four soldiers. What actually happens when they get there is naturally different. But there is the same relationship with the girl, or something approaching it. There is the air of violence from the outside world coming in on a closed community.

You once said that *Serjeant Musgrave* was suggested to you by an American film called *The Raid?*

ARDEN: Yes. I didn't get the idea of the play from the film, merely some hints for setting up the structure. The plan of the film is rather similar: a group of men—Confederate soldiers in disguise—ride into a Northern town. Three-quarters of the film is taken up with their installation in the town, and the various personal relationships they establish. On the appointed morning they all turn out in their Confederate uniforms, hoist a flag in the square, rob the bank and burn the houses. Finally, as in *Serjeant Musgrave,* the cavalry arrives at the last minute although in this case they are too late.

The Happy Haven, which came after *Musgrave,* was a climax in your battle for understanding from the critics. Their chief complaint seemed to be that you never follow the same line twice?

ARDEN: As I see it, there is a lot of similarity between my plays. As has in fact been pointed out—it hadn't occurred to me—the last scene of *The Happy Haven* is practically the same as the last scene of *Serjeant Musgrave,* with the people pinned against the walls while an appalling act takes place in the middle of the stage.

And curiously, both of them end with the woman cradling, in one case, a skeleton, in the other a child.

ARDEN: Yes. Which may be fortuitous—Freudian if you like. The thing about *The Happy Haven* that worried everybody was the fact that nearly all the cast wore grotesque masks throughout the action. This was interesting to do, and may be interesting to do again—but I don't quite see why everybody should have been rocked over backwards by it. It is a valid form of theatrical technique, which I felt could have been accepted a good deal more easily than it was. The point is, we had done some messing about with masks with Bill Gaskill at the Court. It obviously was potentially extremely useful, and I made a mental note that I would do a play for masks when I got a suitable subject. When I began to work on *The Happy Haven,* I found it was developing into a grotesque comedy about an old folks' home—the original idea was for a much more naturalistic play, probably for TV, which would have employed actors about the right age for the characters—and then when the theme seemed to be demanding more stylised treatment, it seemed a good idea to use masks on young actors and actresses. You can't have actors, like say, Edith Evans and Sybil Thorndike in that sort of play, because they are too near the real age, and it becomes cruel in the wrong sense. And also, on a purely technical level, the older the actor the slower they go. If you are writing a comedy, this imposes problems. When you use elderly actors in comedy you nearly always have to have some younger characters as a foil, otherwise the pace is dropped.

So you had written *The Happy Haven* before you had taken up your year's playwriting fellowship at Bristol University?

ARDEN: No. I had already had the idea. When I got to Bristol, I found they had a small experimental theatre with an open stage, so I wrote *The Happy Haven* for it. I feel—and I know a lot of people felt the same—that it was more successful in Bristol than London; it worked better.

Did you like the London production?

ARDEN: Yes . . . well, I had a lot to do with it, because I rewrote a good deal of the play for Bill Gaskill, who directed it, and I had to make certain alterations for the change-over in setting. Also, we felt that some of the earlier part of the play had not worked very well at Bristol—there had been a certain stodginess in the first act, which I had to rewrite. Yes, I liked it, but I merely felt that it showed that if you write a play for the open stage, it is by no means a foregone conclusion that it is going to have anything like the same effect when done in a conventional theatre. The scene where the dog grows back into a puppy worked much better on the open stage—it had much more of the effect that I wanted—it seemed to belong organically to the play.

At Bristol there was no set in the accepted sense of the word —the stage background was built to follow the architecture of the studio theatre anyway. We had a sort of back wall with doors, but the colour scheme followed straight through from that of the auditorium, so that to somebody who didn't know the building at all, you couldn't see where the stage set left off, and where the theatre began. The dog was much more stylised because whereas in London his noises had to be barked by a girl sitting off-stage, into a mike, at Bristol we had the prompter, who being on an open stage had to be in full view of the audience, dressed in a white surgical overall like the doctor, sitting at a desk with his prompt-book, and he just sat there and barked. It was a much more theatrical effect than the London one, and fitted in with the staging and everything so much better.

In *The Happy Haven,* there are a number of purely technical devices, which I introduced simply to see if they would work on the open stage. There is a certain amount of "experiment" in this sense; it doesn't affect the story or plot in any way. The dog is one. Another is—a thing which didn't quite work in London—the doctor's lectures. In Bristol these were very funny because he was in what was practically a lecture-theatre anyway. On the Court stage they were too withdrawn from the audience and therefore rather tiresome.

The language is very simple, pared down?

ARDEN: The masks seemed to demand it. We felt afterwards, Gaskill and I, that it wasn't simple enough. In the Bristol production it certainly wasn't. Between then and London I cut about half the images because I found that an actor with a mask does not need elaborate language—the mask is so powerful in itself that it needs a more naked expression of emotion. But I *am* simplifying my language in general as I go on writing, because I have come to the conclusion that elaborate verbiage on the stage tends to miss a lot of its effects simply because people haven't time to listen and watch at the same time.

On this question of language—you are one of the few writers who uses both prose and poetry. You usually make a distinction between the two?

ARDEN: Yes. I prefer to make a firm distinction. I see prose as being a more useful vehicle for conveying plot and character relationships; and poetry as a sort of comment on them. I find it difficult to carry this out in practice. Brecht, for instance, is usually very, very distinct between the two. I haven't always found it possible to be so. I mean, you are writing a scene, for instance, which seems to call for prose, then you get a heightened emotion, and before you know where you are, the prose has become lyrical, and yet it doesn't seem to warrant a change into verse. Writing heightened prose is a dangerous pastime. Dickens is always doing it. There are whole chunks of his novels that are actually scannable, like the death of Little Nell, when he goes into a sort of sloppy Longfellow verse. I think that a writer should be able to control whatever medium he is working in. Prose that scans is not prose but verse, and it should declare itself as such.

Do you find it easier to use verse in a period play than in a modern one?

ARDEN: Well, yes, because in a modern play one is conscious all the time that this is not the way these people would really be speaking in this situation, whereas no one can really know how men *talked* to each other in the past. In *The Waters of Babylon,* where I used a lot of verse, I feel on rereading it that many of the scenes would have been better if I had gone about it more naturalistically, and used a more natural prose. I think the use of formal verse, and straightforward vernacular prose in juxtaposition is quite a good solution even in a modern play. If people are speaking formal verse with lines that rhyme, the audience does not have to worry whether it sounds natural or not. They are talking poetry. It's with the half and half thing that one is in trouble.

You once said in *Encore* that there was a certain point of emphasis either in the action, or in the development of character, when a character naturally went into verse.

ARDEN: Yes. This depends on the play, of course. I would not lay down hard and fast rules. Some people might have thought that Musgrave's speech in the market place would be a suitable occasion to use verse. I did not, because at that point he has to present a certain amount of factual information concerning the massacre and so forth. Moreover, he is doing it in the role of a recruiting sergeant. Now a recruiting sergeant who speaks verse is a little awkward. What I needed was an ordinary recruiting speech, written in almost a pastiche style, which then gradually, without the audience quite realising when, takes on a different meaning. If Musgrave had suddenly broken off and started talking verse too soon, it would have been wrong. As it is, I go into rhymed verse for the episode one calls his dance —although in fact, in the production it was hardly a dance, but a physical and verbal "demonstration." I did use verse in the first act, where Annie is asked what she thinks of soldiers, and she goes off into a four-stanza spoken ballad. There she was speaking on a subject which is actually the theme for the whole play; she is also speaking out of an emotional pressure, and therefore can drop into verse without any difficulty at all.

In the cases you cite you are using verse in order to heighten the emphasis. Cannot one use verse in a more natural manner?

ARDEN: I think one can—but it's not the way I usually think of its use in the theatre. Also you have to remember that different periods create different conventions. The Elizabethans were able to write largely in verse because the theatre in those days was a much more formal activity than it is now. The further back in history one goes the more formal the verse becomes. Medieval plays were usually written in rhymed stanzas all the way through. Because people were aware of seeing something thoroughly artificial, and the concept of naturalism on the stage was very much in its infancy. Nowadays the prevailing desire for naturalism has resulted in the loss of much of the old theatrical art. On the other hand, the technique of naturalism that has been built up by prose dramatists is both valid and good. I don't see any reason to reject it in order to do the same thing in verse. I have no sympathy with T. S. Eliot's attempts to make verse sound like Noel Coward comedy. It's a way of deceiving the audience. You get them in there and make them think they are listening to a comedy, and then you insert the religion. I find this distasteful. If you want religion in a play, you should make no bones about it. I can't believe that anybody who thought they were going to see a Noel Coward comedy enjoyed themselves very much when they found themselves at *The Cocktail Party.*

In all your plays you use characters who are not readily sympathetic, and force the audience to accept them. Is this conscious?

ARDEN: I have grave objections to being presented with a character on the stage whom you know to be the author's mouthpiece. It can work. Obviously in Shaw's play you know you are going to sympathise with St. Joan. But in a play in which the characters are complete fiction and you don't know beforehand what the story is, I don't see why we should always be given this cosy point of reference. It can produce awful sentimentality, particularly if the play handles any sort of social or personal problem; you have a ghastly feeling that before the evening is over, the sympathetic character and his wife are going to link hands and say, "We march on together, whatever people say against us."

Nearly all the films from Hollywood—*On the Waterfront*, for example—which deal with social problems, invariably have the star playing the part of the fearless newspaperman, or the fearless stevedore, or what have you. The result is that it all becomes predictable. I cannot see why a social play should not be so designed that we may find ourselves understanding the person's problems, but not necessarily approving his reactions to them. After all, this was usually the case with Ibsen. Which character are you supposed to sympathise with in *Ghosts?* Is it the son or is it the mother? Neither of them is completely sympathetic, and I don't think there is anything particularly new about this. It is merely that earlier plays in this manner have now become accepted. The trouble arises in the first performance of such plays, because the audience still looks for the character they are supposed to sympathise with. Once they know the play it is no longer necessary.

Do you find it a temptation to present a character as sympathetic from the start? To make sure that people sympathise with Musgrave, for example, because his message is a good one, although his methods are wrong?

ARDEN: No, I don't think I am tempted in that way. For instance, take the character of Musgrave. I decided what he had to say, and why he had to say it, and roughly what he was going to do about it, before I worked out the character. The character came to fit the actions. I am always being told this is the wrong way to write a play. But with *Serjeant Musgrave* I thought: assume that an army sergeant in a colonial war is sufficiently disgusted with a particular atrocity he has been involved in. He comes back to England to make a demonstration of protest. I don't know at that stage the details of the demonstration, they're not worked out in my mind—well, what sort of man is he likely to be? Granted the period—I began with the scarlet uniforms for purely theatrical reasons—I used my historical imagination, and decided that the most likely character would be one of those Crimean sergeants, who fought with rifle in one hand, and bible in the other. This is not a character I feel particularly sympathetic to—but he seemed to be a plausible historical type. If I had made Musgrave into a straightforward liberal, with whom our modern progressives would immediately feel at home, he would have been historically out of the picture, and most unlikely as a sergeant in the Victorian army.

You did write *Serjeant Musgrave* with a social purpose in mind?

ARDEN: Well, one of the things that set the play off was an incident in Cyprus. A soldier's wife was shot in the street by terrorists—and according to newspaper reports—which was all I had to work on at the time—some soldiers ran wild at night and people were killed in the rounding-up. The atrocity which sparks off Musgrave's revolt, and which happens before the play begins, is roughly similar.

In the Cyprus incident, five people died, one of them a little girl, as in your play. . . .

ARDEN: That was quite deliberate.

Yet in your play, only twenty-five people were injured whereas in Cyprus, the number was more like one hundred and twenty-five. Why did you change one figure and not the other?

ARDEN: I didn't want to overdo the atrocity. You see if you have an enormous massacre in a play that is set in a previous period, people start asking where it was. I had to be very careful all through the play not to make it so documentary that people would start wondering and worrying why they hadn't read about it in history books. This is one of the principal reasons why Musgrave could not massacre the crowd at the end. That would have been altogether too unhistorical. As it was, at least one critic opened his notice by asking, in a jeering sort of way, "When did a sergeant last invade a Yorkshire village with a gatling gun, and hold the town to ransom?" In the film which we mentioned earlier, *The Raid,* the terrorists actually get away with their robbery and violence. The point there is that the raid is historical. They couldn't alter the episode because it was known. I'm sure if *The Raid* had been a fictional film they would probably have had ... well, I don't know what a happy ending is in a Civil War picture, because the films are shown in the North as well as the South. Any play set in a recent historical period which is not actually true is in that trouble. Whereas if you set up a fiction in the immediate present it doesn't matter.

Something which puzzled a lot of people in *Serjeant Musgrave* was the dance at the end. One critic pointed out that when the leading collier joined in the dance around Musgrave, this was a denial of everything that Musgrave believed in. What exactly did you mean to suggest?

ARDEN: This scene didn't quite work in the theatre—for purely economic reasons. What should be happening in that dance is that the audience should be made conscious of the fact that the town has been taken over by the real military—the Dragoons. Now, because the Royal Court couldn't afford more than two dragoons, this effect was somewhat nullified. Ideally there should be a complete force. If I were able to produce the play in a larger theatre, able to pay an enormous cast of supers, the stage would be full of dragoons and the dance would take place in front of them. Then the impression given would be that even the most sympathetic of the colliers, who nearly sides with Musgrave, has no alternative but to take part in the dance, and that law and order have been re-established by force. Which, if you like, is the natural result of Musgrave trying to establish the opposite by force. The dance certainly implies apathy in some of the colliers but there is a stage direction which makes it quite clear that their leader, who is the last to join in, does so unwillingly. This is the sort of detail which, on a small stage covered with people, can easily be missed. With space and more actors, the scene could be a great deal clearer in production.

Does it depress you that none of your stage plays have got through to a wider audience?

ARDEN: Naturally I found it depressing, but one hopes. *Serjeant Musgrave* has been done by three-quarters of the university dramatic societies in the country—it's keeping me in bread and butter at the moment. There has been one repertory production so far—at Lincoln. It must have been a good one, as it caused at least one critic—Laurence Kitchin—to revise his opinion of the play. A lot of critics are taking back what they said at first—Harold Hobson changed his mind after seeing the university production at Leeds. To my annoyance they do so by denigrating the London production which I thought was an excellent one. It is a difficult play, but I wish they would accept the fact that they simply missed the point when they first saw it.

Can one write a play without taking the audience's understanding into consideration?

ARDEN: I think it's probably true, as John Whiting said in a previous interview, that when you write a play, you don't think of the audience. I certainly don't. If I do, I put it out of my mind because I find it depressing. One writes a play for itself, it is an object in itself, and you cannot be thinking all the time of the coming production, because it is very limiting. That's how bad commercial drama gets written.

But here you are—recognised by many people as the most powerful and promising playwright in England—you have had several plays produced and yet not one of them has drawn an audience. Why is this, and do you think it is going to continue?

ARDEN: I don't know—I just don't know. I think a lot of it is to do with the problem of theatre audiences in London. You are not getting an ideal audience—certainly not at the Royal Court. New plays at the Royal Court have always had a difficult time—or nearly always. Even *Look Back in Anger* was only saved by a last minute holding operation, and *The Entertainer* succeeded because they got Laurence Olivier and the play was booked out before the opening. Most of the plays immediately successful at the Court are so for reasons of casting, or some other external factor. N. F. Simpson had a sticky time at first, and then his particular type of humour became fashionable. I don't know whether I shall ever become fashionable or not.

Although as I have said, I can detect certain similarities in my plays, I try not to write the same play twice. Now without being derogatory about it, I think that Simpson probably does. You could take whole chunks out of *One Way Pendulum* and put them in *A Resounding Tinkle,* or vice-versa, and it wouldn't matter. I think you can do the same with *The Entertainer* and *Look Back in Anger. The Entertainer* does have the big difference of the stage show in it, but the family natterings might easily be in either play. When John Osborne tries something completely new, like *Paul Slickey,* then it doesn't go down. With *Luther,* I suspect that he is on a safer wicket just as Whiting is on a safer wicket with *The Devils.* When you write a historical play, the audience has a definite point of reference—they say, we don't know much about the devils of Loudon, but they did really happen, and they have been written up by an established writer like Aldous Huxley. I am quite sure, for instance, that if I had written *Serjeant Musgrave's Dance* not about Serjeant Musgrave, but about, say, the naval mutiny of 1796, I would have done much better. I dare say I could have used a subject like that and said all the things I tried to say. The historical play is a form that people understand, and you don't have to work so hard in the first ten minutes. But I suppose that to ask an English audience to accept a period play that is neither comedy, romance or even history *is* asking rather a lot.

You wrote a Christmas play for the village church here?*

ARDEN: That was a quite straightforward piece of work. A half-hour play that took an hour when we performed it. We hadn't allowed for the Somerset drawl. In many ways it has been my most enjoyable theatrical experience. I wrote it, my wife produced it, and the village people acted it. It was simply a narrative of the Gospel account of the birth of Christ. The central character was Herod, and I suppose the central event of the play, as it transpired, was not the birth of Christ but the massacre of the innocents, which gave it a certain resemblance to *Serjeant Musgrave*. I saw Herod as an administrator, not exceptionally tyrannical in his approach to his job—which is blatantly unhistorical, because, in fact, Herod *was*. But in my play he finds himself in a corner and can see no other way out but to order the massacre.

Is there any modern play which you would particularly like to have written?

ARDEN: *Mother Courage,* I should think. I was very impressed by the German production in London a few years ago. *The Crucible* is another. I'm fond of Osborne and Wesker and so on, but they're too contemporary for me to feel them very strongly as influences. I am very interested in everything they do, but it doesn't immediately impinge on me. Oh, yes—John Whiting's *Saint Day,* which excited me when I saw it in 1952, did have a strong influence on me. Of the older writers, I feel like Robert Bolt does about Shakespeare—you can't get away from him. Ben Jonson I'm very fond of. Earlier on I preferred Marlowe and Webster, but I'm coming more and more to like Jonson. I'm probably more influenced by films, because I don't work for the cinema, and when I go to the pictures I don't have to put preconceptions out of my mind. When I lived in London I went to the cinema nearly every day. I'd like to make a film one day, a big film. At the moment I'm working on a sort of

---

* Brent Knoll, Somerset.

Free Cinema script—but only a half-hour thing. I'd like to have a million pounds and make an epic. I do enjoy small scale films like, say, *Twelve Angry Men*, but I wouldn't have particularly wished to write it. The sort of film I would write might be called "a Northern," a film based on one of the border ballads, using the Northumberland moors. So far, the breakthrough in British cinema has confined itself to films like *Saturday Night and Sunday Morning* and *Room at the Top*, which have been based on novels, and the John Osborne films based on plays. They haven't come up with an original script which gets outside the housing estate. I think this can be done. I don't necessarily mean a period film at all. There are plenty of themes which can be handled in an epic way and the only ones which have been tried are the war films, which are usually of negligible value.

As both architect and playwright do you have any strong views for or against the proscenium arch stage?

ARDEN: I like an open stage, with the audience in the same room as the stage. The proscenium arch is not a very happy medium for staging the sort of plays I want to write: people tell me I am a cold writer anyway. I suspect that one of the reasons why *The Happy Haven* did not do so well in London as in Bristol is simply that the audience was frozen off by the proscenium arch, and the parts of the play that were meant to come out at the audience completely failed to do so. I'm not fond of staging in the round. I hate looking past the actors and seeing the audience. I saw a production of *Phèdre* in the round, and in each speech the actors had to walk round the stage twice so that all the audience could get some of it. This becomes very annoying. I do like a background behind the actors because I like them to be related to an architectural point. You can group actors in relation to a stage-with-corners quite easily, but when the stage is round, there is bound to be an amorphous quality about the visual side of the production.

Have you designed sets yourself?

ARDEN: No. Though Jocelyn Herbert's sets for *Serjeant Musgrave* beautifully fulfilled the mental picture I had while writing the play. The only reservations I had about them were not the designs, but the lengthy scene-changes, caused by the Royal Court's terribly cramped backstage conditions.

Did you in fact write some of the front-stage scenes specially to cover the scene changes?

ARDEN: No. They were organic to the play, although the whole business of the slowness of the scene change made them seem less so. There is a progress of the action during them. If the scenery could have been flown much more quickly at the Court I would have preferred to have had every scene on the full stage. I always dislike actors acting in what amounts to a long corridor between the footlights and the backcloth.

There was however, a certain amount of rewriting during rehearsals concerning the revelation of the soldiers' purpose?

ARDEN: Well they don't reveal enough, actually. I improved the revelation scene in the production, but if it were done again I would improve it still more. The audience was still left too much in the dark. I maintain that no one who really has his ears on him could fail to make out what the soldiers were going to do, but on the other hand, you have got to face the fact that a lot of the audience haven't.

Even listening carefully, the one thing one was doubtful about was what was in the box the soldiers guarded so carefully.

ARDEN: That was intentional. I rather intended the skeleton to remain something of a surprise. There is some dramatic effect to be gained by pulling it out. But I do think that the general purpose of the soldiers' visit should be made much clearer. The real trouble is that in the churchyard scene, where they explain themselves, there is a tremendous amount of emotion being generated. They are all getting angry with each other, and

Musgrave goes off into a religious tirade. The result is that the audience is so busy watching the actors dramatising their emotions that they aren't picking up the plot information which is being conveyed in the dialogue. It would be better if I divided the two parts of the scene, so that the plot is made clear and then the emotion developed from it. Or, if you like, you can have your emotional outburst and then settle down to listen to the plot. You can't have both at the same time, especially in a play where the emotions are so very oversized. I often find, for instance, that in Tennessee Williams, where everybody acts at a high pitch of hysteria throughout the play, you often have no idea what the play is about at any given moment. You can't work out who burnt down whose house or who had lynched who twenty years before.

How do you set about writing a play?

ARDEN: Granted an idea, which may take three or four months to germinate in my mind, I then sit down and write, not a full synopsis, but some very detailed notes. I find I can't satisfactorily write a synopsis for a play to a point much beyond the middle of act two. After that I have to leave it to the characters, as it were, to develop their own action in the last act. I know roughly what the climax is to be, but I can't write it down. For instance, in *Serjeant Musgrave* I knew the climax was the production of the skeleton. I didn't know who was going to be dead by that time, or how the play was going to end. I write down roughly what characters I think I am going to need— lay out a synopsis of the first act, and something of the second act—and then, start writing. Sometimes I pause, after I've written a scene or two and got most of the characters established, to see if they really work and to think about them, to see whether or not they are the sort of people who fit the synopsis I have already sketched. And sometimes, of course, I have to make revisions in either the characters or the plot.

I usually work every day on the play if I can, because if I leave it for any time it tends to get lost. I write in pencil in standard hard cover exercise books. I finish it in the notebooks, then I type it out. I do like to alter as I type, which means I can never employ a typist to do it. At that stage I am ready to send it to someone and wait for their comments before doing anything more.

Do you ever find that, having written a scene in prose, you then have to rewrite that same scene in verse?

ARDEN: No, I don't think so. Once or twice I have gone from verse back to prose. But I don't think I have ever done the other. I usually have a pretty fair idea of what my verse bits are going to be several scenes ahead. When I construct a play I think first in terms of a story, and then the main scenes that will develop out of that story. For *Serjeant Musgrave* I had three main visual images—the big market place scene, the scene with the soldiers in the stable at night, and the soldiers' arrival in the town. I find these almost "given" scenes—from the "muse" if you like—then the intellectual work comes in fitting them together; in finding out which characters are supposed to be in which scene, and how the scenes join up. In a sense this is the relationship with architecture which I mentioned before—I consider these given scenes almost as your client giving you the number of bathrooms he wants, and which you have got to fit into the house. Having first found the story and theme, then the three or four important scenes that are to illustrate them, I reach the hard-work-process of putting them together. This, of course, may result in the alteration of the original conception—indeed it usually does. I have always been surprised at the amount of my original play which has been retained from the draft I sent out. Sometimes I feel that a good deal more could have been changed.

You would have been able to make the alterations if required?

ARDEN: Well, that's the difficulty. I find that once I have worked on a play so much, I can't really do any more until I have seen it on the stage. I wish we could have an experimental theatre with a tiny audience where one could try out every play before presenting it to the public and critics. Even the best directors can't give a reliable judgment simply on a script. A lot of scenes that I think very good in writing turn out to be flat on stage. On the other hand, often something exciting comes up that you never knew was there.

Do you find that your characters begin to dictate a life of their own?

ARDEN: Yes. I try to get the main lines of the personality down on paper in dialogue in the first two or three scenes, and find a rhythm for the character's speech. To my mind one of the most important aspects of character is speech rhythms. I like to give a character a particular turn of phrase, which in life, of course, is always happening—people often use the same two or three little catch phrases—and all this helps to build up a picture. By the end of scene three, you may suddenly find that this character couldn't possibly do what you have laid out for him in scene four. The character now exists as a person, and you must rewrite the action round him rather than adjust him to fit the actions.

A specific example is Sparky—the two important things about him are his death and his loneliness. . . .

ARDEN: Oddly enough, the death of Sparky is one of the things I had not anticipated. I didn't really decide that any of them were to die until I had started the second act. Then it suddenly struck me. I already had the concept of the scene in the stable, with the girl coming and playing a scene with each soldier in turn—given a situation of high tension such as exists in the play, one girl and three men is going to result in something. In this case Sparky's death.

It must have been a very complex generation, because it's his death which brings Annie into the centre of the play's climax.

ARDEN: This is the point. I knew Annie had to be in the centre at the end, but I did not know how I was going to get her there. I also knew she had to be in the centre in the stable scene. To find a connection between the two scenes led me to the death of Sparky. I then went back and rewrote some of the earlier scenes to prepare for it. The same sort of thing happened with each of the three soldiers, in fact. I started off calling them "One Soldier," "Two Soldier," and "Three Soldier," wrote a few scenes, decided they were developing certain characteristics of their own, went back and renamed them "The Joking Soldier," "The Surly Soldier," and "The Grey-Haired Soldier." I finished the play and then when we went into rehearsal decided they had better have names—this was really Lindsay Anderson's idea. He maintained that if you call a character "The Surly Soldier," it is going to make an actor think he has got to be surly all the way through. It was not until they had names that the soldiers really came alive as people.

Did you fill in the theme of loneliness around Sparky?

ARDEN: That came naturally from the "Joking Soldier." I started off with the first scene complete—four men on a canal bank, waiting for a barge, one of them making jokes. This automatically puts him into a sort of isolation—if he is making jokes all the time there must be a failure in communication between him and everybody else. Because you cannot carry on a complete relationship in the form of jokes. Like that American play, *The Kidders.*

What are you working on now?

ARDEN: I'm doing a translation of Goethe's first play, *Goetz von Berlichingen,* which I hope will adapt well for the modern theatre. As far as I know it has never been performed in this country. I have found only one English translation, made by Sir Walter Scott shortly after the play was written, in a rather dull literary style, whereas the original is much more idiomatic and vital. It's an exciting play of medieval action, with a good deal of serious social and historical stuff in it, because it was written about a period of social change. The hero, Goetz, is a romantic conservative, more than a bit out of touch with his times. Also

I have just finished a television play based on my experiences in an architect's office. It is a straightforward story about a building contract and the effect on the personal relationship between the architect and his client when the thing starts to go wrong.

When you write for television do you try to write a more popular play? In other words, do you try to make your TV plays more acceptable?

ARDEN: Well, I think they have to be on television. But I don't think that it in any way implies a degradation of one's talent. Acceptability does not necessarily mean that you have to write what you think people are going to *like*. It merely means you have got to write something they will *understand,* which is slightly different. I don't know how to write a "popular" play. I mean, to know how to write a television play which will reach a large number of people is a technical question affecting the method of expression and not the content, which I don't believe in modifying. I doubt if *Soldier, Soldier,* from the point of view of content is any more commercial than any of my stage plays.

Serjeant Musgrave has been bought for production by Granada TV?

ARDEN: Yes, as an adaptation. The first idea for the play came to me in stage terms partly because of its spectacle. I had seen a number of contemporary plays and felt—particularly with *Live Like Pigs*—well, this is all very nice, I like this play, but I can see, looking at it on the stage, why some people don't like it. It *is* grey. And I suddenly wanted to write a play with a visual excitement as well as a verbal one. I visualised the stage full of scarlet uniforms, and began to get interested from there. Now had *Serjeant Musgrave* come to me in a different way, I might have seen it in terms of television. I am quite sure that the theme I intended to handle would not have put me off writing it for television. But the writing would have been completely different. This might sound as if in some way I write "down" for television. The point is that in writing a television play I am doing something I regard as artistically responsible—that is, purely an adaptation of style to suit the different medium. But to write a play for the theatre to suit what the theatre audiences are alleged to want seems to me quite a different moral question altogether. Once you start this there is a serious danger— though not a foregone conclusion—that you are going to end up with something dishonest. I always do try to make sure that people "get" what I say; if I fail it is because, possibly, I have been more complex in the writing than I had intended. I don't deliberately write for an elite audience. I would like people to understand my plays more. Of course, failure in communication is not always the dramatist's fault. Harold Pinter's *The Birthday Party* was a complete failure. *The Caretaker* is hailed as a masterpiece. I cannot see that the one is so very much better than the other. I like both plays very much but there seems to be no enormous leap forward in quality. Having failed to appreciate *The Birthday Party,* the public and critics had about two years to see more of Pinter in his revue sketches and television plays so that by the time *The Caretaker* was done there was an informed audience understanding his method and willing to meet it halfway. If *The Caretaker* had been produced first, the fortunes of the two plays might well have been reversed. The little play I did at the church here was thought at first by some people to be obscure. The vicar was so sure it was going to flop he washed his hands of the whole business. A number of people came both nights and told me they enjoyed it much more on the second visit. I think most of my plays have the disadvantage that they are more easily understood when you've seen them once.

This is something that bothers you?

ARDEN: It does rather. I would like my plays to be immediately comprehensible. I often do a great deal of rewriting, as with *Serjeant Musgrave,* to make sure that they are. This may sound a bit like commercialism, but when I think of a commercial play I think of a dramatist who knows what he wants to write and then softens it down to what he imagines the audience wants. That seems to me to be a bad thing. I fancy that a dramatist who writes exactly what he wants to write, and then decides that it is too difficult to understand, and so simplifies it, is not doing the same thing at all. The theatre is a "public art," which means that dramatists who get completely out of touch with their public are in a sense failing to practise the art properly: *but* it is often necessary that they *should* get out of touch for a while in order to make some step forward without which the art would atrophy—and they cannot be condemned for this until a sufficient lapse of time has shown whether they have judged correctly or no. To be useful, the critic of experimental theatre must be sufficiently sensitive to see where the dramatist is trying to go and to estimate the value for his audiences of setting out to follow him. Which is asking a lot of a critic. It is asking still more of the dramatist—all the time I write I find I am writing, partly indeed to express what I know, feel, and see, but even more to test the truth of my knowledge, feelings and vision. I did not fully understand my own feelings about pacifism until I wrote *Serjeant Musgrave*; nor about old age until I wrote *The Happy Haven*. Even yet, both plays seem to leave much unresolved about the questions they raise. I see myself as a practitioner of an art which is both public and exploratory: the exploring is done in public and is therefore full of danger—if you fail, it is bound to be a pretty humiliating failure! But if you succeed, you will have done so by presenting, alive, on the stage, a tactile piece of human existence which will be recognised as true and meaningful and illuminating, and the recognition will be almost a ceremonious act between audience, actors and author—it is the possibility of this happening with any play that keeps the business going.

DATE DUE